Lecture Notes of the Institute for Computer Sciences, Social Informatics and Telecommunications Engineering 402

More information about this series at http://www.springer.com/series/8197

Xingliang Yuan · Wei Bao · Xun Yi ·
Nguyen Hoang Tran (Eds.)

Quality, Reliability, Security and Robustness in Heterogeneous Systems

17th EAI International Conference, QShine 2021
Virtual Event, November 29–30, 2021
Proceedings

Springer

Editors
Xingliang Yuan ⓘ
Monash University
Clayton, VIC, Australia

Xun Yi
RMIT University
Melbourne, VIC, Australia

Wei Bao
School of Computer Science
University of Sydney
Camperdown, NSW, Australia

Nguyen Hoang Tran
University of Sydney
Camperdown, NSW, Australia

ISSN 1867-8211   ISSN 1867-822X (electronic)
Lecture Notes of the Institute for Computer Sciences, Social Informatics
and Telecommunications Engineering
ISBN 978-3-030-91423-3   ISBN 978-3-030-91424-0 (eBook)
https://doi.org/10.1007/978-3-030-91424-0

This Springer imprint is published by the registered company Springer Nature Switzerland AG
The registered company address is: Gewerbestrasse 11, 6330 Cham, Switzerland

Preface

We are delighted to introduce the proceedings of the 17th edition of the European Alliance for Innovation (EAI) International Conference on Heterogeneous Networking for Quality, Reliability, Security and Robustness (QShine 2021). This conference has brought researchers, developers, and practitioners around the world to disseminate, exchange and discuss all recent advances related to heterogeneous networking, particularly for quality, reliability, security, and robustness.

The technical program of QShine 2021 consisted of 20 full papers, which were selected from 43 submitted papers. Aside from the high-quality technical paper presentations, the program also featured two keynote speeches from Tianqing Zhu (University of Technology Sydney, Australia), and Jinjun Chen (Swinburne University of Technology, Australia).

The coordination and organization of the steering chairs, Imrich Chlamtac and Bo Li, were essential for the success of the conference. We sincerely appreciate their constant support and guidance. It was also a great pleasure to work with such an excellent Organizing Committee for their hard work in supporting the conference. Moreover, we would like to thank the Technical Program Committee, led by our TPC Co-chairs, Xingliang Yuan and Wei Bao who completed the peer-review process of technical papers and made a high-quality technical program. We are also grateful to conference managers, Natasha Onofrei for her support and all the authors who submitted their papers to the QShine 2021 conference and workshops.

We strongly believe that QShine conference provides a good forum for all researchers, developers and practitioners to discuss all science and technology aspects that are relevant to heterogeneous networking. We also expect that the future editions of the QShine conference will be as successful and simulating, as indicated by the contributions presented in this volume.

November 2021

Xingliang Yuan
Wei Bao
Xun Yi
Nguyen Hoang Tran

Organization

Steering Committee

Imrich Chlamtac	University of Trento, Italy
Bo Li	Hong Kong University of Science and Technology, Hong Kong

Organizing Committee

General Co-chairs

Xun Yi	RMIT University, Australia
Nguyen Hoang Tran	The University of Sydney, Australia

Techncial Program Committee Co-chairs

Xingliang Yuan	Monash University, Australia
Wei Bao	The University of Sydney, Australia

Web Chair

Liming Ge	The University of Sydney, Australia

Publicity and Social Media Chair

Xiaoning Liu	RMIT University, Australia

Workshops Chair

Xuechao Yang	RMIT University, Australia

Sponsorship and Exhibit Chair

Canh T. Dinh	The University of Sydney, Australia

Publications Chair

Shangqi Lai	Monash University, Australia

Local Chair

Shabnam Kasra Kermanshahi   RMIT University, Australia

Technical Program Committee

Sarder Fakhrul Abedin	Mid Sweden University, Sweden
Sharif Abuadbba	CSIRO Data 61, Australia
Jaya Prakash Champati	IMDEA Networks Institute, Spain
Sid Chau	Australian National University, Australia
Chao Chen	James Cook University, Australia
Xiaojiang Chen	Northwest University, China
Helei Cui	Northwestern Polytechnical University, China
Shujie Cui	Monash University, Australia
Linlin Guo	Dalian University of Technology, China
Young Choon Lee	Macquarie University, Australia
Ruidong Li	National Institute of Information and Communications Technology, Japan
Wanyu Lin	Hong Kong Polytechnic University, Hong Kong
Zhen Liu	Shanghai Jiao Tong University, China
Bingxian Lu	Dalian University of Technology, China
Siqi Ma	University of Queensland, Australia
Suryadipta Majumdar	Concordia University, Canada
Reza Malekian	Malmö University, Sweden
Yunlong Mao	Nanjing University, China
Quoc Viet Pham	Pusan National University, South Korea
Zhenquan Qin	Dalian University of Technology, China
Fatemeh Rezaeibagha	Murdoch University, Australia
Abubakar Sadiq Sani	University of New South Wales, Australia
Zhenkui Shi	Guangxi Normal University, China
Chandra Thapa	CSIRO Data 61, Australia
Khan Ferdous Wahid	Airbus Group, Germany
Lei Wu	Zhejiang University, China
Lei Xu	Nanjing University of Science and Technology, China
Phee Lep Yeoh	The University of Sydney, Australia
Dong Yuan	The University of Sydney, Australia
Xu Yuan	University of Louisiana at Lafayette, USA
Sherali Zeadally	University of Kentucky, USA
Leo Zhang	Deakin University, Australia
Yifeng Zheng	Harbin Institute of Technology, China
Zhi Zhou	Sun Yat-sen University, China
Cong Zuo	Nanyang Technological University, Singapore

Contents

IoT Security and Lightweight Cryptography

Network Security

Privacy-Preserving Emerging Networked Applications

Machine Learning in Distributed Networks

FedDICE: A Ransomware Spread Detection in a Distributed Integrated Clinical Environment Using Federated Learning and SDN Based Mitigation

Chandra Thapa[1(✉)], Kallol Krishna Karmakar[2], Alberto Huertas Celdran[3], Seyit Camtepe[1], Vijay Varadharajan[2], and Surya Nepal[1,4]

[1] CSIRO Data61, Marsfield, Australia
chandra.thapa@data61.csiro.au
[2] The University of Newcastle, Callaghan, Australia
[3] University of Zurich, Zürich, Switzerland
[4] Cyber Security Cooperative Research Centre, Joondalup, Australia

Abstract. An integrated clinical environment (ICE) enables the connection and coordination of the internet of medical things around the care of patients in hospitals. However, ransomware attacks and their spread on hospital infrastructures, including ICE, are rising. Often the adversaries are targeting multiple hospitals with the same ransomware attacks. These attacks are detected by using machine learning algorithms. But the challenge is devising the anti-ransomware learning mechanisms and services under the following conditions: (1) provide immunity to other hospitals if one of them got the attack, (2) hospitals are usually distributed over geographical locations, and (3) direct data sharing is avoided due to privacy concerns. In this regard, this paper presents a federated distributed integrated clinical environment, aka. *FedDICE*. FedDICE integrates federated learning (FL), which is privacy-preserving learning, to SDN-oriented security architecture to enable collaborative learning, detection, and mitigation of ransomware attacks. We demonstrate the importance of FedDICE in a collaborative environment with up to 4 hospitals and 4 ransomware families, namely WannaCry, Petya, BadRabbit and PowerGhost. Our results find that in both IID and non-IID data setups, FedDICE achieves the centralized baseline performance that needs direct data sharing for detection. However, as a trade-off to data privacy, FedDICE observes overhead in the anti-ransomware model training, e.g., 28× for the logistic regression model. Besides, FedDICE utilizes SDN's dynamic network programmability feature to remove the infected devices in ICE.

1 Introduction

The latest advancement of computing paradigms and communications is influencing the revolution of many heterogeneous scenarios. Healthcare is one of the most relevant due to its impact on human well-being. Nowadays, hospitals

© ICST Institute for Computer Sciences, Social Informatics and Telecommunications Engineering 2021
Published by Springer Nature Switzerland AG 2021. All Rights Reserved
X. Yuan et al. (Eds.): QShine 2021, LNICST 402, pp. 3–24, 2021.
https://doi.org/10.1007/978-3-030-91424-0_1

are adapting their operating theaters and infrastructure with new paradigms, for example, the Internet of Medical Things (IoMT) [12], and Medical Cyber-Physical Systems (MCPS) [31], to enable open coordination and interoperability of heterogeneous medical devices (e.g., data logging device) and applications (e.g., clinical decision making). These infrastructures are called *Integrated Clinical Environments (ICE)* [14] and hold the promise of providing innovative and optimized ways to monitor, diagnose, and treat patients. Moreover, ICE enables a holistic view of the ongoing condition of a patient and improves the patient's data collection system by creating the IoMT and MCPS around the care of patients. Refer to Fig. 1(a) for the ICE functional architecture.

However, hospitals, including their ICEs, are under cyberattacks. We have been witnessing how hospitals are impacted by multiple types of cyberattacks that expose sensitive data or disrupt critical tasks such as surgeries or treatments [27]. This problem is greatly influenced by having medical devices or computers without enough –or obsolete– cybersecurity mechanisms and connection to the internet. In this context, from current hospitals to the next generation equipped with ICE, the expected healthcare evolution will aggravate the situation because ICE devices have not been designed to satisfy security requirements, and consequently, are vulnerable to cyberattacks such as ransomware.

Ransomware cyberattacks deserve special attention from the research community as they are skyrocketing during this COVID-19 pandemic period in healthcare [16,22]. For example, it is increased by 45% since November 2020 [11]. However, they are not new events. They accounted for 85% of all malware, and more than 70% of attacks confirmed data disclosure based on Verizon in 2018 [34]. In January 2018, the Hancock Health Hospital (US) paid attackers $55,000 to unlock systems following a ransomware infection [7]. Considering all, it is evident that without addressing ransomware attacks impacting clinical scenarios, we cannot achieve the benefits of ICE in healthcare.

For ransomware detection, various mechanisms have been developed. But, the traditional cybersecurity mechanisms based on signatures, e.g., SIDS [18], and rule-based static policies, e.g., traditional policy-based detection in software-defined networks (SDN), are no longer suitable for detecting new ransomware families that have not been seen before or use encrypted communications. To solve this drawback, a vast number of solutions based on machine learning (ML) and deep learning (DL) have been proposed [17]. However, ML/DL requires sufficient ransomware data for training and testing its algorithms. Moreover, data should have a good quality [35], for example, all targeted classes (e.g., ransomware families) to enabling better ML/DL learning on their features.

Unfortunately, it is not easy to find all required ransomware data in one hospital's ICE environment, as one hospital might not suffer from all ransomware families. Thus there is a need for collaboration among hospitals. The straightforward way is to collect the ransomware data directly from the multiple hospital's ICE and perform machine learning. This approach is called *centralized learning* (CL). The challenge here is data privacy since the data from ICE is privacy critical as it can contain patients' health data and can expose the hospitals' internal ICE networks to others (refer to Sect. 3.1 for details). Also, privacy in ICE is recommended by NIST (NIST RISK MANAGEMENT FRAMEWORK, supra note 57, at v) frameworks [2]. Thus hospitals are reluctant to collaborate with direct data sharing. Besides, the hospitals (ICEs) are separated and located at different geo-locations making the raw data sharing difficult.

Overall, a collaborative healthcare framework is needed, where several hospitals (ICEs) work together to create a powerful anti-ransomware model with data privacy. As the collaborative framework has multiple ICEs (hospitals) located in different places, it is called distributed ICE (DICE). Each participating hospital with its local ICE environment can share its locally trained anti-ransomware models instead of raw ransomware data in DICE. They can use those shared models in two ways; (i) use individually, and (ii) aggregate models to form one global model. The former is not preferred because it is a burden to the hospitals as they need to keep, manage, and update these multiple models received from multiple hospitals with time.

In this regard, federated learning (FL) is a suitable candidate. FL aggregates the multiple models to form one global model and updates it with time by considering data privacy in a distributed machine learning. Thus this paper integrates FL to DICE, and the integrated framework is called *FedDICE*. In ransomware attack scenarios, its spread is one of the major concerns in the connected environment [4] such as ICE. So, the FedDICE is investigated by focusing on the detection and mitigation of ransomware spread. Specifically, this work presents the performance of FL in ransomware spread detection considering four popular families, namely WannaCry, Petya, BadRabbit, and PowerGhost. This is not known yet despite FL's widespread use in other healthcare scenarios, such as diagnosing medical conditions from medical imaging like MRI scans and X-rays [29,33]. For the mitigation of the attacks in ICE, SDN policies are applied to separate the ransomware-infected system/device from the network.

For convenience, we list our overall contributions based on the research question (**RQ**) in the following:

- (**RQ1**) **Need of a collaborative framework in ransomware spread detection:** We study how the models trained on one ransomware family, we call *singly-trained models*, perform over other ransomware families. Our results demonstrate that the singly-trained models are not effective in general in detecting different ransomware. Thus collaboration is required if all ransomware data is not available at one hospital. Refer to Sect. 6.5 for details.
- (**RQ2**) **Security architecture of FedDICE:** We present a security architecture of FedDICE for the model development, detection, and mitigation of ransomware spread. The architecture is based on the SDN functionalities and components. Refer to Sect. 5 for details.
- (**RQ3**) **Performance of FedDICE over centralized learning:** This is an important research question highlighting the importance of the FL paradigm in DICE, i.e., FedDICE, both from the requirements and performance sides in ransomware spread detection. Our studies demonstrate that FL achieves the baseline performance, i.e., centralized learning, under both the IID and the non-IID ransomware data distribution in FedDICE. Moreover, FL is even better than centralized learning in some cases. Thus one can avoid using

privacy-unfriendly centralized learning. Besides, our results show that a simple model such as logistic regression performs well in ransomware spread detection in our setup. Refer to Sect. 6.5 for details.

– (**RQ4**) **Mitigation of the ransomware spread:** As the mitigation of ransomware threat is equally important as its detection, we implement policy-based mitigation in the SDN-managed FedDICE. Refer to Sect. 7 for details.

2   Background

This section provides background on the various techniques and frameworks that we are using in this paper.

2.1   ICE Framework

ICE consists of multiple medical and non-medical equipment (including IoMT), their connections, and control systems designed to enable a patient-centric infrastructure. To standardize the ICE framework for interoperability, the American Society for Testing and Materials (ASTM) states a high-level architecture for ICE [14]. The proposed framework is depicted in Fig. 1(a). The framework enables the internal and external medical or relevant devices to connect to the system via *ICE equipment interface* and *external interface*, respectively. All the devices/equipment are connected in a network, and it is managed and monitored by *ICE network controller*. Thus, it has access to the network flow information of the devices in the ICE network. Such information is stored in *data logger* for forensic analysis. For SDN-based infrastructure, the *SDN controller* is kept at the same layer of the ICE network controller, and they operate collaboratively. The medical applications run on the *ICE supervisor* platform. These applications use the data generated by medical devices for medical decisions, in which the devices are operated on the patient, and the clinician makes the decision.

2.2   DICE Framework

DICE is formed by connecting multiple ICE via a trusted party, called supernode. The supernode is connected through the external interface of each ICE. It has some computing power and is responsible only for enabling collaboration among the participating ICEs. A supernode can have an SDN controller to help with the routing of packets between hospitals. Supernode acts only following the commands from the participating ICEs. By default, neither it interferes with the decisions made by the local SDN controller (at each hospital) for its local ICE, nor it sees/collect or transfers data of the connected ICE without their approvals. Figure 1(b) illustrates an example scenario of DICE where three different hospitals in different regions are connected via a supernode to collaborating by sharing their local inferences to improve their local ICE network security. Overall, DICE is better than a single standalone ICE for various aspects, including improved security via knowledge sharing (e.g., models), data sharing, and resource management.

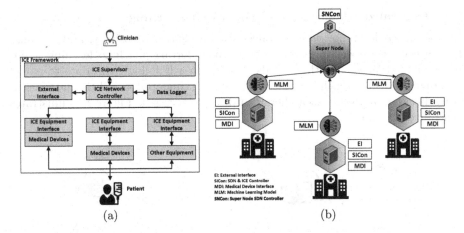

Fig. 1. (a) An ICE framework by ASTM Standard F2671-2009 [14], and (b) an example scenario of DICE with three hospitals. In DICE, each hospital has its local ICE with components such as external interface (EI), SDN and ICE controller (SICon), and medical device interface (MDI). The locally trained machine learning models (MLM) can be shared with the supernode, which also has an SDN controller (SNCon).

DICE Specific Requirements: This work is related to the security and privacy of DICE; thus, we further explore and list its requirements in the following:

1. **Distributed computing:** The underlying structure of the DICE framework has distributed resources, including computation. Thus, the computations, including ML/AI anti-ransomware model training/testing and data pre-processing, are required to do in the local resources of ICEs. Moreover, the distributed computing enables reliability by localizing the possibility of the system failure, e.g., limiting fault to the local ICE, add scalability by allowing more ICEs to the framework, and faster computations due to distributed computing capability.

2. **Local control:** The local ICEs belong to independent hospitals, so the control over their local network and SDN policies execution must remain within. The outsider (e.g., supernode) can only facilitate them to route and share model, data, and knowledge for overall benefit but only with their consent.

3. **Collaborative approach:** DICE needs a collaborative approach to solve various issues, including security. For example, the participating ICEs can share their knowledge on detecting some ransomware to alert or improve the detection capability of other ICEs. Also, this approach enables better Ml/AI threat detection model training by providing access to more data types.

4. **Privacy:** Privacy is another important requirement demanded by regulations (e.g., General Data Protection Regulation of Europe [13] and NIST [2]) and users. In DICE, the information shared between the ICEs of different organizations needs to be protected; the approach should be privacy-by-design and privacy-by-default.

2.3   Centralized Learning and Federated Learning

In centralized learning, data is collected to a central repository, and the ana-
lyst directly accesses those repositories to undertake machine learning training and inferences. In other words, this approach follows the data-to-model
paradigm. This approach is not a privacy-preserving approach if the data is sensitive because analysts/researchers can directly access it. Figure 2(a) illustrates
centralized learning.

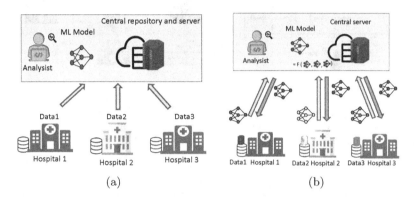

Fig. 2. An illustration of (a) centralized learning (CL), and (b) federated learning (FL)
with three hospitals.

Federated learning [19, 23, 33] follows the model-to-data paradigm in which
the model is sent to the clients (e.g., hospitals) to train/test instead of taking data out from those clients for the machine learning. Precisely, the model
training/testing proceeds as follows: Let W_t be the model parameters at time
instance t at the server. It is broadcast to all N participating clients. Afterward,
each client i trains the model on their local data, and the locally trained model
W_t^i, for $i \in \{1, 2, \cdots, N\}$, is sent back to the server. Then the server aggregates the model, for example by weighted averaging, to form the global model
$W_{t+1} = \sum_i \frac{n_i}{n} W_t^i$, where n_i and n are the number of samples at client i and the
total number of samples considering all clients. This process continues till the
model converges. Figure 1(b) illustrates FL with three clients. As data is always
kept with the clients and the raw data is never seen by the analyst/server, FL
provides privacy-by-design and privacy-by-default.

3   Motivation of FedDICE for the Ransomware Spread Detection

DICE enables collaboration among multiple hospitals to detect ransomware
spread synergetically. In addition, FL enables all the DICE-specific requirements
as listed in Sect. 2.2. This way, the integration of FL to DICE, which is forming FedDICE, is well motivated. Further, we elaborate on the two main reasons
related to privacy and computation in the following.

3.1   Network Flow Dataset and Its Risk

Our dataset uses the network flow (netflow) format of CISCO. The fields include start time, source IP, Destination IP, total packets, total load, and source inter-packet arrival time [1]. Netflow is a protocol for collecting, aggregating, and recording traffic flow data in a network, gives you deep network visibility.

Netflow data of critical infrastructure such as ICE are sensitive. Adversaries can plan for an efficient attack in a network by gathering deep network information from the netflow data of the network. For example, (i) finding a bottleneck of the network can identify the possible target point for the attacker to craft a denial of service attack, and (ii) finding the specific traffic patterns makes it easy for filtering attacks (blocking those traffic in the network). Consequently, a hospital does not want to share their netflow data with outsiders in DICE if raw ransomware data sharing is required. Works have been done to obfuscate the data in network flow [28, 36]. However, the sanitized data either decreases data quality for machine learning or poses some risk of leakage. The best option is not to share the (netflow) data in the first place but allow the machine learning inference. This is done by integrating FL in DICE, i.e., via FedDICE. Besides, FL enables privacy-by-design and privacy-by-default mechanisms, and it is compliant with data protection regulations such as GDPR [13].

3.2   Distributed Computation

The DICE formed by the collaboration of multiple hospitals (ICEs) is distributed and can be spread out to different geo-locations. DICE can leverage the advantages of distributed computing, including horizontal scaling of the network elements, fault tolerance, low latency, and distributed computational requirements. Being a distributed ML approach, FL enables all the benefits of the distributed computation to DICE. Thus FedDICE is promising for ransomware spread detection.

4   Threat Scenario

The threats in DICE can be ICE layer-specific, such as a compromised supervisor in the supervisory layer, malicious or infected devices, and malicious SDN network applications in the controller layer [10]. As the primary threat is usually due to the infected devices in an ICE, we consider only this threat scenario in this paper. In this scenario, firstly, a device is infected by a certain ransomware type. Then the ransomware spreads over the network to infect other devices/systems, including patient health monitoring devices and database servers, within the (local) ICE framework. During the development of the anti-ransomware model collaboratively in DICE, we assume that all participating hospitals are honest-but-curious parties. They behave as per our expectation but are only interested in inferring more on data of other hospitals. Also, they do not maliciously behave to alter or affect the anti-ransomware model training/testing process. We also assume that all the participating hospitals have the same network infrastructure and architecture in our studies for simplicity.

5   Proposed Security Architecture of FedDICE

Considering the threat scenario, we present a security architecture of FedDICE driven by SDN for the detection and mitigation of ransomware spread. This is an answer to **RQ2**. The architecture is depicted in Fig. 3, and it accounts for FedDICE with N hospital ICEs. The major components and their functions in the architecture are presented in the following.

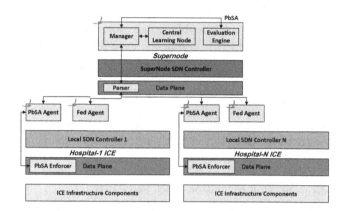

Fig. 3. Security architecture of FedDICE for the detection and mitigation of ransomware spread.

(i) **Manager:** Manager is a software module present in the supernode. It has a collection of scripts that will be executed to manage FedDICE. The manager runs as a northbound application and interacts with the supernode SDN controller through its northbound application programming interface. It maintains communication with the local (leaf) SDN controller agent. Specifically, the manager performs the following tasks: (a) Maintains communication with the agents running on the local SDN controllers and the central learning node, (b) transforms the parser output to a more readable format for other software modules, (c) based on the central learning node feedback, the manager can create policies that can be installed in the policy repository maintained by the evaluation engine – a system administrator can also install such policies in the policy repository – and (d) conveys central learning node decisions to the enforcer module, and enforces appropriate flow rules in the data plane devices.

(ii) **Evaluation Engine:** An evaluation engine is used to evaluate incoming network traffic against the relevant security policy expressions. Following the evaluation, the manager determines the flow rules, which are then conveyed to the enforcer module. This module also maintains a policy database. Our policy database is a simple JSON file; for example, refer to Fig. 6(b).

(iii) **Agents:** Our security architecture uses agents, which are mainly northbound applications, to transfer information between the SDN Controllers. In some cases, they can be a separate application, which only utilises the controller information. This approach helps to build an application that can be used with a heterogeneous controller. The agents are running on each local SDN controller. Moreover, there are two agents; PbSA and Fed agents. PbSA is a policy-based security application running on the top of the local SDN controller. Firstly, it mirrors all the incoming packet information and formats them for machine learning purposes. This module also stores the formatted packet information in a local repository. The fed agent (federated machine agent) uses the local storage's raw data to build the local anti-malware model. Later it coordinates with the manager via parser to forward the local model and receive the global model. The global model is used to detect ransomware spread in local ICEs.

(iv) **Enforcer:** We have modified the data plane devices and introduced an enforcer module. The enforcer module fetches the required information for the agents from the south-bound interface connected to the switches. It enables to enforcing flow rules obtained from the manager and applies the policies at the switching hardware.

(v) **Central Learning Node:** Central learning node is present in the supernode, and it is responsible for the aggregation of the anti-ransomware models received from the local ICEs during federated learning. The node also forms policies considering the aggregated models.

Now we briefly discuss how the overall security components work together in FedDICE. Firstly, each local ICE fed agent regularly trains and updates its anti-ransomware ML model through FL. These models are used as policies in our approach. In contrast to a static policy, which is usually manually updated to detect and mitigate the ransomware spread, the ML model-based policy updates automatically through FL. Then it is applied to detect the ransomware spread in the local ICE. Afterward, the PbSA enforcer executes the policies to remove the infected devices from the ICE if there is any detection.

6   Experiments, Results, and Analysis on the Detection of Ransomware Spread

In this section, we perform various experiments to investigate the performance of FedDICE in ransomware spread detection. This provides answers of **RQ1** and **RQ3**. Before presenting our results and analysis, we provide details on data, models, performance metrics, and implementation in the following sections.

6.1   Data

We use a clinical environment network traffic dataset, where the data is captured in pcap and binetflow format [1]. The dataset has clean and ransomware-generated network traffic information by devices with an operating system, Windows (version: 7 and 10) and Ubuntu (version: 16.04). There are four popular ransomware families, namely *WannaCry* (RW-WC), *Petya* (RW-PY), *BadRabbit* (RW-BR) and *PowerGhost* (RW-PG). The dataset is generated by considering sliding windows of netflows to obtain a total of 520 features related to transmission control protocol (TCP), user datagram protocol (UDP), address resolution protocol (ARP), and flow features. The sliding windows can have various time duration, including 5 s, 10 s, and 20 s. In the feature generation process, aggregated features are generated using the last flow information of the sliding window duration (e.g., 10 s). This is done to collect a wide variety of both the context features and flow features. Refer to [15] for details. The samples refer to the aggregated traffic information at different time frames. There are 150540 samples if we use a 10 s window in our network observations. For all our experiments, we use the dataset split and numbers as depicted in Table 1.

We divide the dataset into two categories during training: clean (label 1) and ransomware (label 0). We consider binary classification because our main task is to detect the ransomware irrespective of its specific type. In FL, the training and validation dataset are local, so it is different in different clients, whereas the test dataset is global and checked on the global model.

Table 1. Dataset (prepared by using 10 s sliding window duration)

Dataset type	Train	Validataion	Test	Total
Clean	80000	10000	10000	100000
RW-WC	20000	2500	2500	25000
RW-PY	784	98	99	981
RW-BR	311	38	40	389
RW-PG	19336	2417	2417	24170
Total	120431	15053	15056	150540

6.2 Model

We consider three different models commonly used in ransomware detection and compatible for FL in our analyses. All are considered for binary classification tasks with an observation window of 10 global epochs in FL.

1. **Logistic regression**: Assume W and b be the weight and bias of the model, respectively. The output of the logistic regression (LR) model is given by: $\sigma(\mathbf{w}^T\mathbf{x} + b)$, where σ is the sigmoid function, $\mathbf{w}$ is the parameter vector, and $\mathbf{x}$ is the input. The sigmoid function maps any real input to the value between zero and one. We consider a binary logistic regression with cross-entropy loss and learning rate $= 0.01$ in our analyses.
2. **Support vector machine**: Support vector machine (SVM) uses the kernel trick (data is projected to higher dimensions) to express its linear function by: $b + \sum_i \alpha_i k(\mathbf{x}, \mathbf{x}^{(i)})$, where $k(\mathbf{x}, \mathbf{x}^{(i)}) = \phi(x).\phi(x^{(i)}$ is called a kernel, $\mathbf{x}^{(i)}$ is a training example, and α is a coefficient vector. The output function is non-linear to x in SVM. We consider the SVM model for binary classification (i.e., $C = 1$) in our analyses. We utilize the skitlearn library to implement the SVM. We use the default parameters (e.g., kernel $=$ rbf, degree $= 3$, gamma $=$ scale, and max_iter $= -1$).

3. **Feedforward Neural Network**: Feedforward neural network (FNN) is formed by the composition of multiple neural network layers, where each layer performs some functions in its input as follows: The first layer output is $\mathbf{h}^{(1)} = g^{(1)}(\mathbf{w}^{(1)\mathrm{T}}\mathbf{x} + b^{(1)})$, the second layer output is $\mathbf{h}^{(2)} = g^{(2)}(\mathbf{w}^{(2)\mathrm{T}}\mathbf{h}^1 + b^{(2)})$, and similar calculations proceeds till the output layer. The layers between the input and output are called hidden layers. In our analyses, we consider a FNN with six hidden layers (each followed by batch-normalization and Relu activation) and softmax output layer. (num features, 1024), (1024, 512), (512, 128), (128, 64), (64, 32), and (32, num class) are the pairs of the number of nodes in hidden layers starting from first to the last, respectively. The cross-entropy loss and learning rate equals 0.01 are used in training.

6.3 Metrics for Performance Measurement

We consider accuracy, precision, recall, F1-score, and false-negative rate (FNR) for performance analysis. In our dataset setup, the ransomware class is labeled 0, and it is a positive class, whereas the normal class is labeled 1, and it is a negative class. Thus, we consider only FNR (not false-positive rate) in our analyses. Moreover, precision, recall, and F1-score are averaged figures (average = 'macro'). Besides, 4 fold validation is carried out in all of our experiments.

6.4 Implementation

The training/testing implementation is done in python programming by leveraging PyTorch library [3]. Moreover, for FL with logistic regression and SVM models, we have used some functions from Sherpa.ai Federated Learning and Differential Privacy Framework [30]. All the programs were executed on a Dell laptop with Intel Core i5-8350U CPU, 8 GB RAM, and x64-based processor.

6.5 Results and Analysis

We present our results and analyze them on the detection of ransomware spread in this section. Firstly, our baseline performance provided by centralized learning is presented, and then we proceed to find the FL performances under three ML models defined in Sect. 6.2.

Table 2. Results summary for centralized learning on testing dataset.

Model	Accuracy	Precision	Recall	F1-score	FNR
LR	0.999768	0.99975	0.999733	0.999738	0.000395
SVM	0.999395	0.999538	0.999105	0.999323	1.78E−03
FNN	0.98954	0.992003	0.98464	0.988185	0.030271

(Baseline Performance) Centralized Learning: Our results on the test dataset (in Table 2) and validation dataset showed excellent similar performance by all three models in centralized learning. For example, we get around 99.9% accuracy for LR and SVM and around 99% for FNN. In addition, all models return almost zero FNR. Relatively, logistic regression is slightly better than others.

(RQ1) Need of a Collaborative Framework in Ransomware Spread Detection: Under **RQ1**, we are aiming to find if a model trained on one ransomware family be still effective in detecting another ransomware family. If the answer is negative in general, then the single client's model and data are insufficient to capture unseen ransomware characteristics. This way, we demonstrate the need for collaborative machine learning such as FL in DICE for the detection.

Now considering each client (i.e., local ICE) is infected by only one ransomware family, we form an experimental setup of the data distribution as depicted in Table 3. Starting from Client1, a model is trained on its training data (consisting of clean and RW-WC), and it is tested against the training data of clients 2, 3, and 4 (that have clean and other types of ransomware samples). Similarly, we carried experiments for all clients. The results for FR, SVM and FNN are presented in Table 4, 5, and 6, respectively.

We summarize our observations based on the empirical results depicted in Tables 4, 5, and 6 in the following:

1. For all our models trained on WannaCry (RW-WC) and clean dataset (i.e., Client1) has shown good performance on PowerGhost (RW-PG) and test dataset, but detect only a few samples of Petya (RW-PY) and BadRabbit (RW-BR). This is indicated by a high FNR greater than 0.98 for the cases.
2. For all our models trained on RW-PG and clean dataset (i.e., Client4) has shown good performance on RW-WC and test dataset. There is a high FNR for RW-PY and RW-BR.

Table 3. Data distribution among clients.

Clients	Client 1	Client 2	Client 3	Client 4
Training data and samples	Clean (20000) RW-WC (20000)	Clean (20000) RW-PY (784)	Clean (20000) RW-BR (310)	Clean (20000) RW-PG (19336)
Training sample size	40,000	20,784	20,310	39,336

Test dataset has 20000 Clean, 5000 RW-WC, 197 RW-PY, 79 RW-BR and 4834 RW-PG samples

Table 4. **(RQ1)** Results for the logistic regression (LR) when training on only one client and testing on the remaining clients for the setup in Table 3.

Training	Testing	Accuracy	Precision	Recall	F1-score	FNR	Misclassified ransomware samples
	Client2	0.96228	0.98114	0.5	0.49039	1	784 out of 784
	Client3	0.98474	0.99237	0.5	0.49615	1	310 out of 310
Client1	Client4	0.99497	0.9951	0.99488	0.99496	0.01024	198 out of 19336
	Test dataset	0.99083	0.99319	0.98635	0.98965	0.0273	276 out of 10110
	Client1	0.93015	0.93865	0.93015	0.92981	0.13945	2789 out of 20000
	Client3	0.9997	0.99665	0.9935	0.99507	0.012903	4 out of 310
Client2	Client4	0.99939	0.99939	0.99939	0.99939	0.000879	17 out of 19336
	Test dataset	0.92016	0.94635	0.88111	0.90419	0.237784	2404 out of 10110
	Client1	0.50255	0.74583	0.50255	0.33902	0.99485	19897 out of 20000
	Client2	0.99682	0.99836	0.95791	0.97721	0.084184	66 out of 784
Client3	Client4	0.52433	0.75832	0.51616	0.37196	0.967677	18711 out of 19336
	Test dataset	0.6716	0.83458	0.51098	0.42238	0.978042	9888 out of 10110
	Client1	1	1	1	1	0	0 out of 20000
	Client2	0.97638	0.98802	0.68686	0.76599	0.626276	491 out of 784
Client4	Client3	0.99301	0.99648	0.77097	0.8497	0.458065	142 out of 310
	Test dataset	0.99415	0.99564	0.9913	0.99342	0.017409	176 out of 10110

3. For all our models trained on RW-PY and clean dataset (i.e., Client2) has shown good performance only on RW-BR (i.e., Client3), and vice-versa.

These results show that there can be some ransomware such as RW-WC and RW-PG, those indicating a possibility of using models trained on network flow information generated by one ransomware to detect each other. However, this is not true in general; for example, models trained on RW-WC or RW-PG have poor performance on RW-PY and RW-BR. This clearly shows that we need collaboration either by direct data sharing or using privacy-preserving techniques such as FL in DICE. The results from the direct data-sharing approach are equivalent to the centralized learning, so we further analyze FL in the following section.

(RQ3) Performance of FedDICE over Centralized Learning: Under **RQ3**, FedDICE, specifically FL, is investigated considering setups with three

Table 5. (RQ1) Results for the SVM when training on only one client and testing on the remaining clients for the setup in Table 3.

Training	Testing	Accuracy	Precision	Recall	F1-score	FNR	Misclassified ransomware samples
Client1	Client2	0.96228	0.98114	0.5	0.49039	1	784 out of 784
	Client3	0.98474	0.99237	0.5	0.49615	1	310 out of 310
	Client4	0.9912	0.9915	0.99105	0.9912	0.017894	346 out of 19336
	Test dataset	0.99083	0.99319	0.98635	0.98965	0.0273	276 out of 10110
Client2	Client1	0.5022	0.73459	0.5022	0.33834	0.99545	19909 out of 20000
	Client3	0.99936	0.9964	0.98221	0.9892	0.035484	11 out of 310
	Client4	0.51993	0.7539	0.51169	0.36262	0.976469	18881 out of 19336
	Test dataset	0.67164	0.83459	0.51103	0.42249	0.977943	9887 out of 10110
Client3	Client1	0.5014	0.75035	0.5014	0.33644	0.9972	19944 out of 20000
	Client2	0.99601	0.99793	0.94707	0.97102	0.105867	83 out of 784
	Client4	0.51792	0.75665	0.50965	0.35812	0.98071	18963 out of 19336
	Test dataset	0.6715	0.83455	0.51083	0.42208	0.978338	9891 out of 10110
Client4	Client1	1	1	1	1	0	0 out of 20000
	Client2	0.96339	0.98167	0.51467	0.51917	0.970663	761 out of 784
	Client3	0.98567	0.99283	0.53065	0.55414	0.93871	291 out of 310
	Test dataset	0.99117	0.99344	0.98684	0.99003	0.026311	266 out of 10110

and four clients, separately. The number of clients is chosen based on possible data distribution and the number of ransomware types. As the FL's performance is dependent on the type of data distribution, we consider both the IID and the non-IID data (representing the heterogeneity of data) distribution among the clients as described in the following:

1. (**CASE-I**) IID data distribution: Each client has clean and all samples of ransomware that are independently and identically distributed. The total sample size in each client is the same. We call **CASE I-A** and **CASE I-B** for three clients and four client setups, respectively.
2. (**CASE-II**) Non-IID data distribution: The distribution of the non-IID datasets is due to the label distribution skew. If three clients, we say **CASE II-A**, where Client1 has normal and RW-WC samples, Client2 has normal, RW-PY and RW-BR samples, and Client3 has normal and RW-PG samples. Another case is with the four clients, we say **CASE II-B**, and its data distribution is depicted in Table 3.

For the **CASE-I**, results (in Table 7(a) and 7(b)) show that FL is effective in ransomware spread detection over the IID data distribution across participating clients. Moreover, its performance is similar to centralized learning (refer to Fig. 4(a)), and all three models achieve the best performance; however, the

Table 6. (RQ1) Results for the Feedforward Neural Network (FNN) when training on only one client and testing on the remaining clients for the setup in Table 3.

Training	Testing	Accuracy	Precision	Recall	F1-score	FNR	Misclassified ransomware samples
	Client2	0.96093	0.55625	0.50298	0.49732	0.992347	778 out of 784
	Client3	0.98336	0.5675	0.50883	0.51295	0.980645	304 out of 310
Client1	Client4	0.97272	0.97438	0.97228	0.97267	0.054096	1046 out of 19336
	Test dataset	0.9903	0.99232	0.986	0.98906	0.027102	276 out of 10110
	Client1	0.5803	0.66871	0.5803	0.51703	0.78165	15633 out of 20000
	Client3	0.94353	0.59966	0.92528	0.64968	0.093548	29 out of 310
Client2	Client4	0.64935	0.72344	0.64437	0.61314	0.650703	12582 out of 19336
	Test dataset	0.79389	0.80031	0.72201	0.73978	0.496835	378 out of 10110
	Client1	0.74245	0.75772	0.74245	0.73858	0.37925	7585 out of 20000
	Client2	0.84729	0.52867	0.59466	0.52663	0.678571	532 out of 784
Client3	Client4	0.76668	0.77746	0.76496	0.76355	0.33704	6517 out of 19336
	Test dataset	0.76008	0.73263	0.7116	0.71925	0.436004	9860 out of 10110
	Client1	0.99292	0.99302	0.99293	0.99292	0	0 out of 20000
	Client2	0.96276	0.74198	0.65957	0.69132	0.668367	524 out of 784
Client4	Client3	0.98124	0.70533	0.78246	0.73744	0.422581	131 out of 310
	Test dataset	0.98482	0.98291	0.98307	0.98299	0.022255	752 out of 10110

Table 7. (RQ3) Results summary for the global model over the testing dataset in federated learning and (a) **CASE I-A**, and (b) **CASE I-B**.

(a)

Model	Accuracy	Precision	Recall	F1-score	FNR
LR	0.999725	0.999728	0.999658	0.99969	0.000544
SVM	0.999453	0.999578	0.999198	0.999385	0.001583
FNN	0.99881	0.999073	0.998263	0.998665	0.003401

(b)

Model	Accuracy	Precision	Recall	F1-score	FNR
LR	0.999675	0.999708	0.999565	0.999635	0.000767
SVM	0.999428	0.999558	0.999163	0.999358	0.001656
FNN	0.998188	0.99854	0.99739	0.99796	0.005007

logistic regression (LR) has a relatively slightly better performance. Usually, FL performance is lower than centralized learning (baseline), but we observe a difference in our results. For example, the performance of FNN in FL is higher than its baseline (see Fig. 4(a)). The possible reason for this result can be the effect of model aggregation in FL. The weighted averaging of the models in model aggregation can stabilize the fluctuations in the model updates to some extent during the model training in FNN and thus contribute to better performance.

Table 8. (RQ3) Results summary for the global model over the testing dataset in federated learning and (a) **CASE II-A**, and (b) **CASE II-B**.

(a)						(b)				
Model	Accuracy	Precision	Recall	F1-score	FNR	Model	Accuracy	Precision	Recall	F1-score	FNR
LR	0.99761	0.99821	0.99644	0.99731	0.007122	LR	0.99768	0.99826	0.99654	0.99739	0.006924
SVM	0.99817	0.99863	0.99728	0.99795	0.00544	SVM	0.99821	0.99865	0.99733	0.99799	0.005341
FNN	0.9911	0.99339	0.98675	0.98996	0.026508	FNN	0.9913	0.99353	0.98704	0.99018	0.025915

For the **CASE-II**, results (in Table 8(a) and 8(b)) show that FL is effective in ransomware spread detection even over the non-IID data distribution across participating clients. Moreover, like in the IID case, its performance is similar to centralized learning (refer to Fig. 4(b)), and all three models achieve the best performance; however, the SVM model has relatively slightly better performance. As expected, due to the skewness in the label distribution over the clients in non-IID data distribution across the participating clients, the FL performance is relatively lower than its IID counterparts. However, the overall maximum degradation is only on a scale of around 2 digits after the decimal, which is insignificant (e.g., 0.01).

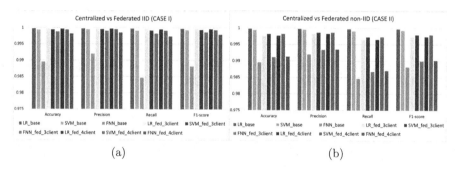

(a)   (b)

Fig. 4. Performances of the centralized and federated learning (a) **CASE-I** and (b) **CASE-II** in bar diagrams where the y-axis's units are shown in the interval of 0.005 units. In labels, the word *"base"* refers to the centralized learning, and *"fed"* refers to the federated learning.

Remark: Based on the overall results obtained with FL in CASE-I and CASE-II, it is clear that FL is effective in the DICE environment for ransomware spread detection. It achieved the baseline (centralized) performance both for the IID and non-IID cases. This suggests that we no longer need to compromise data privacy by using centralized learning. Moreover, we do not need sophisticated models for our cases as a simple model such as logistic regression is sufficient to detect the ransomware spread effectively.

Overhead Time for the Model Training: The anti-ransomware model train-ing time in DICE is also critical as the model needs to be updated regularly to learn about the characteristics of a newly available ransomware spread. As such, we investigate the overhead time for the model development in FL and central-ized baselines.

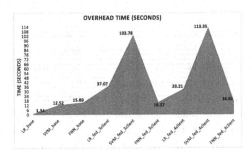

Fig. 5. Overhead time comparison for centralized and federated learning (CASE-I).

Our results are depicted in Fig. 5. It shows that FL has some higher overhead time for model processing (training and testing) than their centralized counter-parts. This can be considered as the trade-off to data privacy and distributed computations. It is known that the overhead depends on the number of clients and data samples in the client; smaller data and higher clients can reduce the overhead time in FL.

We also performed our experiments on the data with sliding window size equals 20 s (besides 10 s) for **RQ1** and **RQ3**. We found similar results and conclusions as above. Unfortunately, the results are excluded due to the page limitation.

7 Experiments on the Mitigation of Ransomware Spread

In this section, we present our policy-based ransomware spread mitigation tech-nique in FedDICE. This is as an answer to **RQ4**. To this end, we have created a small SDN network simulating FedDICE to test our proposed security architec-ture described in Sect. 5. For simulation simplicity, we represent the hierarchy of controllers using SDN data-plane devices, where every single data-plane device hosts an FL module. Our network setup has used four mininet simulated hosts (clients) connected to an ONOS SDN controller. In addition, we have tapped one Raspberry pi virtual machine (VM) as one of the hosts in this network. We consider this as an IoT device connected to a hospital network.

Successful Attack Phase: To simulate the Wannacry ransomware attack in our network, we have used tcpreplay [5]. Normally, a user-driven input initiates ransomware propagation. However, for this simulation purposes, we use a previ-ously recorded set of WannaCry packet traces. We have connected a Raspbian

VM to the network and used tcpreplay to replay the packet trace. Figure 6(a) shows a Wireshark capture of the WannaCry communication in the network.

Detection and Mitigation Phase: The FL models are used as policies to detect the attacks coming towards any hospital node. Our policy syntax is granular and can extend beyond the machine learning model. The policies are extremely customizable. We are using JSON to write the policies. The formulated policies can be used in the SDN controller of any hierarchy. Together with PbSA agent running in the local ICE, the fed agent can automatically forge the policies and install them in the local controller. Also, the FL models get updated in the regular interval from the central learning node located in the supernode, allowing the other lead SDN controller to be aware of the learning model changes. Besides, each policy has multiple sections. Firstly, the source profile (src_profile) refers to the specifics of the packets originating from the source, i.e., from which domain, IP, MAC, and service type the packet is coming from. Secondly, the destination profile (dst_profile) talks about the specifics of the packet destination, i.e., which domain, IP, and MAC address the packet is going to. Thirdly, the flow profile (flow_profile) specifies the flow. A series of packets constitute a flow, and each flow has a specific frequency of packet occurrence that is of specific sizes. Flows can specify payload type in the policy as well. For instance, a policy specifies the flow that needs to be dropped, e.g., flow containing ransomware packets. Fourthly, the machine learning model W_t specifies the model used as the policy for checking the incoming packet flow. Finally, each policy comes with an action. An action can be as simple as dropping a flow, or it can be a complicated one that routes the flows via edge devices. For instance, we can route any sensitive healthcare device flows via trusted switching devices. We can signify a wildcard using "*" in any policy field. Listing in Fig. 6(b) shows a sample policy used to detect the custom ransomware attack simulated by us in the SDN infrastructure. The policy says that any packet originating from any profile targets towards any

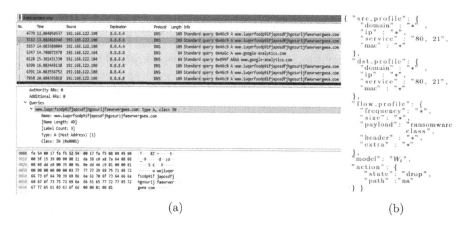

(a)   (b)

Fig. 6. (a) Wireshark capture of the communication, including that from ransomware, and (b) a sample policy in a JSON format.

destination, which is detected as the ransomware payload by the trained model, W_t, then the packets will be dropped. Furthermore, the local SDN controller removes the data source from the network.

8   Related Work

This section reviews the relevant works to cybersecurity in (distributed) ICE, ransomware detection and mitigation in clinical scenarios, and related works to federated learning in ransomware detection.

8.1   Cybersecurity in ICE

An ICE is usually implemented by using OpenICE [6]. Its security is managed partially by the external Data Distribution Service (DDS) middleware. However, these DDS middleware suffered from various difficulties, including complexity and scalability, in implementations [20]. In another work, authors have proposed a cloud-based secure logger as an effective solution against replay, eavesdropping, and injection [25], but the solution is ineffective if there is no message alteration.

8.2   Ransomware Detection

In literature, SDN-based ransomware mitigation solutions had been proposed. One of the works considered SDN redirection capabilities together with a black-list of proxy servers to check if the infected device is trying to connect to one of them to obtain the public encryption key [8]. The mitigation consisted of establishing a flow filter to impede this communication, and thus, the encryption of the files. Here the main drawback is the need to keep a blacklist of proxy servers updated. These servers must be identified utilizing behavioral analysis of known malware, thus making it impossible to detect new campaigns. When compared with our solution, our goal is not to prevent the encryption of the files. We attempt to detect ransomware spreading by using the characteristic traffic patterns generated during that stage. Additionally, our mitigation procedure restores the ICE/DICE system to a clean state. In another work, a deep packet inspection was implemented to identify the HTTP POST messages from ransomware [9]. The authors considered the lengths of each three consecutive HTTP POST messages as a feature vector and train by computing both the centroid of the feature vectors belonging to each ransomware class and a maximal distance to be considered from that class. This approach does not work if the packets are encrypted.

8.3   Related Works to Federated Learning in Ransomware Detection

There are two categories of related works: malware detection and anomaly detection. Various works had been done on the malware detection side, but little attention was given to ransomware detection and mitigation. Usually, these works considered host-based datasets, which are host-based systems' logs, e.g., event logs in a computer. For industrial IoT, FL was used to detect android malware applications in Industrial IoT (host-based data). Moreover, the authors considered data triggered by poisoning attacks based on GAN for robust training [32]. In separate work, host-based activities log datasets of malware (including ransomware) are considered to carry FL on malware classification [21]. On the anomaly detection side, FL was implemented to detect anomalies in IoT [26]. The data streaming from each IoT was considered and analyzed where the laptop was considered a gateway [26]. The IoT was infected with only one malware called Mirai (not a ransomware-type). In contrast, our work has considered the network of networks beyond the gateway (e.g., laptop) and ransomware samples in a DICE environment. In separate work, FL was implemented for network anomaly detection but performed to detect VPN traffic and Tor traffic [37]. Federated deep learning over the network flow dataset, called CIC-IDS2017, using blockchains was implemented for anomaly detection in intrusion detection. Moreover, CIC-IDS2017 did not contain data due to ransomware samples. In our work, we are focused on network security rather than an individual device. Thus, we use a dataset capturing network information (netflow). In contrast to the host-based dataset, our dataset captures completely different characteristics and belongs to a different distribution. It is unclear how the FL approach performs in a network-based ransomware dataset, so we addressed this question in this work.

9   Conclusion and Future Works

In this work, we presented FedDICE, which is federated learning entangled distributed integrated clinical environment. It enables data privacy by leveraging federating learning. Our results demonstrated that FedDICE effectively detects ransomware spread detection of WannaCry, Petya, BadRabbit, and PowerGhost with a testing accuracy of around 99% in the distributed integrated clinical environment (DICE). This performance is similar to the performance achieved by centralized learning, which is not a privacy-friendly approach. Besides, we implemented a policy-based ransomware spread mitigation technique leveraging the software-defined network functionalities. FedDICE is a generic framework and can be potentially used for other applications such as AI-supported medical decisions with data privacy.

This work demonstrated the proof of concept of FedDICE and its application in ransomware spread detection and mitigation. Studies considering a large-scale DICE with a large number of ransomware types are interesting avenues for further explorations. Studying other threat scenarios where attackers influencing the model training, including adversarial federated learning (e.g., FedGAN [32], model poisoning attacks [24]), in the FedDICE system is left as future works.

References

1. The hospital room of the future datasets. http://perception.inf.um.es/ICE-datasets/. Accessed 05 Feb 2021

2. NIST cybersecurity framework. https://www.nist.gov/cyberframework/risk-management-framework

3. Pytorch. https://pytorch.org/

4. Ransomware: Past, present, and future. https://blog.talosintelligence.com/2016/04/ransomware.html#ch3-portent

5. Tcpreplay. https://linux.die.net/man/1/tcpreplay. Accessed 2 Apr 2021

6. Arney, D., Plourde, J., Goldman, J.M.: OpenICE medical device interoperability platform overview and requirement analysis. Biomed. Tech. **63**, 39–47 (2018)

7. Brok, C.: Following ransomware attack Indiana hospital pays $55k to unlock data (2020). https://digitalguardian.com/blog/following-ransomware-attack-indiana-hospital-pays-55k-unlock-data#:~:text=A%20hospital%20in%20Indiana%20paid,stop%20the%20bleeding%20on%20Friday

8. Cabaj, K., Mazurczyk, W.: Using software-defined networking for ransomware mitigation: the case of CryptoWall. IEEE Netw. **30**(6), 14–20 (2016)

9. Cabaj, K., Gregorczyk, M., Mazurczyk, W.: Software-defined networking-based crypto ransomware detection using HTTP traffic characteristics. Comput. Electr. Eng. **66**, 353–368 (2018)

10. Celdran, A.H., Karmakar, K.K., Marmol, F.G., Varadharajan, V.: Detecting and mitigating cyberattacks using software defined networks for integrated clinical environments. Peer-to-Peer Netw. Appl. **14**, 1–16 (2021)

11. CheckPoint: Attacks targeting healthcare organizations spike globally as covid-19 cases rise again (2021). https://blog.checkpoint.com/2021/01/05/attacks-targeting-healthcare-organizations-spike-globally-as-covid-19-cases-rise-again/

12. Dimitrov, D.V.: Medical internet of things and big data in healthcare. Healthc. Inform. Res. **22**(3), 156–163 (2016)

13. EU: Regulation (EU) 2016/679 general data protection regulation. Off. J. Eur. Union (2016)

14. ASTM F2761: Medical devices and medical systems - essential safety requirements for equipment comprising the patient-centric integrated clinical environment (ICE) - part 1: General requirements and conceptual model. ASTM International (2013). https://www.astm.org/Standards/F2761.htm

15. Fernandez Maimo, L., Huertas Celdran, A., Perales Gomez, L., Garcia Clemente, F.J., Weimer, J., Lee, I.: Intelligent and dynamic ransomware spread detection and mitigation in integrated clinical environments. Sensors **19**(5), 1114 (2019)

16. Gallagher, R.: Bloomberg: Hackers 'without conscience' demand ransom from dozens of hospitals and labs working on coronavirus (2020). https://fortune.com/2020/04/01/hackers-ransomware-hospitals-labs-coronavirus/

17. Gibert, D., Mateu, C., Planes, J.: The rise of machine learning for detection and classification of malware: research developments, trends and challenges. J. Netw. Comput. Appl. **153**, 102526 (2020)

18. Khraisat, A., Gonda, I., Vamplew, P., Kamruzzaman, J.: Survey of intrusion detection systems: techniques, datasets and challenges. Cybersecurity **2**(20), 1–22 (2019)

19. Konecný, J., McMahan, B., Ramage, D.: Federated optimization: distributed optimization beyond the datacenter. arxiv (2015). https://arxiv.org/pdf/1511.03575.pdf

20. Köksal, Ö., Tekinerdogan, B.: Obstacles in data distribution service middleware: a systematic review. Future Gener. Comput. Syst. **68**, 191–210 (2017)

21. Lin, K.Y., Huang, W.R.: Using federated learning on malware classification. In: Proceedings of the ICACT, pp. 585–589 (2020)

22. Mathews, L.: Ransomware attacks on the healthcare sector are skyrocketing (2021). https://www.forbes.com/sites/leemathews/2021/01/08/ransomware-attacks-on-the-healthcare-sector-are-skyrocketing/?sh=2c5aa87d2d25

23. McMahan, B., Moore, E., Ramage, D., Hampson, S., y Arcas, B.A.: Communication-efficient learning of deep networks from decentralized data. In: Proceedings of the AISTATS, pp. 1273–1282 (2017)

24. Mothukuri, V., Parizi, R.M., Pouriyeh, S., Huang, Y., Dehghantanha, A., Srivastava, G.: A survey on security and privacy of federated learning. Futur. Gener. Comput. Syst. **115**, 619–640 (2021)

25. Nguyen, H., Acharya, B., et al.: Cloud-based secure logger for medical devices. In: Proceedings of the IEEE CHASE, pp. 89–94 (2016)

26. Nguyen, T.D., Marchal, S., Miettinen, M., Fereidooni, H., Asokan, N., Sadeghi, A.R.: DIoT: a federated self-learning anomaly detection system for IoT. In: Proceedings of the ICDCS, pp. 756–767 (2019)

27. O'Neill, P.H.: A patient has died after ransomware hackers hit a German hospital (2020). https://www.technologyreview.com/2020/09/18/1008582/a-patient-has-died-after-ransomware-hackers-hit-a-german-hospital/

28. Riboni, D., Villani, A., Vitali, D., Bettini, C., Mancini, L.V.: Obfuscation of sensitive data in network flows. In: 2012 Proceedings of the IEEE INFOCOM, pp. 2372–2380 (2012)

29. Sheller, M.J., Edwards, B., Reina, G.A., et al.: Federated learning in medicine: facilitating multi-institutional collaborations without sharing patient data. Sci. Rep. **10**, 12598 (2020). https://doi.org/10.1038/s41598-020-69250-1

30. Sherpa.ai: Federated learning framework. https://github.com/sherpaai/Sherpa.ai-Federated-Learning-Framework

31. Stankovic, J.A.: Research directions for cyber physical systems in wireless and mobile healthcare. ACM Trans. Cyber-Phys. Syst. **1**(1), 1–12 (2016)

32. Taheri, R., Shojafar, M., Alazab, M., Tafazolli, R.: FED-IIoT: a robust federated malware detection architecture in industrial IoT. IEEE TII (2020)

33. Thapa, C., Camtepe, S.: Precision health data: requirements, challenges and existing techniques for data security and privacy. Comput. Biol. Med. **129**, 1–23 (2021)

34. Verizon: DBIR 2020 data breach investigation report (2020). https://enterprise.verizon.com/resources/reports/2020-data-breach-investigations-report.pdf

35. Vogelsang, A., Borg, M.: Requirements engineering for machine learning: perspectives from data scientists. In: Proceedings of the IEEE 27th International Requirements Engineering Conference Workshops (REW) (2019)

36. Wang, L., Dyer, K.P., Akella, A., Ristenpart, T., Shrimpton, T.E.: Seeing through network-protocol obfuscation. In: Proceedings of the 22nd ACM SIGSAC Conference on Computer and Communications Security (CCS 2015), pp. 57–69 (2015)

37. Zhao, Y., Chen, J., Wu, D., Teng, J., Yu, S.: Multi-task network anomaly detection using federated learning. In: Proceedings of the SoICT, pp. 273–279 (2019)

Accelerating TEE-Based DNN Inference Using Mean Shift Network Pruning

Chengyao Xu and Shangqi Lai$^{(\boxtimes)}$ ⓘ

Faculty of Information Technology, Monash University, Clayton, Australia
cxu100@student.monash.edu, shangqi.lai@monash.edu

Abstract. In recent years, deep neural networks (DNNs) have achieved great success in many areas and have been deployed as cloud services to bring convenience to people's daily lives. However, the widespread use of DNNs in the cloud brings critical privacy concerns. Researchers have proposed many solutions to address the privacy concerns of deploying DNN in the cloud, and one major category of solutions rely on a trusted execution environment (TEE). Nonetheless, the DNN inference requires extensive memory and computing resources to achieve accurate decision-making, which does not operate well in TEE with restricted memory space. This paper proposes a network pruning algorithm based on mean shift clustering to reduce the model size and improve the inference performance in TEE. The core idea of our design is to use a mean shift algorithm to aggregate the weight values automatically and prune the network based on the distance between the weight and center. Our experiments prune three popular networks on the CIFAR-10 dataset. The experimental results show that our algorithm successfully reduces the network size without affecting its accuracy. The inference in TEE is accelerated by 20%.

1 Introduction

Deep neural networks (DNNs) have become the mainstream computing model in the artificial intelligence industry [30]. It shows superior performance in many fields such as image recognition [21], speech recognition [8], and natural language processing [48]. Recent advances of Machine Learning as a Service (MLaaS) [3, 4] enable users to deploy DNN models on the cloud and perform complex predication tasks efficiently and economically. However, the use of such cloud services raises privacy concerns. For example, an enterprise may use proprietary networks/datasets to conduct its core business. These networks/datasets are high-value assets for the enterprise and should not be revealed to cloud providers.

To mitigate the above privacy concerns, privacy-preserving machine learning has attracted attention; this approach encrypts the DNN model and dataset and processes machine learning tasks over the encrypted model and data. Existing studies in this area can be classified into software-based [7,10,22,23,27,31] and hardware-based (TEE-based) solutions [14,18,33,41].

© ICST Institute for Computer Sciences, Social Informatics and Telecommunications Engineering 2021
Published by Springer Nature Switzerland AG 2021. All Rights Reserved
X. Yuan et al. (Eds.): QShine 2021, LNICST 402, pp. 25–41, 2021.
https://doi.org/10.1007/978-3-030-91424-0_2

The software-based solutions leverage cryptographic tools like homomorphic encryption [7,10] and secure multiparty computation [20,22,23,27,31]. Those works archive a high level of privacy protection. However, due to the nature of cryptography algorithms, those approaches introduce a large number of computation operations. Thus, those mechanisms are hard to deploy to protect complex DNN models without incurring a significant inference latency.

Hardware-based (TEE-based) solutions rely on the trusted hardware to process sensitive information within an isolated environment (known as enclave). It has been widely used in many application contexts such as encrypted database [5,43,44], secure network functions [9,24,35] and also becomes a promising alternative of cryptographic tools when designing privacy-preserving machine learning schemes [14,18,33,41]. Nonetheless, existing works demonstrate that the limited memory size of the enclave restricts the performance of DNN inference. In specific, VGG-16, one of the most common DNN models, requires approximately 1 GB of memory for inference [26], while the maximum protected memory is only 128 MB in the Intel SGX [1]. Using extra memory in Intel SGX will trigger paging, which requires extra page swapping, data encryption, decryption operations and introduces a noticeable delay on the inference time (5× as shown in [40]).

To alleviate the memory consumption and accelerate TEE-based DNN inference, we present a novel networking pruning algorithm based on the mean shift clustering technique. We implement our algorithm and use it to prune three of the most commonly used DNN models: Res-NET [15], Densenet [17], and VGG-Net [39], trained with CIFAR-10 dataset. Then, we conduct inference tasks over our compressed DNN model inside an Intel SGX runtime called Occlum [37]. Our experimental results show that the proposed algorithm can effectively recognize and remove more than 35% of the redundant parameters for all three networks, together with an approximate 30% reduction in FLOPs. Moreover, compared to the unpruned network, the inference delay of the pruned network is reduced by 20% under the Intel SGX environment, and it only introduces a negligible accuracy loss (only 0.1%).

The rest of this paper is structured as follows. We discuss related work in Sect. 2. Then, we introduce the background knowledge in Sect. 3 and present an overview of our design goals and threat model in Sect. 4. In Sect. 5, we elaborate on the details of the novel network pruning algorithm. Next, we describe the experimental setup and the corresponding result/discussions regarding our solution in Sect. 6 and 7. We give a conclusion in Sect. 8.

2   Relative Work

2.1   Software-Based Secure Machine Learning

Secure machine learning involves protecting the privacy of both the training data and the model. In past years, cryptographic tools such as homomorphic encryption [7,10] and secure multi-party computation [20,22,23,27,31] have been increasingly used to handle this problem. However, the above solutions can only be applied to small-scale problems because the primitives incur intensive computations and introduce a noticeable delay when processing huge tasks.

2.2   TEE-Based Secure Machine Learning

Recently, TEE-based secure machine learning services have been widely studied. Particularly, these services [14,18,33,41] deploy machine learning tasks (can be training, inference or both) inside TEE to protect the privacy of user data and machine learning models. Nonetheless, TEE-based services still suffer the memory access pattern side-channel attacks as well as the performance issue due to the memory size limit of TEE platforms. Several works [33,34] targeting the memory access side-channel attacks have been presented. They leverage oblivious primitives to hide the memory access pattern and prevent the adversary from inferring extra information from the memory trace of machine learning tasks. On the other hand, it is still challenging to mitigate the delay introduced by TEE's memory size limit. For instance, Slalom [41] try to improve the performance of the model inference process in the TEE. It successfully allocates all linear layer calculations in DNN to untrusted but fast hardware, i.e., GPU. However, due to the collaboration between trusted and untrusted hardware, the system can not guarantee the privacy of DNN models. Also, Graviton [45] introduces a TEE on GPUs to speed up the secure inference process on GPUs, but it is just a blueprint feature which does not support by any off-the-shelf GPU.

2.3   Memory Efficient Machine Learning

Several methods have been proposed to optimize DNN models, such as Deep Compression [12], Network Sliming [28], ThiNet [29]. As a result, the amount of parameters required by the network is reduced compared to the original network, thus achieving acceleration and compression. However, those methods, including our approach, only focus on reducing the redundant parts of the model, which still requires a large amount of memory capacity for the calculations. Occlumency [26] proposes a direct way to optimize the memory usage of convolutional layers and achieved considerable speed up for the inference process. Our work can draw on the strengths of Occlumency to achieve better inference performance.

3   Background

3.1   Intel SGX

Intel SGX [1] is an x86 instruction set designed to improve the security of application code and data. On SGX-enabled platforms, applications are divided into trusted and untrusted parts. The trusted part, called enclave, is located in a dedicated part of the physical RAM and is strongly protected by SGX, while the untrusted part is executed as a general process. The untrusted part can only invoke a set of well-defined interfaces (ecall/ocall) to send and receive data from

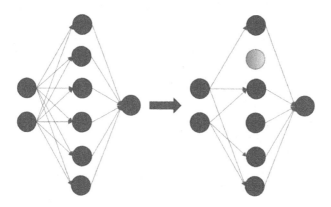

Fig. 1. Network pruning example: the technique prunes neurons (and its input/output) which are classified as "unnecessary" by the algorithm.

the enclave. All other software, including operating systems, privileged software, virtual machine management programs, and firmware, cannot access the enclave memory. SGX uses a remote attestation mechanism to ensure the enclave itself is trusted. The originator of the communication can verify that the SGX enclave is not tampered with against the authentication service provided by Intel.

SGX Runtime. To develop SGX applications, SGX SDK, such as Intel SGX SDK, Open Enclave SDK, Google Asylo, or Apache Rust SGX SDK, has been designed to provide basic supports on high-level languages, APIs and documentation. However, developing an SGX application still involves considerable efforts under the SGX environment. For instance, developers need to decide which components should be placed inside the enclave and outside the enclave and how the two parties should communicate. For complex applications, determining an efficient, logical, and secure partitioning scheme can be challenging in itself. Meanwhile, the developer should consider how to convert the legacy function calls to a secure version because SGX SDK does not support most of the system calls in the legacy system. To simplify the development of the SGX application, researchers have proposed many library OS for Intel SGX, such as SGX-LKL [36], Occlum [37], Graphene-SGX [42], and SCONE [6]. Those library OS contain a group of secure system calls for legacy code. They enable their users to port the entire application into the enclave with few or even no modifications, which highly reduce the development cost of SGX applications.

In this paper, we choose to use Occlum [37] to reduce the development cost. Occlum is the first TEE OS developed in Rust, dramatically reduces the chance of memory security issues, and provides 10-1000× faster process startup and 3× higher throughput for inter-process communication than the previous state-of-the-art open-source TEE OS (Graphene-SGX [42]).

3.2   Network Pruning

Network pruning is a network compression method that removes the redundant parts of the model to make the model more refined and improve the model's generalization performance. It can be classified into two types: unstructured pruning and structured pruning according to the network pruning object. Figure 1 shows the basic idea of Network Pruning.

Unstructured pruning methods [11,13] prune individual neurons (or individual connection weights) in the network and turn the dense connections between the neurons of the original network into sparse connections. Those methods aim to improve the runtime performance of networks by converting the original dense matrix operation into a sparse matrix operation. However, we note that the commonly used hardware in DNN does not provide additional acceleration for sparse matrix operations [28]. Hence, the unstructured pruning methods may not offer any acceleration for DNN but may be slower.

In recent years, structured pruning [29,32] is proposed to prune the network. Compared to unstructured pruning, structured pruning does not focus on the pruning of individual connection weights. Instead, it removes all values on the whole filter (filter-based) or layer (layer-based). Although its degree of freedom of pruning is relatively lower, and the degree of pruning is also lower, it can be more efficient in practice. The reason is that such methods do not require specific hardware platforms or computational libraries for the use of the pruned network. The pruned models can run directly on the mainstream deep learning frameworks nowadays to obtain direct acceleration.

4   Overview

4.1   Design Goals

This work aims to archive the following three goals:

Improved Inference Speed. Our design helps to achieve a low DNN inference latency compared to directly port the deep learning inference in the SGX enclave. Our pruning algorithm can significantly reduce the memory space required for inference service, which can reduce the paging operation of the SGX enclave. Also, by using the algorithm, the Floating Point Operations per second (FLOPs) of the inference process are reduced, which can also reduce the inference latency.

No Accuracy Loss. Our design prunes the DNN model to accelerate the DNN inference. In order to preserve the accuracy of the inference result, we carefully design the algorithm we used for model pruning so the pruned model will not incur any accuracy loss compared to the original model.

Privacy Protection for Whole Inference Service. Our design enables users to fit the entire DNN model into the enclave memory. Thus, the user can send their private data to the enclave for the prediction tasks, and the whole inference service will be shielded by TEE. As a result, our solution can provide efficient

Fig. 2. Flow-chart of pruning procedure.

black-box access to the model and protect the models against white-box level attacks. More privacy-preserving technologies should apply to the models (e.g., differential privacy) to migrate black-box level attacks, but those are beyond the scope of our work.

4.2   Threat Model

In this paper, we consider the scenario that a user subscribes to a DNN inference service on a cloud platform. The user will upload his/her DNN model to the cloud and obtain inference results from the cloud. We assume a powerful adversary who is capable of accessing all the resources running on the cloud, such as software and GPU. The adversary can obtain and analyze the memory trace of all processes except those running within the enclave. The adversary aims to leverage the collected information to infer useful information regarding user's DNN model and data. Our design leverages Intel SGX to protect user's private input (DNN model and data) against the above adversary.

We follow the existing works [5,9,35,43,44] to consider SGX side-channel attacks [25,38,47] and Denial of Services attack out of scope.

5   Mean Shift Network Pruning

To accelerate the DNN inference in the enclave, we design a network pruning algorithm to remove the redundant part of the DNN model. Figures 2 shows the general idea of our pruning algorithm. In the rest of this section, we introduce our proposed mean shift network pruning algorithm in detail.

Select BN Layers. During network training, parameter updates will cause the input data distribution in each layer to change continuously. Whenever the parameters are updated in the upper layer, it will inevitably cause a change in the input data distribution in the lower layer. This creates a complicated data distribution, which makes the analysis of the relationship of the weights a difficult task. In deep neural networks, this phenomenon is more serious. To solve the above issue, the BN algorithm can be applied to normalize the input at each layer and make the input data distribute stably during the training process. The proposed protocol leverages the benefit of using the Batch normalization (BN) [19] to prune the unnecessary channel. After loading the pre-trained models, the algorithm selects Batch normalization (BN) layers from the whole model for the pruning process. BN helps to improve the performance of our design because the training process with BN produces a more stable data distribution, which reduces the difficulty of analyzing the relationship of the weights. Moreover, the convolutional weights associated with BN are cut off, eliminating the need to re-analyze the association between each layer.

Mean Shift Clustering Algorithm. After selecting the BN layer, we choose to apply the mean shift clustering algorithm to cluster the weight value of the BN layer and prune out the unnecessary channel based on the cluster.

Clustering is a machine learning technique that involves the grouping of data points. Given a set of data points, we can use a clustering algorithm to divide data points into several groups. Theoretically, data points in the same group should have similar attributes and features, while data points in different groups should have highly different attributes and features. Clustering is an unsupervised learning method and is a standard statistical data analysis technique used in many fields. There are many clustering algorithms such as K-Means, K-Means++. In the K-Means algorithm, the final clustering result is influenced by the initial clustering center. The K-Means++ algorithm is proposed to provide a basis for choosing a better initial clustering center. However, the number of classes of clusters in the algorithm still needs to be formulated in advance. It will be challenging to solve K-Means and K-Means++ accurately for data sets with an unknown number of classes in advance.

The mean shift algorithm is a clustering algorithm based on the cluster center, like K-Means, but the difference is that the mean shift algorithm does not require a priori knowledge about the number of categories. Specifically, the mean shift algorithm employs an iterative step in which the offset mean of the current point is calculated. The point is moved to this offset mean, and then this is used as the new starting point to continue moving until the final condition is satisfied. For n sample points $x_i, i = 1, ..., n$ in a given d-dimensional space R^d, the formula of the mean shift vector for point x is:

$$M_h(x) = \frac{1}{k} \sum_{x_i \in S_h} (x_i - x), \tag{1}$$

where S_h refers to a high-dimensional spherical region of radius h, and adding all the points in it to the vector starting from the center of the circle is the mean shift vector (M_h).

Then, for each element in the set, the algorithm moves the element to the position of the mean of the eigenvalues of all elements in its neighborhood. The above step repeats until convergence. The element is marked as being in the same class when the element is in its convergence position.

A problem when solving the mean shift vector is that the algorithm assumes each sample point x_i contributes the same amount to sample X in the region of S_h. In practice, the contribution of each sample point x_i to sample X is different, and a kernel function can measure such sharing. A kernel function is a common approach used in machine learning. Suppose that the kernel function is added to the basic M_h to make each sample point x_i contribute differently to the sample X within a range S_h of radius h. The influence of distance is considered when calculating M_h. It can also be assumed that the importance is not the same for all sample points X. Therefore, a weighting factor is also introduced for each sample. In this way, the M_h form can be extended as follows:

$$M_h(x) = \frac{\sum_{i=1}^{n} G(\frac{x_i-x}{h})w(x_i)(x_i - x)}{\sum_{i=1}^{n} G(\frac{x_i-x}{h})w(x_i)}, \tag{2}$$

where $G(\frac{x_i-x}{h})$ is the kernel function and $w(x_i)$ is a weight assigned to the sampling points. The pseudocode for mean shift can be seen in Algorithm 1:

Algorithm 1. mean shift clustering algorithm

1: **Input:** Data set D, Radius h
2: **Output:** Cluster C
3: **Initialization:** Cluster C, Threshold t
4: **repeat**:
5: Select a random point in the unlabeled D as $center$
6: Initialize cluster C_n
7:    **repeat**:
8:       Find all points that are within radius h from $center$, denoted as the set S.
9:       Sum up the vectors from $center$ to all elements in the S as M_h
10:       Update all points to C_n with the w (in formula 2) that these points belong to C_n
11:       $center \leftarrow center + |M_h|$
12:    **until**: M_h converge
13:    **if** the distance between C_n's $center$ and C_{n-1}'s $center$ smaller then t **then**
14:       merge C_n to C_{n-1}
15:    **else** add C_n to C
16: **until** all points in D have be accessed.
17: Classify each points to their cluster based on the largest w

---

In this work, the algorithm will take inputs as the weight data of each BN layer (data set) and the automatically detected radius from the build-in function *estimate_bandwidth* with default quantile value. After getting the results of the clustering, the information is passed onto the next stage.

Channel Pruning. In the above steps, our approach generates the mean shift clusters. Next, it selects the pruned channels by referring to use the minimum value among all cluster centers. The weight value smaller than the minimum center value will be pruned out. In the pruning phase, our approach will prune channels by removing all their incoming and outgoing connections and corresponding weights.

Advantages of Channel-Wise Pruning. As discussed in Sect. 3.2, network pruning can be divided into two categories: unstructured pruning and structured pruning. Unless the lower-level hardware and computational libraries better support it, it is not easy to get substantial performance gains with unstructured pruning. Therefore, much of the research in the past few years has focused on the structured pruning. The structured pruning methods can be further subdivided to layer-wise, channel-wise and filter-wise.

The pruning object of the layer granularity-based pruning algorithm is the entire network layer. The purpose of pruning is to make a deep neural network into a relatively shallow network. This pruning method's advantages are undeniable, as the use of pruned networks does not require any unique toolkit for inference acceleration. However, apart from this advantage, the limitations and drawbacks of this approach are also obvious. The direct pruning of the network layers makes the method extremely inflexible, and it is only effective when a network model is deep enough (more than 50 layers) to trim off some layers [46]. We also found that layer-based network pruning algorithms are inflexible; the sparse operations of weight-based pruning (unstructured pruning) algorithms cannot be accelerated directly on existing hardware platforms and computational libraries.

On the other hand, recent network pruning algorithms based on convolutional kernel and channel achieves a balance in flexibility and implementation. Moreover, it can be applied to any typical CNN or fully connected layer (treating each neuron as a channel). The resulting network is also essentially a thin network that can be reasoned quickly on CNN platforms. Since cropping a feature map is equivalent to cropping the connected convolutional kernels together, channel-wise and filter-wise pruning is in the same class of algorithms.

6   Experiment

We evaluate the performance of our works in terms of the number of model parameters, FLOPs, model accuracy and inference latency with a variety of DNN models. We have implemented our work based on PyTorch [2].

6.1   Experiment Setup

Dataset. We evaluated our work upon the CIFAR-10 dataset. The CIFAR-10 dataset is a small dataset for identifying common objects containing 10 categories of color images, including airplanes, cars, birds, cats, etc. There are 60,000 images in the dataset. Each category contains 6,000 images, of which 5,000 images are used for training, and another 1,000 images are used for testing. The size of all images is 32×32 pixels.

Models. We use three well-known CNN models to evaluate our design, VGG, ResNet, and DenseNet.

VGG. VGG is a deep convolutional neural network for image recognition developed and trained by the Computer Vision Group at the University of Oxford, which achieved second place in the classification event and first place in the localization event ILSVRC2014 competition. Commonly used versions of the VGGNet structure are VGG-16 and VGG-19. To facilitate comparisons with existing methods, the experiments in this section use the VGG-16 network, which

Table 1. The result on the CIFAR-10 dataset.

Model	Accuracy	Parameters	Pruned	FLOPs	Pruned	Pruned ratio
VGGNet (Baseline)	94.2%	14.72M	-	313.75M	-	-
VGGNet (Pruned)	84.2% (94.0%)	7.07M	52.1%	237.36M	24.3%	38.2%
ResNet-164 (Baseline)	95.0%	1.70M	-	253.95M	-	-
ResNet-164 (Pruned)	87.3% (94.8%)	1.11M	34.7%	173.40M	31.7%	33.2%
DenseNet-40 (Baseline)	94.2%	1.06M	-	287.71M	-	-
DenseNet-40 (Pruned)	87.0% (94.1%)	0.69M	34.9%	204.71M	28.9%	31.9%

"Baseline" denotes the pre-trained model we used in the experiment without any pruning operation. In the 2nd column, "84.2% (93.9%)" indicates the pruned model has 84.2% accuracy, and fine-tuned pruned model has 93.9% accuracy. The 4th and 6th columns show the pruned ratio of parameters and FLOPs. The total pruned ratio of the model is in the 7th column.

consists of 16 layers, including 13 convolutional layers and 3 fully connected layers. For network pruning, we pre-trained the VGG-16 net with CIFAR-10, and the test accuracy is 94.20%.

ResNet. In order to verify the effectiveness of pruning for more compact networks, the experiments further continue to validate the pruning method on the CIFAR-10 dataset based on the ResNet, a deep convolutional neural network, which won the championship in three categories of image classification, detection, and localization in ILSVRC2015. The ResNet-164 network is used in this experiment. Unlike the single-branch VGG16 network, Res Net-164 is a multi-branch network with many more layers, consisting of 163 convolutional layers and a fully connected layer for classification. The trained benchmark model was tested on CIFAR-10 with 95% accuracy after the training.

DenseNet. DenseNet was proposed after ResNet and combining the ideas of ResNet. One of the advantages of DenseNet is that the network is narrower and has fewer parameters. In this paper, we use DenseNet-40 consisting of 39 convolutional layers and a fully connected layer. The benchmark model we used in this part was trained on CIFAR-10 with 94.2% accuracy.

Running Environment. We used a Google Cloud virtual instance as the platform to test our design. The instance equips an Intel Cascade Lake C2 CPU platform with 4 vCPU and 16 GB memory. As the virtual instance does not support SGX hardware mode, the experiment was tested under SGX simulation mode. For SGX runtime, we choose to use Occlum. Occlum is a multi-process library OS (LibOS) for Intel SGX. It provides a container-like, user-friendly interface that allows applications to run on SGX with little or no source code modification. Moreover, Occlum is the first TEE OS developed using the Rust language, significantly reducing memory security issues.

6.2 Result

Parameters and FLOPs Reductions. Our work aims to reduce the number of computational resources required for DNN inference. From Table 1, we can see that each model has over 35% unnecessary channel pruned, and the model accuracy is slightly different from the baseline after the fine-tuning process. For VGGNet, we can find that over 50% of redundant parameters can be pruned, while for ResNet and DenseNet, the pruned ratio on parameters is relatively miniature, just around 34%. We believed this is because those two networks are more compact than VGGNet and the structure already provides some channel selection function. Figure 3 provides a clear view of the Parameter and FLOPs reductions in three models.

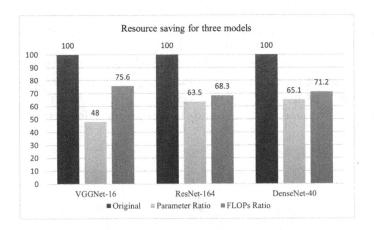

Fig. 3. Comparison of pruned models

We choose Network Slimming [28] (Slim) as the comparison method, and the evaluation metrics include accuracy, pruning rate, reduction in the number of parameters, and FLOPs. We only compare the result on ResNet and DenseNet. Since our method is an adaptive pruning method, it is hard to control the pruning rate compared to Slim's brutal pruning. Thus, the pruning performance on VGGNet is hard to compare.

The result is in Table 2 and 3. From the result, we can observe that our work performed better on ResNet, while on DenseNet, our approach only outperformed on FLOPs reduction. However, the total pruned ratio for our approach is only around 32%, but for Slim, the set pruned ratio is 40%. It shows that our approach uses a lower pruning rate to achieve the effectiveness of Slim's 40% pruning rate. The experiment also shows that iIf we could increase the pruning rate, we can save more resources as more neurons will be removed from the network. However, the high pruning rate may eliminates some important channels hence affect the accuracy of the model. In the next section, we will discuss more details about the pruning rate.

Inference Latency. We compare our work with two baselines. The first one (*SGX*) runs the model inference in the enclave but does not prune the model. We use this baseline to show the effectiveness of our approach in reducing the wait time for model inference in the enclave. In the second baseline (*Native*), the model inference is running as a general program without the protection of SGX. We use this baseline to investigate the overhead of our work.

Table 2. Experimental results of ResNet-164 pruning on CIFAR-10

Method	FLOPs reduction (%)	Params reduction (%)	Accuracy (%)
Slim (40%)	23.7	14.9	**+0.34**
Our work	**31.7**	**34.7**	−0.2

Table 3. Experimental results of DenseNet-40 pruning on CIFAR-10

Method	FLOPs reduction (%)	Params reduction (%)	Accuracy (%)
Slim (40%)	28.4	**35.7**	**+0.92**
Our work	**28.9**	34.9	−0.1

"Slim (40%)" denotes the pruning rate in Network Slimming method is 40%

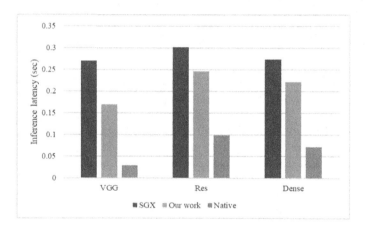

Fig. 4. Inference latency of various deep-learning models in native environment, Occlum runtime (SGX) and our work (Occlum + pruning)

We evaluate the three models' inference times for the experiments in the Native and SGX environments in the unpruned case. The results are shown in Fig. 4. We can see that DNN inference has a significant latency in the SGX environment and up to 9× in VGGNet inference. From the figure, we can see that the inference speed of the pruned model running on SGX is significantly improved. For the VGG-16 network, the redundant parameters are reduced due to the higher pruning rate. The inference speed is improved by 37% compared to the unpruned model. On the other hand, the speedups of ResNet-164 and DenseNet-40 were minor but also improved about 20% for each. Figure 4 also compares the inference speed of the unpruned model running in a native operating environment with the pruned model running in the SGX enclave. It shows that although our solution incurs an extra inference latency, it is still a significant improvement compared to directly port the inference service into SGX.

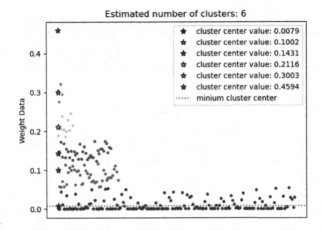

Fig. 5. Clustering result on weight data

7   Discussion

Pruning Rate. As mentioned, our proposed algorithm is an adaptive pruning algorithm based on mean shift clustering. We choose to use the minimum point in the clustering result as the pruning criterion in our experiments. The algorithm runs clustering on the weight value of the BN layer. The relationship between weight value and channel importance is proportional. The smaller the weight value is, the less impact on the overall network structure. Thus, we choose to prune off the channels with a weight value smaller than the minimum centroid value. The experiments show that the pruning rate for the three networks is between 30% and 40% when we use the minimum value. Figure 5 shows the weight distribution after mean shift clustering. In order to improve the pruning rate further, we have considered using the mean value of all cluster centroids as the pruning criterion. However, we can see from the figure that most weight distributions are below the average, leading to a significant pruning rate. On VGGNet, we used the average value for pruning which led to some layers being completely pruned, thus destroying the entire network structure. In ResNet and DenseNet, we can achieve a higher pruning rate by using the average value. However, the model's accuracy is greatly affected due to the reduction of channels. To sum up, mean shift clustering helps us classify the weight values effectively, but it is challenging to filter out more irrelevant weights from the cluster classes and increase the pruning rate.

Another point to mention is that this work is tested on the popular CNN networks. Evaluating the effect of algorithms on DNN models is our future research direction.

Flexibility. The existing structured pruning algorithms are usually based on sparse parameters for pruning. For example, Network Slimming adds a channel-wise scaling factor to the BN layer and applies an L1 regularizer to obtain sparse parameters. Network Trimming [16] tends to produce sparse activation values for activation functions such as RELU to perform pruning. Although good results can be achieved, pruning involves more or less the setting of hyperparameters in algorithm implementation, such as determining the pruning dimension of the model or pruning rate of the model. Moreover, most of the models need to be retrained to get the sparse parameters.

We also compared our work with [49] which archived a better pruning rate than ours with similar accuracy loss. In [49], the authors claim that the L1 regularisation technique would cause all scale coefficients to converge to zero. Instead, their solution aims to reduce the scale coefficients of the "unimportant" channels only while keeping the other coefficients large. However, this technique still requires retraining the model to polarise the weight distribution of the BN layer before pruning, which can take a much longer time to proceed comparing to our solution. On the other hand, our algorithm relies only on the benefits of the BN layer and mean shift clustering, which significantly reduces the preprocessing requirements of the model and can directly prune most existing models and achieve a notable pruning rate. In future work, we will replicate their algorithm and perform mean shift clustering on the polarised weights and then prune them to compare the experimental results.

Another benefit of our work is that by modifying the code, we believe that our algorithm can provide a TEE-based privacy-preserving network pruning service that allows people to compress their own trained models without any relevant knowledge. This could be a future research direction for us.

Inference Acceleration. As in the experimental result, our method can improve the inference speed of the model in SGX and does not affect the model's accuracy. However, our experiments are only based on the CIFAR-10 dataset, which is difficult to compare with the ImageNet dataset used in other papers. Moreover, our method only reduces the number of parameters and FLOPs of the model and does not fundamentally solve the memory occupation problem faced by DNN model inference in SGX. There have been some studies on memory optimization for using DNN models in SGX. Occlumency [26] proposed Partitioned Convolution to replace the traditional im2col convolutional computation, which greatly reduces the memory required for convolutional computation. At the same time, they observe that most models sequentially compute each layer and leverage this feature to optimize the feature maps of the convolution layer output. Particularly, they discard the feature maps that are no longer used to relieve the memory pressure of SGX. However, their approach requires extensive modifications to the underlying framework of deep learning and is more restrictive to the models used. Using GPU acceleration is currently the mainstream acceleration approach for DNN models. Nonetheless, the traditional SGX does not support the use of GPU. SLALOM [41] proposes a DNN inference acceleration using both GPU and SGX. But their approach requires part of the computation to be performed on an unprotected GPU, which can lead to some privacy issues. Memory optimization for DNN and establishing trust execution environments for GPU DNN inference service still be the critical research direction.

8 Conclusion

This paper presents an unsupervised clustering pruning algorithm based on mean shift clustering, which can effectively compress the existing DNN models. Our evaluations over CIFAR-10 dataset with three models, VGG-16, ResNet-164, and DenseNet-40, show that our pruning algorithm can reduce FLOPs and parameters by more than 30%. After deploying the pruned models to SGX, our method speeds up about 20% compared to the traditional DNN inference service in SGX. The proposed algorithm enables complicated DNN models to be fit into the constraints of memory under the SGX environment. Furthermore, it successfully reduces the inference latency in the SGX while preserving the privacy of users' data and models.

References

1. Intel Software Guard Extensions. https://software.intel.com/content/www/us/en/develop/topics/software-guard-extensions.html [online]
2. PyTorch. https://pytorch.org [online]
3. Azure Machine Learning (2021). https://azure.microsoft.com/en-au/services/machine-learning/
4. Google Vertex AI (2021). https://cloud.google.com/vertex-ai
5. Amjad, G., Kamara, S., Moataz, T.: Forward and backward private searchable encryption with SGX. In: EuroSec 2019 (2019)
6. Arnautov, S., et al.: SCONE: secure linux containers with intel SGX. In: USENIX OSDI 2016 (2016)
7. Chabanne, H., de Wargny, A., Milgram, J., Morel, C., Prouff, E.: Privacy-preserving classification on deep neural network. IACR Crypto ePrint: 2017/035 (2017)
8. Deng, L., Hinton, G., Kingsbury, B.: New Types of deep neural network learning for speech recognition and related applications: an overview. In: IEEE ICASSP 2013 (2013)
9. Duan, H., et al.: LightBox: full-stack protected stateful middlebox at lightning speed. In: ACM CCS1 2019 (2019)
10. Gilad-Bachrach, R., et al.: CryptoNets: applying neural nnetworks to encrypted data with high throughput and accuracy. In: ICML 2016 (2016)
11. Guo, Y., Yao, A., Chen, Y.: Dynamic network surgery for efficient DNNs. arXiv preprint:1608.04493 (2016)
12. Han, S., Mao, H., Dally, W.J.: Deep compression: compressing deep neural networks with pruning, trained quantization and Huffman coding. arXiv preprint:1510.00149 (2016)
13. Han, S., Pool, J., Tran, J., Dally, W.J.: Learning both weights and connections for efficient neural networks. arXiv preprint:1506.02626 (2015)
14. Hashemi, H., Wang, Y., Annavaram, M.: DarKnight: a data privacy scheme for training and inference of deep neural networks. arXiv preprint:2006.01300 (2020)
15. He, K., Zhang, X., Ren, S., Sun, J.: Deep residual learning for image recognition. arXiv preprint:1512.03385 (2015)
16. Hu, H., Peng, R., Tai, Y.W., Tang, C.K.: Network trimming: a data-driven neuron pruning approach towards efficient deep architectures. arXiv preprint:1607.03250 (2016)

17. Huang, G., Liu, Z., Van Der Maaten, L., Weinberger, K.Q.: densely connected convolutional networks. In: IEEE CVPR 2017 (2017)
18. Hunt, T., Zhu, Z., Xu, Y., Peter, S., Witchel, E.: Ryoan: a distributed sandbox for untrusted computation on secret data. In: USENIX OSDI 2016 (2016)
19. Ioffe, S., Szegedy, C.: Batch normalization: accelerating deep network training by reducing internal covariate shift. In: ICML 2015 (2015)
20. Juvekar, C., Vaikuntanathan, V., Chandrakasan, A.: GAZELLE: a low latency framework for secure neural network inference. In: USENIX Security 2018 (2018)
21. Krizhevsky, A., Sutskever, I., Hinton, G.E.: ImageNet classification with deep convolutional neural networks. In: NIPS 2012 (2012)
22. Lai, S., et al.: Enabling efficient privacy-assured outlier detection over encrypted incremental datasets. IEEE Internet of Things J. 7(4), 2651–2662 (2019)
23. Lai, S., et al.: GraphSE^2: an encrypted graph database for privacy-preserving social search. In: ACM ASIACCS 2019 (2019)
24. Lai, S., et al.: OblivSketch: oblivious network measurement as a cloud service. In: NDSS 2021 (2021)
25. Lee, S., et al.: Inferring fine-grained control flow inside SGX enclaves with branch shadowing. In: USENIX Security 2017 (2017)
26. Lee, T., et al.: Occlumency: privacy-preserving remote deep-learning inference using SGX. In: ACM MobiCom 2019 (2019)
27. Liu, J., Juuti, M., Lu, Y., Asokan, N.: Oblivious neural network predictions via MiniONN transformations. In: ACM CCS 2017 (2017)
28. Liu, Z., et al.: Learning efficient convolutional networks through network slimming. In: IEEE ICCV 2017 (2017)
29. Luo, J.H., Wu, J., Lin, W.: ThiNet: A Filter level pruning method for deep neural network compression. In: IEEE ICCV 2017 (2017)
30. Masi, I., Wu, Y., Hassner, T., Natarajan, P.: Deep face recognition: a survey. In: SIBGRAPI 2018 (2018)
31. Mishra, P., Lehmkuhl, R., Srinivasan, A., Zheng, W., Popa, R.A.: DELPHI: a cryptographic inference service for neural networks. In: USENIX Security 2020 (2020)
32. Molchanov, P., Tyree, S., Karras, T., Aila, T., Kautz, J.: Pruning convolutional neural networks for resource efficient inference. arXiv preprint:1611.06440 (2016)
33. Ohrimenko, O., et al.: Oblivious multi-party machine learning on trusted processors. In: USENIX Security 2016 (2016)
34. Poddar, R., Ananthanarayanan, G., Setty, S., Volos, S., Popa, R.A.: Visor: privacy-preserving video analytics as a cloud service. In: USENIX Security 2020 (2020)
35. Poddar, R., Lan, C., Popa, R.A., Ratnasamy, S.: Safebricks: shielding network functions in the cloud. In: USENIX NSDI 2018 (2018)
36. Priebe, C., et al.: SGX-LKL: securing the host OS interface for trusted execution. arXiv preprint:1908.11143 (2020)
37. Shen, Y., et al.: Occlum: secure and efficient multitasking inside a single enclave of intel SGX. In: ACM ASPLOS 2020 (2020)
38. Shinde, S., Chua, Z.L., Narayanan, V., Saxena, P.: Preventing page faults from telling your secrets. In: ACM AsiaCCS 2016 (2016)
39. Simonyan, K., Zisserman, A.: Very deep convolutional networks for large-scale image recognition. arXiv preprint:1409.1556 (2014)
40. Taassori, M., Shafiee, A., Balasubramonian, R.: VAULT: reducing paging overheads in SGX with efficient integrity verification structures. In: ACM ASPLOS 2018 (2018)

41. Tramer, F., Boneh, D.: Slalom: fast, verifiable and private execution of neural networks in trusted hardware. In: ICLR 2019 (2019)
42. Tsai, C.C., Porter, D.E., Vij, M.: Graphene-SGX: a practical library OS for unmodified applications on SGX. In: USENIX ATC 2017 (2017)
43. Vo, V., Lai, S., Yuan, X., Nepal, S., Liu, J.K.: Towards efficient and strong backward private searchable encryption with secure enclaves. In: ACNS 2021 (2021)
44. Vo, V., et al.: Accelerating forward and backward private searchable encryption using trusted execution. In: ACNS 2020 (2020)
45. Volos, S., Vaswani, K., Bruno, R.: Graviton: trusted execution environments on GPUs. In: USENIX OSDI 2018 (2018)
46. Wen, W., Wu, C., Wang, Y., Chen, Y., Li, H.: Learning structured sparsity in deep neural networks. arXiv preprint:1608.03665 (2016)
47. Xu, Y., Cui, W., Peinado, M.: Controlled-channel attacks: deterministic side channels for untrusted operating systems. In: IEEE S&P 2015 (2015)
48. Young, T., Hazarika, D., Poria, S., Cambria, E.: Recent trends in deep learning based natural language processing. IEEE Comput. Intell. Mag. **13**(3), 55–75 (2018)
49. Zhuang, T., Zhang, Z., Huang, Y., Zeng, X., Shuang, K., Li, X.: Neuron-level structured pruning using polarization regularizer. In: NeurIPS 2020 (2020)

Towards Secure and Trustworthy Crowdsourcing with Versatile Data Analytics

Rui Lian[1,2], Anxin Zhou[1,2], Yifeng Zheng[3], and Cong Wang[1,2(✉)]

[1] City University of Hong Kong, Kowloon Tong, Hong Kong
{rui.lian,anxin.zhou}@my.cityu.edu.hk, congwang@cityu.edu.hk
[2] City University of Hong Kong Shenzhen Research Institute, Shenzhen, China
[3] Harbin Institute of Technology, Shenzhen, China
yifeng.zheng@hit.edu.cn

Abstract. Crowdsourcing enables the harnessing of crowd wisdom for data collection. While being widely successful, almost all existing crowdsourcing platforms store and process plaintext data only. Such a practice would allow anyone gaining access to the platform (e.g., attackers, administrators) to obtain the sensitive data, raising potential security and privacy concerns. If actively exploited, this not only infringes the data ownership of the crowdsourcing requester who solicits data, but also leaks the privacy of the workers who provide data. In this paper, we envision a crowdsourcing platform with built-in end-to-end encryption (E2EE), where the crowdsourced data remains always-encrypted secret to the platform. Such a design would serve as an in-depth defence strategy against data breach from both internal and external threats, and provide technical means for crowdsourcing service providers to meet various stringent regulatory compliance. We will discuss the technical requirements and related challenges to make this vision a reality, including: 1) assuring high-quality crowdsourced data to enhance data values, 2) enabling versatile data analytics to uncover data insights, 3) protecting data at the front-end to fully achieve E2EE, and 4) preventing the abuse of E2EE for practical deployment. We will briefly overview the limitations of prior arts in meeting all these requirements, and identify a few potential research directions for the roadmap ahead.

Keywords: Crowdsourcing · Confidential computing · Data protection

1 Introduction

In the era of big data, healthcare, marketing, government policies and more all heavily rely on data for decision-makings and innovations. Such data demand drives the growth of crowdsourcing platforms (e.g., MTurk, Appen, and Freelancer), which can help a requester solicit data for various applications ranging from image annotation [9] to opinion collection [36].

© ICST Institute for Computer Sciences, Social Informatics and Telecommunications Engineering 2021
Published by Springer Nature Switzerland AG 2021. All Rights Reserved
X. Yuan et al. (Eds.): QShine 2021, LNICST 402, pp. 42–53, 2021.
https://doi.org/10.1007/978-3-030-91424-0_3

However, the accumulation of large-scale data makes crowdsourcing platforms lucrative targets for attackers [40]. This security concern poses strong demands on data protection at the platforms. Meanwhile, the increasingly strict legal regulation on data privacy and ownership, like the GDPR [13], also makes such data protection a crucial necessity.

Existing crowdsourcing platforms have adopted many methods to thwart external attacks [3]. However, these platforms still store and process data in clear plaintext, opening potential pathways to data breach incidents [1,37]. In this paper, we envision a crowdsourcing platform with built-in end-to-end encryption (E2EE), where the crowdsourced data remains always-encrypted secret to the platform. Such a design would serve as an in-depth defence strategy against data breach from both internal and external threats, and provide technical means for crowdsourcing service providers to meet various stringent regulatory compliance.

While directly adopting E2EE ensures data security in transit and at rest [11], E2EE alone is not yet sufficient to meet versatile data utility demands at the crowdsourcing platform. Indeed, E2EE is just a starting point. For secure and trustworthy crowdsourcing with versatile data analytics, we must also leverage latest advancement in computing over encrypted data, aka confidential computing. There are two general lines of approaches for data processing in the context of E2EE: cryptographic techniques like e.g., homomorphic encryption, secure multi-party computation, etc., and hardware-assisted designs like secure enclave, which provides a hardware-supported trusted execution environment (TEE) for isolated confidential data processing. For the former, while steady advancements have been made over the years, it is still not yet suitable to meet the practical performance and versatile utility demand in realistic workload. For the latter, even though it relies on a slightly different trust model, i.e., fully trusting the hardware vendor that facilitates the TEE, it promises much better performance and is easier to be deployed in practice. The E2EE application like Signal[1] is one such illustrating example.

In light of these observations, we will follow the line of hardware-assisted designs in our subsequent discussion. Particularly, we will leverage TEE as a starting point for data processing on the E2EE crowdsourcing platform to offer utilities equivalent to those of today's crowdsourcing platforms.

Assuring High-Quality Crowdsourced Data. The collected data may be unreliable due to factors like varied worker skills, ambient noises, and personal bias [28], raising a need to put quality assurance in the first place [8]. To assure data quality, a common strategy is to mine ground truth from unreliable data with aggregation mechanisms. Specifically, most crowdsourcing platforms assign the same task to multiple workers and aggregate their data as the result. To retain this utility in the context of E2EE, we can directly utilize TEE to aggregate encrypted crowd data. While conceptually simple, TEE is not a panacea due to its own limitations, such as the limited memory space, costly enclave interaction, and side-channel attacks [7]. Without correctly taking care of the limitations, the security and efficiency features of TEE will not be convincingly

---

[1] https://signal.org/blog/private-contact-discovery/.

justified. In addition, we believe the status quo of quality assurance can also be improved. The conventional aggregation mechanisms (e.g., averaging, majority voting) consider all data from workers are equally reliable. The equal treatment of the experts and novice workers may make the aggregation ineffective and produce low-quality data [8]. To reduce the error between the aggregated result and the ground truth, we aim to integrate cutting-edge reliability-aware aggregation mechanisms [48] into our platform. We also aim to adopt quality-aware incentives [34] for encouraging workers to contribute high-quality data.

Enabling Versatile Data Analytics. Normally, the data produced from the quality assurance phase are stored at the back-end database systems (e.g., relational databases). Data consumers[2] usually need to conduct data analytics to uncover data insights[3]. Data analytics is often done with statistics functions, which can be easily facilitated by off-the-shelf databases running SQL queries [4,17,49]. In our aforementioned E2EE settings, the data will be stored in always-encrypted form. Thus, the back-end databases are also expected to fully support the versatile SQL queries directly over the encrypted data. Moreover, such an encrypted database design, if successful, should be fully compatible with today's applications, expected to serve as a drop-in replacement to today's widely deployed industrial-grade database systems. Today's TEE-based encryption-in-use databases [2,43,46] largely match the aforementioned functionality requirements. With TEE, they also provide a natural benefit that allows the public to verify the results without revealing sensitive data [54]. This can be very benefitial to researchers of computational social science for reproducible research from crowdsourcing data [25]. However, there are still limitations on security and performance respectively. For security, it has been shown that there are various exploitable leakage profiles during query processing, which could be utilized to recover the ciphertext relations [43]. For performance, the frequent context switch from inside the enclave to the external could be very costly for certain queries [46]. Besides, recent results have shown that malicious consumers might infer private information of workers from the analytics results [39], which further raises the privacy-preserving demand when releasing the analytics results.

Beyond preserving the utilities, we have identified some deployment considerations that are necessary but usually overlooked by prior E2EE crowdsourcing works [29,30,52,53].

Protecting Data at the Front End. While the platform stores and processes encrypted data, data protection on its front-end also matters for fully achieving E2EE. If not handled well, the crowdsourced data might be leaked at the front-end without user consent. The web browser, as the widely-used front-end of crowdsourcing platforms, is vulnerable to many attacks. One of the main security culprits in the browser is the malicious browser extension that is often granted excessive privileges. This allows them to access and modify data by executing JavaScript code stealthily [6,20,41,50]. What makes matters worse through

---

[2] Here, data consumers can be anyone authorized by the requester.
[3] https://www.surveymonkey.com/apps/categories/analytics-reporting.

browser extensions is malvertising that may induce users to install malware and control their machines [23]. Therefore, it is important to raise the security bar to prevent malicious browser extensions from stealing the data residing at the front-end. Ideally, we can create an isolated environment for data processing in the browser, where malicious browser extensions cannot access the data. Towards this demand, cutting-edge methods [12,21,31,47] include developing web proxies, browser extensions, and hardware-assisted components. Besides technical perspective, we believe securing the front-end also needs to take into account various usability perspectives from the users. As such, we propose to follow the line of developing a dedicated browser extension for our easy-to-adopt defence, and will discuss various pros and cons following this path for the E2EE crowdsourcing platform.

Preventing the Abuse of E2EE. The adoption of E2EE, however, exacerbates the abuse issue in crowdsourcing. Since E2EE ensures that the platform does not have access to the contents, malicious users can "legitimately" abuse the platform to conduct illicit activities and spread misinformation. For example, a terrorist may post a crowdsourcing task to spread recruiting imagery. Such circumstances may have serious consequences, putting societies at risk (like impacts on democratic elections and terrorism [16,19]). Some legal and social organizations thus have been pushing for a suspension of adopting E2EE for applications [33,42]. Therefore, it is necessary to consider how to prevent the abuse of E2EE. Today's ongoing explorations of content moderation in E2EE respond to this issue [24,44]. These works either rely on user self-reporting to trace back the source of abusive data or maintain a blacklist to filter out malicious data. We will follow this line of work and continuously explore more possibilities.

To our best knowledge, currently, there is no viable crowdsourcing platform that can provide end-to-end data protection while preserving the aforementioned utilities or fully addressing the deployment challenges. In subsequent sections, we will briefly overview the E2EE crowdsourcing framework, present a comprehensive study on the existing landscape, with limitations in meeting all requirements as introduced above, and identify a few potential research directions for the roadmap ahead.

2   Overview

The crowdsourcing scenario involves four parties: the requester, workers, the data consumer, and the platform. At a high level, the requester publishes tasks on the platform, and workers participate in the tasks, who submit data under the protection of a browser extension. The platform firstly detects whether the submitted data include harmful contents, and then executes quality assurance mechanisms and stores the data in databases. Afterwards, an authorized data consumer can query the database and obtain the analytics results that protect individual privacy. Throughout the processing pipeline, the platform only sees encrypted data and enforces the correctness of all computations.

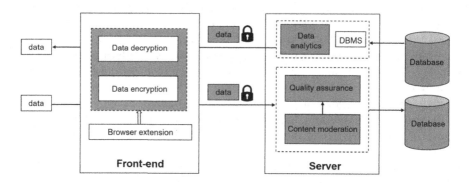

Fig. 1. Our envisioned system architecture.

Concerning the above requirements for crowdsourcing with E2EE, we propose an architecture for the system building, as illustrated in Fig. 1. From a high-level point of view, the architecture consists of a front-end component and a server-side component. The front-end component performs data encryption and decryption under the protection of a browser extension, while the server-side component performs content moderation, quality assurance, and data analytics in the encrypted domain. Below we dwell on the existing landscape of techniques related to the design for supporting the target requirements and present the roadmap ahead.

3   Design Space of E2EE-Crowdsourcing

3.1   Assuring High-Quality Crowdsourced Data

Existing Landscape. The processes of quality assurance govern the design and assignment of tasks, data aggregation, and more. Here, we introduce the data aggregation that is typically a core service of the platform. We refer the reader to the works [8,27] for more details. Most crowdsourcing platforms assign each task to multiple workers and infer its result by aggregating all of its data from these workers (e.g., averaging, majority voting). However, crowdsourcing has some complex tasks like medical data labeling, in which the majority of workers may provide inaccurate data. This causes errors between the aggregated result and ground truth. Although various reliability-based aggregations have emerged for this issue, there are still many underexplored areas. Most aggregation approaches deal with structured data, while more and more crowdsourcing applications collect unstructured data such as text. For example, researchers often use crowdsourcing surveys to collect opinions from workers.

Existing works on E2EE quality assurance in crowdsourcing target specific mechanisms (e.g., majority voting, golden question, truth discovery) by using different cryptographic primitives [29,30,52,53]. They do not flexibly support various quality assurance mechanisms for different crowdsourcing applications. Due to heavy cryptography, they usually incur high overheads, which limit their deployments in practice. For example, the work [29] makes the data requester cost 56 GB memory and 2 h to prove whether an encrypted answer is the majority voting result. Therefore, an approach to achieve diverse quality assurance mechanisms in the context of E2EE remains underexplored.

Roadmap Ahead. To reduce errors between the aggregated result and ground truth, we resort to cutting-edge reliability-based aggregation mechanisms. We will extend them to support multiple data types in crowdsourcing applications. To further encourage workers to contribute high-quality data, we plan to mine and combine the reliability of workers with quality-aware incentives. To develop and deploy diverse and efficient quality assurance mechanisms in the context of E2EE, we plan to explore the hardware-assisted TEE (e.g., Intel SGX) to better support the computation-based quality assurance mechanisms, without violating data confidentiality.

As mentioned before, we need to carefully address the limitations of SGX to guarantee security and performance: 1) The large volume of encrypted crowdsourced data is in conflict with the restricted memory space (e.g., 256 MB for current SGX), which is shared by all enclaves on the same processor. Naively pulling data into the enclave would incur expensive page-swapping overheads. Thus, when designing the secure aggregation algorithms, we should carefully balance the volume size of each batch of data, which might have different impact on the accuracy of aggregations, affecting our quality assurance objective. 2) The interactions between the enclave and untrusted memory can be relatively costly. Thus, besides choosing the appropriate data batch size, even from the algorithm design point of view, we must ensure that frequent switches should be largely avoided when refactoring computation-based quality assurance mechanisms into the enclave. 3) SGX is susceptible to various side-channel attacks (e.g., cache-timing attacks, page-fault attacks), which may expose sensitive information about the data being processed. Subject to the sensitivity of crowdsourcing tasks, we believe it's necessary for the platform to provide tradeoff options to adopt various side-channel defence mechanisms, which can further mitigate undesired information leakages, but with extra cost.

3.2   Enabling Versatile Data Analytics

Existing Landscape. Existing encrypted databases[4] are built by using special cryptographic primitives or TEE. As mentioned earlier, cryptographic-based designs often support only a limited subset of SQL queries, while possibly being subject to various leakage-abuse attacks. For practical consideration, we follow the line of work leveraging TEE for encrypted database systems with rich SQL queries [2,43,46]. The first proposal [35] suggests storing the whole database engine into the enclave for strong security, but it incurs heavy overheads of extending memory space. Later, subsequent works consider optimizations of storage or computation with the assistance of enclaves. Some works design specified

---

[4] We do not provide an exhaustive list here.

key-value storage structures to overcome the enclave memory limitation [5], but they do not support mutually distrusting users to share one database instance. Others use SGX as add-on extensions that assist the query processing over encrypted data entries on demand through the enclave. While functionally intuitive, the designs might lead to considerable information leakages subject to different query types [2,43,46].

Roadmap Ahead. We believe the prior arts leveraging SGX as add-on extensions [2,43,46] are on the right directions, for the flexble encrypted query support and easy deployment in practice. But there are still security and performance gaps to be fulfilled. 1) Partitioning various modules of query processing into the enclave can have broad design choices, with various tradeoffs among security, efficiency, and query expressiveness. The query processing consists of a series of modules such as query parser, translator, optimizer, etc. Existing practices that utilize the enclave as database extensions could reveal exploitable leakage profiles during query processing, exposing ciphertext relationships [43]. Moving more modules into the enclave will naturally help reduce the exploitable leakage profiles. But in doing so, we must also deal with the limited enclave space (e.g., 256 MB), and costly engineering efforts for the lack of I/O support and system calls in enclave. 2) For certain queries, existing designs, e.g., [46], might lead to frequent enclave context switches with observable performance downgrade. Thus, it is important to study how to build secure indexing designs to speed up the query processing over current practices, yet without sacrificing security. Among the observable leakage profiles, access pattern leakages [32,51] are with the top priority to address. Existing general ORAM and oblivious algorithms are often not economically viable. We believe random obfuscation based design, which disrupts the access pattern on demand, can potentially mitigate the concern, while preserving sufficient efficiency for the roadmap ahead to pursue. 3) In addition, for the aforementioned concerns on inference threats from analytical results, we believe the adoption of differential privacy mechanisms in encrypted database is a must for result release control [22]. However, it is not yet clear whether all kinds of queries can be supported, in a scalable and dynamic encrypted database. 4) As for verification of the analytics results, we consider dedicated designs are also necessary. We propose to follow the latest arts [54], and further investigate the compatibility of those verification designs with respect to all the aforementioned security and privacy considerations.

3.3   Protecting Data at the Front-End

Existing Landscape. To enhance data security in the browser, most works develop dedicated components such as a web proxy or a browser extension to isolate and process data. The work [18] leverages encapsulated DOM subtrees and attaches them to untrusted DOM. However, it is still susceptible to various web attacks such as XSS attacks and SQL injection [14]. Later, works in [26,38] develop browser extensions to identify and protect sensitive data. This line of work requires web developers to identify sensitive data fields manually on each webpage, which could be error-prone and introduce additional trust issues. To isolate and process sensitive data, they need to leverage corresponding iframes and develop specified APIs. However, malicious extensions might still be able to inject scripts inside a targeted iframe so as to break the security feature. Other works [10,12,15] protect data with the assistance of hardware (e.g., Intel SGX). But it seems not a viable option in crowdsourcing platforms, where it's not easy to assume millions of workers to readily have the complex hardware-assisted environments by themselves.

Roadmap Ahead. As mentioned earlier, from the usability and easy-for-adoption point of view, we consider a dedicated browser extension for the E2EE crowdsourcing platform is a more rational design choice to protect the data at the Frond-end. Since browser extensions usually have high privileges of accessing and modifying sensitive data, we need to have a comprehensive understanding about various methods of privilege exploitation, before finalising the design choices of building such a secure extension. Common methods of privilege exploitation are code execution, web interception, content scripts injection, etc. Note that simply disabling these methods may not be recommended, as they might inadvertently affect the functionalities of other benign browser extensions. Thus, we must treat these design choices with care, so as to avoid any undesirable side effect. From the data protection perspective, we need an isolated environment for web data processing. The browser extension sandbox can be a safe mechanism for this purpose. Based on that, our preliminary work [47] has shown promising result to establish a software-based web enclave. We shall continue the exploration, e.g., by identifying all input data fields on different task webpages of the crowdsourcing platform, and establish a full-fledged system with secure front-end.

3.4 Preventing the Abuse of E2EE

Existing Landscape. Current data-driven platforms often fill many harmful contents. For instance, Facebook reported more than 8,000 reports that some users tried to induce children to share imagery in 2018[5]. It is hard to detect such content in the encrypted context. Apple iMessage[6] claiming E2EE creates a backdoor to identify harmful content sharing with children. It violates the objective of E2EE that prevents the platform from accessing plaintext data. How to fight against the potential abuse or exploitation of E2EE is an open problem, and there are many unsolved challenges in properly answering the question.

Roadmap Ahead. Building on the insights from prior arts, we believe there are currently two possible ways for the ongoing exploration: reactive designs and proactive mechanisms. First, drawing on the insight from [44], one feasible approach is to enable the traceback property of the content distribution at the E2EE crowdsourcing platform, where users are allowed to report harmful data to the platform for the possible harmful source identification. This approach, reactive

---

[5] https://www.justice.gov/opa/press-release/file/1207081/download.
[6] https://www.apple.com/privacy/features/.

in nature, would naturally require one of the data receipients as trustworthy and capable of identifying the harmful content, which might not always be true in reality. How to realise those assumptions in practice in a large-scale crowd-sourcing system can be the possible direction ahead. Second, following the latest result by [24], another possible direction is to proactively conduct the harmful content detection directly over encrypted data. One example is to rely on perceptual hash matching [24] over unwanted/illegal images. Intuitively, one could potentionally store the blacklist of the hash digest of those pre-defined harmful contents in advance, and check any subsequent content before distribution on demand. One could further leverage secure enclave to achieve privacy-preserving content moderation. But such a proactive approach might face limitations of pre-defined content list, which could be easily bypassed with newly generated harmful content in different forms. More recently, the community has also be exploring possible machine learning based techniques for content moderation [45] in plaintext domain. With secure enclave, one could possibly deploy well-trained models (e.g., Natural Language Processing) to flag the potentially harmful texts in a privacy-preserving manner over the E2EE crowdsourcing platform.

4   Conclusion

In this paper, we present the vision for a secure and trustworthy crowdsourcing platform with functionality, scalability, and practicality. By investigating the current practice of crowdsourcing platforms and literature, we explore the cutting-edge security techniques and dwell on the possibility to put them together towards the realization of our vision. For future work, we will develop a full-fledged crowdsourcing platform by realizing the various proposed components, with comprehensive evaluations to examine the practical usability.

Acknowledgment. This work was supported in part by the RGC of HK under GRF projects CityU 11217819 and 11217620, RIF project R6021-20, the NSFC under Grant 61572412, and by Shenzhen Municipality Science and Technology Innovation Commission (grant no. SGDX20201103093004019, CityU).

References

1. Abrams, L.: Hacker leaks 386 million user records from 18 companies for free (2020). https://www.bleepingcomputer.com/news/security/hacker-leaks-386-million-user-records-from-18-companies-for-free/
2. Antonopoulos, P., et al.: Azure SQL database always encrypted. In: Proceedings of ACM SIGMOD (2020)
3. Appen: data-security (2021). https://appen.com/data-security/
4. Armbrust, M., et al.: Spark SQL: relational data processing in spark. In: Proceedings of ACM SIGMOD (2015)
5. Bailleu, M., Thalheim, J., Bhatotia, P., Fetzer, C., Honda, M., Vaswani, K.: {SPEICHER}: Securing ISM-based key-value stores using shielded execution. In: Proceedings of USENIX FAST (2019)

6. Chen, Q., Kapravelos, A.: Mystique: uncovering information leakage from browser extensions. In: Proceedings of ACM CCS (2018)
7. Costan, V., Devadas, S.: Intel SGX explained. IACR Cryptol. ePrint Arch. **2016**(86), 1–118 (2016)
8. Daniel, F., Kucherbaev, P., Cappiello, C., Benatallah, B., Allahbakhsh, M.: Quality control in crowdsourcing: a survey of quality attributes, assessment techniques, and assurance actions. ACM Comput. Surv. **51**(1), 1–40 (2018)
9. Deng, J., Dong, W., Socher, R., Li, L.J., Li, K., Fei-Fei, L.: Imagenet: a large-scale hierarchical image database. In: Proceedings of IEEE CVPR (2009)
10. Dhar, A., Ulqinaku, E., Kostiainen, K., Capkun, S.: Protection: root-of-trust for in compromised platforms. In: Proceedings of NDSS (2020)
11. Ermoshina, K., Musiani, F., Halpin, H.: End-to-end encrypted messaging protocols: an overview. In: Proceedings of INSCI (2016)
12. Eskandarian, S., et al.: Fidelius: protecting user secrets from compromised browsers. In: Proceedings of IEEE SP (2019)
13. eugdpr.org: The EU general data protection regulation (GDPR) is the most important change in data privacy regulation in 20 years (2021). https://eugdpr.org/
14. Freyberger, M., He, W., Akhawe, D., Mazurek, M.L., Mittal, P.: Cracking shadowcrypt: exploring the limitations of secure i/o systems in internet browsers. In: Proceedings of PETS (2018)
15. Goltzsche, D., Wulf, C., Muthukumaran, D., Rieck, K., Pietzuch, P., Kapitza, R.: Trustjs: trusted client-side execution of javascript. In: Proceedings of EuroSys (2017)
16. Graham, R.: How terrorists use encryption. CTC Sentinel **9**(6), 20 (2016)
17. Grandl, R., Singhvi, A., Viswanathan, R., Akella, A.: Whiz: data-driven analytics execution. In: Proceedings of USENIX NSDI (2021)
18. He, W., Akhawe, D., Jain, S., Shi, E., Song, D.: Shadowcrypt: encrypted web applications for everyone. In: Proceedings of ACM CCS (2014)
19. Isaac, M., Roose, K.: Disinformation spreads on Whatsapp ahead of Brazilian election (2018). https://www.nytimes.com/2018/10/19/technology/whatsapp-brazil-presidential-election.html
20. Jagpal, N., et al.: Trends and lessons from three years fighting malicious extensions. In: Proceedings of USENIX Security (2015)
21. Johns, M., Dirksen, A.: Towards enabling secure web-based cloud services using client-side encryption. In: Proceedings of ACM CCS Workshop (2020)
22. Johnson, N., Near, J.P., Hellerstein, J.M., Song, D.: Chorus: a programming framework for building scalable differential privacy mechanisms. In: Proceedings of IEEE EuroS&P (2020)
23. Kanich, C., Checkoway, S., Mowery, K.: Putting out a hit: crowdsourcing malware installs. In: Proceedings of USENIX WOOT (2011)
24. Kulshrestha, A., Mayer, J.: Identifying harmful media in end-to-end encrypted communication: efficient private membership computation. In: Proceedings of USENIX Security (2021)
25. Lazer, D., et al.: Social science. Computational social science. Science **323**(5915), 721–723 (2009)
26. Légaré, J.S., Sumi, R., Aiello, W.: Beeswax: a platform for private web apps. In: Proceedings of PETS (2016)
27. Li, G., Wang, J., Zheng, Y., Franklin, M.J.: Crowdsourced data management: a survey. IEEE Trans. Knowl. Data Eng. **28**(9), 2296–2319 (2016)
28. Liu, Q., Ihler, A.T., Steyvers, M.: Scoring workers in crowdsourcing: how many control questions are enough? In: Proceedings of NIPS (2013)

29. Lu, Y., Tang, Q., Wang, G.: Zebralancer: Private and anonymous crowdsourcing system atop open blockchain. In: Proceedings of IEEE ICDCS (2018)
30. Lu, Y., Tang, Q., Wang, G.: Dragoon: private decentralized hits made practical. In: Proceedings of IEEE ICDCS (2020)
31. Mozilla: Mozilla rally (2021). https://rally.mozilla.org/how-rally-works/
32. Ohrimenko, O., Costa, M., Fournet, C., Gkantsidis, C., Kohlweiss, M., Sharma, D.: Observing and preventing leakage in mapreduce. In: Proceedings of ACM CCS (2015)
33. Patel, P.: International statement: end-to-end encryption and public safety (2021). https://www.justice.gov/opa/pr/international-statement-end-end-encryption-and-public-safety
34. Peng, D., Wu, F., Chen, G.: Pay as how well you do: a quality based incentive mechanism for crowdsensing. In: Proceedings of ACM MobiHoc (2015)
35. Priebe, C., Vaswani, K., Costa, M.: Enclavedb: a secure database using SGX. In: Proceeding of IEEE SP (2018)
36. Redmiles, E.M., Kross, S., Mazurek, M.L.: How well do my results generalize? comparing security and privacy survey results from mturk, web, and telephone samples. In: Proceedings of IEEE SP (2019)
37. Redrup, Y.: Freelancer contests $20,000 privacy breach fine from OAIC (2016). https://www.afr.com/markets/business/freelancer-contests-20000-privacy-breach-fine-from-oaic-20160112-gm4aw2
38. Ruoti, S., Andersen, J., Monson, T., Zappala, D., Seamons, K.: Messageguard: A browser-based platform for usable, content-based encryption research. arXiv preprint arXiv:1510.08943 (2015)
39. Sannon, S., Cosley, D.: Privacy, power, and invisible labor on amazon mechanical turk. In: Proceedings of ACM CHI (2019)
40. Securitymagazine: nearly 80% of companies experienced a cloud data breach in past 18 months (2020). https://www.securitymagazine.com/articles/92533-nearly-80-of-companies-experienced-a-cloud-data-breach-in-past-18-months
41. Starov, O., Nikiforakis, N.: Extended tracking powers: measuring the privacy diffusion enabled by browser extensions. In: Proceedings of WWW (2017)
42. Statement, N.: National center for missing and exploited children (2021). https://missingkids.org/blog/2019/post-update/end-to-end-encryption
43. Sun, Y., Wang, S., Li, H., Li, F.: Building enclave-native storage engines for practical encrypted databases. In: Proceedings of VLDB Endowment (2021)
44. Tyagi, N., Miers, I., Ristenpart, T.: Traceback for end-to-end encrypted messaging. In: Proceedings of ACM CCS (2019)
45. Ueta, S., Nagaraja, S., Sango, M.: Auto content moderation in c2c e-commerce. In: Proceedings of USENIX OpML (2020)
46. Vinayagamurthy, D., Gribov, A., Gorbunov, S.: Stealthdb: a scalable encrypted database with full SQL query support. In: Proceedings of PETS (2019)
47. Wang, X., Du, Y., Wang, C., Wang, Q., Fang, L.: Webenclave: protect web secrets from browser extensions with software enclave. IEEE Trans. Depend. Secure Comput. https://doi.org/10.1109/TDSC20213081867 (2021, accepted)
48. Wang, Y., Wang, K., Miao, C.: Truth discovery against strategic sybil attack in crowdsourcing. In: Proceedings of ACM KDD (2020)
49. Xin, R.S., Rosen, J., Zaharia, M., Franklin, M.J., Shenker, S., Stoica, I.: Shark: SQL and rich analytics at scale. In: Proceedings of ACM SIGMOD (2013)
50. Xing, X., et al.: Understanding malvertising through ad-injecting browser extensions. In: Proceedings of WWW (2015)

51. Xu, Y., Cui, W., Peinado, M.: Controlled-channel attacks: deterministic side channels for untrusted operating systems. In: Proceedings of IEEE SP (2015)
52. Zheng, Y., Duan, H., Wang, C.: Learning the truth privately and confidently: encrypted confidence-aware truth discovery in mobile crowdsensing. IEEE Trans. Inf. Forensics Secur. **13**(10), 2475–2489 (2018)
53. Zheng, Y., Duan, H., Yuan, X., Wang, C.: Privacy-aware and efficient mobile crowdsensing with truth discovery. IEEE Trans. Depend. Secur. Comput. **17**(1), 121–133 (2020)
54. Zhou, W., Cai, Y., Peng, Y., Wang, S., Ma, K., Li, F.: Veridb: an SGX-based verifiable database. In: Proceedings of ACM SIGMOD (2021)

Blockchain Networks
and Blockchain-Based Applications

Blockchain for IoT: A Critical Analysis Concerning Performance and Scalability

Ziaur Rahman[✉], Xun Yi, Ibrahim Khalil, and Andrei Kelarev

RMIT University, Melbourne, VIC 3000, Australia
{rahman.ziaur,xun.yi,ibrahim.khalil,andrei.kelarev}@rmit.edu.au

Abstract. The world has been experiencing a mind-blowing expansion of blockchain technology since it was first introduced as an emerging means of cryptocurrency called bitcoin. Currently, it has been regarded as a pervasive frame of reference across almost all research domains, ranging from virtual cash to agriculture or even supply-chain to the Internet of Things. The ability to have a self-administering register with legitimate immutability makes blockchain appealing for the Internet of Things (IoT). As billions of IoT devices are now online in distributed fashion, the huge challenges and questions require to addressed in pursuit of urgently needed solutions. The present paper has been motivated by the aim of facilitating such efforts. The contribution of this work is to figure out those trade-offs the IoT ecosystem usually encounters because of the wrong choice of blockchain technology. Unlike a survey or review, the critical findings of this paper target sorting out specific security challenges of blockchain-IoT Infrastructure. The contribution includes how to direct developers and researchers in this domain to pick out the unblemished combinations of Blockchain enabled IoT applications. In addition, the paper promises to bring a deep insight on Ethereum, Hyperledger blockchain and IOTA technology to show their limitations and prospects in terms of performance and scalability.

Keywords: Distributed ledger · Public consensus · Blockchain

1 Introduction

Blockchain and IoT have been able to show immense effectiveness and potential for future improvements to productivity when being applied in collaboration. Therefore, how they could be employed to install end-to-end secure and sensor embedded automated solutions has become a frequently asked question. The world has already been surprised to experience the beautiful adaptations of different IoT solutions, ranging from healthcare-warehousing to transportation-logistics [1]. Existing centralized Edge and Fog based IoT infrastructure may

---

Supported by RMIT RTS Program.

X. Yuan et al. (Eds.): QShine 2021, LNICST 402, pp. 57–74, 2021.
https://doi.org/10.1007/978-3-030-91424-0_4

not be that scalable, secure and efficient to mitigate broader enterprise challenges. Mostly, emerging IoT solutions concern network of sensor-enabled smart appliances where it facilitates the services on the cloud of physical devices varies from modern car to smart-home utensils. In essence, an immutable timestamp ledger used for distributed data including either payment, contract, personal sharing and storing or supply chain and health care expected to impact several sectors due to its salient features such as immutability, distributed structure, consensus-driven behavior and transparency [2].

1.1 Blockchain's Potentials to Be Peer with IoT

There are several reasons why blockchain can be very promising to ensure efficiency, scalability and security of the IoT arrangement. Firstly, it has a proven cryptographic signing capability to perform end-to-end cryptographic message transfer. It is able to enable asset functionality to provide good governess [3,4]. Moreover, it can address custodial tracking of asset transmission in a global logistic phenomenon. Besides, next we give a list of several emerging issues and their corresponding blockchain potentials as follows.

i Free global infrastructure that offers
   – Blockchain is leveraging and reliable
ii Data belonging in the Edge-Network the final destination to the appliances
   – Blockchain has the ability to be replicated rapidly and consistently to every closest node for which it will certainly will be cost-effective
iii Hack-proof cryptography eliminating attacks
   – Already proven to be resilient to the popular attacks - for example: if you are looking to protect a power grid or if you are looking to protect high value asset it becomes natural to use blockchain
iv Record proof of life for industrial assets in an irreversible ledger
   – people can even associate it to an asset to verify its validity which might be increasing the revenue of the company as there is no counterfeiting.
v Track-chain of custody assets on Transportation or sale
   – we not only can verify but also can track when those are sold to a different individuals allowing us to gain the types of metrics that we would necessarily lose thus we can provide insight to companies.
   – Full redundancy providing a hundred percent uptime and assuring message delivery

The contribution of this work is to figure out those trade-offs the IoT ecosystem usually encounters because of the wrong choice of blockchain technology. Unlike a survey or review, the critical findings of this paper target sorting out specific performance and scalability challenges of blockchain-IoT Infrastructure. The contribution includes how to direct developers and researchers in this domain to pick out the unblemished combinations of Blockchain enabled IoT applications. The claimed contributions are justified through the respective sections of the paper. The Sect. 3 of this paper discusses Blockchain suitability to eliminate the problems that emerges because of Blockchain and IoT integration [5]. The later sections explains how existing solution namely Microsoft Azure adopts different Blockchain platforms such as Ethereum, Hyperledger, etc. The following section illustrates Blockchain potentials for specific IoT issues. The challenges come to light while a sensor-enabled system finds its devices, managing access control, etc. through respective use-case anaysis. Furthermore, the analysis justifies the smart contract compliance for IoT system along with data integrity and confidentiality loop-holes.

Therefore, the article is organized as follows: the preceding section and the introduction throughout its subsections talk about why blockchain is necessarily applicable in the Internet of Things (IoT) [6]. Section 2 is a bit about blockchain internal design and its tailored categories leading with part 3 where an OSI like blockchain open system structure redrawn following some previous works. Sections 4, 5, and 6 portray the comparative analysis with contemporary technologies including Hyperledger, IOTA and Microsoft Azure IoT architecture. Then the following section summaries with a brief table and graphs showing the challenges and proposed solutions at a glance as well as its applicability concerning the throughput and latency. A set of use cases where blockchain is an inevitable peer of IoT mentioned before the conclusion on top of advantages & application.

2   Blockchain Preliminaries

The blockchain is a means of removing the need of traditionally created trust created through intermediaries in the distributed systems. A blockchain enables trusts among untrusting entities within a common interest. Thus, it helps to form a permanent and transparent record of exchange of processing, ignoring the need for an intermediary. The terms blockchain and distributed ledger often used interchangeably, but they are not always the same thing. Blockchain is about the exchange of value instant, decentralized, pseudonymous value transfer which is now possible. It can ensure ledger building by preserving a set of transactions shared to all participating users, where the new one is necessarily verified and validated by others [7,8]. Adjoining brand-new transaction usually called mining demands solving the complex and substantial computational puzzle which in nature is a complicated answer but simplest to authenticate using a chosen consensus mechanism in the network of untrusted and anonymous nodes. That indeed has brought enormous transparency for a BC-enabled applications. Significant resource constraints required to facilitate the consensus algorithm by which it restricts unauthorised blocks from joining the network. Besides, communication among nodes are encrypted by changeable public keys (PK) to prevent tracking itself, thus it has been able to draw attention in non-monetary application [4,9].

A sample chain of blocks can be delineated where each block depicts the hash of the previous block, time stamp, transaction root and nonce created by the miner [10].

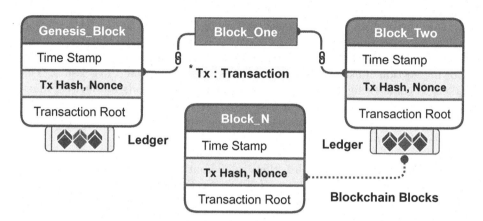

Fig. 1. At a glance view of chain of different blocks with nones, time stamp, transaction data and hashes

It has already been able to show its potentials in particular in this field by super setting secure smart device authentication to ensure uncompromised communication, decentralized data formulation or even automatic data purchasing and others. Thus, we can conceivably estimate that an emerging phenomenon of IoT utensils would be equipped with the Internet to ease every aspect of human life [11].

2.1   Blockchain Category

The following Fig. 2 shows the comparative classification of blockchain ledger concerning the considered ledger accessibility.

Public Ledger Based Blockchain. It is also often known as permissionless blockchain as anyone can send, verify and read transactions on the network even able to get and run the codes on their machine to take part in mining process using consensus [9] algorithms. It has the maximum anonymity and transparency even though any user unidentified are allowed to send, read and validate the incognito transaction. Ethereum and Bitcoin are the typical examples of public blockchain. **Private Ledger Based Blockchain.** It controls the access privileges by restricting read and modification right to a particular organization; thus, it does not require a consensus mechanism or mining to ensure anonymity. In some instances, the read authority kept restricted to an arbitrary level, but mostly the transaction editing is strictly permissioned. The ledger-building process for coin supervised by Eris and Monax or the Multichain could be said to have private-typed blockchain techniques [8]. It dserve mentioning that Ethereum now has permissioned Blockchain, such as Quorum. **Protected Ledger Based Blockchain.** Protected Blockchain is also known as Consortium/federated [12] or and in some cases it is called hybrid or publicly permissioned blockchain which is maintained within the authority of a group of owner or users [13]. Hyperledger by Linux Foundation and IBM [1], Services of R3 with

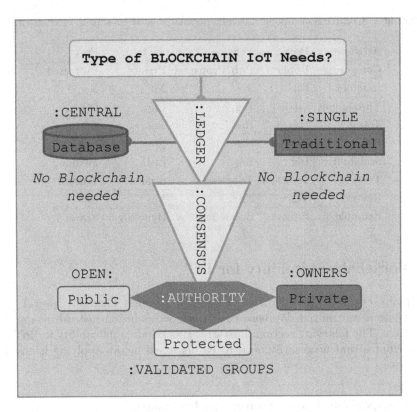

Fig. 2. Blockchain grouping according to the requirement analysis. It shows either the need of the particular type of blockchain or the usual approach is able to meet the demand

Corda or Energy Web Foundation are example of protected type of Blockchain [14]. However, the required blockchain type shown through Fig. 5 based after the ledger, consensus and the dependability of the type of authority. Figure 2 shows that if the system has a centralized or single ledger system, no category of the blockchain is needed there. However, if the authority is restricted within a validated group, then protected one seems to suit more than public or private ledger based blockchain system [15]. Beside, above types of Blockchain, this manuscript explains performance comparison of IOTA. The founders of IOTA have described its ledger as a public permission-less backbone for the Internet of Things that enables interoperability between multiple devices [12]. That means, it will enable transactions (tx) between connected devices, and anyone on the network can access its ledger.

Table 1. Comparison among different popularly used consensus mechanisms

Attributes	PoW	PoS	BFT	PoA
Category	Public	Pub/Protected	Private	Protected
Random	No	Yes	No	No
Throughput	Little	Big	Big	Big
Token	Has	Has	Not	Native
P-Cost	Has	Has	Not	Not
Scalability	Big	Big	Little	Medium
Trust	Trustless	Trustless	Semi	Trusted
Reward	Yes	No	No	No
Example	Bitcoin	Ethereum	Hypeledger	Kovan

3   Blockchain Suitability for IoT

As explained earlier, Blockchain can solve all IoT issues. There are several problems where a centralized database can be a good solution instead of applying blockchain. The following section illustartes Blockchain applicability for IoT and the attributes that necessarily need to be discussed before applying it any IoT use cases.

3.1   Comparison Among Consensus Protocols

Table 1 shows the comparison among different consensus mechanism. It illustrates that Proof of Work (PoW) or Proof of Stake (PoS) require significant computational resource, whereas Byzantine Fault Tolerance (BFT) and Proof of Authority (PoA) have higher throughput in comparison to its peers. But in either case of BFT and PoA scalability can be a challenge. Another thing is that they have a token in dependability, which seems to be working fine for IoT nodes. In case of scalability and Overheads, blocks are broadcast to and verified by all nodes with a quadratic increment of the traffic, and intractable processing overheads that demand huge extensibility whereas IoT devices (e.g., LORA) have limited Bandwidth connections [11]. For delay/latency: IoT devices have stricter delay requirement (e.g., Smart Home Sensor unlikely to wait) whereas BTC can take approximately 30 min to confirm a transaction. Even it has security overheads as it has to protect the double spending seems inapplicable for IoT. For bitcoin, the throughput is 7/Transaction which would go beyond such limit due to huge interaction among nodes in IoT. Therefore, after bitcoin many have been opted for BFT based Hyperledger [1,9] or non-consensus driven approach such as IOTA [16]. The applicability of different blockchain platforms based on those consensus protocols and non-consensus approach discussed with this [17].

BC Type	Consensus	Delay & SC		Distinct Features
IOTA	No [DAG]	10 ms	No	Light computation, low Network use
HYPERLEDGER	PBFT	10-100 ms	Yes	High computation intensive
ETHEREUM	Ethash	10k ms	Yes	Light computation, high network use

Fig. 3. The both part of the above figure shows the comparative analysis among Ethereum [18], Hyperledger [1] and IoTA [16] and before applying those as a mean of IoT performance and scalability

3.2   Etherem, Hyperledger and IOTA

Ethereum emerged intending to compete with bitcoin is a flexible blockchain platform with required smart contracts and proof-of-work consensus mechanism called Ethash. This associates with Directed Acyclic Graphs (DAG) [16] to generate the probabilistic hash. It ensures robust extensibility for the IoT applications, including some efficiency trade-offs. As Ethash works upon PoW, Ethereum requires around 20 s to append a new block after mining [4,9]. Secondly, **Hyperledger** is a permissioned and protected type of blockchain. It commonly applies access control, along with chaincode-based smart contracts and consensus with existing Practical Byzantine Fault Tolerance (PBFT) [9,19]. It includes anchors of trust to base certificate-authorities as an increment to the asymmetric cryptographic approach and digital signature properties with SHA3 or ECDSA. Hence, its smart contracts implementation involves the chaincode that has a self-execution ability such as asset or resource transferring among network-peers in huge time. This latency is low among comparative distributed ledger implementations. Fabric has been chosen as blockchain medium by IBM in their Bluemix-Watson IoT architecture, which has been shown by the respective section hereafter. **IOTA** which a unique distributed ledger in that it does not utilize an explicit blockchain at all; instead, it implements a directed acyclic graph of transactions – instead of blocks of multiple transactions that link together, each transaction approves and links back to two other transactions. IOTA Tangles has immense potentials to be efficiently adapted with IoT to ensure security and privacy by ensuring maximum throughput. Figure 3 shows the comparative analysis among Ethereum, Hyperledger and IOTA in terms of performance and scalability.

3.3   Azure IoT Workbench

Figure 4 illustrates the Azure IoT workbench that facilitates client-side application for both mobile and web system depending on the smart-contract. It purposes to verify, retrieve and test applications or entertain new use-cases there. It brings a user-interface to interact with the end-user for appropriate tasks. Besides, entitled individuals are given to permission accessing the administrative console with different functionalities such as uploading and deploying smart contracts depending on certain roles. As depicted in the figure, the workbench has a gateway-service API standing on the representational state transfer (REST) API reproduces and delivers messages to event-broker while attempting to append data to blockchain. Queries are submitted to off-chain-database when data is requested. The database mostly the SQL contains a replication of all chained meta-data and bulk data that issues relevant configuring context for the smart contracts supported. Thus, the users with developer role are allowed to get accessed the gateway servicing API to develop blockchain apps without depending on the client/end-user solutions. In case of message breaking for incoming data, users who desire to circulate messages thoroughly to the Azure workbench can submit data directly to the service bus there. For illustration, this API solutions for system integrated confederation or sensor based tools. Apart from this events are held during the life-time of the application. It can be caused by the gateway API or even inside ledger and its alerting trigger downstream-code based on the event so far occurred. Microsoft Azure consortium usually able to locate two different kinds of event consumers. First one gets activated by the events lies on the blockchain to manipulate the off chain SQL storage while the rest responds capturing meta-data for the events brought by document upload and storage related API. Figure 4 shows how Microsoft (MS) Azure IoT work bench adapts different Blockchain farmeworks. It also portrays that MS Azure architecture can facilitate Hyperledger Fabric (HLF), CORDA R3, or IOTA. The IoT Hub is connected to the IoT sensors and its bus is enjoined to the Transaction Builder. MS Azure can be proof that how exisiting IoT workbench can be implemented for the scalable and secure IoT service.

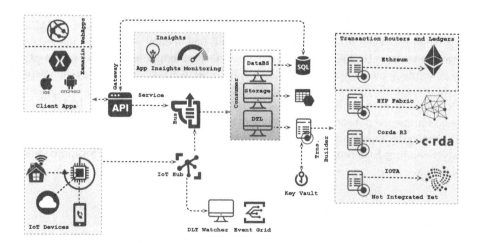

Fig. 4. Microsoft Azure Blockchain Architecture that has been integrated with Ethreum for securing IoT appliances. The COrda, Hyperledger and IOTA could be incorporated just like Ethreum as said by Azure

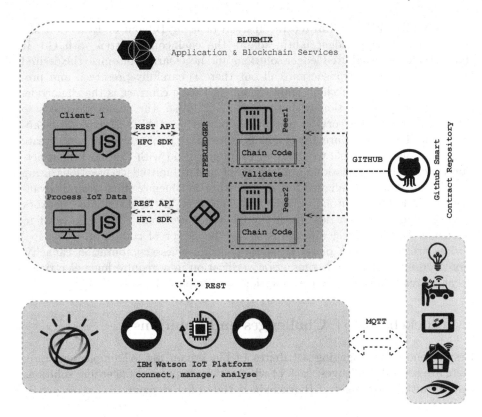

Fig. 5. IBM Watson and Bluemix Integration for IoT-Blockchain Service. Watson communicates the IoT devices, where Bluemix facilitates Blockchain network on top of smart contarct repository from Github

3.4   IBM Blockchain Integrated IoT Architecture

The IBM Blockchain architecture for IoT solutions comprises three principal tiers; each has customized roles in its own side. The Fig. 5 depicts the high level IoT architecture incorporating Hyperledger Fabric as Blockchain service, Watson as IoT Platform and Bluemix as cloud environment [1,20]. The IBM IoT architecture can be divided into several components as shown by Fig. 5. It has been discussed with its three tiers, service execution process and along with the challenges it encounters. It also shows the IBM Blumix IoT working procedure. During execution, data collected from smart devices and intelligent sensors are dispatched to Watson using ISO standard (Message Queuing Telemetry Transport (MQTT) protocol. Specific blockchain proxy works to send data from Watson to the chain-code of the Hyperledger Fabric depending on the settlement. Hence, the transactions get executed in the Cloud. The solution-components associated in the execution process have been enlisted as below:

Smart Contarct as Chaincode. Instead of using Bitcoin or Ethereum like smart contract Hypeledger fabric adapts the chaincode written with Go. It shapes the core distributed ledger solutions and necessarily epitomize the desired business logic. Each transaction call out there is carefully preserved and prevailed as expected blockchain transaction. As Fabric contract is the chaincode, it requires implementation with the certain APIs so, the chaincode needs to get registered with the services using those pre=defined APIs. Hyperledger Fabric Client (HFC) Software Development Kits (SDK) ease developers to create Node.js applications able to maintain communication with the blockchain network. Here, the applications are registered and submitted transactions using APIs. IBM Blockchain aligned IoT Architecture on Bluemix offers several advantages such as trust, autonomy, scalability, security in the distributed network comprising multiple parties. Even though there are some challenges need to overcome. One of the significant issues is the power of computation, as IoT devices are usually low powered devices and have less computation capacity. Moreover, encrypting and transaction verification may require huge electricity. It can increase both energy consumption and expenses as well [4].

4   Blockchain-IoT Challenges and Solutions

Despite enormous engaging attributes of blockchain for IoT implementation, there are several challenges; each of which deserves proper concerning solutions before fruitful lodgement of Blockchain in the of IoT domain.

4.1   Storage, Throughput and Latency Challenges

Ethreum and Bitcoin have storage and Latency challenges as discussed earlier. The storage size has been increasing day by day as shown by Fig. 6. It represents the incremental storage amount from 2015 to quarter August 2021. Blockchain platform that requires higher storage has lesser suitability for real-time system such as IoT. IoT system generates huge and voluminous data which indulges the chances of failure because of storage overhead. Figure 6 shows that in terms of storage the Ethereum seems more suitable than Bitcoin. Though only storage overhead is not the only standard to decide whether a particular Blockchain is suitable or not. But surely, it affects both the performance and scalability of the system. Whereas, the following Fig. 7 shows a comparison among Ethreum, Parity and Hyperledger with per second transaction amount labelled beside the bars. The data were found from [9]. They worked with blockbench collecting data from Yahoo Cloud Serving Benchmark (YCSB) a and Smallbank. It concludes by showing Hypeledger has the maximum throughput. While the second part shows Hyperledger works fine under 16 Nodes. The challenge is here how it can be improved when more nodes will be incorporated as depicted by Fig. 7. Figure 7 shows the throughput Comparison among Ethreum, Ethereum (ETH) Parity and Hyperledger (HLF) fabric based on the Data found on using Blockbench. Though Parity is one of several implementations of Ethereum, it was considered as alternative Blockchain solution for IoT. Therefore, the Figure illustrates both the Ethereum (ETH) and ETH Parity. Hyperledger is a multi-project open source collaborative effort hosted by The Linux Foundation, created to advance cross-industry blockchain technologies [12]. In this comparison we consider Hyperledger (HLF) Fabric only. The scalability challenges as figured out needs proper attention, otherwise the large-scale IoT system not that type of Blockchain after a certain volume of sensor integration.

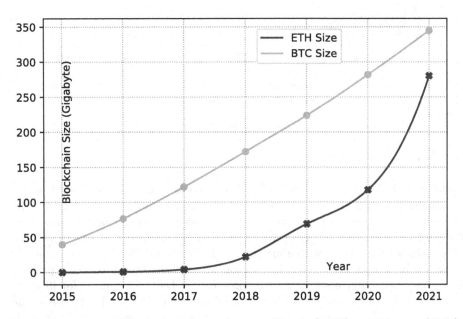

Fig. 6. Comparison of Chain-data storage between Bitcoin (BTC) and Ethreum (ETH) based on the online data provided by blockchain and statista and etherscan.io website

4.2 Prominent Challenges and Solutions

As IoT systems vary from smart coffee machines to complex automobiles, it is difficult to generalize all challenges in one table. The following Fig. 9 describes some inevitable challenges and their possible solutions, respectively [20]. We have so far included seven possible challenges and respective blockchain solutions may require considerations before applying it for IoT architecture [21].

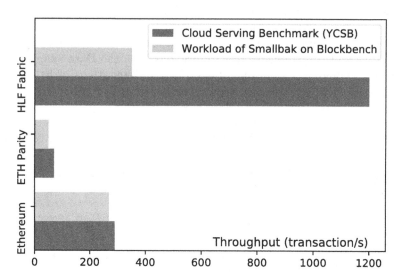

Fig. 7. Throughput (Performance Efficiency) comparison among Ethreum, Ethereum (ETH) Parity and Hyperledger (HLF) fabric based on Data in [9] using Blockbench framework.

5   Use Case Analysis

According to a review [3], the research on blockchain and distributed ledger in association with the several mobile operators conducted by GSMA [3], the emerging application of distributed ledger for blockchain can be put into three different sets ordering as Areas with common IoT Controls, Areas where IoT Appropriates and Areas with Particular IoT Solutions. The Fig. 8 shows a relative study comparing among application areas with respect to three priority interests- maximum, medium and minimum. For Data Sharing as for illustration, three operators recommends it as medium while five of all suggests as the maximum priority of interest, leaving the access control application with minimum priority. As claimed by GSMA, data were collected with sincerely exploring all operators, still it deserves further before assessing for technical and industrial implementation. Considering conciseness and brevity, four use cases directly relating to performance, security and sclability that have been discussed in the following sections.

5.1   Use Case: Finding IoT Devices

Retrieving and tracking identity information of the devices has been influencing factor with the growth of IoT enabling. The following cases will describe examples of finding intelligent devices in the IoT Network.

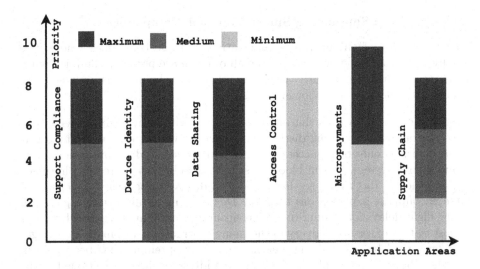

Fig. 8. Applicability of six considered Blockchain aligned IoT usecases according to the review by 10 operators plotting with their priority and applicability. The problems as illustrated through the usecases can be solved after incorporating Blockchain technology.

Case 1: Storing the original data and device status toward authentication. For example- For example identifying the manufacturing company or party if it has quality assurance accreditation including the life cycle status and validating the serial numbers provided.

Case 2: Issuer signature verification according to the information stored in the ledger to make sure software updates from trusted sources.

Case 3: Preserving and ownership device information such as hardware configuration, version information, boot code installation purposing to ensure privacy status check.

5.2   Use Case: IoT Access Control

A Monitoring and recording access control in inevitable in IoT network to preserve access control details for both physical and virtual resources. Therefore, the use-case for this can be as below-

Case 1: Virtual File sharing server uses the ledger to preserve identity of the individuals and application by securely assigning printing, saving or editing accessibility rights. For example – while a consumer made order for a good online is away from home, there is a risk in deliveries. So, customers can get benefit of using distributed ledger, instead of giving access to their home by using keys/address/codes prone to be misused.

Case 2: Issuer signature verification according to the information stored in the ledger to make sure software updates from trusted sources.

5.3   Use Case: Supporting Smart Contract Compliance

There are a lot of circumstances associating multiple companies where it is equally important to know whether the all of those are properly complied with. Thus, compliance is efficiently activated using blockchain smart contract. For example, let consider the following cases.

Case 1: Certain Individual sharing personal data with their health provider can control accessibility using distributed ledgers to make sure good data governance if it is only being accessed by the authorized medical professionals. In multiparty system, patient blood pressure should be only shared by pharmacy and general practitioner so that prescribed drugs can be easily dispensed.

Case 2: Suppose a person has to pay 2 Dollar extra for airport taxi pickup if the flight delays for 30 min. In a micro-insurance premium case like this lower cost feature of service delivery in the smart contract can automatically trigger it on arrival by determining whether that extra premium has been paid in order. Blockchain can play a vital role to address the issues mentioned in the use-cases.

Case 3: Driving particulars including license information, previous record of traffic rules violation, health and safety compliance either of a person or car need to get verified before one can drive a connected hire car. Even the car can upload journey information, servicing history, faults made by itself. In a case where hundreds of thousand cars and drivers are affiliated with, smart contract and blockchain can easily provide required information within least hardship and delay.

5.4   Use Case: Data Integrity and Confidentiality

It is often desired that the data sharing with keeping it confidential enough would be remarkably plausible in a distributed ledger framework [22]. One of the significant features of blockchain is it can be applied to assert data integrity and IoT affiliated data effectively by maintaining the sequence of digital signatures and data hashes. A use case for this can as following [23]. Selected challenges are outlined in the Fig. 9.

Case 1: IoT Devices are expected to transfer information to the servers belongs to the manufacturing company. For example- intelligent thermostat connected with cloud services determines when to switch on and off depending of the current weather status can send data to the company about component wear. Existing solution such as Public Key Infrastructure (PKI) driven techniques can solve issues like this but Blockchain seems to more efficient deterring the need to reinvent processes with integrity and confidentiality.

Case 2: Home or office alarm machines can be controlled by different entity as per their access privileges assigned. In case of it is compromised by intruders it may require to remotely access by law enforcing agencies. Distributed Ledger could be a very useful to handle this case with integrated with millions of devices [12, 24].

CHALLENGES	KEY ATTRIBUTES	SOLUTIONS
Transaction Throughput	The transaction confirmation time of different public ledger ranges from 100 to 2000 TPS (Transaction Per Second) seems infeasible for transferring real time IoT data which may lead to data loss.	In compare to *Bitcoin*, *Ethreum*, *Corda* and *Quorum Ripple* eats up lesser time per transaction as claimed
Energy Comsumption	IoT appliances are mostly light weight and it should have required power capacity to pursue cryptographic algorithms.	Could be adapted with planned manufacturing considering potential energy usage mechanisms.
Confidential Private Key	DTL often exercises asymmetric encryption approach where private keys should keep confidential and the preservation should be resilient to potential adversaries due to open accessibility of IoT ends.	Ledgers in the distributed IoT infrastructure could be designed in a way therefore the complete ledger does not require replication either
Network Bandwidth	If the block sizes 1 Megabyte require typically 10 Minutes meaning the data rate could be near about 150 Megabytes per day that demands significant bandwidth which seems not reasonable for small IoT Wide Area Network such as *Sigfox/LORA*.	Ledgers in the distributed IoT infrastructure could be designed in a way therefore the complete ledger does not require replication either
Transaction Congestion	If the transaction receives exceed the maximum throughput limit of the ledger transaction may occurred which may lead additional incremental user expenses. Even the limit offered by ripple or ethereum is still not that enough to meet up real time requirement	The zero fee transactions approach of non-Mining tangle based *IOTA* could be applied
Mining Expenses & Price Volatility	Public blockchains inevitably engage with the consensus mining and rewarding demands high priced dedicated hardware arrangement relying on high power arise suitability issues for sensitive IoT devices.	Low power consensus approach, private blockchain or *non mining DTL* could be considered as alternatives
Data Chain Storage & Scalability	*Bitcoin, Ethreum* and *IOTA* have reached respectively 200, 125 and 25 gigabytes by January 2019 as comparison shown by the figure which clearly rise voluminous storage management for 75 billion of potential intelligent devices with an unavoidable scalability challenges	It could be mitigated by introducing bigdata handling strategies incorporated with distributed ledger

Fig. 9. Blockchain implementation challenges in the IoT and probable solutions identified

Case 3: Let us consider a personal fitness tracker regularly recording health care dart demands to share with the individual whom it belongs, researcher and medical personnel. Besides, individual may be willing to get services accordingly from manufacturer with micro premium business relationship. The similar scenario could be though when smart homes have weather station/air monitoring IoT appliances shared with several parties. In a case where a machine-manufacturer-practitioner-researcher network seems excessively large distributed ledger may be only smooth solution confronting challenges.

Case 4: Even blockchain cand be put in the smart electricity grids to read the total amount of energy produced by the micro-generator such as solar farm or wind turbines and also can record the dissipation time period based which net supplier payment would be issuing. Here distributed ledger can provide immutable records auditable from either ends and smart contract can make sure efficient payment process according to the stipulated rate.

6   Conclusion

Applying Blockchain towards efficient and scalable solution of smart and sensor based appliances of Internet of things is an emerging research area that have been rapidly evolving with an immense potentials and brand-new challenges [25]. There are huge skepticism with on how efficiently it could be incorporated with usual IoT appliances by ensuring maximum throughput and anonymity. The effort so far made throughout this article can help novice research and developers in this arena by introducing different extant blockchain platforms and some concerning challenges in general before adopting with IoT devices. Lastly, it has brought some relevant use cases that could be considered while working on IoT leading blockchain. The paper brings a critical analysis on how Blockchain platform such as Bitcoin, Ethereum, and IOTA can be adopted for IoT applications. It concludes that all of those have immense potentials to be used as a development platform purposing to enable effective and real time deployment of smart devices on the distributed network. IOTA has been sought to be more efficient to solve transaction-latency and mining reward issue, which could be promising in different relevant use cases to save cost by bringing throughput and efficiency. As private, public and protected blockchain have respective merits and trade-offs in different cases, therefore further research could be made to specify the exact gaps in between [26]. If the challenges and issues aroused could be minimized, it could be a great mean and benefactor of the future technology driven world.

References

1. Griggs, K.N., Ossipova, O., Kohlios, C.P., Baccarini, A.N., Howson, E.A., Hayajneh, T.: Healthcare blockchain system using smart contracts for secure automated remote patient monitoring. J. Med. Syst. **42**(7), 130 (2018)
2. Nakamoto, S.: Bitcoin: a peer-to-peer electronic cash system (2008)

3. O. G. S. M. Global system for mobile communications association: opportunities and use cases for distributed ledger technologies in IoT. https://www.gsma.com/iot/opportunities-distributed-ledger-in-iot/. Accessed Jan 2019 [survey made by gartner]
4. Ferrag, M.A., Derdour, M., Mukherjee, M., Derhab, A., Maglaras, I., Janicke, H.: Blockchain technologies for the internet of things: research issues and challenges. IEEE Internet of Things J. **6**. 2188– 2204 (2018)
5. Butun, I., Österberg, P.: A review of distributed access control for blockchain systems towards securing the internet of things. IEEE Access **9**, 5428–5441 (2021)
6. Yang, X., et al.: Blockchain-based secure and lightweight authentication for internet of things. IEEE Internet of Things J. pp. 1–1 (2021)
7. Salman, T., Zolanvari, M., Erbad, A., Jain, R., Samaka, M.: Security services using blockchains: a state of the art survey. IEEE Commun. Surv. Tutor. **21**, 858–880 (2018)
8. Fernández-Caramés, T.M., Fraga-Lamas, P.: A review on the use of blockchain for the internet of things. IEEE Access **6**, 32979–33001 (2018)
9. Dinh, T.T.A., Liu, R., Zhang, M., Chen, G., Ooi, B.C., Wang, J.: Untangling blockchain: a data processing view of blockchain systems. IEEE Trans. Knowl. Data Eng. **30**(7), 1366–1385 (2018)
10. Minoli, D., Occhiogrosso, B.: Blockchain mechanisms for IoT security. Internet of Things **1**, 1–13 (2018)
11. Hammi, M.T., Hammi, B., Bellot, P., Serhrouchni, A.: Bubbles of trust: a decentralized blockchain-based authentication system for IoT. Comput. Secur. **78**, 126–142 (2018)
12. Rahman, Z., Khalil, I., Yi, X., Atiquzzaman, M.: Blockchain-based security framework for a critical industry 4.0 cyber-physical system. IEEE Commun. Mag. **59**(5), 128–134 (2021)
13. Saraf, C., Sabadra, S.: Blockchain platforms: a compendium. In: 2018 IEEE International Conference on Innovative Research and Development (ICIRD), pp. 1–6. IEEE (2018)
14. Abdella, J., Shuaib, K.: Peer to peer distributed energy trading in smart grids: a survey. Energies **11**(6), 1560 (2018)
15. Kshetri, N.: Can blockchain strengthen the internet of things? IT Profess. **19**(4), 68–72 (2017)
16. Popov, S., Saa, O., Finardi, P.: Equilibria in the tangle. arXiv preprint arXiv:1712.05385 (2017)
17. Dorri, A., Kanhere, S.S., Jurdak, R.: Towards an optimized blockchain for IoT. In: 2017 IEEE/ACM Second International Conference on Internet-of-Things Design and Implementation (IoTDI), pp. 173–178. IEEE (2017)
18. Buterin, R., et al.: A next-generation smart contract and decentralized application platform. Ethreum White Paper (2014)
19. Aitzhan, N.Z., Svetinovic, D.: Security and privacy in decentralized energy trading through multi-signatures, blockchain and anonymous messaging streams. IEEE Trans. Depend. Secur. Comput. **15**(5), 840–852 (2018)
20. Eckhoff, D., Wagner, I.: Privacy in the smart city—applications, technologies, challenges, and solutions. IEEE Commun. Surv. Tutor. **20**(1), 489–516 (2017)
21. Ferrag, M.A., Derdour, M., Mukherjee, M., Derhab, A., Maglaras, L., Janicke, H.: Blockchain technologies for the internet of things: research issues and challenges. IEEE Internet of Things J. **6**(2), 2188–2204 (2019)

22. Dorri, A., Kanhere, S.S., Jurdak, R.,Gauravaram, P.: Blockchain for IoT security and privacy: the case study of a smart home. In: 2017 IEEE International Conference on Pervasive Computing and Communications Workshops (PerCom workshops), pp. 618–623. IEEE (2017)
23. Yu, B., Wright, J., Nepal, S., Zhu, L., Liu, J., Ranjan, R.: Iotchain: establishing trust in the internet of things ecosystem using blockchain. IEEE Cloud Comput. **5**(4), 12–23 (2018)
24. Hossain, M.S., Waheed, S., Rahman, Z., Shezan, S., Hossain, M.M.: Blockchain for the security of internet of things: a smart home use case using Ethereum. Int. J. Recent Technol. Eng. **8**(5), 4601–4608 (2020)
25. Rahman, A., Hossain, M.S., Rahman, Z., Shezan, S.A.: Performance enhancement of the internet of things with the integrated blockchain technology using RSK sidechain. Int. J. Adv. Technol. Eng. Explor. **6**(61), 257–266 (2019)
26. Yang, R., et al.: Public and private blockchain in construction business process and information integration. Autom. Constr. **118**, 103276 (2020)

Toward Achieving Unanimity for Implicit Closings in a Trustless System

Mitsuyoshi Imamura[1]([✉]) and Kazumasa Omote[1,2]

[1] University of Tsukuba, Tennodai 1-1-1, Tsukuba 305-8573, Japan
s1730148@s.tsukuba.ac.jp, omote@risk.tsukuba.ac.jp
[2] National Institute of Information and Communications Technology,
4-2-1 Nukui-Kitamachi, Koganei, Tokyo 184-8795, Japan

Abstract. Blockchain, which has a decentralized management structure, is a technology that challenges conventional wisdom about the availability and durability of an unstable structure, because the network system is managed by volunteers, as opposed to cloud- and network-service providers that leverage centralized management structures. The most popular services based on blockchain (e.g., Bitcoin and Ethereum) have structures that make it challenging to close or discontinue services unless all users agree, no matter if they are honest or malicious. Remarkably, this structure shows stable availability and durability, even now. Considering that unpopular services are eventually terminated, there are more than 2,000 service projects forked from Bitcoin and Ethereum, and it is not realistic to expect all of them to operate in the same manner. When users abandon services like these because of low interest, the blockchain, which depends on volunteers to maintain the system, is affected by reduced availability and durability until it is finally closed. However, unlike centralized management organizations, for service closings, both the indicator and closing mechanism are unclear, because management depends on user dynamism. Therefore, we investigate the mechanism of public blockchain closing by focusing on three decentralized roles of blockchain users. Then, we discuss the closing implication of blockchain-based services using the empirical analysis of 200 different systems.

Keywords: Blockchain · Cryptocurrency · Consensus of closing blockchain

1 Introduction

More than 10 years ago, Satoshi Nakamoto first published the now well-known blockchain whitepaper [20] as a new paradigm of a trust structure that differed from the previous centralized trust structures. The technological challenge of managing a system used by an unspecified number of non-trusted users has been commonly encountered over the past few years. Every year, the self-sovereignty of

X. Yuan et al. (Eds.): QShine 2021, LNICST 402, pp. 75–93, 2021.
https://doi.org/10.1007/978-3-030-91424-0_5

end-users over their devices and data has accelerated the adherence to decentralized structures, because distrust has grown around centralized ones. Although previous studies [1] have reported that blockchains are potentially excellent technology, as the number of users increase, participants face greater uncertainty of performance, because the operation reflects the harmony of all users. With centralized structures, keep in mind that a planned-performance design is curated.

Typically, cloud- and network-service providers use centralized structures to control performance and availability via the direct management of resources, and they systematically abandon the durability of infrequently used services. In contrast, the public blockchain has an unstable structure, because performance, availability, and durability depend on user behavior. From their decentralized natures, leading blockchain-based services (e.g., Bitcoin and Ethereum) experience project forking caused by disagreements within the community. This cannot be prevented unless all users agree to closing. Hence, various projects persevere without losing the original data.

In particular, we focus on the fixing of the blockchain at Ethereum that triggered "The DAO attack," during which, vast amounts of assets were stolen on July 20, 2016, owing to a vulnerability in the program [9]. This incident is a notable example of how difficult it can be to close a service without the full agreement of all users of the blockchain. Looking back on the situation at the time, although 80% of users managing Ethereum nodes used a ledger that allowed modifications, another group continued to use the original ledger that did not apply it. Currently, each exchange lists Ethereum Classic based on their unmodified ledger, and the community declared independence from the modified version on the official website, and the developer was also informed that the project would continue to be developed individually on August 2016. Therefore, Ethereum Classic remains robustly available and persistent, despite Ethereum being a majority opinion project.

Because there are more than 2,000 blockchain projects derived from Bitcoin, it is not realistic to expect all projects to continue running in the same manner, despite being difficult to close or modify. This is rational, given the physical resources and costs shouldered by users to maintain the blockchain. Unlike a planned closing promulgated by a centralized management organization, the mechanisms leading to decentralized closings remain unclear, because management depends on user dynamism.

The conclusion that networks lacking interest and dynamism are closed is intuitively easy to understand. However, researching the validity of this conclusion is outside of the scope of this study and irrelevant to our focus of understanding the process of this closure, including the signs of closure and the impact of closure on the network. Our intended scope is beneficial because of two reasons.

First, understanding the closure process will help in designing blockchains that have strict closure mechanisms. Although it may seem strange to incorporate an erasure mechanism into a blockchain that is data-robust, we have encountered several situations where closure is necessary. In a hard fork, which requires the approval of a large number of stakeholders, a mechanism of fork location is necessary to avoid the confusion caused by value dichotomization. Public blockchains must completely close, owing to security risks, such as the misuse of blockchain availability [2, 6] and the poisoning of ledgers [16, 19]. Additionally, a general data protection regulation (GDPR) that includes the right to be forgotten [22] should be achieved, even under a decentralized system having no party responsible for protecting users from data embedded in the ledger. This means that the issue occurs after the service is used. Hence, consolidating the majority agreement for the ledger is very time consuming. Thus, a substantial amount of time must pass before everyone loses interest, leaving zero users for consensus. However, in previous blockchain communities, this situation has indeed been left to the passage of time, owing to the decentralized responsibility. Reducing this time not only minimizes the loss of service caused by community disruption, but it also reduces the ongoing risk present in the ledger. It should be noted that although implementing a mechanism for global consensus may seem difficult, this type of closure mechanism already exists. For example, forking occurs daily and is commonplace owing to competition in mining. However, the reason why forked blocks do not remain in the network is that a clear closure mechanism exists between the distributed nodes maintaining the ledger, which keeps only the longest blocks. In summary, we aim to extend this mechanism via this study.

The second benefit is that understanding the closure process provides a benchmark against which continuity can be measured. The paper deals primarily with public-cryptography-focused blockchains, but we envision business, commercial, and industrial compliance as well. Future works can expand the research scope of permitted blockchains. For example, researchers should seek to determine whether or not, if one of the main partners drops, the continuity of the blockchain will be affected. In other words, how do user critiques manifest in the system when there is no price to be linked to cryptocurrencies or tokens. Additionally, we assume that understanding the closure process helps define the user policy of blockchains for the industrial use case if metrics were to exist that could be used to finally close the service forms between users prior to releasing the service. As is evident in public blockchains [9], it is very difficult to achieve consensus after a service has been launched. Therefore, postponing the issue presents risk to all participants by wasting time and money owing to confusion.

In this paper, closing public blockchains has been discussed and the setups required to do so on a trustless network have been summarized. Our proposal entails a using a method that applies a time constraint on the validity of the user's traceability and consensus. It clarifies the rational framework under which an unspecified number of users agreed to terminate blockchain ledger, rather than it being modified or deleted by some strong authority, such as consortium or private blockchain.

We begin by investigating the mechanisms of service closure by focusing on the three decentralized user roles in the blockchain (i.e., sender, miner, and recorder). Then, we discuss network dynamism and the consensus models behind the blockchain system by leveraging the empirical analysis of 200 different systems. The main contributions to our research are as follows:

- We propose a new framework for blockchain-closing consensus.
- We analyze the transactions and block trends of near-closure blockchains.
- We visualize the propagation flow toward consensus of blockchain closure.
- We discuss the implementation of the modeled consensus-closing mechanism.

The remainder of this paper is organized as follows. Section 2 presents the blockchain mechanism, focusing on the distributed user roles to understand the consensus required for closing. Section 3 introduces previous research related to closing blockchains. In Sect. 4, we propose a framework for reconsidering this consensus. Section 5 analyzes real networks to validate the new framework. Section 6 presents new implementation ideas based on the framework and empirical analysis. Finally, we present our conclusions in Sect. 7.

2   Blockchain Mechanism

This section introduces the necessary blockchain components and operational mechanisms necessary to form a unanimity for closing. We emphasize the cycle of roles in the blockchain network to demonstrate the user motivation and rational behavior mechanisms for system continuity. Furthermore, we explain the common cryptocurrency-type blockchain that we target in our empirical analysis.

2.1   Blockchain Overview

The key components of a blockchain are the transaction and the block. In this section, we explain the common components of public blockchains based on Bitcoin. A transaction consists of ledger data and inputs of the transferred value. It is the smallest data-structure unit in the blockchain. The block also contains the block version, the height, Merkle tree root hash value, and timestamp in addition to the verified transactions and a hash value calculated from the previous block. Among all blocks, a "genesis block" is a pointer that defines the initial position in the list structure that connects future blocks. The blocks linked by the hash are continuous, characterizing the blockchain's unchanging data structure, and this characteristic structure contributes to its tamper-resistance feature. Distributed nodes that replicate all blocks support the network's worldwide data consistency, and consistent storage is provided by users connected to the network. Transaction creation and block storage are thus repeated across the network.

According to previous research [14], the flow that the original paper [20] describes as a step on the system, structured as a user's roles, is represented by the cyclic structure shown in Fig. 1. Blockchain users have three roles: the sender generates transactions; the miner verifies the transactions and stores it in a block; and the recorder saves the latest blocks. Note that users may have duplicate roles. In the cycle presented in Fig. 1, the function of the three roles as follows:

- The sender obtains the block required for signature from the recorder, creates new transactions, and sends these to the miner.

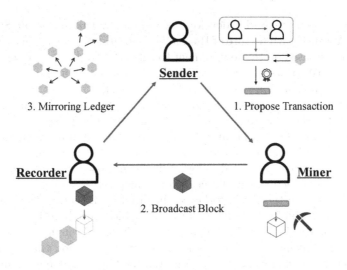

Fig. 1. Cycle of user roles in blockchain.

- The miner collects the new transactions to store in a block and locates a nonce of proof-of-work (PoW) for its block to store the transaction. When the miner finds a nonce, it broadcasts the block back to the recorder.
- The recorder accepts the block only if all transactions therein are valid and not already spent. It then mirrors the latest block status to other nodes on the network. The recorder's mirroring path duplicates the ledger and creates a propagation path that is used in transaction passing by the sender and the miner on the blockchain network.

We focus on the driving force of the cycle in which the blockchain network operates. For a blockchain to exist, miner and recorder roles are required to validate and store transactions. The miner receives a fee from the sender with a reward for the verification work, thereby providing the miner with motivation to play the role. However, the recorder can only use the correct data and will never receive any money for broadcasting the latest blocks to the network. Therefore, the recorder tries to work at a low cost to maintain storage via the same behavior that the miner uses to work at a low cost to receive more rewards. If recorders give up managing the ledger due to maintenance costs, the availability and durability of the network is reduced. Then, the sender regards the service as unlikely to survive. Consequently, we can understand the non-programmable background mechanism by which the users on the blockchain network tend to behave rationally.

2.2 Cryptocurrency

Widely known as the original cryptocurrency, Bitcoin started on January 9, 2009, when Satoshi Nakamoto, who is an anonymous developer, announced the concept in an email[1] to the developer community, sharing it on SOURCE-FORGE[2]. A well-known feature of Bitcoin is its limitation on the participation of malicious users based on the requirement to solve the Byzantine consensus problem using a PoW process, referred to as HashCash [5]. This protocol provides a defense mechanism that prevents Sybil attacks [4] and a lottery mechanism that selects a random leader at each round via competition among users. For this reason, the PoW is known as the "Nakamoto Consensus." It is also an aspect of financial services, because the numbers generated mathematically and cryptographically inside the blockchain have a quantitative meaning. Using this concept as a baseline, several developers have proposed new cryptocurrencies adapted to new challenges and functional expansions.

Cryptocurrencies that were forked or inspired by Bitcoin are classified into two main types. The first is such as Litecoin, which only inherits the currency implications of the blockchain and improves Bitcoin throughput. Because we know that the Nakamoto Consensus requires low-transaction throughput, high latency, and energy inefficiency, PeerCoin was the first to implement an alternative consensus algorithm (Proof-of-Stake). Other cryptocurrencies include Dash, Monero, and Zcash, which provide more anonymity in transactions.

Another type of cryptocurrency is the implementation of roles and functions, instead of just monetary implications. Ethereum is a leading cryptocurrency that implements smart contracts and has generic functions. Furthermore, Storj provides cloud-storage capabilities, and Namecoin has the equivalent of a domain name service.

3   Related Work

Although there are mechanisms for closing the consortium blockchain because of resource limitations [8], we could not find any direct research related to the requirements of closing public blockchains. However, we located secondary research that included the context of blockchain closing.

Bartoletti et al. [7] measured project mortality based on source-code updates from 120 blockchain-related social-good projects on GitHub. The projects were declared "abandoned" by a third party if their websites were down or if old content was not updated. Fantazzini et al. [10] estimated credit risk in financial-asset portfolios for cryptocurrencies. In their model design, they considered "coin death." If the value drops below one cent with no trading volume and no nodes on the network, no active community, no listing from all exchanges, and no thresholds for price peaks, it dies. However, the death is not permanent. A coin can revive many times. Guo et al. [12] investigated whether wealth distribution was an important factor in determining whether a cryptocurrency survives and gains popularity using a power-law model for Bitcoin and Auroracoin. They showed that some features leading to the death of many coins included complexity of the design of the block-reward scheme, disappearance of the developer, and malware

---

[1] https://www.mail-archive.com/cryptography@metzdowd.com/msg10142.html.

[2] sourceforge.net.

attacks set up by keyloggers and wallet thieves. They also showed that cryptocurrencies were unique and not clones or forks of other cryptocurrencies. The names were not duplicated, and the timing of the listing on the exchange was not bad.

Secondary research shows a common trend of using external information and financial data rather than referring to the system's running status. DeadCoins[3] and Coinopsies[4] are the leading external sources for identifying and locating dead coins. Both media published their lists with evidence, including screenshots and links submitted by users. These studies do not necessarily imply closings in the blockchain, however, we found that they provide empirical evidence of closing consensus in the community.

Studies on the blockchain network availability suggest the state of the system when discussing closing, and research that targets user mechanisms in the system is helpful in understanding the triggers and dynamics of stopping use. In addition, although our study assumes that users do not voluntarily use the blockchain based on the perspective that it is not available, malicious attacks on availability help our discussion as they create a similar situation.

Imamura et al. [14] reported that user behavior was based on economic rationality, owing to storage costs and network maintenance. This means that maintaining a system that is almost dead is irrational because the rational user behavior was positive. Motlagh et al. [17] used continuous-time Markov chains to cover four states (i.e., sleep, getting headers, waking up, and operationally modeling the churning process of nodes). Referring to their research, understanding the potential churn process is an essential milestone in considering the unanimity required to close a blockchain.

Heilman et al. [13] reported an Eclipse attack that isolated nodes by blocking peer-to-peer (P2P) network connections. Apostolaki et al. [3] reported a border-gateway-protocol hijacking attack that similarly caused a partition of the P2P network, leading to the isolation of a specific attack target. Tran et al. [21] reported an extended Erebus attack that partitioned the network without routing manipulations of the larger network. These studies did not express closings, but they reported situations that were more-or-less equivalent in that the volunteer nodes were no longer connected, and the nodes could not refer to the original ledger. The discovery of new blocks and nodes is an empirical factor related to closing a blockchain. The difference between these attacks and the closing blockchain is that they are not temporarily unreferenced, but they are instead permanently unreferenced.

In terms of new-block propagation, a block-delay attack represents a similar situation. Gervais et al. [11] proposed a method to reduce availability without splitting the network by exploiting the application's protocol to delay the propagation of blocks to the attack-target nodes. Walck et al. [23] reported a high-probability block-delay attack by hiding malicious nodes near the network in which the attack-target nodes were built. Based on these reports, even if a

---

[3] https://deadcoins.com/.
[4] https://www.coinopsy.com/dead-coins/.

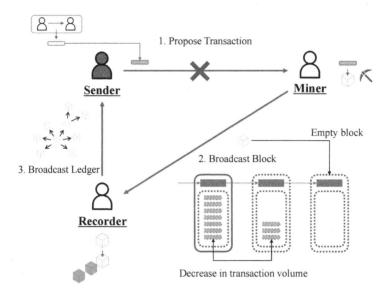

Fig. 2. Cycle of user role when the sender's consent is in the blockchain.

relay network is maintained, network availability can be reduced to nearly zero if there are problems with block propagation.

In summary, the availability of the network is achieved by rational property. Therefore, our starting point for thinking about closing blockchain is to model the processes that lead to irrational conditions. The properties needed to model closing blockchain is referred to as the block and node states in an attack.

4 New Framework for Closing Blockchains

To discretize the unanimity of closing blockchains within the community and to organize the contributing factors, we propose a framework based on the cycle described in Sect. 2.

First, closing the blockchain requires all users to agree with. However, there are no explicit rules on how to gain this unanimity. One method is to build rules around user behavior (e.g., joining and leaving) that can represent implicit user consent. According to Fig. 1, the three user roles include sender, miner, and recorder. If all three roles continue to be filled, they essentially agree to maintain the blockchain, and the cycle runs smoothly. However, if one of these user roles goes unfilled, the closing process begins. The abandonment of all three roles is equivalent to unanimity. The following subsections describe each step of closing a blockchain as implied by the three user roles, focusing on abandonment behaviors and the impact on the cycle.

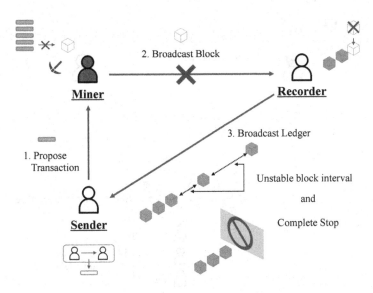

Fig. 3. Cycle of user role when the miner's consent is in the blockchain.

4.1 Sender's Consent

Here, we explain the case where only the sender consents to closing the blockchain. Because the sender's role is to propose transactions, giving up the role means that transaction proposes will cease. Figure 2 shows how the cycle is affected by the sender's role going unfilled, thus stopping the proposes.

First, when the sender stops proposing, the number of transactions stored by the miner in the block gradually reduces. Eventually, an empty block is created. The cost of storing an empty block is lower than that of storing a full block, because the recorder always keeps an empty block. This means that, in many of the protocols applied by the blockchain, the miner does not receive a transfer fee, which is economically damaging. In the case of the recorder, the cost of storage is lower than when storing a full block, because the recorder always saves an empty one. Regardless, it is significant that the largest user role, the sender, no longer exists. Importantly, the miner and the recorder roles recognize the lack of sender participation by examining the number of transactions. In conjunction with the sender's implied signal of closing consent, this suggests that the miner and the recorder will be close behind.

4.2 Miner's Consent

When only miners imply their closing consent, it helps to understand the hard-fork situation that occurred with Ethereum. The role of the miner is to validate the broadcast transactions in the blockchain and to record them in a new block. Hence, giving up the role means that new blocks will cease to be created. Figure 3 shows how the cycle is affected by the miner ceasing activity. When this occurs,

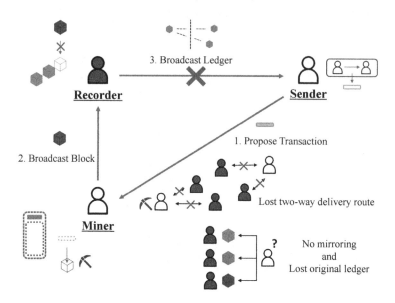

Fig. 4. Cycle of user role when the recorder's consent is in the blockchain.

time lags appear in the block interval, and the block updates eventually stop. The recorder is not able to chain the new blocks, and the block header stops updating. Shortly thereafter, the recorder will not be able to determine whether the block was stopped, or the PoW difficulty was delayed block creation. No matter how many transactions the sender broadcasts, they will not be verified. The recorder's resources are then overloaded, and all transactions are pooled. The miner's consent is easier to determine than the sender's consent.

4.3   Recorder's Consent

When only the recorders agree to closing the blockchain, it represents a final consent, unlike those of the sender and the miner. The recorder's role is to store all data to the initial block and update the ledger with new blocks validated by the miner and to maintain the route by which transactions and blocks are propagated. To lose the recorder role means that data cannot be recorded, and they are thus destroyed. Figure 4 shows the impact on the cycle that occurs when a recorder stops maintaining a distributed ledger. When recorder gives up, the sender can no longer determine the network status. The miner cannot catch new transactions and continues to generate empty blocks through self-mining. When this occurs, it is difficult to determine whether there is a network or software problem, compared with the sender's and the miner's consent. No longer able to validate the original block, the blockchain reaches its final closing state.

5   Empirical Analysis

In this section, we confirm the closing blockchain framework defined in the previous section against the actual state of a public blockchain to support an empirical understanding of the application research and to analyze the characteristics of each type of consent.

5.1   Data Collection

Our analysis covers 219 minor cryptocurrencies listed in cryptoID[5], including those listed in the middle of the period from June 1, 2019 to May 31, 2020. cryptoID provided the dataset for the blocks, transactions, and nodes on the blockchain network. We covered the entire observation period for blocks and transactions, but we only collected node information on the network from every 10 min and only for the most-recent month's data. The dataset about nodes in the network is minimal, owing to the limitations of the data source. Note that the theme of this analysis has potential limitations, unlike typical cryptocurrencies (e.g., Bitcoin and Ethereum). We targeted cryptocurrencies that cannot be observed stably. This is because of the need to continuously acquire the data source in a self-consistent manner; however, this data source may be lost in the near future.

5.2   Characteristics of Transactions and Blocks

Our framework proposed for finding unanimity for closing the blockchain focuses on the number of transactions included in a block and the new blocks. Note that checking the recorder's consensus is not measurable, because we need to observe that there were no nodes in the network, according to the framework. Thus, Fig. 5 shows a period of zero transactions and zero blocks in a day to confirm the status of the defined sender's and miner's consent. For the number of transactions, we did not include transactions that transferred generated mined coins to separate the cases where the number of transactions was zero but blocks were mined. The white area indicates a period where more than one transaction or block was identified in a day, and the black line indicates a period of zero transactions or blocks in a day. The periods with zero blocks matches the period with zero transactions.

As shown in the linear pattern, 124 currencies did not contain a single transaction during the day in the observation period. There were 46 cryptocurrencies for which no new blocks were created at least once during the day. Note that, even with Bitcoin, there were blocks that did not contain transactions, depending on the timing. However, they did not last all day. The decline in the number of transactions is a well-known cause of coin death in the community, but we can classify it into more detailed stages using the empirical results shown in Fig. 5. If we match the notation of the closing consensus with the notation of death, it

---

[5] https://chainz.cryptoid.info/.

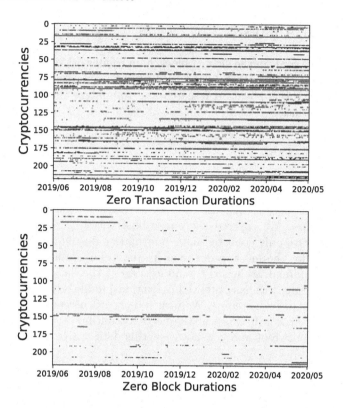

Fig. 5. Zero transactions and zero block duration in cryptocurrencies.

means that there is a stage of death in which there is not only a superficial death where the transaction is zero, but there is also an even deeper death where the block is zero. We arrive to this fact from the result that the pattern in the top figure showing the zero transactions does not match the pattern in the bottom figure showing the zero blocks.

Following the proposed framework, zero transactions depend on the actions of the sender, and zero blocks depend on the miner. As confirmed by the cycle flow, the creation of empty blocks has validity, reflecting that the sender had no intention of using the system. However, the miner intended to maintain the system to contribute to the cycle. Meanwhile, with the refusal to create a new block, there was an improvement in the investigation that required checking that transactions were sent throughout the network to determine which one the sender was on.

5.3 Case of Closing a Blockchain

To provide a concrete example, Fig. 6 shows an excerpt of the NPCcoin transactions and blocks included in zero transactions and zero blocks. The history of NPCcoin is an example of how, during the observation period, their genesis

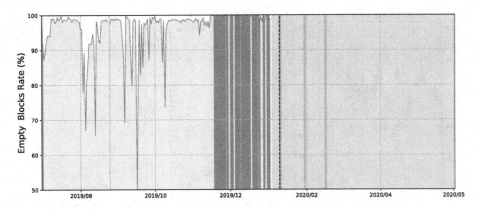

Fig. 6. Transaction and block lifecycle in NPCcoin. (Color figure online)

block of June 30, 2019, started. However, after about 6 months of operation, the developers announced that the community would shut down on January 10, 2020. The gray area in the figure shows the case where the empty block rate was less than 100% during the daytime. The blue area shows 100%, and the red area shows the period when no new blocks were created. The black dotted line represents January 10, 2020, the day the shutdown took place. The two vertical lines around February 2020 are blue. The blue area just before the shift to the red area starts on November 18, 2019. The most continuous period lasts 8 days, from December 10 through 17, 2019. Note that the blue area is not continuous.

We found two interesting things about closing consensus in Fig. 6. One is that the creation of a new block stops after an empty block. Of course, it is possible that this result is based on the announcement on the official site. However, there were no senders when mining resumed in February, 2020, after mining new blocks stopped. If the sender's broadcasted transaction was in the transaction memory pool, a new block that included transactions would be generated at this point. However, an empty block was generated. In other words, a sender could not be shown to exist; thus, the miner stopped mining. This is a good case of reproducing the cycle of propagation in which the sender first loses interest, then the miner loses interest. Additionally, the tendency for the number of transactions to gradually decrease, as the state just before the number of transactions reaches zero, is intuitively consistent with the situation where users gradually stop using the system when they lose interest. The other thing is that it is difficult to reach unanimity on a minor currency that is as close to closure as possible. As we find from the fact that mining has resumed, the ledger maintained an average of five servers until recently, regardless of the announcements. Thus, the cycle of unanimity remains consistent with the rotation of sender, miner, and recorder. Moreover, we focused on the timing of the block's delivery stoppage to clarify the potential signs of the dynamism that drove the closing blockchain.

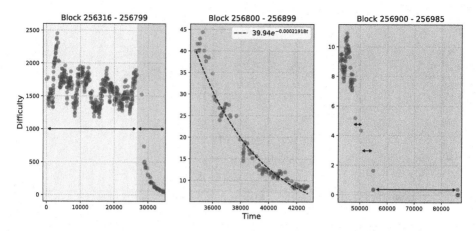

Fig. 7. Relationship trend between mining difficulty and mining interval just before the block mining stops.

Figure 7 shows the relationship between mining difficulty and mining interval from Block 256,985 on January 3, 2020, which is the day before block mining stopped. This confirms the trend. Each figure is empirically classified into three levels based on changes in the level of mining difficulty and interval. The left figure shows the discontinuous stage at which mining stopped after a period of continuous mining. The middle figure shows a stage in which the mining difficulty decreased in conjunction with the decrease in hash power caused by mining stoppage. The right figure shows the last stage at which a critical hash power was reached, at which point mining became difficult.

These results provide us with a useful empirical rule for isolating the early states. Thus, we can assume that following a model in which mining difficulty is stable and mean-regressive, a non-sequential change in mining difficulty that exponentially decreases can be an indication of miner dropout. The critical point is shown in the figure. We expected instability during stops in the framework. We confirmed that, in the last stage just before the mining stopped, the block interval was longer, and the block delivery speed as less stable.

We should note that our target blockchain implemented a block-by-block difficulty adjustment. However, we can assume that, even in the case of a blockchain, the difficulty adjustment occurs at constant intervals, similar to Bitcoin. The change in hash power is not immediately reflected as an exponential function, but it is similar to a change in the step function. From these results, we believe that there is validity in considering the proposed framework in the order of the cycle and for each role.

5.4   Characteristics of Nodes

As noted in the previous sub-section, the nodes that maintain the ledger are the root of the system, and the recorder is the final voter in blockchain closure. Here,

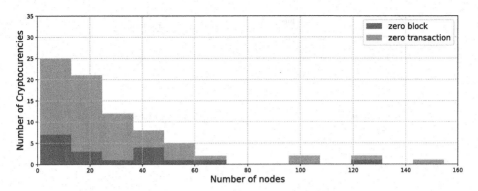

Fig. 8. The number of nodes in the cryptocurrency network with zero transactions and zero blocks.

we understand the characteristics of the unanimity by analyzing the distribution of the most recent orders. Figure 8 represents the distribution of the average number of nodes found on May 31st for the 80 cryptocurrencies that experienced an empty block or a new block suspended during the most recent period from May 1 to 31, 2020. The 80 cryptocurrencies were broken down into 60 empty blocks and 20 new blocks that were suspended.

First, for statistical information, we found 2,344 unique nodes, of which 2,174 (92.75%) were unduplicated, and the rest contained two or more duplicates. The largest duplicate nodes were duplicated in 35 cryptocurrencies. We noted that this is the server provided by the data-source site, which is used for this research. The regions in which the nodes were located were in 90 countries, with the most node-rich regions being, in order, the United States (530), Germany (469), Russia (103), The Netherlands (97), and Italy (92). Minor providers, including Hetzner, Choopa, OVH, and Contabo, were selected as node providers. These providers tended to be less expensive than major providers, such as Amazon Web Services, Microsoft Azure, or the Google Cloud Platform. This result is not significantly different from those reported in previous studies [15, 18] that investigated the node distribution of networks in major cryptocurrencies.

Next, we found that more than half of the cryptocurrencies that created an empty block or stopped a new block maintained an average of fewer than 40 nodes. The distribution trends were the same in both cryptocurrencies, and they were maintained with fewer nodes. This number of nodes was less than 1% of those maintained by Bitcoin and Ethereum, each. This number approximates the final number of users. Thus, we controlled the availability of data with this unanimity to the number of people. However, we are certain that it was not easy to execute, because, even if one unit was running, it would be very difficult to close.

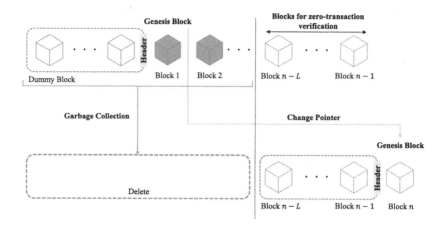

Fig. 9. Dynamically changing genesis block.

6   Discussion

From the framework and empirical analysis, we found that the number of transactions and blocks was significant for the closing unanimity. In this section, we discuss the method of embedding closure mechanisms into the blockchain based on this trend. In the design, full closure of the blockchain is needed to ensure that there are zero nodes storing the ledger. However, this situation means that we must verify that there are zero users in the network. Thus, we note that the mechanism that reduces availability is challenging and very difficult to implement. Therefore, we aim to achieve closing unanimity via the lack of new transactions and blocks, wherein the sender and the miner' agrees to close the blockchain by relaxing the conditions.

Focusing on the agreement of no new blocks, we find that this state is equivalent to the first time the blockchain is launched. In other words, we can create the same situation as closing through initialization, which overwrites the data previously stored in the ledger and erases the historical data. The idea of this mechanism is illustrated in Fig. 9, which demonstrates the change of a genesis block to a dynamic pointer.

As a necessary configuration, we set a threshold of block-length L, which describes a block with zero transactions when the blockchain is launched. The first time the block is judged, it is handled with L dummy blocks, and these correspond to the header to which the genesis block points. Note that the block headers (L blocks) are necessary to judge the changing pointer.

After building the block, if all L blocks are zero-transaction blocks at the creation of the nth block, the genesis block is changed to the nth block, and the blocks before $n - L$ are deleted. This behavior is similar to unused allocated values in memory being removed via garbage collection.

The initialization of the ledger propagates to all existing recorders in the network by the nth block. When a new recorder connects to the network, the existing recorder mirrors the initialized ledger, so that the discarded blocks are never restored. The configuration of the basic blockchain is the same as the basic blockchain structure, excluding the design of the timing for block deletion. Thus, this design is equivalent to a blockchain having no block destruction by setting the value of L to 0.

Unlike the case of hard-coding the genesis block, using it as a dynamic pointer in the network intentionally limits its integrity and the design lifetime. Here, we consider the block length, L, using empirical values for a deeper discussion. Referring to the number of blocks from 8 days and the longest period of zero transactions in the empirical analysis of Fig. 6, the block length, L, is about 10,000, because the mining interval is 60 s. However, considering the verification of every block propagation, we assume that we need to set a shorter L. Of course, it is difficult to delete after data are deployed on the network. However, this idea is an effective approach to stop them from being propagated to new users. We also assume that, if an update occurs, we can consequently follow the same path as the original block shown in Fig. 4 of the recorder in the framework, where we cannot prove that any past block is the original.

7   Conclusion

In this research, to deepen the discussion on finding the unanimity required to close blockchains, we proposed a framework for mechanism analysis that focuses on the three user roles (i.e., sender, recorder, and miner) in the blockchain. We considered user behavior that did not contribute to the cycle of roles as "voting without interest" and visualized the impact of the flow of blocks and transactions in the system. Then, we confirmed the validity of the proposed framework on the minor cryptocurrencies using a blockchain that we assumed to be near closing.

We confirmed the empirical consistency of our proposed framework in which the flow of the block stopped when the flow of the transaction reached zero, using the target measured from the launch to the mining stop of the block during the observation period. We also reported on discontinuous connections of mining difficulty and changes in decay and mining intervals that made them unstable at the critical point at which the miner stopped a new block. We noted the difficulty of stopping and the high remaining block availability, because some nodes still maintained ledgers, even after excluding duplicate nodes, despite the zero flow of transactions and blocks.

Finally, based on the framework and empirical analysis, we discussed methods of implementing a mechanism for closing the blockchain. Because it is the closing that is the target of this paper, we emphasized the approach via initialization rather than modification or deletion.

In a future work, it will be necessary to clarify the operational issues using a pilot implementation program that applies a stopping mechanism. We assume that discussions are necessary for businesses to responsibly close-out decentralized data using the blockchains across companies in view of security risks and data protection. To achieve this, we must set limits on the integrity of data in the blockchain and implement a system lifetime.

Acknowledgement. This work was partly supported by Grant-in-Aid for Scientific Research (B) (19H04107).

References

1. Al-Jaroodi, J., Mohamed, N.: Blockchain in industries: a survey. IEEE Access **7**, 36500–36515 (2019)
2. Ali, S.T., McCorry, P., Lee, P.H.J., Hao, F.: Zombiecoin 2.0: managing next-generation botnets using bitcoin. Int. J. Inf. Secur. **17**(4), 411–422 (2018)
3. Apostolaki, M., Zohar, A., Vanbever, L.: Hijacking bitcoin: routing attacks on cryptocurrencies. In: IEEE Symposium on Security and Privacy (S&P), pp. 375–392. IEEE (2017)
4. Babaioff, M., Dobzinski, S., Oren, S., Zohar, A.: On bitcoin and red balloons. In: Proceedings of the 13th ACM Conference on Electronic Commerce, pp. 56–73. ACM (2012)
5. Back, A., et al.: Hashcash-a denial of service counter-measure (2002). http://www.hashcash.org/papers/hashcash.pdf
6. Baden, M., Torres, C.F., Pontiveros, B.B.F., State, R.: Whispering botnet command and control instructions. In: 2019 Crypto Valley Conference on Blockchain Technology (CVCBT), pp. 77–81. IEEE (2019)
7. Bartoletti, M., Cimoli, T., Pompianu, L., Serusi, S.: Blockchain for social good: a quantitative analysis. In: Proceedings of the 4th EAI International Conference on Smart Objects and Technologies for Social Good, pp. 37–42. ACM (2018)
8. Cunico, H.A., Dunne, S., Harpur, L.S., Silva, A.: Blockchain lifecycle management. US Patent App. 15/848,036. 20 June 2019
9. DuPont, Q.: Experiments in algorithmic governance: a history and ethnography of "the DAO," a failed decentralized autonomous organization. Bitcoin and beyond, pp. 157–177 (2017)
10. Fantazzini, D., Zimin, S.: A multivariate approach for the simultaneous modelling of market risk and credit risk for cryptocurrencies. J. Ind. Bus. Econ. **47**(1), 19–69 (2020)
11. Gervais, A., Ritzdorf, H., Karame, G.O., Capkun, S.: Tampering with the delivery of blocks and transactions in bitcoin. In: Proceedings of the 22nd ACM SIGSAC Conference on Computer and Communications Security, pp. 692–705. ACM (2015)
12. Guo, L., Li, X.J.: Risk analysis of cryptocurrency as an alternative asset class. In: Härdle, W.K., Chen, C.Y.-H., Overbeck, L. (eds.) Applied Quantitative Finance. SC, pp. 309–329. Springer, Heidelberg (2017). https://doi.org/10.1007/978-3-662-54486-0_16
13. Heilman, E., Kendler, A., Zohar, A., Goldberg, S.: Eclipse attacks on bitcoin's peer-to-peer network. In: 24th USENIX Security Symposium, pp. 129–144. USENIX Association (2015)
14. Imamura, M., Omote, K.: Difficulty of decentralized structure due to rational user behavior on blockchain. In: Liu, J.K., Huang, X. (eds.) NSS 2019. LNCS, vol. 11928, pp. 504–519. Springer, Cham (2019). https://doi.org/10.1007/978-3-030-36938-5_31
15. Kim, S.K., Ma, Z., Murali, S., Mason, J., Miller, A., Bailey, M.: Measuring Ethereum network peers. In: Proceedings of the Internet Measurement Conference 2018, pp. 91–104. ACM (2018)

16. Matzutt, R., et al.: A quantitative analysis of the impact of arbitrary blockchain content on bitcoin. In: Meiklejohn, S., Sako, K. (eds.) FC 2018. LNCS, vol. 10957, pp. 420–438. Springer, Heidelberg (2018). https://doi.org/10.1007/978-3-662-58387-6_23

17. Motlagh, S.G., Misic, J., Misic, V.B.: Modeling of churn process in bitcoin network. In: 2020 International Conference on Computing, Networking and Communications (ICNC), pp. 686–691. IEEE (2020)

18. Park, S., Im, S., Seol, Y., Paek, J.: Nodes in the bitcoin network: comparative measurement study and survey. IEEE Access **7**, 57009–57022 (2019)

19. Sato, T., Imamura, M., Omote, K.: Threat analysis of poisoning attack against ethereum blockchain. In: Laurent, M., Giannetsos, T. (eds.) WISTP 2019. LNCS, vol. 12024, pp. 139–154. Springer, Cham (2020). https://doi.org/10.1007/978-3-030-41702-4_9

20. Satoshi, N.: Bitcoin: a peer-to-peer electronic cash system (2008). http://www.bitcoin.org/bitcoin.pdf

21. Tran, M., Choi, I., Moon, G.J., Vu, A.V., Kang, M.S.: A stealthier partitioning attack against bitcoin peer-to-peer network. In: IEEE Symposium on Security and Privacy (S&P). IEEE (2020)

22. Voigt, P., Von dem Bussche, A.: The EU General Data Protection Regulation (GDPR). A Practical Guide, 1st edn, Springer International Publishing, Cham (2017)

23. Walck, M., Wang, K., Kim, H.S.: Tendrilstaller: block delay attack in bitcoin. In: 2019 IEEE International Conference on Blockchain (Blockchain), pp. 1–9. IEEE (2019)

DBS: Blockchain-Based Privacy-Preserving RBAC in IoT

Xianxian Li[1,2], Junhao Yang[1,2], Shiqi Gao[1,2], Zhenkui Shi[1,2(✉)], Jie Li[1,2], and Xuemei Fu[1,2]

[1] College of Computer Science, Guangxi Normal University, Guilin 541000, GX, China
lixx@mailbox.gxnu.edu.cn, shizhenkui@gxnu.edu.cn
[2] Guangxi Key Lab of Multi-source Information Mining and Security, Guilin, China

Abstract. In this paper, we propose a new privacy-preserving scheme for access control in IoT based on blockchain technology and role-based access control (RBAC). The decentralized property and reliability of the blockchain platform make the proposed solution fit the geographically distributed scenario for IoT better. We extend the traditional RBAC with a new device domain to realize more flexible and manageable access control for the diverse IoT devices. Besides, the scheme takes advantage of zero-knowledge proof and the trusted execution environment (TEE) to ensure the transaction information is confidential, to protect the privacy of the details of access control including information of roles, devices, and policies. To demonstrate the feasibility and effectiveness of the architecture, we implemented our scheme and evaluated on the Ethereum private chain to achieve privacy-preserving access control for IoT. The results show that our scheme is feasible and the cost is acceptable.

Keywords: Internet of Things · Privacy-preserving · Access control · Smart contract · Blockchain

1 Introduction

According to the prediction of the American Computer Industry Association (CompTIA), the number of IoT devices will increase to 50.1 billion by 2025. The ubiquitous IoT is affecting all aspects of our lives, such as intelligent transportation, smart home, environmental monitoring, street lighting system, food traceability, medical health, and so on.

The work is partially supported by the National Natural Science Foundation of China (No. 61672176), the Guangxi "Bagui Scholar" Teams for Innovation and Research Project, the Guangxi Talent Highland Project of Big Data Intelligence and Application, the Guangxi Science and Technology Plan Projects No. AD20159039, the Guangxi Young and Middle-aged Ability Improvement Project No. 2020KY02032, the Innovation Project of Guangxi Graduate Education No. YCSW2020110.

Due to the IoT devices are globally distributed and the scale of managed devices may be from hundreds to millions for different organizations, companies, or institutions, how to access control these devices efficiently, conveniently, and securely become an important problem. In IoT, access control is used to grant or revoke the permission to a specified user to have access to the specified IoT devices. It consists of a set of concepts such as access control policies, authorization, granting, revoking, etc. The traditional centralized access control systems are for the human-machine oriented Internet scenarios where devices are within the same trust domain and can not meet the needs of access control of the IoT. In addition, IoT devices may be dynamic and abundant, there may be a single point of failure, and other issues such as the constrained CPU, memory, power.

The emerging technology of blockchain [1] may provide viable schemes for IoT access control. The blockchain is a distributed digital ledger. The decentralized architecture of the blockchain reduces the pressure of the old central computing of the IoT. The data is no longer controlled by the center alone, but also provides more possibilities for the innovation of the organizational structure of the IoT. The accuracy and non-tamper ability of blockchain records make the data available and more secure. And some architectures for IoT access control have been proposed [2–4]. But the current schemes of IoT access control still face the following challenges.

- Management. In most proposed schemes, the solutions to manage these access policies don't consider the scale of devices and are not flexible or efficient enough. The number of IoT devices may be from hundreds to millions for an organization. For example, considering the scenario when a device manager quits from an organization, they should execute the function of removing manager from device n times where n is the number of devices the manager controls. Similarly, when a new manager checks in, they should execute the function of adding a manager to device n times. For an access policy always indicates a relation between a device manager and a device in most current schemes [2]. Such a solution is not flexible or efficient. Besides, massive IoT devices are being deployed every day. The access policies should be updated efficiently and adaptively. Existing solutions maybe not applicable.
- Security and privacy. Some schemes are based on public blockchains. The information is public. This means all access policies are public and may face severe privacy issues for the organizations.
- Cost. Some schemes may be based on private chains. These chains need to invest a lot of nodes to satisfy the blockchain and fit the distribution of the IoT.

To address the above issues, we propose DBS, which is a privacy-preserving RBAC architecture based on blockchain in IoT. Comparing with previous work where an access policy indicates a manager's access authority to a single device, we extend the traditional RBAC with a new domain and make DBS fit the access control of IoT. Through this methodology, we ca manage the access policy in a batch manner. And it can deal with the scenarios by calling about two functions when many access policies should be changed. DBS leverages zero-knowledge proof to protect the privacy of transactions and combines with the TEE to ensure the confidentiality and integrity of the smart contract. DBS consists of double access control contracts, one authorization contract, and one authentication contract. Authorization contract is used to assign a role to the requester and provides functions for adding, updating, and deleting access control policies. An authentication contract is used to check the access right of the requester and prevent unauthorized access. Finally, we implemented and evaluated our scheme. And the results show that by introducing the RBAC model, it can simplify management, preserve the privacy of access policies, and achieve convenience and flexibility to access and manage the IoT devices.

2   Related Work

Access Control Schemes Based on Blockchain

Due to the excellent features of blockchain such as decentralization, tamper-proof, traceability, etc., at present, many researchers have leveraged blockchain to solve the access control of IoT. The decentralized peer-to-peer network can well conform the distribution of IoT. Because of the three problems that must be solved in access control under the IoT (the lightweight terminal devices, the massive terminal nodes, and the dynamic nature of the IoT), the survey [5,6] summarized how to solve these problems and the advantages of using blockchain.

For the access model, we will take the most common models like Attribute-based access control (ABAC), role-based access control (RBAC) [7], etc. as our study cases. [8] proposed a scheme based on the ABAC. It can create, manage, and implement access control policies by using blockchain technology, which allows to access resources in a distributed manner. But this method is not completely decentralized. The scheme needs authorization centers for policy implementation points, policy management points, and policy decision points. And the policies and the rights exchange are publicly visible. These may breach the privacy of related parties. [9] also proposed an ABAC model based on a decentralized blockchain, but it is in a big data scenario that is similar to the Internet of things.

Role-based access control (RBAC) is another common access, management model. [10] uses smart contract and role-based access control to realize cross-organization role verification. [4] proposed a framework of arbitration roles and permission. Users can manage IoT devices through a single smart contract.

In terms of blockchain technology, the current schemes can fall into two categories: transaction-based access control and smart contract-based access control [11]. FairAccess in [3] uses new types of transactions to grant, get, delegate, and revoke access. [12] proposed a novel decentralized record management system to handle electronic medical records using blockchain technology. The system uses three smart contracts: register contract, patient-provider relationship contract, and summary contract to control access to electronic medical records. And [13] realized access control of IoT devices through multiple different smart contracts including register contracts, access control contracts, and judge contracts to accomplish the functions of registration, access verification, and audit in the access control process. [14] provides a specific case to realize the application of access control to smart homes based on the smart contract.

There are few of the currently proposed schemes which considered the policies management of massive IoT devices and users. And there are a large number of new IoT devices deployed or upgraded every day. New schemes should be essential to manage access policies conveniently and efficiently.

Privacy-Preserving Schemes for IoT

Although, the anonymity of blockchain may protect a user's privacy to a certain extent, and the distributed nodes of blockchain can prevent a single point of failure. In the era of big data, attackers can still identify some user's blockchain transaction information and IP [15], leaving users' critical information exposed to the shadow of privacy disclosure.

For the privacy and security of blockchain, Microsoft [16] proposed a framework to protect the privacy of blockchain by using a trusted execution environment (TEE). The Confidential Consortium framework includes a set of key and permission management mechanisms, which can ensure that only encrypted transactions can be processed in a trusted execution environment, and only users with corresponding permissions can view the relevant status. TEE can not only prove the correctness of the code, but also ensure that the internal data is invisible to the outside and not tampered with when running, and then ensure the confidentiality and integrity of the key code and data of the blockchain protocol, so that the application of the blockchain can run efficiently on the fully trusted member nodes. And [17] also uses a hardware enclave to ensure the confidentiality of smart contracts. After the verification on the blockchain, the smart contract is put into the offline distributed TEE platform for execution and storage to maintain the integrity and confidentiality of the smart contract. For the privacy problem of smart contracts, [18] proposed a distributed smart contract system with privacy protection. Through zero-knowledge proof [19,20], the scheme can ensure that the transactions will not be disclosed. Similar privacy schemes include zerocoin and zerocash [21,22].

However, all the above schemes are not dedicated to IoT and cannot be applied directly in access control for IoT. The access policies may include information about IoT devices and users. These may raise critical privacy concerns. And new privacy-preserving access control schemes should be proposed to protect the privacy of related users and devices.

3 System Architecture

We propose a new architecture in this paper which is a distributed privacy-preserving access control system. In the scheme, access control information is stored and authenticated via blockchain and smart contract.

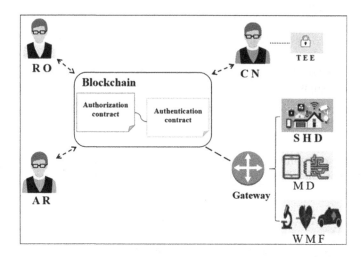

Fig. 1. Access control system overview of DBS.

3.1 Architecture Component

The architecture of our system is illustrated in Fig. 1. The architecture includes six different components: Resource owner, access requesters, consensus nodes, and smart contracts, which connect through P2P networks. At the same time, there are a large number of IoT devices (e.g. mobile devices (MD), smart home devices (SHD), wearable medical facilities (WMF), etc.), which are connected to the P2P network via the gateways. Such mechanism is common in many work [3,13]. The different components of the architecture can be explained in detail as follows.

1) *Resource owner (RO)*: RO is the owner of the IoT devices, responsible for managing the access control permission of a set of IoT devices, and has the highest management rights. Any entity can become a resource owner by registering its own IoT device on the deployed smart contract.
   RO defines access control policies and various operations in the authorization contract and deploys the authorization contract on the blockchain to realize the function of the authorization contract. By invoking the authorization contract, RO can assign different roles to different access requesters to achieve permission management. At the same time, RO deploys an authentication contract to check the role and operation of the access requester to realize access management.

2) *Access requester (AR)*: AR refers to the people who want to access the IoT devices to obtain relevant data, operate and manage IoT devices. There are two types of access requesters, the access requester in the domain, and the cross-domain access requester, such as family members and non-family members, or company employees and non-company employees.

There are different authorization methods for different access requesters. For the access requester in the domain, RO can directly assign the corresponding roles to the members and add user-role-permission-devices information to authorization contract by invoking the contract. However, the cross-domain access requester needs to apply for a role from the authorization contract. When the access control policies defined by the RO are met, the authorization contract will assign corresponding roles to the cross-domain access requesters.

3) *Consensus node (CN)*: CN is a specific blockchain node in our architecture. It is not only responsible for verifying and processing transactions but also for deploying and executing smart contracts.

To guarantee the confidentiality of the code and data of smart contracts, these consensus nodes need trusted execution environments (TEE). TEE can provide a secure enclaved space for data and code to ensure their confidentiality and integrity. The contract will be encrypted before transferring and can only be decrypted inside the corresponding enclave. TEE will generate a key-pair for this contract and publish the public key. The invocation arguments are encrypted with the contracts public key which can only be decrypted within the enclave. The return value will be encrypted by a user-provided key which is delivered along with calling arguments. During the whole process, anyone even the CN cannot leak the internal executing state.

4) *Smart contract (SC)*: We define management operations in smart contracts to manage the access control. All the operations allowed in the access management system are triggered by blockchain transactions. We utilize two smart contracts, an authorization contract and an authentication contract to assign roles and check access rights respectively.

- Authorization contract: RO defines access control policies and management operations in the authorization contract. The management operations include *Addrole()*, *Deleterole()*, *Grantrole()*, *PolicyAdd()*, *PolicyUpdate();* and *PolicyDelete()*, etc. For the access requester in the domain, RO calls the *Addrole()* operation to assign the corresponding role to the access requester directly. For cross domain access requesters, who needs sends a transaction application role to the authorization contract, and the authorization contract will judge whether it meets the requirements of role assignment according to the access control policy. If the policies are satisfied, the access requester's information is added to the authorization contract with operation *Grantrole()*.

- Authentication contract: is responsible for preventing unauthorized access and checking the access permission of the access requester. The operation of authentication contract includes *FindRole()*, *FindDevice()* and *Judge()*, etc. When the access requester sends an access request to the IoT device, the authentication contract will invoke the authorization contract by executing the *FindRole()* operation to determine whether the access requester is a legitimate user. Then, the authentication contract will execute the *FindDevice()* operation to determine whether the access requester can access the corresponding IoT devices. Finally, the authorization contract will execute

Judge() operation to match role-permission-device to determine whether the access request meets the access control policy.

5) *Gateway*: As mentioned before, IoT devices do not belong to the blockchain network. The majority of IoT devices are very constrained in terms of CPU, memory, and battery. Those limitations restrict IoT devices to be part of the blockchain network. Like previous work, we use a gateway to connect the blockchain network and IoT devices. Gateway is an interface that transforms the information of IoT devices into messages that can be understood by blockchain nodes. Multiple IoT devices can be connected to a gateway and multiple gateways can also be connected to multiple blockchain nodes. The gateway cannot be a constrained device. Such devices need high-performance features to be able to serve as many simultaneous requests as possible from IoT devices.

6) *IoT devices*: can be smart home devices, mobile devices, wearable medical devices, industrial sensor devices, etc. IoT devices connects to the gateway via short-range communication technologies like Bluetooth, Wi-Fi, and Zigbee, and etc. Then interact with the blockchain network via the gateway to execute access control operations.

IoT devices do not belong to the blockchain network. Consequently, one of the requirements of our architecture is that all the devices will have to be uniquely identified globally in the blockchain network. Public key generators can provide a feasible solution for the problem by producing acceptable large and unique random numbers. Typically, we can use the existing IoT cryptographic technologies to create a public key for every device.

3.2 Improved Role Based Access Control Model

Due to the constrained nature of IoT devices can not achieve accurate access management, such as sensors. We have improved the RBAC model. There are three sets: U, R and P in traditional RBAC models. We add a device set D on this basis. The improved RBAC relationship is shown in Table 1. Through this methodology, we can manage the access policy in a batch manner. And it can deal with the massive IoT device policy managements by calling about two functions.

Table 1. Relationship of user-role-permission-devices

User	Role	Permission	Device
Address 1	Role 1	execute	$d_1, d_2, d_3, ...d_n$
Address 1	Role 1	write	$d_1, d_2, d_3, ...d_n$
Address 1	Role 1	store	$d_1, d_2, d_3, ...d_n$
Address 1	Role 2	write	$d_1, d_2, d_3, ...d_{n-1}$
Address 1	Role 2	store	d_1, d_2, d_3
Address 2	Role 3	write	$d_1, d_2, d_3, d_4, d_5,$
Address 2	Role 4	read	$d_1, d_2, d_3, ...d_{n-2}$
Address 3	Role 5	read	$d_1, d_2, d_3, ...d_{n-3}$

4   Privacy-Preserving

In this part, we introduce how our scheme preserve the privacy. We describe three main parts: encryption and decryption system, zero-knowledge proof process, trusted execution environment (TEE) protocol.

4.1   Encryption and Decryption System

The key system of DBS is shown in Fig. 3. Where A represents a sender, which can be the resource owner or access requester in the system. B stands for a receiver, which can be a smart contract in the system.

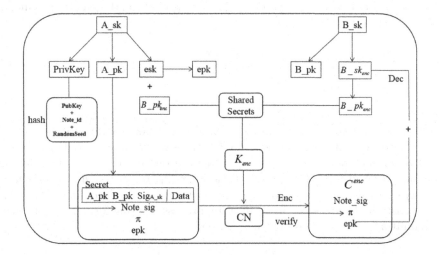

Fig. 2. Encryption and decryption system.

1) *Encryption* is used to protect the privacy of both parties and the confidentiality of the transaction. First, Sender A will obtain public key B_{pk} and encrypted public key $B_{pk_{enc}}$ of receiver B. Then the sender will generate an asymmetric key pair *esk* and *epk* temporarily. *esk* and $B_{pk_{enc}}$ are used to generate a sharedSecret, and then a symmetric key K_{enc} is generated. The sender can encrypt the transaction with symmetric secret key K_{enc} to protect the privacy of both parties and the confidentiality of the transaction.

At the same time, to ensure the integrity of the transaction and prevent Man-in-the-middle Attack, the sender will temporarily generate another asymmetric key pair PrivKey and PubKey to sign the transaction before encrypting the transaction. The signature Tx_{sig} is generated by hashing PubKey, RandomSeed and $Note_{id}$.

Before sending the transaction, the sender will generate a zero-knowledge proof π about the transaction amount to hide the transaction amount. To ensure the correctness of the transaction amount and prevent double flower transactions, the proof π and random public key epk are write to the transaction.

2) *Decryption*: After the transaction is verified, it will be stored on the blockchain in an encrypted form. The receiver can leverage the encrypted private key $B_{sk_{enc}}$ and random public key *epk* to generate the symmetric secret key K_{enc} which can be used to decrypt the transaction.

4.2   Zero Knowledge Proof Process

This part introduces the application of zero-knowledge proof in DBS. Let s be a safety parameter, n be a large prime number, p,q be two random large prime numbers. n, λ and k are calculated by formulas (1), (2), and (3) respectively. g is an element with larger order in the Z_n^*, and g_1, g_2, h_1 and h_2 are the elements in the cyclic group generated by g.

$$n = pq \tag{1}$$

$$\lambda = lcm(p-1, q-1) \tag{2}$$

$$k = g^\lambda \quad mod \quad n^2 \tag{3}$$

1) Proof of equal transaction amount: Formula (4) takes parameters r_1, g_1, h_1 and n to generate commitment C_1 for transaction amount t. Formula (5) takes parameters r_2, g_2, $h2$ and n to generate commitment C_2 for transaction amount t. And formula (6) takes parameters r_1, r_2, g_1, g_2, h_1, h_2 and n to generate evidence *eproof* for the equivalence of transaction amount t. The consensus node performs the verification process by using formula (7) through commitment C_1, C_2 and evidence *eProof*.

$$C_1 = g_1^x h_1^x \quad mod \quad n \tag{4}$$

$$C_2 = g_2^x h_2^x \quad mod \quad n \tag{5}$$

$$eProofGen = (t, r_1, r_2, g_1, g_2, h_1, h_2, n) \tag{6}$$

$$eProofVer = (eProof, C_1, C_2, g_1, g_2, h_1, h_2, n) \tag{7}$$

2) Proof of transaction amount greater than 0: Formula (8) takes the parameters r, g, h and n as the secret transaction amount t to generate commitment C. Formula (9) takes parameters a, r, g, h and n as secret transaction amount t to produce proof *gproof* larger than parameter a. Formula (10) takes the proof gproof, parameter, a, r, g, h, C, n to judge whether the secret amount in commitment C is greater than parameter a.

$$C = g^x h^r mod n \tag{8}$$

$$gProofGen = (t, a, r, g, h, n) \tag{9}$$

$$gProofVer = (gProof, a, C, g, h, n) \tag{10}$$

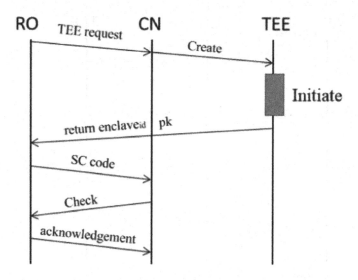

Fig. 3. Contract deployment.

4.3 Trusted Execution Environment Protocol

To protect the privacy of smart contract and access control process. We use trusted execution environment technology in DBS. In this part, we will introduce the details of the trusted execution environment (TEE) protocol. We use TEE protocol in two scenarios: contract deployment and contract invocation.

1) Contract Deployment: The RO write contract code on their clients using native languages (like C/Solidity), then compiles the code, and deploys them to TEE. Figure 3 shows the protocol process for deploying contracts.
   Firstly, the RO will request the TEE from the CN through a secure channel. The CN initializes an enclave in the local TEE. The enclave will generate an asymmetric key pair, of which the private key is only kept by the enclave, so that the subsequent invocation can be protected by the public key.
   After receiving the enclave information and public key, the RO will upload the hash of the contract binary code. After confirming the contract, the CN loads the binary code of the contract into the previously initialized enclave.
   Finally, after the contract deployment transaction is acknowledged, the contract information and enclave public key will be broadcast to all nodes of the blockchain.
2) Contract Invocation: Once the contract is deployed, the AR can send an access request to invoke the smart contract. Figure 4 shows the protocol process of invoking the contract.

First, the access requester sends the access request to the smart contract. The consensus is found in the trusted enclave.

After receiving the access request, the CN will find the enclave where the invoked contract is located, and then load the encrypted access request into the

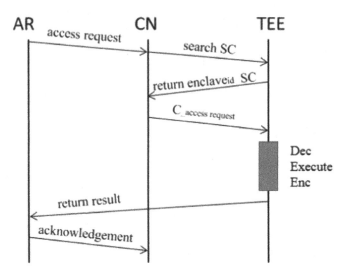

Fig. 4. Contract invocation.

target enclave. The enclave will decrypt the access request with the private key, and then take the data in the access request as the input to execute the contract. The execution result is encrypted with the public key of the AR and returned.

At last, after the access request transaction is acknowledged, the encrypted access results will be broadcast to all nodes of the blockchain.

5   Access Control Process

This section presents the smart contract-based distributed access control process. We introduce the access control flow of two different access requesters in the same domain and cross domain. The optimization of the IoT access control system can be realized with the help of an authorization contract and authentication contract.

To protect the privacy of transactions, each entity conducts a one-time setup phase that results in two public keys: a proving key pk and a verification key vk before sending the transaction. The proving key pk is used to encrypt the transaction and produce a proof π. The non-interactive proof π is a zero-knowledge proof. Then the encrypted transaction (Tc) and proof π are uploaded to the blockchain. The encrypted transaction address, transaction amount, and transaction information cannot be visible. CN uses the verification key vk to verify the proof π; in particular zk-SNARK proofs are publicly verifiable: anyone can verify π, without interacting with the prover that generated π.

5.1   Access Control Process Within the Domain

For requesters in the domain access, the RO generates an invoke transaction including user ID, role, permission, and devices, which is encrypted with the public key of the authorization contract, then sends to the blockchain. After the invocation transaction is acknowledged, the *Addrole()* operation will add the information to the access control list of the authorization contract. The access requester sends an encrypted access request to the authentication contract, which will identify the access requester. The access control flow of the access requester in the domain is shown in Fig. 5.

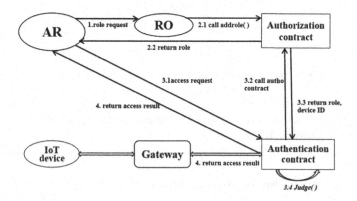

Fig. 5. Access control process within the domain.

- Step 1: The AR sends the role request to the RO.
- Step 2: The RO assigns the role to the AR after receiving the role request.
- Step 3: The AR sends an encrypted access request to the authentication contract.
- Step 4: The authentication contract returns the encrypted access result.

5.2   Access Control Process Cross Domain

For the cross-domain access requester, the RO will add the newly defined access control policy to the authorization contract after receiving the signature of the cross-domain access requester for identification. The cross-domain access requester sends an encrypted role request to the authorization contract, including signature and user ID. The authorization contract assigns roles to cross-domain access requesters according to the defined access control policies, and adds the information of cross-domain access requesters to the access control list by using the *Grantrole()* operation. The cross-domain access requester sends an encrypted access request to the authentication contract, which will identify the cross-domain access requester. The access control flow of the cross-domain access requester is shown in Fig. 6.

- Step 1: The AR sends the signature to the RO.
- Step 2: The RO adds a new access control policy to the authorization contract.

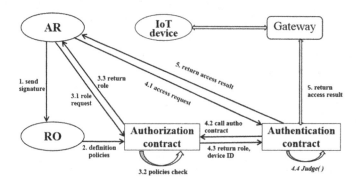

Fig. 6. Access control process cross the domain.

- Step 3: The AR sends a role request transaction encrypted with the contract public key to the authorization contract.
- Step 4: The AR sends an encrypted access request to the authentication contract.
- Step 5: The authentication contract returns the encrypted access result.

6 Implementation

6.1 Hardware and Software

In our experiment, the specifications of the devices used are listed in Table 2. The station plays the role of RO, desktops plays the role of CN, laptops play the role of AR due to their relatively large computing and storage capability, and the Raspberry function plays as local gateways. On each device, a geth client is installed as an Ethereum node.

Table 2. Specification of devices

	CPU	Operating system	Memory	Hard disk
Lenovo ThinkStation P910	Intel Xeon E5-2640 v4, 2.4 GHz	Window 10 (64bit)	64 GB	2 TB
Lenovo 10N9CTO1WW	Intel Core i7-7700, 3.6 GHz	Window 7 (64bit)	8 GB	2 TB
Lenovo N50	Intel Core i5-4210, 1.7 GHz	Window 7 (64bit)	4 GB	500 GB
Raspberriy ModelB	Contex A53, 1.2 GHz	Raspbian GNU/Linux 8	1 GB	16 GB

6.2 Experiment

The experiments were done on an Ubuntu-16.4.3 desktop with Intel Core i7-7700, 3.6 GHz. We used Truffle to deploy and invoke smart contracts, which is a development framework based on Ethereum's solidity language. We use Ganache to develop and test local blockchain, which simulates the functions of a real Ethereum network, including multiple accounts and ether for testing.

In the experimental case, we completed the establishment of local blockchain, the compilation and deployment of authorization contract, and authentication contracts to achieve fine-grained access control between entities. To verify the feasibility of the access, the access requester sends an access operation to the IoT device, and the result of the access request is shown in Fig. 7. To verify the privacy of the transaction, the consensus node verifies the proof pi, and the verification result is shown in Fig. 8.

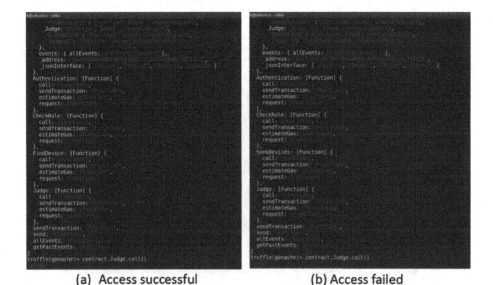

(a) Access successful   (b) Access failed

Fig. 7. Access result.

6.3   Performance

Because of the mass of IoT devices, the local gateway needs high-performance features to serve as many requests from IoT devices at the same time as possible. We tested the throughput and bandwidth of the local gateway, and the results are shown in Fig. 9. We also tested the response time required for the access request from the local gateway to the IoT device. As the number of access requests increases, the response time also increases, as shown in Fig. 10.

(a) Verification pass   (b) Verification failed

Fig. 8. Verification result.

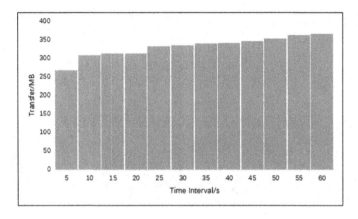

Fig. 9. Throughput of local gateway.

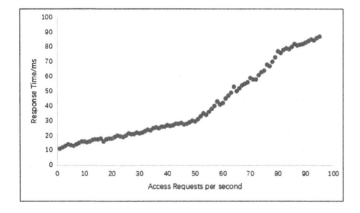

Fig. 10. Response time.

7   Conclusion

In this paper, we investigated the privacy issue of access control schemes based on blockchain in the IoT and proposed an architecture with privacy-preserving based on blockchain to achieve distributed, trustworthy, secure, and convenient access control. The architecture consists of two parts: an access control part, and a privacy protection part. The access control part includes double smart contracts to grant roles and check access rights respectively. The privacy part includes transaction privacy and smart contract privacy. The transaction information is kept secret by zero-knowledge proof algorithm, and the smart contract is protected by TEE. Also, we performed the deployment and invoke of smart contract on the local private chain Ganache and implemented zero-knowledge proof algorithm on Ubuntu. The results demonstrated the feasibility and confidentiality of the proposed architecture in achieving distributed and trustworthy access control for the IoT.

References

1. Nakamoto, S.: Bitcoin: a peer-to-peer electronic cash system (2008)
2. Novo, O.: Blockchain meets IoT: an architecture for scalable access management in IoT. IEEE Internet Things J. 5(2), 1184–1195 (2018)
3. Ouaddah, A., Abou Elkalam, A.: Fairaccess: a new blockchain-based access control framework for the IoT. Security 9, 5943–5964 (2017)
4. Du Rhuizhong, L.Y., Liu, A.D., Du, X.H.: An access control method using smart contract for Internet of Things. J. Comput. Res. Dev. 56(10), 2287 (2019)
5. Reyna, A., Martin, C., Chen, J., Soler, E., Diaz, M.: On blockchain and its integration with IoT. Challenges and opportunities. Future Gener. Comput. Syst. 88, 173–190 (2018)
6. Konstantinos Christidis, M.D.: Blockchains and smart contracts for the Internet of Things. IEEE Access 4, 2292–2303 (2016)
7. Sandhu, R.S., Feinstein, H.L., Coyne, E.J.: Role-based access control models. IEEE Comput. 29(2), 38–47 (1996)
8. Di Francesco Maesa, D., Mori, P., Ricci, L.: Blockchain based access control. In: Chen, L.Y., Reiser, H.P. (eds.) DAIS 2017. LNCS, vol. 10320, pp. 206–220. Springer, Cham (2017). https://doi.org/10.1007/978-3-319-59665-5_15
9. Ding, S., Cao, J., Li, C., Fan, K., Li, H.: A novel attribute-based access control scheme using blockchain for IoT. IEEE Access 7, 38431–38441 (2019)
10. Cruz, J.P., Kaji, Y.: RBAC-SC: role-based access control using smart contract. IEEE Access 6, 12240–12251 (2018)
11. Buterin, V.: A next-generation smart contract and decentralized application platform (2016)
12. Azaria, A., Ekblaw, A., Vieira, T., Lippman, A.: Medrec: using blockchain for medical data access and permission management. In: 2016 2nd International Conference on Open and Big Data (OBD), pp. 25–30, August 2016
13. Zhang, Y., Kasahara, S., Shen, Y., Jiang, X.: Smart contract-based access control for the Internet of Things. IEEE Internet Things J. 6(2), 1594–1605 (2019)
14. Dorri, A., Kanhere, S.S., Jurdak, R., Gauravaram, P.: Blockchain for IoT security and privacy: the case study of a smart home, pp. 618–623 (2017)

15. Meiklejohn, S., Pomarole, M., Jordan, G., Levechenko, K.: A fustful of bitcoin: characterizing payments among men with no names. In: Internet Measurment Conference, pp. 127–140 (2013)
16. Russinovich, M., Ashton, E., Avaessians, C., Castro, M.: CCF: a framework for building confidential verifiable replicated services (2019)
17. Yuan, R., Xia, Y.-B., Chen, H.-B., Zang, B.-Y., Xie, J.: Shadoweth: private smart contract on public blockchain. J. Comput. Sci. Technol. **33**(3), 542–556 (2018)
18. Kosba, A., Miller, A., Shi, E., Wen, Z., Papamanthou, C.: Hawk: The blockchain model of cryptography and privacy-preserving smart contracts, pp. 839–858 (2016)
19. Ben-Sasson, E., Chiesa, A., Tromer, E., Virza, M.: Succinct non-interactive zero knowledge for a von Neumann architecture, pp. 781–796 (2014)
20. Parno, B., Howell, J., Gentry, C., Raykova, M.: Pinocchio: nearly practical verifiable computation. In: 2013 IEEE Symposium on Security and Privacy, pp. 238–252 (2013)
21. Miers, I., Garman, C., Green, M., Rubin, A.D.: Zerocoin: anonymous distributed e-cash from bitcoin. In: 2013 IEEE Symposium on Security and Privacy, pp. 397–411 (2013)
22. Ben Sasson, E., et al.: Zerocash: decentralized anonymous payments from bitcoin. In: 2014 IEEE Symposium on Security and Privacy, pp. 459–474 (2014)

Achieving Fair and Accountable Data Trading Scheme for Educational Multimedia Data Based on Blockchain

Xianxian Li[1,2], Jiahui Peng[1,2], Zhenkui Shi[1,2(✉)], and Chunpei Li[1,2]

[1] College of Computer Science, Guangxi Normal University, Guilin, China
lixx@mailbox.gxnu.edu.cn
[2] Guangxi Key Lab of Multi-source Information Mining Security, Guilin, China
shizhenkui@gxnu.edu.cn

Abstract. Educational resources have a higher need for copyright protection to avoiding illegal redistribution. The transactions of educational multimedia data resources can effectively promote the development of educational informatization and solve the island situation of educational resources. In the process of traditional transactions for educational multimedia data, there is always a third parties, which may lead to dispute and distrust. And the copyright is not well protected. In this paper, we propose a fair and accountable trading scheme for educational multimedia data. The scheme is based on blockchain to achieve accountability and secure storage with IPFS. And we aim to construct a relatively strong copyright protection model through digital fingerprint and watermark technology. We implemented and evaluated the scheme in Ethereum. The results show that our scheme can achieve well copyright protection and preserve the users' privacy. The overall overhead is reasonable.

Keywords: Blockchain trading · Educational multimedia data · Copyright confirmation

1 Introduction

The era of big data has promoted the development of online education. More and more students would like to obtain knowledge through the Internet. Digital educational resources such as teaching plans, handouts, teaching videos and other multimedia data become the key to the development of online education. The transactions of high quality resources have become one of the effective

The work is partially supported by the National Natural Science Foundation of China (No. 61672176), the Guangxi "Bagui Scholar" Teams for Innovation and Research Project, the Guangxi Talent Highland Project of Big Data Intelligence and Application, the Guangxi Science and Technology Plan Projects No. AD20159039, the Guangxi Young and Middle-aged Ability Improvement Project No. 2020KY02032, the Innovation Project of Guangxi Graduate Education No. YCSW2020110.

X. Yuan et al. (Eds.): QShine 2021, LNICST 402, pp. 111–125, 2021.
https://doi.org/10.1007/978-3-030-91424-0_7

ways to solve the island of educational multimedia data. Educational multimedia resources are easy to be copied. This will lead to them to be pirated easily [1]. Many challenges need to be solved in the transaction of multimedia data in the network, such as the fairness of educational multimedia data transaction, the digital copyright protection after the transaction of educational multimedia data, and the large storage problems of educational multimedia data. It will affect the development of educational informatization to some extent.

Our scheme focuses on multimedia data in the transaction of educational resources, which includes educational audios and videos, teaching plans. Whereas handouts are not considered in our scheme. We summarize the challenges of educational multimedia data transaction as follows:

- **Copyright confirmation:** When the data owner wanted to sell data in our system, he may only want to sell right to buyers to use data instead of data ownership. That is, the data consumers are not allowed to sell data for the second time after getting the data. The data consumers can sell the data again after obtaining the permission of the data owner, who needs to purchase ownership of the data before them can sell the purchased data, otherwise buyers can only have the right to use the data.
- **Secure storage:** Educational multimedia data is mainly based on teaching videos which are generally generated through the whole school year and teaching books. And the contents are very rich. These educational multimedia data need to use large storage resources. It is obviously impractical to store such huge multimedia data directly on the blockchain. And it is also not secure to store in the cloud server because of the dishonest or curious cloud server. There may be security issues [2,3].
- **Reasonable pricing:** In the current scheme of data trading, the price of data is set by the data owner. Unreasonable price will affect the profit of data, the higher price will lead to unsatisfactory data sales, on the contrary, lower price will also affect the income of data owner. Data buyers also hope to have a price negotiation mechanism, which can realize the bargaining process of commodities trading in order to achieve the best balance of both sides.
- **Fair transaction and privacy.** In the traditional multimedia data transaction process, privacy and fairness is an issue that has to be considered. The fairness we mentioned is defined as follows:

- **Real-time.** The data owner obtained the token and buyer got the data completing their act of trading. After the buyer passed the verification, the data owner should obtain the transaction amount corresponding to the data immediately.
- **Independence.** Cheating by one of the parties in the transaction will not affect the other party's benefits negotiated before the transaction.
- **Reasonable rewards and punishments.** Users who have participated in transactions in the system can apply for arbitration for cheating during the transaction. Once it is determined to be cheated, the cheating party will be punished (such as forfeiting the deposit).

As one of the most representative emerging technologies in the 21st century, blockchain has become an indispensable technology for distributed transactions because of its decentralized, traceable and tamper proof characteristics. The use of blockchain technology can help to realize the fairness of the transaction process and can effectively prevent security and privacy issues caused by tampering of transaction data. The role of blockchain technology is not only limited to transactions, but also helps to confirm and trace data rights in the process of transactions. At present, copyright protection works focus on digital fingerprint and digital watermark technology. The digital watermark can confirm the ownership of copyright, and digital fingerprint can confirm the owner of copyright [4]. Combining blockchain and digital fingerprint can help the confirmation work of copyright in the process of transaction more credible.

Our scheme realizes a fair and accountable transaction process of educational multimedia resources, and uses blockchain combined with digital fingerprint and watermark technology to confirm copyright of educational data. In terms of privacy protection, we use the enclave module of SGX to protect the privacy of smart contracts, which protects users' private information, and proves the feasibility of our proposed scheme through efficiency. Our contributions mainly include the following:

- Compared with the previous work requiring the participation of a trusted third party, our scheme uses blockchain technology to realize a decentralized data right confirmation model. The symmetric fingerprint scheme is optimized by homomorphic encryption to protect the privacy of transaction participants, and the process of right confirmation and accountability is completed by smart contract;
- Reasonable pricing model combines with fair mechanism of trading were designed by using smart contract, and our scheme used Trusted Execution Environment SGX to protect users' privacy.
- We implement and evaluate our scheme on Ethereum. The results show the solution works well.

2   Related Work

Blockchain technology was first proposed by Nakamoto in his paper [5] in 2008. The emergence of the first Genesis block marks that blockchain technology has entered the development of Internet, blockchain technology has been developed for thirteen years. Smart contract [6] and the consensus mechanism [7,8] is the key technologies of blockchain. In particular, the use of smart contract makes blockchain not only used for transaction bookkeeping, but also provides blockchain with the ability to deal with complex computer problems, which provides a good technical foundation for the application of blockchain.

Blockchain technology has been used for transactions since its inception, the recent works were more about privacy and security issues in the transaction process [9,11]. For example, [12] uses the anonymous mechanism which is implemented on the blockchain to protect users' privacy, and the dynamic price negotiation model is implemented by using the Robin Stein bargaining model, and the proxy re-encryption technology is used to realize the secure storage of data. The work is completed by smart contract, but the smart contract has the problem of privacy leakage in the process of public operation because it is publicly executed. The anonymous mechanism is implemented by elliptic curve encryption algorithm, and each execution of the smart contract needs to verify the identity information. So it may be not efficient enough. [13] proposed an auction transaction framework with copyright protection, and blockchain is used to implement the copyright protection protocol. However, the complexity of the protocol is $log(m)$ in the process of right confirmation, and m is the number of users who participated in the transaction. If the number of users is large, the protocol will be inefficient and cannot meet the requirements of actual transaction application scenarios. [14] uses the trusted execution environment SGX combined with blockchain technology to implement a secure transaction scheme. The scheme puts the smart contract into Software Guard Extensions (SGX) for execution, which protects the privacy of sensitive information of the smart contract. SGX is responsible for outputting the final result, while the execution process is confidential to all participants.

The main current works of copyright protection are through digital fingerprint and watermark. Digital watermark technology can confirm the ownership of copyright, but it can not confirm the responsible person in the process of piracy tracking [15]. On the contrary, digital fingerprint technology can determine the owner of copyright which can be divided into three kinds: symmetric fingerprint [16], asymmetric fingerprint [17] and anonymous fingerprint [18]. Symmetric fingerprint may lead seller to frame the buyer, while the asymmetric fingerprint refers to the asymmetric encryption technology to solve the problem of anti frame, and the anonymous fingerprint realizes the identity hiding on the basis of the asymmetric fingerprint. In copyright protection aspect, there are some work combined with Digital Rights Management (DRM) system [19–21]. But DRM system is a centralized management system, privacy information may be tampered by administrator. Meanwhile, DRM system will charge the management fee, which will add the transaction cost to a certain extent. In the copyright confirmation work, we hope to achieve a copyright management system without the third party, which can protect users' privacy and finish the transaction with fair process.

Due to its technical characteristics, the copyright protection work of blockchain technology combined with digital fingerprint and watermark is less. The representative work is the work [22] which used zero knowledge proof, protocol of oblivious transfer, secret sharing and digital watermark technology to realize data tracking. This work can still track the copyright in the case of partial data leakage. However, it used many encryption technologies, the scheme is inefficient in the case of large volume data. It can not be applied to the scene of multimedia data which is large. [23] uses local sensitive hashing and traditional hashing technology to achieve copyright detection, but this work introduces a third-party organization for copyright confirmation, which deviates from our efforts to achieve the copyright confirmation without the third party. [13] as we said before, because it needs to compare with all the users participating in the transaction in the detection process, it can not be applied to the actual scenarios.

To sum up, there is a lot of work on the blockchain transaction, but there is little work on the data right confirmation in the transaction process. Copyright protection researches have been carried out for many years, and digital fingerprint and watermark technology have been mature. How to combine the blockchain technology with digital fingerprint and watermark technology to realize a data transaction scheme with right confirmation can help solve the increasingly obvious piracy in the process of trading for educational resources, so as to improve motivation of resources providers and promote a better and faster development of educational informatization.

3   Proposed Framework

3.1   Preliminaries

Blockchain and Smart Contract: Blockchain technology [24] is widely used in data transactions due to its decentralized, tamper-proof, and traceable characteristics. Blockchain is a distributed shared ledger and database, which can effectively solve the problem of information asymmetry, and achieve collaborative trust and concerted action among multiple subjects.

Smart contracts are a computer program that automatically executes after setting predetermined rules and terms. It is used to process transaction steps in the blockchain, which was the key to the development of blockchain to the 2.0 stages, which can help blockchain to realize more complex program and provide a good foundation for large-scale application to real scenes.

Bilinear Map: Suppose there is a mapping e: $G_1 \times G_2 \rightarrow G_t$ is bilinear map, it has properties as follow:

- There is the same order g which is shared by G_1 and G_2.
- If there have $x, y \in \mathbb{Z}_q$ and $g, q \in G_1, e(g^x, q^y) = e(g, q)^{xy}$ can be calculated correctly.
- If there have g belong to G_1 and q is generated by be $G_1, e(g,q)$ is generated by G_2.

Homomorphic Encryption: Using the Homomorphic Encryption [25] base on RSA, which can perform operations without decrypting them. When give the key K, it satisfies: $H(Enc(M_1, M_2)) = Enc(f(M_1, M_2))$, where H() and f() can be seen as the addition and multiplication operations. Let $\otimes$ and $\oplus$ represents addition and multiplication operations. For $\forall x, y \in$ prime field $\psi_q, x \otimes y \overset{def}{=} xy$ mod q and $x \oplus y \overset{def}{=} x + y$ mod q.

Diffie-Hellman Key Exchange Protocol: Diffie-Hellman key exchange protocol can exchange secret keys in non-secure channels for encrypting subsequent communication information.

- **Setup:** In order to exchange the shared secret key, both parties of the exchange rely on a finite cyclic group G and the generator g of the group, and both parties also need to generate random numbers x and y respectively.
- **Exchange:** Alice generates a random number x and sends g^x to Bob. Similarly, Bob generates a random number y and sends g^y to Alice. Alice calculates $Key_{AB}Y_{B^x}(modp) = (g^y)^x modp$ and Bob calculates $Key_{BA}Y_{A^y}(modp) = (g^x)^y modp$, where p is a large prime number.
- **Verify:** Both parties judge whether they have received the correct parameters by calculating $Key_{AB} = Key_{BA}$.

  The Diffie-Hellman key exchange protocol can effectively solve the problem of safe key transmission in the transaction process and further enhance the reliability of the transaction.

Trusted Execution Environment: Intel Software Guard Extensions (SGX) [26] are currently under investigation in the area of privacy protection. SGX provides a hardware environment where code runs in a memory area known as an enclave. SGX is currently used to perform some privacy protection for smart contracts which involved sensitive information [27].

IPFS: InterPlanetary File System is a File System that enables distributed storage of large files, with technical features that are faster, more secure, and more open. The goal of IPFS protocol is to replace the traditional Internet protocol HTTP and store large files on IPFS in the system. Blockchain only stores the address hashes returned by IPFS. The integration with blockchain technology can effectively reduce the pressure of storage on blockchain [27].

RobinStein Model: In 1982, Rubinstein proposed the bargaining model of alternating offers [28], which belongs to the cooperative model of game. The simplified scenario assumes that there are two players 1 and 2 who shared the cake with a size of 1 unit. 1 moves first and puts forward the allocation plan, which is called "bid first". 2 then chosen to accept or reject the proposal proposed by 1 after finishing step. If the proposal is rejected, 2 will propose his own proposal of allocation, which is called the "counter-offer" of 2, and then 1 will consider whether to accept it or not. If 1 accepts, the game is over, otherwise 1 bid again,......, until one party's offer is accepted by the other.

3.2   The Overview of Our Scheme

As shown in Fig. 1, our framework consists of five entities: Schools/Teachers, Data Buyers, SGX enclave, smart contracts, and IPFS.

Schools/Teachers (ST): The ST collects and sells educational multimedia data in the system, participates in data processing, stores data, and initiates smart contracts for data transactions to complete the transaction process.

Data Buyers (DB): The DB searches the data in the blockchain network according to the data description to meet the purchase requirements, then purchases the data, verifies the data and completes the transaction process.

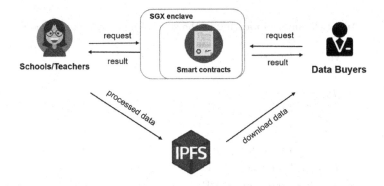

Fig. 1. System framework

Smart Contract: Smart contract completes the execution of the steps of the transaction process. Our scheme includes the following smart contracts:

- **Query:** The DB searches for data that met the requirements.
- **Bargaining process:** Execute the process of ST and DB's bargaining game on data price, in which each bid is protected by SGX to protect the privacy of both parties, in order not to be cheated after the other party knows its price.
- **Data trading:** Perform fair steps of data transaction.
- **Transaction receipt store:** Perform transaction receipt store.
- **Private key verification:** Smart contract uses zero knowledge proof to verify whether the private key of DB meets the transaction requirements. It should be noted that because there are many secret keys in system, using zero-knowledge proof can quickly identify whether the private key meets the requirement.
- **Piracy detection:** Fingerprint comparison of pirated multimedia data to determine if there is a piracy behavior.

SGX Enclave: Since the execution of smart contracts is public, enclave is used to help prevent privacy issues during the execution of smart contracts and to prevent cheating during transactions.

IPFS: Distributed storage of large-capacity educational multimedia data. After the storage is complete, return an address hash to smart contract for saving.

4   Our Fair and Copyright-Preserving Data Trading Scheme

This section elaborates on our fair and copyright-protected data transaction framework. Table 1 lists the symbols used in scheme and their specific meanings. Figure 2 shows the workflow of our scheme.

Table 1. Symbols appearing in the scheme and their explanation

Symbol	Description
FP_{ST}	ST's fingerprint
FP_{DB}	DB's fingerprint
dep_{ST}	ST's deposit
dep_{DB}	DB's deposit
PK_{ST}	Public key of ST
SK_{ST}	Secret key of ST
PK_{DB}	Public key of DB
SK_{DB}	Secret key of DB
encFP	DB's fingerprint used private key to encrypt
$Receipt_0$	Receipt required by DB to purchase data
$Receipt_1$	Receipt required for ST to withdraw tokens
Add_{Hash}	Hash of data storage address returned by IPFS
Price	The price of the data

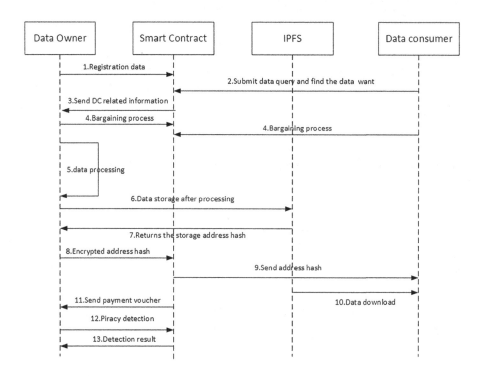

Fig. 2. System workflow

4.1   Participants Registration

If DB wants to buy data in system, he submitted search request to query SC, SC returns the most similar data to DB. Before the transaction, data should be processed as following:

1. ST and DB register in the blockchain network, and obtain a public-private key pair $(PK_{ST}, SK_{ST} || PK_{DB}, SK_{DB})$ issued by the CA center by Bilinear Map by the following formula:$SK = a, PK = a * G$, a is a prime number. The public-private key pair will be used in data processing and transaction processes.

2. If the DB wants to buy data, he should submit the set$\{dep_{DB}, encFP_{DB}\}$ to smart contract, deposit dep_{DB} which is equal to the data price, $EncFP_{DB}$ is the encrypted fingerprint.

3. If the ST wants to sell educational multimedia data, he needs to register in the blockchain and submit the set$\{FP_{ST}, dep_{ST}, price\}$to smart contract.

Before the data is submitted, our scheme allows the price to be agreed as follows:

DB invokes the remote enclave for executing the bargain smart contract. Because our pricing is the priority of the seller, the price at the beginning is set by the seller, which means that the seller always makes the first bid, and each bid of the seller cannot be higher than the price of the previous round. The price offered by the buyer each time cannot be lower than the last price. We define the authentication of the bidding parties as following:

$$Verify_{ybar} = (Bid, Hash(Bid), Sig_{SK}(Hash(Bid))) \qquad (1)$$

According to Rubinstein bargaining game theory, the perfect equilibrium of the price negotiation between the two parties is calculated as:

$$M = \frac{(1 - \delta_2)(S_i^{ST} - S_{i+1}^{DB})}{1 - \delta_1 \delta_2} + S_{i+1}^{DB} \qquad (2)$$

The recommended bidding mechanism for the contract is based on predicting that both parties have enough patience to participate in the data negotiation process, so the selected initial discount factor for both parties is $\delta_1 = \delta_2 = 0.9$.

The recommended price of the smart contract guides the bidder's quote in the next stage to reach the perfect equilibrium price as soon as possible, helping both parties complete the price negotiation efficiently and fairly. When both parties complete the stage of bidding, the discount factor will change, representing that the best balance of the price negotiation between the two parties decreases.

4.2   Data Trading

Setup: ST invokes the remote enclave for trading smart contract execution. ST and DB exchange shared key g^{xy} through the Diffie-Hellman key exchange method, where x and y correspond to random numbers generated by ST and DB, respectively. The ST and DB verify to each other by the shared key which received by each other using formulas 3 and 4.

$$Enc(g^{xy}, Sig(SK_{ST}, H(g^x) || H(g^y))) \qquad (3)$$

$$Enc(g^{xy}, Sig(SK_{DB}, H(g^y)||H(g^y))) \tag{4}$$

DB can decrypt x generated by the ST through the random number: $x = SK_{DB} * r^{-1}(mod\varphi(n))$, where $r * r^{-1} \equiv 1(mod\varphi(n))$.

Payment Receipt Generation:

1. Generated payment receipt for DB's purchase data:

$$Receipt_0 = PK_{DO}||Price_{Data}||Time||E_{PK_{DB}}(r)||Hash(r) \tag{5}$$

Where $Time$ is the time when the receipt is generated, $E_{PK_{DB}}(r)$ is the random number r encrypted with the DB's public key, which is generated by the traditional random number algorithm, and $Hash(r)$ is the hash value of the random number r.

2. The DB uses his private key to sign the receipt and send it to the smart contract for transaction authentication.

$$Receipt_1 = Sig(Receipt_0, SK_{DB}) \tag{6}$$

Data Exchange: After the above steps, ST and DB will exchange the data.

1. The ST and the DB should submit deposit dep_{ST} and dep_{DB} for corresponding data price respectively.

2. The DB queries the SC to find the matching data, initiates the transaction request, and confirms the matching ST via the random number x of the Diffie-Hellman key exchange method.

3. The ST initiates the transaction, encrypts the hash value Add_{Hash} of the data address using the shared key g^{xy}, and sends it to SC.

4. DB sends $Receipt_1$ and PK_{DB} to SC.

5. The ST uses PK_{DB} to verify $Receipt_1$ to get $Receipt_0$ from SC, uses SK_{ST} to decrypt $E_{PK_{DB}}(r)$ to get r', and sends r' to SC for verification.

6. SC compares r'with $Hash(r)$, the purpose is to identify the ST. The tokens in the receipt will be sent to the ST account if the verification is successful.

7. The ST confirms the transaction, the SC sends the encrypted address and data hash value to the DB, and the DB decrypts the data, verifies the data hash to confirm the data which he bought, and finally closes the transaction.

8. Both the ST and the DB can initiate arbitration before closing the deal. The arbitration contract validates the process and cheating party will forfeit the deposit.

4.3   Traitor Tracing

Like work [13], we also divide the piracy tracking process into two examples. It should be noted that an ST may correspond to multiple data, but since the fingerprint embedded in each data is unique in our scheme, there is no problem that the fingerprint of each file is different.

Case 1: When a data owner finds illegal pirated data $data_{pira}$ after the trading. He gets the fingerprint $FP^* = $ extract$(data_{pira})$. Find the illegal consumer from on-chain trading records and the request of the corresponding ID user, then gets $EncFP_{DB}$ according to the request, if $EncFP_{DB} = Enc(FP^*, PK_{DB})$ the consumer is the pirate. Then the seller submits the evidences to the arbiter for accountability. Arbiter verifies the evidences through the Ethereum to make a judgment.

Case 2: When a seller uploads the data hash path to smart contract: data owner downloads the $data_i$ from IPFS. If data owner can detect a encrypted fingerprint FP' that: $FP' = Enc(FP_{ST}, PK_{DB})$ which can show this seller is a pirate because he wanted to resell the data from others.

5 Security Analysis

In this chapter, we will carry out security analysis on the proposed scheme and give corresponding defense scheme against the attack.

Single Point of Failure: Single point of failure refers to the failure or outage of some nodes of the system that affects the operation of the whole system. Our scheme is implemented with pow consensus algorithm for data synchronization, allowing up to $1/2$ of the nodes to fail.

Users' Info Security and Privacy: All smart contracts designed for user privacy or affecting the fairness of transactions are executed in SGX Enclave. The transaction parties or other participants can only see the final result of the transaction rather than the data information of the transaction process, which greatly protects the privacy of parties and guarantees the security of the transaction.

Problem of Framing: Our copyright confirmation scheme uses homomorphic encryption combined with digital fingerprint, which is similar to asymmetric fingerprint. In addition, the information of both sides of the transaction is stored on the blockchain to prevent tampering, and there is no case of the seller embedding other fingerprints to frame the buyer.

6 Performance Evaluation

We test our scheme on Ethereum with Intel Core i7 CPU with 16 GB RAM with 1 TB hard drive with bandwidth 50 Mbps and 100 Raspberry Pi Nodes. We tested the efficiency of 1 GB–6 GB of educational multimedia data stored in IPFS to evaluate whether our proposed solution can meet actual needs.

6.1 Smart Contract Efficiency

We tested the gas consumption and execution time of the smart contracts in the Ethereum environment, where we used Ganache to create private chain and maintained the account using MetaMask. Tables 2 shows the execution results and gas costs of smart contracts and Fig. 3 shows the execution time. The 1–6

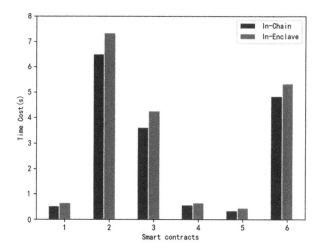

Fig. 3. Smart contracts perform

Table 2. Gas consumption of smart contracts

	Gas used	Gas cost (Ether)
Data query	98525	0.0019
Bargaining process	3029521	0.0589
Data trading	254253	0.0050
Transaction receipt	39558	0.0007
Private key verification	39000	0.0007
Piracy detection	2959512	0.0563

abscissas of Fig. 3 respectively represent the smart contract: Data query, Bargaining process, Data trading, Transaction receipt, Private key verification and Piracy detection. Through the chart analysis, we can know that our scheme meets the efficiency requirements of actual transaction scenarios.

6.2 IPFS Storage Data Efficiency

In order to show the efficiency of IPFS in storing large-capacity educational multimedia resources, we tested the upload speed of IPFS, and the data size of tested was 1 GB–5 GB as shown in Fig. 4. In the evaluation, the upload time of 1 GB compressed data is 16 s, and the upload time of 5 GB compressed data is 68 s. The experiment shows the efficiency and feasibility of using IPFS to store large data. In addition, ours also tested the impact of the number of folders on the storage efficiency of IPFS. Experiments show that the number of folders has little effect on upload speed, and the time efficiency of the impact is within the acceptable range.

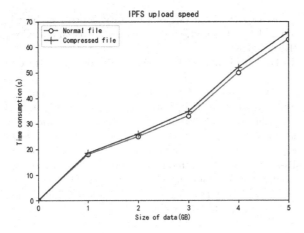

Fig. 4. IPFS upload speed

7   Conclusion

In this article, we propose a fair and accountable educational multimedia data transaction scheme based on blockchain. A detailed solution is designed using Ethereum, smart contract, IPFS, digital fingerprint/watermark technology to provide a safe and reliable educational multimedia data transaction and traceability digital copyright protection scheme. Blockchain technology mainly provides decentralized traceability, using smart contracts to complete the entire transaction process, some transactions using SGX to complete the privacy protection of sensitive information, and testing the feasibility of the entire platform through the implementation of smart contracts. In future work, we plan to continue to improve the platform performance and security.

References

1. Zhao, H.L., Xu, Y.P., Yang, Y.: Technology research of mobile internet digital rights management security authorization. In: Proceedings of the 19th National Youth Communication Academic Conference, pp. 299–309 (2014)
2. Song, H., Li, J., Li, H.: A cloud secure storage mechanism based on data dispersion and encryption. IEEE Access **9**, 63745–63751 (2021)
3. Shi. Z., Fu, X., Li, X., et al.: ESVSSE: enabling efficient, secure, verifiable searchable symmetric encryption. IEEE Trans. Knowl. Data Eng. (2020)
4. Shen, J.: Blockchain technology and its applications in digital content copyright protection. In: Yuan, C., Li, X., Kent, J. (eds.) Proceedings of the 4th International Conference on Economic Management and Green Development. AEPS, pp. 18–25. Springer, Singapore (2021). https://doi.org/10.1007/978-981-16-5359-9_3
5. Nakamoto, S.: Bitcoin: a peer-to-peer electronic cash system. Manubot (2019)
6. Mermer, G.B., Zeydan, E., Arslan, S.S.: An overview of blockchain technologies: principles, opportunities and challenges. In: 2018 26th Signal Processing and Communications Applications Conference (SIU), pp. 1–4. IEEE (2018)

7. Fullmer, D., Morse, A.S.: Analysis of difficulty control in bitcoin and proof-of-work blockchains. In: 2018 IEEE Conference on Decision and Control (CDC), pp. 5988–5992. IEEE (2018)

8. Castro, M., Liskov, B.: Practical byzantine fault tolerance. In: OSDI, vol. 99, pp. 173–186 (1999)

9. Li, Z., Kang, J., Yu, R., et al.: Consortium blockchain for secure energy trading in industrial Internet of Things. IEEE Trans. Ind. Inform. **14**(8), 3690–3700 (2017)

10. Gai, K., Wu, Y., Zhu, L., et al.: Privacy-preserving energy trading using consortium blockchain in smart grid. IEEE Trans. Ind. Inform. **15**(6), 3548–3558 (2019)

11. Aitzhan, N.Z., Svetinovic, D.: Security and privacy in decentralized energy trading through multi-signatures, blockchain and anonymous messaging streams. IEEE Trans. Dependable Secure Comput. **15**(5), 840–852 (2016)

12. Hu, D., Li, Y., Pan, L., et al.: A blockchain-based trading system for big data. Comput. Networks **191**, 107994 (2021)

13. Sheng, D., Xiao, M., Liu, A., et al.: CPchain: a copyright-preserving crowdsourcing data trading framework based on blockchain. In: 2020 29th International Conference on Computer Communications and Networks (ICCCN), pp. 1–9. IEEE (2020)

14. Dai, W., Dai, C., Choo, K.K.R., et al.: SDTE: a secure blockchain-based data trading ecosystem. IEEE Trans. Inf. Forensics Secur. **15**, 725–737 (2019)

15. Savelyev, A.: Copyright in the blockchain era: promises and challenges. Comput. Law Secur. Rev. **34**(3), 550–561 (2018)

16. Tulyakov, S., Farooq, F., Govindaraju, V.: Symmetric hash functions for fingerprint minutiae. In: Singh, S., Singh, M., Apte, C., Perner, P. (eds.) ICAPR 2005. LNCS, vol. 3687, pp. 30–38. Springer, Heidelberg (2005). https://doi.org/10.1007/11552499_4

17. Charpentier, A., Fontaine, C., Furon, T., Cox, I.: An asymmetric fingerprinting scheme based on Tardos codes. In: Filler, T., Pevný, T., Craver, S., Ker, A. (eds.) IH 2011. LNCS, vol. 6958, pp. 43–58. Springer, Heidelberg (2011). https://doi.org/10.1007/978-3-642-24178-9_4

18. Farooq, F., Bolle, R.M., Jea, T.Y., et al.: Anonymous and revocable fingerprint recognition. In: 2007 IEEE Conference on Computer Vision and Pattern Recognition, pp. 1–7. IEEE (2007)

19. Liu, Q., Safavi-Naini, R., Sheppard, N.P.: Digital rights management for content distribution. In: Proceedings of the Australasian Information Security Workshop Conference on ACSW Frontiers 2003-Volume 21, pp. 49–58 (2003)

20. Ma, Z., Jiang, M., Gao, H., et al.: Blockchain for digital rights management. Future Gener. Comput. Syst. **89**, 746–764 (2018)

21. Kenny, S., Korba, L.: Applying digital rights management systems to privacy rights management. Comput. Secur. **21**(7), 648–664 (2002)

22. Huang, C., Liu, D., Ni, J., et al.: Achieving accountable and efficient data sharing in industrial Internet of Things. IEEE Trans. Ind. Inform. **17**(2), 1416–1427 (2020)

23. Chen, Z., Wang, Y., Ni, T., et al.: DCDChain: A Credible Architecture of Digital Copyright Detection Based on Blockchain. arXiv preprint arXiv:2010.01235 (2020)

24. Underwood, S.: Blockchain beyond bitcoin. Commun. ACM **59**(11), 15–17 (2016)

25. Yi, X., Paulet, R., Bertino, E.: Homomorphic encryption. In: Homomorphic Encryption and Applications. SCS, pp. 27–46. Springer, Cham (2014). https://doi.org/10.1007/978-3-319-12229-8_2

26. Brasser, F., Müller, U., Dmitrienko, A., et al.: Software grand exposure: SGX cache attacks are practical. In: 11th USENIX Workshop on Offensive Technologies (WOOT 17) (2017)

27. Bowman, M., et al.: Private data objects: an overview. arXiv preprint arXiv:1807.05686 (2018)
28. Rubinstein, A.: Perfect equilibrium in a bargaining model. Econometrica J. Econometric Soc. 97–109 (1982)

5G Networks and Security

A Lightweight Authentication Protocol for 5G Cellular Network Connected Drones

Siyu Chen, Shujie Cui$^{(\boxtimes)}$, and Joseph Liu

Faculty of Information Technology, Monash University, Melbourne, Australia
csiy0001@student.monash.edu, {shujie.cui,joseph.liu}@monash.edu

Abstract. Drones are being diversely used in various areas due to their low price. Most of the use cases demand a secure and reliable wireless communication infrastructure to ensure the quality of service. Such demand boosts the deployment of drones in 5G cellular network. The ground base station (BS) is the main component associated with drones in the 5G cellular network. However, the BS in 5G currently broadcasts the system information message without authentication protection. This poses serious security concerns as the system information message will be used to build connection between the BS and cellular devices. Particularly, adversaries can masquerade as BSs, connect drones, and obtain the data captured by them. Although some attacks have been prevented due to the recent enhancements for 5G cellular protocols, the root vulnerability for the bootstrap phase between drones and the BS still existed and not fixed yet.

In this work, we consider a scenario where drones are used in a sport venue to capture the match and 5G cellular network is used to disseminate the live stream. To protect drones from fake BSs, we adopt and optimise the authentication protocol proposed by Singla *et al.* in [26]. Basically, we modify its architecture by deploying aerial balloon drone BSs over the sport venues to provide more reliable communication service. Moreover, we optimise the verification process in order to reduce the computation overhead on drones. We implemented a prototype of the protocol and evaluated its performance. The experiment results show our authentication protocol is practical to be adopted.

Keywords: Drones · 5G security · Multi-tier architecture · Authentication protocol · Elliptic curve cryptography

1 Introduction

Since the first commercial drone, or unmanned aerial vehicle (UAV), was introduced at CES 2010 by Parrot, drones have been adopted to undertake various services, such as delivery [20], filming movies [28], and post-disaster rescue [12], due to their reasonable price and diverse uses. To ensure quality of the services

X. Yuan et al. (Eds.): QShine 2021, LNICST 402, pp. 129–143, 2021.
https://doi.org/10.1007/978-3-030-91424-0_8

provided by drones, those emerging usages of drones demand a secure and reliable wireless communication infrastructure for control commands and information dissemination. On the one hand, the drones need to get time critical control and safety commands to maintain the flight operations. On the other hand, the drones have to disseminate collected data so as to pertain their mission. For instance, in a surveillance operation, drones need to transmit real time video to the ground station/remote pilot, and the underlying transmission medium should be able support high data rates (often higher in full HD video transmission or wireless backhauling).

Utilizing the cellular network for positioning, navigation, and communication of drones has gained significant interest in recent years, as it provides an effective solution for establishing reliable wireless connectivity with ground cellular Base Stations (BSs) [29]. Specifically, due to the rising adoption of 5G and the need for real-time systems, the global Cellular-Connected (CC) drone market is expected to generate $592.1 million in 2023 [23].

In this work, we consider the usage of 5G CC drones in sport venues for live stream. Basically, the drones are equipped with cameras to capture the real-time sport event and the components for 5G connection. Using small drones with cameras in a stadium would explore an advanced perspective that never seen before with the new vantage points and breathtaking views. By connecting drones with 5G cellular network, which is about 3 times faster than generic WiFi on average, drones can transfer high-resolution video signal more efficiently (up to 8k) [27]. The audience can get an immersive and high-quality live broadcast experience.

Since the communication between drones and 5G BSs are wireless in nature, different kinds of attacks, such as replay, man-in-the-middle, impersonation, privileged insider and password guessing are possible in our scenario. A major risk of a drone is getting out of the control due to malicious masquerade attacks. An adversary could create a fake BS nearby the stadium and induce CC drones to connect it and make them becomes rogue drones. In the worst case, the adversary might send malicious commands to compromised drones to interrupt the sport events, ask them to forward live stream to unsubscribed entities, or steer them to destroy assets or injure athletes and audience [18]. It is necessary to design a secure authentication scheme for drones to authenticate the messages from the BS, especially the broadcast system information message that used to set connection between drone and BS. Moreover, considering the CC drone has relatively low computation ability and battery life [19], the authentication protocol cannot induce heavy communication and computation overhead to the drones.

In [26], Singla et al. design a lightweight authentication protocol to secure the initialization connection between 5G network BSs and cellular devices. However, their protocol cannot be applied into our scenario directly. On the one hand, compared with 4G, 3G and 2G cellular networks, 5G base-stations use much higher frequency radio waves (e.g., millimeter waves) to offer faster communication but with much smaller coverage area. The sport venues are typically located in urban area and surrounded with high-rise buildings, which affects the connection between drones and the 5G network. Whereas, the live stream of sport events has strong requirement for the stability of the communication. On the other hand, the computation run in drones should be more lightweight than that run in other type of cellular devices, like smartphones. The reason is that a sport match in a sport venue, such as football match, usually takes several hours, and during the match the drones have to keep flying in the air to record the match, which is much more power-consuming than other devices. Any significant computation overhead will decrease the endurance of the CC drone. The computation overhead on drones required by the protocol should be reduced in order let the drones work for longer period.

In this paper, we adapt the authentication protocol proposed in [26] to allow drones to authenticate 5G BSs. Moreover, we modify the protocol in two aspects in order to make it suitable for our scenario. Specifically, to address the first problem, we deploy an aerial balloon drone over the sport venue to provide the BS service, *i.e.,* broadcast system information messages and collect live streaming to and from the drones under its coverage. Compared with the ground BS outside of the sport venue, our aerial balloon drone BS has much better coverage and is much closer to the drones working within the venue. Moreover, this deployment can increase signal quality and reduce signal attenuation. By doing so, the drones can connect to the 5G network more easily and stable, and the live stream can be transmitted with better guarantee. Moreover, we optimise the protocol to reduce the computation overhead in drones. Precisely, we simplify the signature verification process on drones. Our experiment results show the protocol is practical for our scenario.

2   Preliminary

This section briefly describes the architecture of our protocol for stadium live stream (Fig. 1). We also introduce the basic building block for our proposed protocol, hierarchical identity-based signatures (HIBS).

2.1   Multi-tier Drone in 5G Cellular Network

Our architecture consists of three main components: 5G core network (5GC), next-gen radio access network (Next-gen RAN), and CC drones. In the following, we will mainly discuss the components involved in the authentication protocol.

5GC. 5GC manages several components that provide service to CC drones. Our protocol mainly involves the 5GC Private Key Generator (5GC-PKG) and the Access and mobility Management Function (AMF). 5GC-PKG is a new component introduced by our scheme. It generates private-public key pair for the AMF. The functionality of AMF is similar to the mobility management entity (MME) in the 4G network [14]. Its core function in our scenario is to manage BSs, including the ground BSs and the aerial BS balloon drone. Specifically, AMF generates private-public key pairs for BSs under its coverage.

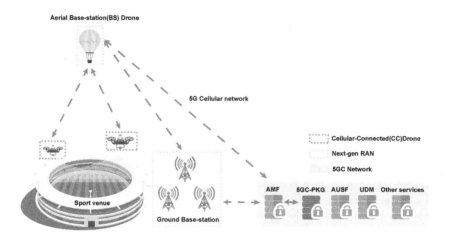

Fig. 1. The architecture of our protocol in 5G cellular network

Next-Gen RAN. It consists of the ground BSs and aerial BS balloon drones at its coverage. In our scenario, the aerial BS balloon drone is in charge of receiving the video signal from CC drones and transferring data for live stream purpose. It also directly controls the CC drones below its coverage by sending commands. The BS balloon drone needs to broadcast the Master Information Block (MIB) message and the System Information Blocks type 1 (SIB1) message to CC drones at regular intervals. MIB and SIB1 messages are the most important information that will enable further communication between the CC drone and the BS balloon drone. Precisely, MIB contains the necessary parameters required to decode SIB1, and SIB1 contains the essential parameters for setting the connection. The connection between a CC drone and the aerial BS balloon drone will be secure as long as the MIB and SIB1 messages are authenticated. Therefore, in our protocol the CC drones only need to verify SIB1 messages broadcast from the BS balloon drone.

CC Drones. They access the 5G cellular network using the Universal Subscriber Identity Module (USIM) card, which is provisioned by a cellular network operator. It contains a 5G Subscription Permanent Identifier (SUPI) [9], which also known as the International Mobile Subscriber Identifier (IMSI) in 4G LTE and 3GPP cellular network. Once CC drones received the broadcast messages from the BS balloon drone, they would verify the information by using our HIBS scheme. Also, our CC drones would be mainly responsible for high-resolution video recording in a sport venue and send the stream to aerial BS balloon drone through the secure communication channel.

2.2   Hierarchical Identity-Based Signatures

Notation. p and q are primes. We define a group $\mathbb{Z}_q$ and a finite field $\mathbb{F}_p$ for HIBS and use an elliptic curve (EC) over $\mathbb{F}_p$ as $E(\mathbb{F}_p)$. P is the generator points on $E(\mathbb{F}_p)$. $x \leftarrow S$ defines a random x is selected from a set S uniformly. $\parallel$ is denoted as string concatenation. $x \times P$ is represented elliptic curve scalar multiplication and all operations for EC utilise an additive notation. We use a hash function $H_1 : \{0,1\}^{i_1} \rightarrow \mathbb{Z}_q$, where i_1 denotes the identity space.

The hierarchical identity-based signatures [8] eliminates the requirement for certificates. It is a generalization of identify-based cryptography that deploys multiple PKGs in tree structure. Precisely, the upper-trier PKG generates the private key for lower-tier entities. In our scheme, we use a 2-tier hierarchical architecture, where 5GC-PKG is the root PKG and generates keys for AMFs, and AMFs are the lower-trier PKGs that generate keys for aerial balloon BS drones. Every entity has a position the tree. The identifies of 5GC-PKG, AMF and the aerial balloon BS drone are ID_0, ID_1, and ID_2, respectively. Specifically, we define $\mathbf{ID}_s = (ID_1, ..., ID_s)$, which is a set of identities of the entities lead up to ID_s, from the node directly following the root. We formally define the HIBS in the following.

Definition 1 (Hierarchical Identity-based Signatures). *A hierarchical identity-based signature scheme is defined as $HIBS = \{Setup, Extract, Sign, Verify\}$.*

- *$(sk, mpk, params) \leftarrow Setup(1^k)$. Given the security parameter k, the 5GC-PKG chooses the master secret key sk, computes system parameters $params$ and its master public key mpk. Only the 5GC-PKG knows the sk, and $params$ and mpk will be publicly available.*
- *$(sk_{ID_s}, \mathbf{Q}_{ID_s}) \leftarrow Extract(\mathbf{ID}_s, sk_{ID_{s-1}}, \mathbf{Q}_{ID_{s-1}})$. Given identity tuple $\mathbf{ID}_s = (ID_1, ..., ID_s)$ at level s, and the commitment value $\mathbf{Q}_{ID_{s-1}}$ the private key $sk_{ID_{s-1}}$ of the entity at depth of $s-1$, it returns the private key for the entity ID_s and its commitment value tuple $\mathbf{Q}_{ID_s} = (Q_{ID_1}, ..., Q_{ID_s})$.*
- *$\sigma \leftarrow Sign(m, sk_{ID})$. Given private key sk_{ID}, message m, and it outputs a signature sigma.*
- *$r \leftarrow Verify(m, \sigma, \mathbf{ID}_s, \mathbf{Q}_{ID_s})$. It takes message m, signature σ, $\mathbf{ID}_s$, $\mathbf{Q}_{ID_s}$ as input, and returns $r = 1$ or $r = 0$ to represent the signature is valid or not, respectively.*

3   Overview of Our Solution

3.1   Threat Model

In this work, we consider the widely-knowledge Dolev-Yao threat model where the adversary could inject, drop, or modify messages sent by legitimate entities through the public radio channel. We consider the adversary targets at attacking CC drones. In particular, an adversary could inject and tamper the messages sent by the legitimate aerial BS drone, and masquerade as a BS and induce the CC drone to connect it. For example, the adversary can create a fake BS and force the CC drones to connect it over legitimate one by controlling the radio signal strength [14]. Then, the adversary can send malicious commands to CC drones and ask them to forward the living stream to an unsubscribed entity. Moreover, the adversary can mount different attacks on CC drones, such as man-in-the-middle, replay [16], and bidding down [25] attacks. However, the adversary can not physically tamper or access the legitimate aerial BS balloon drone, CC drones or 5GC infrastructure. It can not also access their private keys stored in BS drone or CC drones.

3.2   Scope of Our Solution

Our scheme enables CC drones to authenticate their upper-tier BS balloon drone before establishing a connection by verifying the SIB1 messages broadcast from the BS balloon drone. We do not consider DoS attacks, such as forcing the CC drone to disconnect our original network and registering to a fake BS using an RF jammer [7]. We also do not consider the passive eavesdropping attack [9] on the communication between the CC drone and the BS balloon drone.

Moreover, our scheme is envisioned for sport venues using drones for transmitting video data. Indeed, our scheme can be extended to many other scenarios, such as deployment in disaster relief. For instance, if an earthquake happens in an area and local architectures have been destroyed, CC drones can provide cellular network support to the survivor immediately below its coverage [19]. It can also record the video for the site condition and transmission to the ground control station and help to search for survivors.

Lastly, our solution can be extended to a 4G LTE or lower protocol cellular network with minimal modifications. This allows our system to become more flexible and increase its commercial competitiveness.

3.3   Overview of Our Protocol

Our authentication protocol allows CC drones to authenticate the aerial BS balloon drone's identity by verifying the SIB1 messages sent by it. Our authentication protocol is basically built based on top of the HIBS scheme, and it consists of 3 layers of components: 5GC-PKG, AMF, and BS balloon drone. We supply a high-level overview of our proposed authentication protocol.

The 5GC-PKG generates its private-public key pairs(PK_{5GC}, sk_{5GC}) at the initialisation phase. Its public key PK_{5GC} is pre-installed inside the USIM of all CC drones during their registration. The AMF sends its identifier AMF_ID and key generation request periodically to 5GC-PKG and receives (sk_{AMF}, PK_{AMF}, ID_{AMF}) from 5GC-PKG. ID_{AMF} is a concatenation of expire timestamp for its key-pair and AMF_ID. Similarly, the BS balloon drone sends a key generation request and NCI_ID to the AMF and receives (PK_{BSD}, sk_{BSD}, ID_{BSD}). ID_{BSD} is a concatenation of the expiration timestamp for its key pair and NCI_ID. The BS balloon drone uses its assigned sk_{BSD} to sign the SIB1 message and generates the signature $Sign\{SIB_1\}$. The BS balloon drone sends $Sign\{SIB_1\}$, PK_{AMF}, ID_{AMF}, ID_{BSD}, and PK_{BSD} to CC drone. Then, the CC drone utilizes obtained information to verify the signature, timestamps of key pairs for the BS balloon drone and the AMF. If the timestamps are still valid and verification is successful, the CC drone would connect to the BS balloon drone.

4 Protocol Description

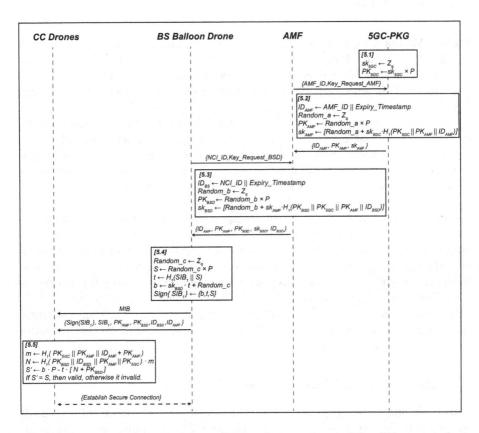

Fig. 2. Our proposed protocol for multi-tier drone system in 5G cellular networks

In this section, we first present the key management mechanism. Second, we give the way to prevent relay attack. Finally, we describe our authentication protocol for different phases. The specific computation performed by each entity and the communication between entities are shown in Fig. 2.

Key Management. We assign different validity period time for each generated private-public key pair of each entity instead of using complicated key revocation techniques. For example, we can set one year validity time for 5GC-PKG's key pair, and set one day for AMFs' keys. Both the 5GC-PKG and the AMFs are located in the 5G core network which are generally carefully protected, thus they cannot be tampered with easily and we can set longer period of validity for their keys. In contrast, the BS balloon drones are much easier to be attacked. We assign a shorter validity time, such as 5 min, for their keys. These validity periods for each entity's key pair can be configured by the network operator based on the situation.

Relay Attack Countermeasure. Our protocol provides mechanisms against illegitimate BSs by allowing the CC drone to authenticate the SIB1 messages. However, the adversary can eavesdrop on such messages and re-transmit them to CC drones. This relay attack can induce CC drones to connect the illegitimate BS.

To prevent relay attack, we propose to bind time to the SIB1 messages broadcast from the aerial BS balloon drone. Specifically, we append two additional fields to the broadcast SIB1 message: T_{sign} denotes when the SIB1 message is being signed; $\triangle T$ denotes the validity period of our signature, and it is location dependent. If CC drones start to verify the SIB1 message at time T_v, the message is valid if $T_v - T_{sign} < \triangle T$. A successful fake BS attack requires to relay the SIB1 message within $\triangle T$ time of T_{sign}. However, to determine an appropriate $\triangle T$ value requires taking account of location-dependent signal interference, which is hard to estimate due to environmental dynamics. Our idea is to measure the maximum time the SIB1 message taken from the legitimate BS balloon drone to CC drones and the minimum time required for a fake BS to execute a successful relay attack, and define them as t_{min} and t_{max}, respectively. t_{max} value must be larger than t_{min} as the fake BS requires an extra round of transmission. $\triangle T$ should be in (t_{min}, t_{max}), i.e., $t_{min} < \triangle T < t_{max}$. We leave a better solution to our future work.

4.1   5GC-PKG Initialisation Phase

During the initialization phase, the 5GC-PKG chooses a random value from $\mathbb{Z}_q$ as its private key sk_{5GC} and generates $sk_{5GC} \times P$ as its public key PK_{5GC} (as shown in Eq. 1). The 5GC-PKG is mainly responsible for generating the private-public key pairs for AMFs of a particular network operator. As mentioned, we also set a validity period for PK_{5GC} and sk_{5GC} in the 5G cellular network such as one year. PK_{5GC} is pre-installed in USIM [9,14] of the CC drones along with the expiry date, which waits to be refreshed once the connection has been established. When its public-private key pair expires, the 5GC-PKG updates and refreshes its new key pair and then delivers its new public key to lower-tier parties. This communication procedure can be executed using a confidential and integrity protection channel among each entity in the system.

$$sk_{5GC} \leftarrow \mathbb{Z}_q, PK_{5GC} \leftarrow sk_{5GC} \times P \tag{1}$$

4.2 AMF Key Generation

AMF gets its key pair from 5GC-PKG by sending a key generation request and its identifier AMF_ID to 5G-PKG. After getting the request from AMF, 5GC-PKG computes $PK_{AMF} \leftarrow Random\_a \times P$, where $Random\_a$ is randomly sampled from $\mathbb{Z}_q$. AMF's private key sk_{AMF} is generated based on sk_{5GC} and PK_{5GC}. Meanwhile, sk_{AMF} should be specific to PK_{AMF} and ID_{AMF}. Therefore, as shown in Eq. 3, sk_{5GC}, PK_{5GC}, PK_{AMF} and ID_{AMF} are all involved in the generation of sk_{AMF}. Once the 5GC-PKG generates private-public key pair for the AMF, it delivers ID_{AMF}, sk_{AMF}, PK_{AMF} to the AMF. When the AMF receives the key pair from 5GC-PKG, it first verifies the expiry timestamp embedded in AMF_ID. This procedure can ensure that the AMF receives valid private-public key pair for itself. We also set a validity period such as 24 h for PK_{AMF} and sk_{AMF} in the AMF component. If the key pairs expire, the AMF will request a new pair of key.

$$Random\_a \leftarrow \mathbb{Z}_q, PK_{AMF} \leftarrow Random\_a \times P \tag{2}$$

$$sk_{AMF} \leftarrow [Random\_a + sk_{5GC} \cdot H_1(PK_{5GC}\|PK_{AMF}\|ID_{AMF})] \tag{3}$$

4.3 BS Balloon Drone Key Generation

The AMF serves the BS balloon drones under its tracking area. The BS balloon drone first sends the key generation request to AMF. The AMF chooses a random value $Random\_b$ from $\mathbb{Z}_q$ and takes $Random\_b \times P$ as the BS balloon drone's public key PK_{BSD}. The secret key sk_{BSD} for BS balloon drone is derived from $Random\_b$, ID_{BSD}, PK_{BSD}, PK_{5GC}, and PK_{AMF} (Eq. 5). The AMF sends ID_{AMF}, PK_{AMF}, PK_{BSD}, sk_{BSD}, ID_{BSD} to the BS balloon drone. The BS balloon drone's key pair also has a validity period, such as 5 min. The ID_{BSD} concatenates the expiration timestamp for its key-pair and BS balloon drone's NCI_ID, so the BS balloon drone verifies the validity period time of its public-private keys by checking the timestamp. A BS balloon drone might under the tracking areas of multiple AMFs [24], thus it can send key generation requests to multiple AMFs. The BS balloon drone can only keep one of the key pairs and discard the other key pairs from AMFs, and it also can keep all the key pairs until they expire.

$$Random\_b \leftarrow \mathbb{Z}_q, PK_{BSD} \leftarrow Random\_b \times P \tag{4}$$

$$sk_{BSD} \leftarrow [Random\_b + sk_{AMF} \cdot H_1(ID_{BSD}\|PK_{BSD}\|PK_{5GC}\|PK_{AMF}] \tag{5}$$

4.4 Message Signing at BS Balloon Drone

For signing a SIB1 message, the BS balloon drone first randomize SIB1 by concatenating it with a random EC point S. Second, the randomized SIB1 is hashed into t with the hash function H_1, and it signs over the hash value t with its private key sk_{BSD}, rather than the original or the randomized SIB1, and get b (see Eq. 7). The final signature consists of b, t, and S. Later on, it broadcasts the signature along with the SIB_1, ID_{BSD}, PK_{BSD}, ID_{AMF} and PK_{AMF} to CC drones. Once the CC drones receive those broadcast messages, they use HIBS to verify the signature.

$$Random\_c \leftarrow \mathbb{Z}_q, S \leftarrow Random\_c \times P \tag{6}$$

$$t \leftarrow H_1(SIB_1 \| S), b \leftarrow sk_{BSD} \cdot t + Random\_c \tag{7}$$

$$Sign\{SIB_1\} \leftarrow (b, t, S) \tag{8}$$

4.5 Signature Verification at CC Drones

Finally, CC drones verify the signature with obtained messages. Recall that, the CC drone receives PK_{5GC}, PK_{AMF}, ID_{AMF}, ID_{BSD} and PK_{BSD} from the upper layer. First, the CC drone checks the identity ID_{AMF} and ID_{BSD} and the expiry timestamps embedded in them. If all the public keys are valid, the CC drone will verify the signed SIB1 message, and the details are shown in Eq. 9–12. In the verification phase, the keys of all the entities in upper layers are involved, which means only when all the keys of the entities in upper layers are valid, the verification could pass.

$$m \leftarrow H_1(ID_{AMF} \| PK_{AMF} \| PK_{5GC}) + PK_{AMF} \tag{9}$$

$$N \leftarrow H_1(PK_{BSD} \| ID_{BSD} \| PK_{AMF} \| PK_{5GC}) \cdot m \tag{10}$$

$$S' \leftarrow b \cdot P - t \cdot [N + PK_{BSD}] \tag{11}$$

$$S' \stackrel{?}{=} S \tag{12}$$

Notably, we optimise the verification process on CC drones compared with the protocol proposed by Singla et al. [26]. Precisely, in our scheme, the BS Balloon Drone also sends the intermediate value S to the CC drone. During the verification phase, the CC drone just computes S' with the messages received from the BS Balloon Drone in the same way as the generation of S, including the signed message b, and verifies if $S = S'$. By doing so, our scheme saves a step of computing a hash value compared with [26].

5 Performance Analysis

5.1 Experiment Setup

We implemented a prototype of our scheme in Python 3.7 [22] using Crypto 2.6.1 library [21]. The performance of each entity involved in the scheme was evaluated on a Macbook Pro laptop with 2.5 GHz 4-core Intel Core i7 processor and 16 GB 1600 MHz DDR3 memory.

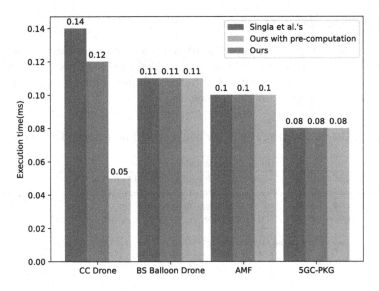

Fig. 3. Execution time for each entity in our proposed protocol

5.2 Computation Overhead

We evaluate the key generation time on 5GC-PKG and AMF, the signing time on the balloon drone BS, and the verification time on drones, and the results are shown in Fig. 3. All the results shown in Fig. 3 are the average of 10 times execution. For the test, we set the key size to 256-bit, which achieves 128-bit symmetric key security according to NIST recommendations [3]. From Fig. 3, we can see that, although the verification process on CC drones takes the longest time among all the entities, it only takes 0.12 ms to verify the signature, which is nearly negligible compared with the time of a sport match.

We also compare the performance of our scheme with the one proposed by Singla *et al.* in [26] in Fig. 3. We can see for the execution time in 5GC-PKG, AMF, and BS Balloon Drone, there is no big difference between the two schemes. However, the verification on CC drones of our scheme is more efficient due to our optimisation, which outperforms the verification of [26] by 14.3%.

We also optimize our proposed protocol by pre-computing the values of m and N at the CC drone. They can be pre-computed due to the fact that both m and N are independent on the SIB1 message, and they are derived from the public keys and identifies of AMF and BS balloon drone. As mentioned, the key pairs of each entity in our scheme have validity period. As long as all the keys involved in the computation of m and N are all valid, they will be the same and the CC drone can pre-compute them offline. When m and N are pre-computed, it only takes 0.05 ms to verify the signature from the BS balloon drone. In this case, the verification phase of our scheme outperforms [26] by 2.4×.

5.3   Communication Overhead

We also evaluate the communication volume for different phases of our protocol, and the result is shown in Table 1. For the authentication, the CC drone only receives 149 bytes from the BS balloon drone, which is a relatively low communication overhead for CC drones.

Table 1. Communication volume for our proposed protocol in different phases

Entity name	Communication volume (B)	Total (B)
AMF → 5GC-PKG	$AMF\_ID(7)$, $Key\_Request\_AMF(2)$	9
5GC-PKG → AMF	$ID_{AMF}(7)$, $PK_{AMF}(32)$, $sk_{AMF}(34)$	73
BS Balloon Drone → AMF	$NCI\_ID(5)$, $Key\_Request\_BSD(2)$	7
AMF → BS Balloon Drone	$ID_{AMF}(7)$, $PK_{AMF}(32)$, $PK_{BSD}(32)$, $sk_{BSD}(42)$, $ID_{BSD}(9)$	122
BS Balloon Drone → CC Drone	$MIB(3)$, $Sign\{SIB_1\}(64)$, $SIB_1(2)$, $PK_{AMF}(32)$, $PK_{BSD}(32)$, $ID_{BSD}(9)$, $ID_{AMF}(7)$	149

The communication overhead between other entities is smaller as they only communicate for keys. The validity period of the private-public key for each entity can affect the communication volume the entities other than the CC drones. The shorter the valid time for private-public key pair for each entity, the more communication volume in a specific time. For example, suppose a BS balloon drone's private-public key is only valid for 5 min. In that case, it indicates that every 5 min passed, the BS balloon drone needs to repeat the key generation request to the AMF, so it requires to send the request 288 times for one day. However, if the key pair for the BS balloon drone is valid for 10 min, the communication volume for that phase would be half the amount compared with the valid period of 5 min.

6   Related Work

Commercial Cellular-Connected Drones. Google Loon project [10] aims to provide cellular network connectivity in remote areas. It has been achieved by utilizing stratospheric balloons to replay radio communication links from ground stations to end user's devices. Facebook's project, called Aquila [17], built a drone BS at a high altitude and provided internet coverage below its flight path. Later on, Huawei wireless X Lab [11] initiated the Digital Sky Initiative in 2017 to investigate the specific use cases associated with multi-tier drones system in the cellular network. Those prototypes utilized multi-tier drones connected to terrestrial networks via an air-to-ground wireless link or a satellite link to provide the 3GPP cellular network or WiFi signal to ground users.

Authentication Methodologies. 3GPP specifications [1] proposed three authentication solutions to verify the authenticity of BSs. The first solution is to verify the system information (SI) messages with identity-based cryptography and using the keys provisioned by the cellular network operators or digital signatures. In this solution, the BS cannot be authenticated during the initialization registration process, and it can only authenticate the BS during cell re-selection. The second one is to use a certification authority (CA) [1], where the BS is assigned a certificate to sign its broadcast messages [5]. However, sending CA certificates can cause significant communication overhead. The last method is to sign the BS's broadcast messages using identity-based signature schemes, which are more lightweight than the CA-based solution. However, the recommended identity-based schemes, SM9 [6] and Boneh-Lynn-Shacham (BLS) [4], from IEEE standard require costly pairing computations on the CC drones.

Attack Mitigation. To address fake BS, many solutions, such as [1], suggest only sending broadcast messages after building a secure communication connection between BS and end devices. The secure communication connection provides integrity and confidentiality protection. However, the adversary still can mount bidding-down attacks where the end devices are forced to use older cellular network protocols, such as 4G LTE, 3G, or 2G. Another typical way utilises machine learning technologies [13,15] to collect and analyse surrounding cellular network signal from legitimate BSs, end devices, and other deployed hardware in the cellular network [16], and white-list trusted BSs. However, in those methods, the adversary can easily bypass such detection by using a legitimate device as a covert channel. Similarly, the scheme also gives in [2] collects numerous regional legitimate BSs' characteristics and builds a unique cell print for authentication.

Although some prevention mechanisms already developed in 4G LTE/3GPP, they are not practical for drones due to the heavy computation and communication overhead. In particular, the masquerade attack is still a problem in the 5G cellular network. It poses an obstacle to developing a secure multi-tier drone system in the 5G cellular network. Our proposed protocol allows the drones to detect fake BS and it is lightweight and efficient.

7   Conclusion and Future Work

We propose to use 5G cellular network connected drones to capture real-time live streaming in sport venues. To provide more stable network connection, we deploy an aerial balloon drone to provide the 5G base station service in our architecture. More importantly, we propose a lightweight and efficient authentication protocol to secure the connection between CC drones and the BS balloon drone so as to prevent fake BSs from stealing the live stream or sending malicious commands to drones. Our evaluation results shown that the proposed protocol has a relatively low communication and computation overhead.

For our future work, on the one hand, we will evaluate the performance of our protocol in real CC drones. On the other hand, we will optimise the protocol further to make it more lightweight. For instance, we will modify the protocol so that more computation can be processed offline for drones.

References

1. Specification number TR 33.809 version 0.8.0. In: Study on 5G security enhancements against false base stations. 3GPP (2020)
2. Alrashede, H., Shaikh, R.A.: IMSI catcher detection method for cellular networks. In: 2019 2nd International Conference on Computer Applications and Information Security (ICCAIS), pp. 1–6. IEEE (2019)
3. BlueKrypt: Cryptographic key length recommendation. https://www.keylength.com/en/4/. Accessed 14 June 2021
4. Boneh, D., Lynn, B., Shacham, H.: Short signatures from the Weil pairing. J. Cryptol. **17**(4), 297–319 (2004). https://doi.org/10.1007/s00145-004-0314-9
5. Boyd, C. (ed.): ASIACRYPT 2001. LNCS, vol. 2248. Springer, Heidelberg (2001). https://doi.org/10.1007/3-540-45682-1
6. Cheng, Z.: The SM9 cryptographic schemes. IACR Cryptol. ePrint Arch. 2017, 117 (2017). http://eprint.iacr.org/2017/117
7. Dabrowski, A., Pianta, N., Klepp, T., Mulazzani, M., Weippl, E.R.: IMSI-catch me if you can: IMSI-catcher-catchers. In: Jordan, C.N.P., Hahn, A., Butler, K.R.B., Sherr, M. (eds.) Proceedings of the 30th Annual Computer Security Applications Conference, ACSAC 2014, New Orleans, LA, USA, 8–12 December 2014, pp. 246–255. ACM (2014). https://doi.org/10.1145/2664243.2664272
8. Gentry, C., Silverberg, A.: Hierarchical ID-Based cryptography. In: Zheng, Y. (ed.) ASIACRYPT 2002. LNCS, vol. 2501, pp. 548–566. Springer, Heidelberg (2002). https://doi.org/10.1007/3-540-36178-2_34
9. Gharsallah, I., Smaoui, S., Zarai, F.: A secure efficient and lightweight authentication protocol for 5G cellular networks: Sel-aka. In: 2019 15th International Wireless Communications and Mobile Computing Conference (IWCMC), pp. 1311–1316. IEEE (2019)
10. Google loon project main page (2011). https://loon.com/. Accessed 23 April 2021
11. Mbbf2017 connected aerial vehicle live (2017). https://www.huawei.com/au/technology-insights/industry-insights/outlook/mobile-broadband/xlabs/use-cases/mbbf2017-connected-aerial-vehicle-live. Accessed 23 April 2021
12. Huo, Y., Dong, X., Lu, T., Xu, W., Yuen, M.: Distributed and multi-layer UAV network for the next-generation wireless communication (2018)
13. Hussain, S.R., Echeverria, M., Chowdhury, O., Li, N., Bertino, E.: Privacy attacks to the 4G and 5g cellular paging protocols using side channel information. In: 26th Annual Network and Distributed System Security Symposium, NDSS 2019, San Diego, California, USA, 24–27 February 2019. The Internet Society (2019)
14. Hussain, S.R., Echeverria, M., Singla, A., Chowdhury, O., Bertino, E.: Insecure connection bootstrapping in cellular networks: the root of all evil. In: Proceedings of the 12th Conference on Security and Privacy in Wireless and Mobile Networks, WiSec 2019, Miami, Florida, USA, 15–17 May 2019, pp. 1–11. ACM (2019). https://doi.org/10.1145/3317549.3323402

15. Jin, J., Lian, C., Xu, M.: Rogue base station detection using a machine learning approach. In: 28th Wireless and Optical Communications Conference, WOCC 2019, Beijing, China, 9–10 May 2019, pp. 1–5. IEEE (2019). https://doi.org/10.1109/WOCC.2019.8770554

16. Lilly, A.: IMSI catchers: hacking mobile communications. Netw. Secur. **2017**(2), 5–7 (2017). https://doi.org/10.1016/S1353-4858(17)30014-4

17. Maguire, Y.: Building communications networks in the stratosphere (2015). https://engineering.fb.com/2015/07/30/connectivity/building-communications-networks-in-the-stratosphere/. Accessed 23 April 2021

18. Mortimer, G.: Stadiums and arenas are keeping the good drones in, and the spies out with dedrone (2017). https://www.suasnews.com/2017/03/stadiums-arenas-keeping-good-drones-spies-dedrone/. Accessed 23 April 2021

19. Naqvi, S.A.R., Hassan, S.A., Pervaiz, H., Ni, Q.: Drone-aided communication as a key enabler for 5G and resilient public safety networks. IEEE Commun. Mag. **56**(1), 36–42 (2018). https://doi.org/10.1109/MCOM.2017.1700451

20. Nassi, B., Shabtai, A., Masuoka, R., Elovici, Y.: Sok - security and privacy in the age of drones: Threats, challenges, solution mechanisms, and scientific gaps. CoRR abs/1903.05155 (2019). http://arxiv.org/abs/1903.05155

21. Pycrypto 2.6.1. https://pypi.org/project/pycrypto/. Accessed 14 June 2021

22. Python 3.7.0. https://www.python.org/downloads/release/python-370/. Accessed 14 June 2021

23. Research, Markets: Global cellular-connected drone market analysis and forecast, 2020–2023 and 2030 (2020). https://www.globenewswire.com/en/news-release/2020/10/30/2117598/28124/en/Global-Cellular-Connected-Drone-Market-Analysis-Forecast-2020-2023-2030.html. Accessed 13 June 13 2021

24. Shaik, A., Borgaonkar, R., Park, S., Seifert, J.: On the impact of rogue base stations in 4G/LTE self organizing networks. In: Papadimitratos, P., Butler, K.R.B., Pöpper, C. (eds.) Proceedings of the 11th ACM Conference on Security and Privacy in Wireless and Mobile Networks, WiSec 2018, Stockholm, Sweden, 18–20 June 2018, pp. 75–86. ACM (2018). https://doi.org/10.1145/3212480.3212497

25. Shaik, A., Borgaonkar, R., Park, S., Seifert, J.: New vulnerabilities in 4G and 5G cellular access network protocols: exposing device capabilities. In: Proceedings of the 12th Conference on Security and Privacy in Wireless and Mobile Networks, WiSec 2019, Miami, Florida, USA, 15–17 May 2019, pp. 221–231. ACM (2019). https://doi.org/10.1145/3317549.3319728

26. Singla, A., Behnia, R., Hussain, S.R., Yavuz, A.A., Bertino, E.: Look before you leap: Secure connection bootstrapping for 5g networks to defend against fake base-stations. In: Cao, J., Au, M.H., Lin, Z., Yung, M. (eds.) ASIA CCS 2021: ACM Asia Conference on Computer and Communications Security, Virtual Event, Hong Kong, 7–11 June 2021, pp. 501–515. ACM (2021)

27. Ullah, H., Nair, N.G., Moore, A., Nugent, C.D., Muschamp, P., Cuevas, M.: 5G communication: an overview of vehicle-to-everything, drones, and healthcare use-cases. IEEE Access **7**, 37251–37268 (2019). https://doi.org/10.1109/ACCESS.2019.2905347

28. Yang, G., et al.: A telecom perspective on the internet of drones: From LTE-advanced to 5G. CoRR abs/1803.11048 (2018)

29. Zeng, Y., Lyu, J., Zhang, R.: Cellular-connected UAV: potential, challenges, and promising technologies. IEEE Wirel. Commun. **26**(1), 120–127 (2019)

Anti-eavesdropping Proportional Fairness Access Control for 5G Networks

Shankar K. Ghosh[1][(✉)], Avirup Das[2], Sasthi C. Ghosh[2], and Nabanita Das[2]

[1] Presidency University, Bangalore 560064, India
[2] Indian Statistical Institute, Kolkata 700108, India
{sasthi,ndas}@isical.ac.in

Abstract. Due to the open access nature, communication over unlicensed band, suffers from security threats like eavesdropping. Eavesdroppers are unwanted nodes, attempting to overhear the signal transmitted between two legitimate mobile terminals (MTs), often for malicious purposes. Apart from security issues, it results in significant degradation of secrecy throughput, i.e., the throughput achieved by a legitimate user without being overheard by eavesdroppers. Since with the present technology, it is quite difficult to identify the eavesdroppers even in 5G, the average throughput of the legitimate MTs decreases when the serving base station schedules the eavesdroppers as well, based on the channel condition only. So far, the issue of eavesdropping has rarely been considered in the context of scheduling. In this paper, we propose an anti-eavesdropping proportional fairness (APF) mechanism considering the possibility of eavesdroppers. Our proposed APF technique first estimates a set of suspected eavesdroppers based on sleep mode information, and then reduces the possibility of scheduling these eavesdroppers by imposing penalties. Penalty assignments are based on past average throughput, current channel conditions and modulation/coding schemes. Both Hidden Markov model based analysis and simulations confirm that the proposed APF technique outperforms the traditional proportional fairness protocol in terms of anti-eavesdropping efficiency and secrecy throughput.

Keywords: Eavesdropping · Secrecy throughput · Proportional fairness scheduling · Hidden Markov model · Physical layer security

1 Introduction

To deal with the increasing demand for wireless data traffic in the upcoming fifth generation (5G) cellular networks, unlicensed band communication has been evolved as a promising solution. Recently, the applicability of new radio (NR), the radio access technology (RAT) for 5G systems, has been extended to unlicensed band spectrum by 3rd generation partnership project (3GPP) [1]. It is expected that the large amount of spectrum available in 2.4 GHz, 5 GHz, 6 GHz and 60 GHz unlicensed

© ICST Institute for Computer Sciences, Social Informatics and Telecommunications Engineering 2021
Published by Springer Nature Switzerland AG 2021. All Rights Reserved
X. Yuan et al. (Eds.): QShine 2021, LNICST 402, pp. 144–158, 2021.
https://doi.org/10.1007/978-3-030-91424-0_9

bands will significantly increase user throughput in NR systems. Although high user throughput can be ensured in unlicensed band communication, it suffers from security threats due to its open access nature [3]. Previously, Shannon's work has been extensively used to secure communication systems using shared secret keys. However, these works have several drawbacks including complexities associated with key management, distribution and key length [2]. To address these drawbacks, a new keyless information theoretic security paradigm namely *physical layer security* has been emerged. In Wyner's work [4], it has been shown that confidential communication between legitimate mobile terminals (MTs) is possible without sharing a secret key if the eavesdropper's channel is a degraded version of the intended receiver's channel. In this regard, *secrecy throughput* has been defined as the difference between the throughput obtained by the intended receiver from the system and the throughput obtained by the eavesdroppers by overhearing the receiver's channel. In presence of eavesdroppers, efficient resource allocation policy is essential to ensure high secrecy throughput. But since, with present technology, exact identification of eavesdroppers is difficult, the problem is still challenging to the research communities [2, 3].

Eavesdroppers are often registered in the network as subscribed MTs and exchange signaling messages with serving base stations (BS) [5]. In such a scenario, the objective of these malicious MTs is to decode private message of any legitimate user. Since the exact identifications of eavesdroppers are not known, the serving BS often schedules eavesdroppers having good channel conditions. This in turn results in starvation of legitimate MTs. It may be noted that secrecy throughput of a legitimate user may degrade in two ways: Firstly, due to eavesdropping, i.e., the signal transmitted to the legitimate user is overheard by the eavesdroppers. Secondly, due to starvation of legitimate MTs, i.e., the average throughput obtained by the legitimate user is much less due to the resource scarcity caused by the eavesdroppers. Although exact identification of eavesdroppers' is quite difficult, the number of such malicious MTs may be known to the BS through various mathematical techniques based on random matrix theory and hypothesis testing [6]. In such a prevailing situation, it is worthy to think of a scheduling mechanism which can *reduce the possibility* of an eavesdropper being scheduled by the serving BS. It may be considered as a penalty for eavesdropping that helps to improve the secrecy throughput of good users by reducing the tendency of overhearing.

To improve user throughput in wireless data networks, a number of scheduling mechanisms have been proposed in literature. A survey of such algorithms can be found in [7]. Among these existing mechanisms, proportional fairness (PF) scheduling is of particular interest due to its ability to strike a trade-off between throughput and fairness. The goal of traditional PF scheduling is to maximize the cell throughput while ensuring fairness among the MTs. A number of variations of traditional PF have also been proposed to deal with the drawbacks incurred by traditional PF such as throughput degradation due to poor channel condition at the cell edges, blockage of signals by obstacles in millimeter wave communications (mmWave) and signal fading caused by mobility of MTs. For example, in [8], an enhanced PF mechanism has been proposed for mmWave. Here the past average throughput decreases exponentially with current throughput degradation. Consequently, the priority of MTs residing in non line of sight region increases. The predictive finite horizon PF mechanism proposed in [9] deals with the fast fading caused by mobility of MTs by employing a data rate prediction and a future channel estimation mechanism. It may be noted that designing scheduling mechanism to reduce the performance degradation caused by eavesdroppers is quite limited in the preceding literature. In [10], a scheduling mechanism has been proposed to improve the security level in cognitive radio network. Here, the cognitive user that maximizes the achievable secrecy rate is scheduled to transmit its data packet. In [11], an optimal transmission scheduling scheme has been proposed to maximize the security of ad hoc network against eavesdropping. Here the scheduling scheme opportunistically selects a source node with the highest secrecy rate to transmit its data. In [13], the probability of success in opportunistic stationary eavesdropping attacks has been analyzed, however nothing has been suggested as preventive measure. These existing mechanisms [10,11,13] are not suitable for upcoming 5G cellular network scenarios as they are designed specifically for ad hoc and cognitive radio networks respectively.

In this work, our *objective* is to propose an anti-eavesdropping PF (APF) scheduling mechanism which can *reduce the possibility* of an eavesdropper being scheduled significantly, and therefore penalizes the eavesdroppers to reduce the tendency of overhearing. Our *contributions* are summarized as follows.

- We propose a new scheduling mechanism namely, the anti-eavesdropping proportional fairness (APF) scheduling which explicitly considers the possibility of throughput degradation by eavesdroppers. The goal of APF is to eliminate eavesdroppers while scheduling different MTs in the system. The APF mechanism first determines the set of suspected eavesdroppers based on *sleep mode information* obtained through co-operative detection [17]. In 5G systems, sleep mode is used by the MTs to save power and to increase battery life. An MT switches to sleep mode when there is no data to be transmitted [19], or to be received. In our proposed mechanism, MTs spending *less time* in sleep mode than the estimated value have higher chance of being an eavesdropper. Then *penalty coefficient* for each of the suspected eavesdropper is determined based on their past average throughput values. Here, the penalty coefficient represents the extent by which the possibility of scheduling the concerned eavesdropper need to be reduced. Next, *individual penalties* for each of the suspected eavesdroppers are determined based on their penalty coefficients, past average throughput values, channel conditions and modulation/coding schemes (MCS). While scheduling different MTs, individual penalties are added to the past average throughput values of the corresponding eavesdroppers. As a result, the possibility of the eavesdropper being scheduled reduces.
- We analyze the performance of our proposed APF based on Hidden Markov model (HMM). Here the sequence of scheduled MTs over an arbitrary time interval has been considered as the *hidden sequence* of legitimate MTs and eavesdroppers. In our developed model, the sequence of secrecy throughput

values has been considered as *observed sequence* and *observation likelihoods* has been computed in proportion to the secrecy throughput values. Finally, anti-eavesdropping efficiency (AE) has been computed as the probability of occurring the observed sequence from a hidden sequence consisting of *only* legitimate MTs. In other words, AE is a measure of *how close a scheduling mechanism is to the ideal situation.*
- Extensive system level simulations have been carried out to compare the performance of APF with traditional PF [7]. The HMM based analyses and simulations confirm that our proposed APF significantly outperforms the traditional PF in terms of AE, secrecy throughput and Jain's fairness index.

The rest of the paper is organized as follows. Section 2 presents the system model considered here. Section 3 describes the proposed scheduling policy with the analytical framework included in Sect. 4. Section 5 presents the simulation results and Sect. 6 concludes with future direction of research.

Table 1. List of important notations

Notation	Description
$(.)$	Indicator of scheduling mechanism (p for PF or a for APF)
$R_u^{(.)}(t)$	Past average throughput of user u at time t
$S_u^{(.)}(t)$	Secrecy throughput of user u at time t
$r_u(t)$	Achievable throughput by user u at time t
$\gamma_u(t)$	SINR received at user u at time t
$P_u(t)$	Power received by user u at time t
$N(t)$	Received noise power at time t
b	Bandwidth of a resource block
$p_k(t)$	Penalty coefficient for eavesdropper k at time t
α	Severity index
Q	Set of all users
ξ	Set of all eavesdroppers
$\tau_{ku}(t)$	Overheard throughput by eavesdropper k from legitimate user u at time t

2   System Model

Our system model consists of a new radio (NR) base station (BS) and Q the set of MTs. Within the coverage region of the BS, MTs are uniformly distributed. We consider that there exists a group of eavesdroppers that wish to decode secret messages. The individual identities of the eavesdroppers are not known to the BS. However, side information is available regarding $|\xi|$ the cardinality of the set of all potential eavesdroppers ξ. Such information is typically available through different statistical characterizations [5,6]. Based on the channel quality information (CQI) values reported by the MTs, the BS assigns resource blocks (RBs) to the MTs based on (.), a predefined scheduling mechanism. In our case, (.) may be either p (for PF) or a (for APF).

Secrecy throughput $S_u^{(\cdot)}(t)$ obtained by a legitimate user u ($u \in Q \setminus \xi$) at time t when (.) is used to schedule MTs has been measured as the difference between $R_u^{(\cdot)}(t)$, the average throughput obtained by MT u from the BS upto time t and $\sum_{k \in \xi} \tau_{ku}(t)$, the total throughput obtained by all eavesdroppers by overhearing the transmitted signal to the legitimate MT u at time t. Here $\tau_{ku}(t)$ represents the individual throughput obtained by eavesdropper k by overhearing the transmitted signal to the legitimate MT u at time t. Since, channel gains of eavesdroppers' channels are much lower compared to that of the legitimate MT's channel, $R_u^{(\cdot)}(t)$ is usually higher compared to that of $\sum_{k \in \xi} \tau_{ku}(t)$. The secrecy throughput $S_u^{(\cdot)}(t)$ obtained by MT u at time t has been computed as:

$$S_u^{(\cdot)}(t) = R_u^{(\cdot)}(t) - \sum_{k \in \xi} \tau_{ku}(t) \tag{1}$$

$\gamma_u(t)$, the signal to interference plus noise ratio (SINR) received at user u at time t has been computed as:

$$\gamma_u(t) = \frac{P_u(t)}{N(t)} \tag{2}$$

$P_u(t)$ is the power received by MT u situated at distance $d(t)$ from the BS at time t and $N(t)$ is the noise power received by MT u at time t. Here $P_u(t)$ has been computed using free space path loss model. Based on $\gamma_u(t)$, achievable throughput by user u through an RB at time t has been computed as:

$$r_u(t) = b \times \log_2\left(1 + \gamma_u(t)\right) \tag{3}$$

where b is the bandwidth of an RB in the NR base station. Based on this system model, in the next section, we propose the APF mechanism. Important notations used in this work have been summarized in Table 1.

3   Proposed APF Scheduling

In this section, we propose the APF mechanism which explicitly consider the possibility of throughput reduction due to the presence of eavesdroppers. The goal of our proposed APF mechanism is to reduce the chance of an eavesdropper being scheduled by the serving BS. We assume that $|\xi|$ the number of eavesdroppers present in the system are known to the serving BS. Such assumption is very common as can be found in [5]. Detailed operation of the proposed scheduling mechanism is described below.

Determining the Set of Suspected Eavesdroppers

In this phase, the set of suspected eavesdroppers $\xi'(t)$ is determined from the set of MTs Q based on sleep mode information obtained through energy detection technique. In 5G systems, sleep mode is used by the MTs to save power and increase battery life. An MT switches to sleep mode when there is no data to be transmitted [19]. Since, eavesdroppers have an intention to sense other MT's downlink channel, transceivers of the eavesdroppers will remain active even when there is no data to be transmitted. As a result, the transceiver will emanate a *leakage power* which may be detected by MTs residing in close proximity using energy detection technique [17].

In our proposed algorithm, a set of trusted MTs (e.g., closed access group MTs) collects the sleep mode information of their nearby MTs through energy detection technique [17] and sends that information to the BS. The BS then computes the time spent in sleep mode by correlating the measurements of various trusted MTs [18]. Once the time periods spent in sleep mode by individual MTs are computed, the set $\xi'(t)$ is determined by including $|\xi|$ MTs in *ascending order* of their sleeping time.

Remark 1. Most of the Internet traffic is variable bit rate (VBR) traffic. In case of VBR traffic call holding time is assumed to follow Pareto principle [20]. As per the Pareto principle, every call has a minimum duration of survival (say x_m) and the probability of survival of a call decreases exponentially beyond x_m. In contrast to legitimate users, the receiver of an eavesdropper remains active even when they do not have data to send. Hence, MTs spending less time in sleep mode is more probable of being an eavesdropper.

Determining the Penalty Coefficients

In this phase, $p_k(t)$ the penalty coefficient for eavesdropper k at time t is determined based on $R_k^a(t-1)$. *Penalty coefficient of eavesdropper k represent the extent by which the possibility of scheduling eavesdropper k needs to be reduced.* The value of $p_k(t)$ has been computed in proportion to $R_k^a(t-1)$, i.e., $p_k(t) = \dfrac{R_k^a(t-1)}{\sum\limits_{k' \in \xi'(t)} R_{k'}^a(t-1)}$. This is quite reasonable because a higher $R_k^a(t-1)$ implies a higher possibility of having good channel conditions in recent past. Consequently, throughput degradation caused due to scheduling eavesdropper k is also expected to be high. Hence, to minimize throughput degradation, the serving BS should defer the scheduling of eavesdropper k in proportion to its past average throughput.

Determining Individual Penalty

In this phase, we determine the individual penalty for each eavesdropper k based on the penalty function $p_k(t) \times [r_k(t)]^\alpha$, where α is the severity index based on MCS. It may be noted that the penalty function explicitly considers the effect of past average throughput, present channel condition and MCS. The individual penalty of eavesdropper k increases with $p_k(t)$ which in turn is proportional to the past average throughput. This is because an eavesdropper with high past

---

Algorithm 1: Proposed APF mechanism

Input   : Q, $|\xi|$, $R_u^a(t-1) \ \forall u \in Q$, $r_u(t) \ \forall u \in Q$, α.
Output: User u^* to be scheduled at time t.

1 $\xi'(t) = \phi$
2 **for** *all* $u \in Q$ **do**
3 | Determine sleep time of u based on leakage power measurement.
4 **end**
5 $\xi'(t)$ = The set of $|\xi|$ MTs taken in ascending sequence of their sleep time.
6 Compute $p_k(t) = \dfrac{R_k^a(t-1)}{\displaystyle\sum_{k' \in \xi'(t)} R_{k'}^a(t-1)} \ \forall k \in \xi'(t)$.

7 Set $p_k(t) = 0 \ \forall k \in Q \setminus \xi'(t)$.
8 Compute $C_u(t) = p_u(t) \times [r_u(t)]^\alpha \ \forall u \in Q$.
9 Determine the user u^* to be scheduled:

$$u^* = \arg\max_{u \in Q} \frac{r_u(t)}{R_u^a(t-1) + C_u(t)}$$

10 Return u^*

---

average throughput is expected to have good channel conditions in recent past, causing significant reduction in secrecy throughput. The individual penalty also increases with increasing $r_k(t)$ which is computed based on current SINR of the channel. This is because an eavesdropper having good channel condition at present is more likely to reduce throughput of legitimate MT, if scheduled by the serving BS. For a given SINR, throughput achieved by an user increases with improved MCS. To take care of this effect, our proposed APF increases the individual penalty exponentially with α. In our proposed scheme, the value of α is 1 for binary phase shift keying (BPSK), 2 for quadrature phase shift keying (QPSK), 3 for 16 quadrature amplitude modulation (QAM) and 4 for 64 QAM.

Assignment of RB

In this phase, RBs are assigned to the MTs based on their current throughput, past average throughput and individual penalties. It may be noted that individual penalties for all legitimate MTs are 0, i.e., $p_k(t) \times [r_k(t)]^\alpha = 0$ for all $k \in Q \setminus \xi'(t)$. An RB is assigned to the user u^* if the following condition holds:

$$u^* = \arg\max_{u \in Q} \frac{r_u(t)}{R_u^a(t-1) + p_u(t) \times [r_u(t)]^\alpha} \tag{4}$$

Thus the probability of scheduling an eavesdropper is reduced as the past average throughput value is increased by the individual penalty. The overall algorithm has been depicted in pseudo code format in Algorithm 1. The time complexity of the proposed APF is $O(|Q|^2)$.

4   Analytical Framework

In this section, we analyze the performances of our proposed APF and traditional PF [7] mechanisms based on Hidden Markov models (HMM). A HMM enables us to talk about some underlying *hidden events* based on some *observed events* and *observation likelihoods*, where the hidden events are considered as causal factors for the observed events. Observation likelihood is defined as the probability of an observation being generated from a particular *hidden state*. Here an output observation depends only on the state that produced the observation and not on any other states or observations. A detailed description of HMM can be found in [16].

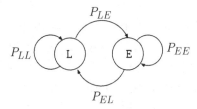

Fig. 1. Hidden Markov model

It has been assumed that time is discrete, and, in every time step t, the BS schedules an MT which may be a legitimate MT or an eavesdropper. However, the characteristic of the scheduled MT is completely unknown to the BS. Hence, the sequence of scheduled MTs over an *arbitrary time interval I* can be considered as a hidden sequence of legitimate MTs and eavesdroppers. On the other hand, the number of existing eavesdroppers and their channel gains can be known to the BS through different statistical tests [3,5]. Hence, at every time t, the BS can record $S^{(\cdot)}(t)$ the secrecy throughput of the scheduled MT at time t. Since, the exact identity of the scheduled MT is less significant in our analysis, we are omitting the subscript in the notion of secrecy throughput for the sake of simplicity. A sequence of such secrecy throughput $S^{(\cdot)}(t)$ over the time interval I can be considered as the observed sequence. Since, the secrecy throughput increases when the BS schedules a higher number of legitimate MTs, the observation likelihoods over I has been computed in proportion to the $S^{(\cdot)}(t)$ values.

In ideal case, for a given observation, the hidden sequence consists of all legitimate MTs, i.e., no eavesdroppers are scheduled by the BS. Keeping this in mind, we define *anti-eavesdropping efficiency* (AE) of a scheduling mechanism as the probability of occurring the observed sequence from a hidden sequence consisting of *only* legitimate MTs. In other words, AE is a measure of *how close a scheduling mechanism is to the ideal situation*. A higher AE indicates the hidden sequence is more close to all legitimate MT sequence, i.e., the corresponding scheduling mechanism is more efficient to eliminate eavesdroppers from being scheduled. In subsequent subsections, we derive the expressions for AE.

4.1   Analyzing AE of PF

We characterize the operation of PF by an HMM consisting of two states namely L and E (shown in Fig. 1). Here the states L and E represent the states that the BS is currently serving a legitimate MT and an eavesdropper respectively. In the considered model, P_{ij}s indicate the transition probabilities from state i to state j where $i, j \in \{L, E\}$. We assume that the time interval I has n equally spaced time steps $t_1, t_2, \ldots, t_n$. Observed sequence over the time interval I is $S^p(t_1)$, $S^p(t_2), \ldots, S^p(t_n)$. Based on the observed sequence, observation likelihoods can be computed as:

$$P\left(S^p(t_i)|L\right) = \frac{S^p(t_i)}{\sum\limits_{k=1}^{n} S^p(t_k)}, \forall i \in [1, n]. \tag{5}$$

Since, the system consists of $|\xi|$ number of eavesdroppers, the probabilities of staying in state L and E are $1 - \frac{|\xi|}{|Q|}$ and $\frac{|\xi|}{|Q|}$ respectively. Hence, the initial probability distribution π can be computed as $\pi = (\pi_L, \pi_E)$, where $\pi_L = 1 - \frac{|\xi|}{|Q|}$ and $\pi_E = \frac{|\xi|}{|Q|}$. Following similar logic, the self transition probability P_{LL} in state L can be computed as $P_{LL} = 1 - \frac{|\xi|}{|Q|}$.

Now, AE of PF is the probability of getting the observation $S^p(t_1)$, $S^p(t_2)$, $\ldots$, $S^p(t_n)$ from a hidden sequence of all Ls, i.e., $P\left(S^p(t_1), S^p(t_2), \ldots, S^p(t_n)|L, L, \ldots, L\right)$. To compute this probability we have adopted the formation presented in [16]. We compute V^p, the AE of PF, i.e., $P\left(S^p(t_1), S^p(t_2), \ldots, S^p(t_n)|L, L, \ldots, L\right)$, as follows:

$$V^p = \pi_L \left[P_{LL}\right]^{n-1} \prod_{i=1}^{n} P\left(S^p(t_i)|L\right) \tag{6}$$

$$= \left(1 - \frac{|\xi|}{|Q|}\right)^n \prod_{i=1}^{n} \frac{S^p(t_i)}{\sum\limits_{k=1}^{n} S^p(t_k)}$$

4.2   Analyzing AE of APF

The operation of our proposed APF can also be characterized by a two state HMM as described for PF, however the transitions probabilities P'_{ij}s are different from PF. At each time t, the APF determines a suspected set of eavesdroppers $\xi'(t)$ and imposes penalties on each of these eavesdroppers. As a result, at most $\xi \cap \xi'(t)$ set of eavesdroppers may be eliminated from being scheduled. Hence, at least $\xi \setminus \xi \cap \xi'(t)$ set of eavesdroppers are present for being scheduled at time t. Accordingly, for APF mechanism, the self transition probability $P'_{LL}(t)$ for state L at time t can be computed as $P'_{LL}(t) = 1 - \frac{|\xi \setminus \xi \cap \xi'(t)|}{|Q|}$. It may be noted that $P'_{LL}(t)$ boils down to P_{LL} when $\xi \cap \xi'(t) = \phi$, the null set. Hence, the average self transition probability over the time interval I can be computed as $P'_{LL} = \frac{1}{n} \sum_{i=1}^{n} P'_{LL}(t_i)$. Since, $P'_{LL}(t_i) \geq P_{LL} \; \forall i \in [1, n]$, we get $P'_{LL} \geq P_{LL}$.

The computation of initial probability distribution is similar to that of PF, i.e., π'_L the probability of starting from state L in APF can be computed as $\pi'_L = 1 - \frac{|\xi|}{|Q|}$. Denoting by $S^a(t_1)$, $S^a(t_2)$, $\ldots$, $S^a(t_n)$ the observation sequence for APF mechanism, V^a the AE for APF mechanism can be computed as:

$$
\begin{aligned}
V^a &= P\left(S^a(t_1), S^a(t_2), \ldots, S^a(t_n) | L, L, \ldots, L\right) \\
&= \pi'_L \left[P'_{LL}\right]^{n-1} \prod_{i=1}^{n} P\left(S^a(t_i) | L\right) \\
&= \left(1 - \frac{|\xi|}{|Q|}\right) \left[\frac{1}{n} \sum_{k=1}^{n} \left(1 - \frac{|\xi \setminus \xi \cap \xi'(t_k)|}{|Q|}\right)\right]^{n-1} \\
&\quad \times \prod_{i=1}^{n} \frac{S^a(t_i)}{\sum_{k=1}^{n} S^a(t_k)}
\end{aligned}
\tag{7}
$$

5 Results and Discussions

In this section, we evaluate the performance of our proposed APF mechanism based on HMM based analysis and system level simulations. We consider secrecy throughput, AE and Jain's fairness index (J) as performance evaluation metrics. Secrecy throughput and AE have already been defined in Sects. 2 and 4 respectively. To measure fairness in achieved throughput among the legitimate MTs we have used the well known *Jain's fairness index* (J) [14]. Here J has been computed as:

$$
J = \frac{\left(\sum_{i \in Q \setminus \xi} R_i^{(\cdot)}(t)\right)^2}{|Q| \sum_{i \in Q \setminus \xi} R_i^{(\cdot)}(t)^2}
$$

5.1 Simulation Setup

To evaluate the performance of our proposed scheme, we have prepared a MATLAB based simulator. We consider a simulation environment similar to that of [12]. Our simulation environment consists of a cell with radius 500 m. Within the coverage region of the cell, MTs are distributed uniformly. We vary the number of MTs from 10 to 100. We have considered an NR BS situated at the center of the cell. Height of the BS measured from the ground has been set to 2 m. All

Table 2. Parameter settings

Parameters	Values	Parameters	Values
Cell radius	500 m	Number of MTs	10–100
Eavesdropper (%)	30%	BS height	2 m
Bandwidth	20 MHz	Transmit power	24 dBm
Noise power	−90 dBm	α	2

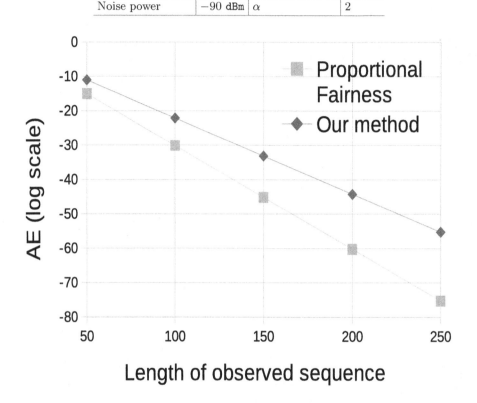

Fig. 2. AE vs. length of observed sequence (analysis)

MTs are equipped with an omni-directional transceiver, and are served by the common BS. We consider that all MTs are in line of sight with the serving BS. Transmitting power of the AP has been set to 24 dBm. The carrier frequency of the AP has been set to 28 GHz according to the 5G NR FR2 band standard [15]. We have considered *free space path loss model* to calculate the received signal strength at the MT end. In the considered simulation environment, MTs are moving according to *random way point* mobility model. While computing past average throughput at time t, we have given same weight to the current throughput and past average throughput at time $t - 1$. We consider that the channel gain of an overheard channel is exponentially distributed with parameter β, where β is uniformly random within $[1 \times 10^{-7}, 2 \times 10^{-7}]$ [3]. In our considered scenario, 10%

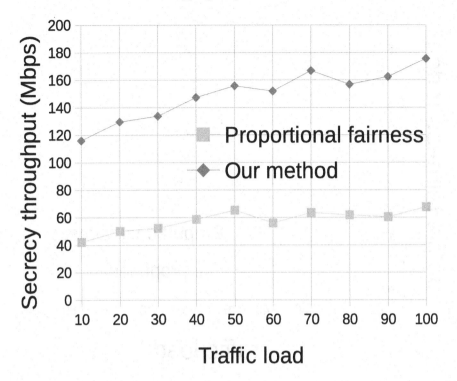

Fig. 3. Secrecy throughput vs. traffic load (simulation)

of the total MTs have been considered as *trusted nodes*. The trusted nodes send the sleep mode status of their neighboring MTs to the BS in every transmission time interval (TTI). The BS decides the sleep mode status of an MT depending upon the majority neighbor's decision. Important parameters considered in our simulations are depicted in Table 2.

5.2   Results

Figure 2 depicts the effect of the length of the observed sequence on AE. Here the results have been obtained based on the analytical models developed in Sect. 4. Results show that the AE decreases with increasing the length of observed sequence for both approaches. However, our proposed APF outperforms the traditional PF [7] in terms of AE. The performance gain in our approach increases with increasing length of the observed sequence. The reasons behind are as follows. The probability of at least one eavesdropper being scheduled increases with increasing the time interval I. As a result, the AE decreases for both the approaches. However, the proposed APF can eliminate eavesdroppers from being scheduled by imposing penalties. Such probability of elimination increases in larger time intervals. As a result, the performance gain in APF increases monotonically with the length of the considered time interval.

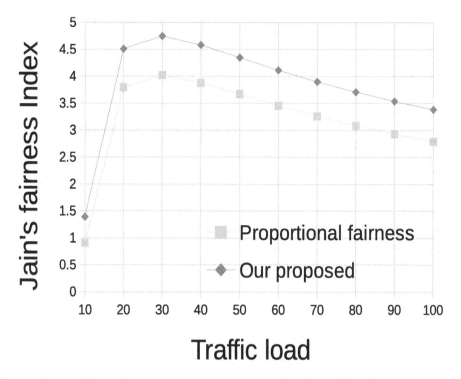

Fig. 4. Jain's fairness index vs. traffic load (simulation)

Figure 3 depicts the effect of traffic load on secrecy throughput. Here the traffic load varies from 10 MTs to 100 MTs with a step of 10 MTs. Results reported in this section represent the average results obtained from 10000 independent runs. The result shows that our proposed APF mechanism significantly outperforms the traditional PF mechanism. The reasons behind are as follows. The secrecy throughput depends on two factors: (a) the throughput obtained by the legitimate MTs from the system, and (b) the throughput obtained by the eavesdroppers by overhearing the transmitted signal to the legitimate MTs. Since, the channel gain of the overheard channel is significantly lower compared to the original channel allocated to the legitimate MTs, throughput obtained by the legitimate MTs takes the decisive role towards determining secrecy throughput. Since, our proposed approach can eliminate eavesdroppers while scheduling different MTs as obtained from the analytical results (Fig. 2), throughput obtained by the legitimate MTs in APF is better compared to that of traditional PF. This results in higher secrecy throughput in our proposed approach. *Both analysis and simulation results generate a consensus that our proposed APF can effectively eliminate eavesdroppers while scheduling different MTs.*

Figure 4 shows the effect of traffic load on the Jain's fairness index. Here also the traffic load varies from 10 MTs to 100 MTs with a step of 10 MTs. The result shows that our proposed APF mechanism significantly improves the Jain's fairness index compared to the traditional PF mechanism as the traffic load increases beyond 20 MTs. The reason behind is as follows. The traditional PF often schedules eavesdroppers having good channel conditions. This results in starvation of some legitimate MTs when the traffic load is beyond a certain threshold (20 MTs in our case). On the other hand, being equipped with side information such as time spent in sleep mode and number of eavesdroppers, our proposed APF reduces the chance of scheduling an eavesdropper. Consequently, in our approach, possibility of starvation is quite low. As a result, the APF mechanism outperforms the traditional PF in terms of Jain's fairness index. The possibility of starvation increases with increasing traffic load for both the approaches, resulting in decreasing trend for J.

6   Conclusions and Future Research Scope

In this work, APF scheduling mechanism has been proposed to avoid eavesdroppers while scheduling different MTs in the system. Moreover, the anti-eavesdropping efficiency of the proposed APF has been analyzed based on HMM. The APF mechanism reduces the chance of an eavesdropper being scheduled by assigning penalties to a suspected set of eavesdroppers. Both analysis and simulation results confirm that the APF mechanism significantly outperforms the traditional PF in terms of secrecy throughput, anti-eavesdropping efficiency and Jain's fairness index.

To determine a more accurate probability distribution to capture the exact set of eavesdroppers, we are planning to employ the carrier frequency offset (CFO) information. The CFO information is related to the user specific transceiver and is less affected by the environment. For further characterization of eavesdropping behaviours, we aim to deploy random matrix theory (RMT) to analyze the multidimensional CFO data.

References

1. Lagen, S., et al.: New radio beam-based access to unlicensed spectrum: design challenges and solutions. IEEE Commun. Surv. Tutor. **22**(1), 8–37 (2020)
2. Hamamreh, J.M., Furqan, H.M., Arslan, H.: Classifications and applications of physical layer security techniques for confidentiality: a comprehensive survey. IEEE Commun. Surv. Tutor. **21**(2), 1773–1828 (2019)
3. Wu, Y., Zheng, J., Guo, K., Qian, L.P., Shen, X., Cai, Y.: Joint traffic scheduling and resource allocations for traffic offloading with secrecy provisioning. IEEE Trans. Veh. Technol. **66**(9), 8315–8332 (2017)
4. Wyner, A.D.: The Wire-tap channel. Bell Syst. Tech J. **54**(8), 1355–1387 (1975)
5. Chorti, A., Perlaza, S.M., Han, Z., Poor, H.V.: Physical layer security in wireless networks with passive and active eavesdroppers. In: Proceedings of IEEE Global Communications Conference (GLOBECOM), pp. 4868–4873 (2012)

6. Chen, H., Tao, X., Li, N., Xia, S., Sui, T.: Physical layer data analysis for abnormal user detecting: a random matrix theory perspective. IEEE Access **7**, 169508–169517 (2019)

7. Capozzi, F., Piro, G., Grieco, L.A., Boggia, G., Camarda, P.: Downlink packet scheduling in LTE cellular networks: key design issues and a survey. IEEE Commun. Surv. Tutor. **15**(2), 678–700 (2013)

8. Ma, J., Aijaz, A., Beach, M.: Recent results on proportional fair scheduling for mmWave-based industrial wireless networks. arXiv:2007.05820 (2020)

9. Margolies, R., et al.: Exploiting mobility in proportional fair cellular scheduling: measurements and algorithms. IEEE/ACM Trans. Netw. **24**(1), 355–367 (2016)

10. Zou, Y., Wang, X., Shen, W.: Physical-layer security with multiuser scheduling in cognitive radio networks. IEEE Trans. Commun. **61**(12), 5103–5113 (2013)

11. Yajun, W., Tongqing, L., Chuanan, W.: An anti-eavesdrop transmission scheduling scheme based on maximizing secrecy outage probability in ad hoc networks. China Commun. **13**(1), 176–184 (2016)

12. Firyaguna, F., Bonfante, A., Kibilda, J., Marchetti, N.: Performance evaluation of scheduling in 5G-mmWave networks under human blockage. arXiv:2007.13112v1 (2020)

13. Balakrishnan, S., Wang, P., Bhuyan, A., Sun, Z.: On success probability of eavesdropping attack in 802.11ad mmWave WLAN. In: Proceedings of IEEE International Conference on Communications (ICC), pp. 1–6 (2018)

14. Guo, C., Zhang, Y., Wang, X.: A Jain's index perspective on α fairness resource allocation over slow fading channels. IEEE Commun. Lett. **17**(4), 705–708 (2013)

15. Carfano, G., Murguia, H., Gudem, P., Mercier, P.: Impact of FR1 5G NR jammers on UWB indoor position location systems. In: Proceedings of International Conference on Indoor Positioning and Indoor Navigation (IPIN), pp. 1–8 (2019)

16. Jurafsky, D., Martin, J.H.: Hidden Markov Models. Speech and Language Processing, Draft of October 2, 2019

17. Sawant, R., Nema, S.: SNR analysis in cooperative spectrum sensing for cognitive radio. In: International Conference on Advances in Communication and Computing Technology (ICACCT). Sangamner 2018, pp. 392–396 (2018). https://doi.org/10.1109/ICACCT.2018.8529340

18. Armi, N., Saad, N.M., Zuki, Y.M., Arshad, M.: Cooperative spectrum sensing and signal detection in cognitive radio. In: 2010 International Conference on Intelligent and Advanced Systems, Kuala Lumpur, Malaysia, 2010, pp. 1–5. https://doi.org/10.1109/ICIAS.2010.5716151

19. Lauridsen, M., Berardinelli, G., Tavares, F.M.L., Frederiksen, F., Mogensen, P.: Sleep modes for enhanced battery life of 5G mobile terminals. In: The proceedings of IEEE Conference on Vehicular Technology (VTC) (2016)

20. Chang, B., Chen, J.: Cross-layer-based adaptive vertical handoff with predistive RSS in heterogeneous wireless networks. IEEE Trans. Veh. Technol. **57**(6), 3679–3692 (2008)

Joint Relay Selection and Frequency Allocation for D2D Communications

Rathindra Nath Dutta$^{(\boxtimes)}$ and Sasthi C. Ghosh

Indian Statistical Institute, Kolkata, India
{rathin_r,sasthi}@isical.ac.in

Abstract. High demand for bandwidth has been the primary motivation for device to device (D2D) communication. In cases where direct communication is not possible, two D2D devices are allowed to communicate via relay nodes. The relay selection problem is concerned with the selection of suitable relay device for each such D2D pairs while frequency assignment problem aims to optimally share the available spectrum resources among the active devices satisfying their quality of service requirements. In this work, we present a joint approach to solve the relay selection and frequency allocation problem in context of D2D communications. We incorporated a network coding strategy into our problem formulation which halves the required time slots for a two-way D2D communication. Considering the underlying problem is NP-Complete, we formulated a linear programming based greedy method which shows near-optimal performance with polynomial time complexity. We also compare our proposed algorithm with two existing works and show throughput improvement.

Keywords: D2D communications · Channel assignment · Relay selection

1 Introduction

The increase of various smart handheld devices, together with their bandwidth hungry applications like video calls, high definition television, video streaming services, mobile gaming etc., demand high data rate which is beyond the limits of conventional cellular network. To cope up with ever increasing data rate demands, several schemes for cooperative communication have already been proposed , chief among them being fixed terminal relaying through small base stations (BSs) to assist the communications [6]. Although these strategies show significant improvements in spectral and energy efficiency as well as in user quality-of-service (QoS), the current capacity is no where close to being enough to meet the required demand. To this end, communication using the millimeter-wave (mmWave) frequency has aroused considerable interest for providing device-to-device (D2D) communication in next generation cellular networks to provide such high data rate [13, 16].

© ICST Institute for Computer Sciences, Social Informatics and Telecommunications Engineering 2021
Published by Springer Nature Switzerland AG 2021. All Rights Reserved
X. Yuan et al. (Eds.): QShine 2021, LNICST 402, pp. 159–173, 2021.
https://doi.org/10.1007/978-3-030-91424-0_10

In D2D communications, two nearby devices are allowed to directly communicate with each other with limited or no involvement of BS. D2D communication enables dramatic improvements in spectral reuse. The close proximity of devices comes with the promises of higher data rates, lowers delays, and reduced power consumption. In fact, communicating with giga-Hertz frequencies having small wavelength, typically measured in millimeters, can offer very high speed data in the range of gigabits per second [13]. However, these signals suffer from higher transmission and penetration losses than their low frequency counterparts making them apt for close proximity communications [12].

In D2D communications, if the source and destination devices are not in the vicinity of one another or suffering from inferior direct link quality, it is possible to establish a D2D connection with one or more relay devices in between. More often than not, a relay based communication having a few shorter links offer more throughput than a traditional communication via the base station, thus such relay based D2D communications has gained popularity over the past few years. The full potential of cooperative communication can be utilized by device relaying [16]. A D2D device pai may have multiple candidate relay devices in its vicinity. Whereas, a relay device might be candidate for many D2D pairs, but it cannot serve more than one D2D pairs simultaneously. Figure 1a shows a sub-optimal scenario where relay R_2 is assigned to D2D pair A_1–A_2 whereas D2D pair B_1–B_2 has no relay allocated to it while relay R_1 is not utilized. In Fig. 1b relay R_1 has been assigned to D2D pair A_1–A_2 and relay R_2 is assigned to D2D pair B_1–B_2. Figure 1b thus depicts an ideal relay assignment for this example. By Fig. 1 it is evident that, optimal relay selection is a 2-dimensional matching problem where a D2D pair is matched with a suitable relay device, assuming a valid frequency allocation is always feasible.

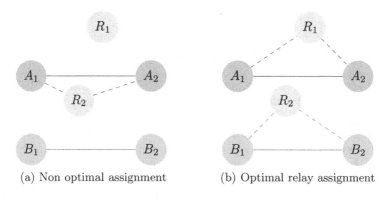

(a) Non optimal assignment   (b) Optimal relay assignment

Fig. 1. Optimal relay selection as matching problem

With limited number of available frequency channels in a licensed band and plenty of requesting D2D users in a service area, the spectrum sharing is a must and thus induces interference. The objective of the frequency channel allocation problem is to assign frequency channels to the requesting D2D users in such a way that their data rate requirements are satisfied. Consider the scenario given in Fig. 1b once again, assuming relay R_2 is in close proximity of the A_1–A_2 D2D pair, the QoS offered by the relay R_2 to the D2D pair B_1–B_2 is dependant of their frequency assignment. Therefore, the relay selection and frequency channel assignment are dependent on each other making them computationally hard to deal with. More precisely, the combined problem of relay selection and frequency allocation has been shown to be NP-complete [8].

Thus, the relay selection and frequency allocation must be dealt jointly, otherwise like in any multistage strategies, result of a former stage will heavily influence the quality of the solution obtained at the end of the subsequent stages. Even if one solves the former stage optimally there is no guaranty of it being part of the overall optimal solution of the joint problem. One can easily come up with instances where doing relay selection independent of frequency allocation in two stages produces non-optimal results and vice-versa.

Furthermore, a two-way communication via a relay, takes four time slots using store and forward method where the first two time slots are used to send data from one device of a D2D pair to the other via the intermediate relay device, and the subsequent two time slots are required to send data in the other direction. Application of efficient network coding can bring this down to two time slots [7], where the relay device receives data simultaneously from the two devices in a D2D pair in the first time slot and transmits back the combined data in the next time slot. Both the receivers receive the data simultaneously and decode its required data from it with negligible overhead.

In this work, we aim to maximize the number of activated links which in turn improves the overall system throughput for relay aided two-way D2D overlay communications. For this, we propose an algorithm to jointly solve the relay selection and frequency allocation problem for two-way communication with reduced time slots using network coding. We allow reusing a channel among many D2D pairs as long as the required signal to interference plus noise ratio (SINR) is satisfied. Our proposed algorithm is a greedy approach based on linear programming (LP) relaxation of the underlying hard problem. Simulation results show near optimal performance of our proposed algorithm in terms of number of links activated. We also show that our proposed algorithm outperforms a state-of-the-art classical algorithm as well as one recent algorithm in terms of overall system throughput.

The rest of the paper is organized as follows. The literature review is given in Sect. 2. Section 3 presents the system model. The joint problem formulation is given in Sect. 4. Our proposed solution is given in Sect. 5 followed by its simulation results in Sect. 6. We conclude this work with Sect. 7.

2   Related Works

In D2D communications, one of the challenging tasks is to optimally allocate resources to the devices [17]. The main objective of the frequency allocation and power control is to maximize the SINR or minimize the interference value to improve link quality. Channel assignment for orthogonal frequency division multiple access (OFDMA) based D2D systems has been studied in [5,8,16,17]. The resource allocation problem for D2D communications has been investigated in [3]. Here the problem has been solved in successive stages. It first selects admissible D2D pairs satisfying the QoS requirements and then allocates powers to the devices. Next, a maximum weight bipartite matching is employed to allocate frequency to each admissible D2D pair in order to maximize the overall system throughput.

In [5] authors have formulated a mode selection and resource allocation problem to maximize the system throughput of D2D and cellular links satisfying minimum rate requirements of the links. To solve this problem, optimal power requirements of the D2D links operating in the direct or relay mode have been calculated. Then, using these power allocations, the joint mode selection and relay assignment has been formulated as a job assignment problem whose optimal solution can be obtained in polynomial time. Various challenges for relay selection have been mentioned in [16]. Authors of [19] proposed a joint relay selection and resource allocation algorithm, which first allocates resources to relay links based on maximum received SINR values and then determines the optimal relay device fulfilling the QoS requirement of D2D users. In [9], authors formulated a mixed integer non-linear programming problem for the joint power and channel allocation in relay-assisted D2D communications and proposed two heuristic algorithms. One algorithm first allocates optimal powers to the links under given channel assignment followed by channel allocation, while the other one does the same in reverse order. In [4] authors proposed a two stage process for relay selection and resource allocation in which first the relay candidates are shortlisted by their position in the sectored cell and then relays and frequencies are selected. In [2], relaying based on D2D communication in an integrated mmWave 5G network has been considered. In [18], a coding technique has been used to improve reliability of the communication. Here first an integer non-linear programming problem has been formulated for the joint resource allocation, later it is converted into binary integer linear programming problem using a concept of D2D cluster and solved using branch-and-cut algorithm.

Both in [8] and [15], the joint relay selection along with related sub-channel and power allocation problem has been investigated. The proposed scheme in [8] first allocates power to the devices then formulates the relay selection and channel allocation problem as a 3-dimensional matching problem which is known to be NP-complete. They proposed an iterative technique to near-optimally solve the matching problem which decomposes the 3-dimensional matching problem into a sequence of 2-dimensional matching problems by fixing one dimension in each stage of an iteration. While in [15], authors aim to maximize the system throughput by considering the relay-aided communications. For this they have considered four subproblems, namely power control, relay selection with area division, mode selection, and finally link selection for activation.

Most of the studies above does not allow reusing the same channel among multiple D2D pairs. We also found that most of the works considers one-way communication scenarios, while many modern applications like video calling requires two-way communication in which high data rate is needed in both directions. In this work, we jointly deal with the problems of relay selection and frequency allocation for two-way communications, where we allow reusing the same channel among many D2D pairs as long as the required SINR is satisfied. Moreover, we make use of network coding to provide two-way communication with reduced time slots which in turn increases the number of activated links and hence the overall system throughput.

3   System Model

We assume a single cell BS controlled D2D overlay scenario where we have M pairs of D2D user equipments (UEs) and N number of idle UEs. Some of these D2D pairs can directly communicate with each other whereas others need an intermediate relay device for their communication. We are only considering one hop relay assisted D2D communications in such cases. We further assume that an idle UE can serve as a relay between only one D2D pair. Figure 2 depicts such a scenario. All these devices need to be allocated spectrum resources where we have F number of dedicated orthogonal sub-channels available for the D2D communications. We assume time is discretized into time slots $\{t_0, t_1, t_2, \dots\}$ with small Δt time span for each time slot. We denote a pair of successive time-slots as a *superslot*. We denote $\mathscr{D}$ as the set of D2D pairs requiring a relay and $\mathscr{D}'$ as the set of D2D pairs communicating directly.

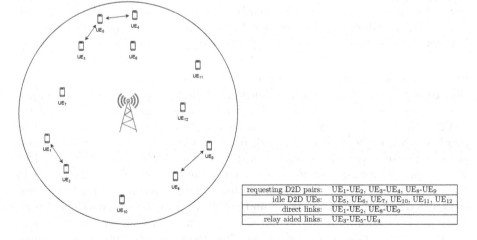

requesting D2D pairs:	UE_1-UE_2, UE_3-UE_4, UE_8-UE_9
idle D2D UEs:	UE_5, UE_6, UE_7, UE_{10}, UE_{11}, UE_{12}
direct links:	UE_1-UE_2, UE_8-UE_9
relay aided links:	UE_3-UE_5-UE_4

Fig. 2. System model

Mobility Consideration. We consider the nodes to be pseudo-stationary, that is they do not change their position for the duration of a superslot. As we solve the problem for a superslot, therefore their movement in between superslots do not affect our proposed solution. For a particular superslot, position of an UE can be determined with great accuracy [11] and is available to the BS.

Candidate Relays. Similar to [4] and [14], we assume all idle D2D UEs are capable and willing to participate in device relaying. Furthermore, we assume that a D2D pair can communicate among each other via a single relay making a one-hop relay assisted communication in cases where direct communication link is poor or does not exist. For a D2D pair, all idle devices within its vicinity, thus possibly having good SINR values, are eligible for being a candidate relay for that pair. An idle device can be in more than one such candidate list, but can only be assigned to a single D2D pair for relaying. We denote $\mathscr{R}$ to be the set of all candidate relay nodes in the service area.

Frequency Allocation. We need to allocate frequency channels to each of the D2D links and also to their relay link (if any). With limited number of frequency channels we need to employ frequency reuse keeping the SINR values above the required QoS threshold. We denote $\mathscr{F}$ to be the set of available orthogonal frequency channels.

Power Allocation and Channel Gain. We assume all transmitter devices are transmitting at a fixed power P. As in [3], for pathloss model we consider both the fast fading due to multi-path propagation and slow fading due to shadowing. Thus, the channel gain between device a and device b can be expressed as $h_{a,b} = K\beta_{a,b}\zeta_{a,b}L_{a,b}^{-\alpha}$, where K is a constant determined by system parameters, $\beta_{a,b}$ is fast fading gain with exponential distribution, $\zeta_{a,b}$ is the slow fading gain with log-normal distribution, α is the pathloss exponent, and $L_{a,b}$ is the distance between devices a and b.

Slot Reduction. In [7], it is shown that for a two-way communication it is possible to reduce number of required time slots by use of network coding technique. System requirements to support such channel coding is given in [1,7]. As shown in Fig. 3a it would take two time slots to send A's data to B via relay R and another two time slots for sending B's data to A via R. The data transmissions are denoted by directed arrows, marked with slot numbers, in the figure. But with proper network coding R can receive from both A and B simultaneously in one time slot and sends back the combined received data in the next time slot as depicted in Fig. 3b. Here both A and B receive the combined data simultaneously from R and decodes the required data from it. This shows a clear benefit in reduction of number of time slots from four to two which supersedes the small overheads incurred for use of this network coding [7]. We assume relay nodes have limited memory thus the data in a time slot must be sent out in next time slot. Our task thus reduces to solving the problem just for a single superslot.

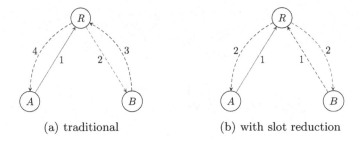

(a) traditional   (b) with slot reduction

Fig. 3. Slot reduction using network coding for two-way communication

Interference Consideration. Consider a D2D pair A-B communicating via a relay R. As shown in Fig. 4a, in the first time slot, both A and B will act as transmitter and R will act as receiver. Both A and B will contribute to interference of all other devices, such as P, receiving using the same frequency in which both A and B transmit. Similarly, all other devices, such as Q, transmitting in the same frequency will cause interference at R. Whereas in second time slot, receiving/transmitting role of the devices reverses. As shown in Fig. 4b, R now becomes transmitter and relays back the data to B and A, both of which are now in receiving mode. Thus A and B get interference from all other devices, such as P, transmitting using the same frequency. Similarly, R causes interference to all other devices, such as Q, receiving in the same frequency.

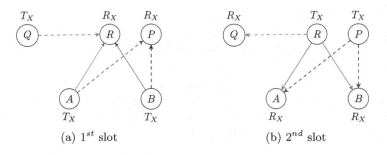

(a) 1st slot   (b) 2nd slot

Fig. 4. Interference from other transmitters for the two time slots

4 Problem Formulation

Assuming all devices transmit using fixed power P, we define received power from device a to device b as $R(a, b) = P \times h_{a,b}$. We define binary allocation matrices $X \in \{0,1\}^{|\mathscr{D}| \times |\mathscr{R}| \times |\mathscr{F}|}$ and $Y \in \{0,1\}^{|\mathscr{D}'| \times |\mathscr{F}|}$ of which entries $X_{i,r,f}$ and $Y_{k,f}$ are defined as follows.

$$X_{i,r,f} = \begin{cases} 1 & \text{if i-th D2D pair communicate via} \\ & \text{relay } r \text{ using frequency } f \\ 0 & \text{otherwise} \end{cases}$$

$$Y_{k,f} = \begin{cases} 1 & \text{if k-th D2D pair communicate directly} \\ & \text{using frequency } f \\ 0 & \text{otherwise} \end{cases}$$

We denote $i = (i_1, i_2)$ for a D2D pair i consisting of devices i_1 and i_2. In the first time slot, for a D2D pair $i = (i_1, i_2)$ communicating via relay r, both i_1 and i_2 act as the transmitters and r acts as the receiver. Even with all transmitters transmitting with same fixed power P, the received signal strength will vary due to different gain obtained at different positions. Thus to ensure *no buffering* is needed at the receiver r, the effective received power at r is set as the minimum of the received powers from the two transmitters i_1 and i_2, that is, $min(R(i_1, r), R(i_2, r))$. The total interference for D2D pair i from all other D2D pairs $j = (j_1, j_2) \in \mathscr{D}$ and $k = (k_1, k_2) \in \mathscr{D}'$ operating on the same frequency f is given in equation (1) where sum of received power from a D2D pair j to a device a is defined as $R_s(j, a) = R(j_1, a) + R(j_2, a)$.

$$Int_{i,r,f} = \sum_{\substack{j \in \mathscr{D} \ r' \in \mathscr{R} \\ j \neq i \ r' \neq r}} R_s(j,r)X_{j,r',f} + \sum_{k \in \mathscr{D}'} R(k_1,r)Y_{k,f} \tag{1}$$

Therefore, SINR for the D2D pair i communicating via relay r using frequency channel f can be given as

$$SINR_{i,r,f} = \frac{min(R(i_1,r), R(i_2,r))}{\eta_0 + Int_{i,r,f}}$$

where η_0 is the thermal noise. Furthermore, for D2D pair i the SINR value must be larger than or equal to the required SINR threshold th_i whenever $X_{i,r,f} = 1$. We can write this as linear inequalities (2) and (3), where M is a suitably large constant value, representing positive infinity.

$$(1 - X_{i,r,f})M + R(i_1, r) \geq (\eta_0 + Int_{i,r,f})th_i \tag{2}$$
$$(1 - X_{i,r,f})M + R(i_2, r) \geq (\eta_0 + Int_{i,r,f})th_i \tag{3}$$

In the second slot, the role of transmitters and receivers reverses. That is, both i_1 and i_2 act as the receivers and r acts as a transmitter. We calculate the interference at i_1 and i_2 in equations (4) and (5) respectively.

$$Int'_{i_1,r,f} = \sum_{\substack{j \in \mathscr{D} \ r' \in \mathscr{R} \\ j \neq i \ r' \neq r}} R(r', i_1)X_{j,r',f} + \sum_{k \in \mathscr{D}'} R(k_2, i_1)Y_{k,f} \tag{4}$$

$$Int''_{i_2,r,f} = \sum_{\substack{j \in \mathscr{D} \ r' \in \mathscr{R} \\ j \neq i \ r' \neq r}} R(r', i_2)X_{j,r',f} + \sum_{k \in \mathscr{D}'} R(k_2, i_2)Y_{k,f} \tag{5}$$

Thus effective SINR in second time slot is given as

$$SINR'_{i,r,f} = min\left(\frac{R(r,i_1)}{\eta_0 + Int'_{i_1,r,f}}, \frac{R(r,i_2)}{\eta_0 + Int''_{i_2,r,f}}\right).$$

This SINR value must also be larger than th_i whenever $X_{i,r,f} = 1$. We can similarly write this as linear inequalities (6) and (7).

$$(1 - X_{i,r,f})M + R(r,i_1) \geq (\eta_0 + Int'_{i_1,r,f})th_i \tag{6}$$

$$(1 - X_{i,r,f})M + R(r,i_2) \geq (\eta_0 + Int''_{i_2,r,f})th_i \tag{7}$$

For a D2D pair $k = (k_1, k_2)$ communicating directly using frequency f, interference at k_2 in slot 1 and at k_1 in slot 2 are given in equations (8) and (9) respectively.

$$Int'''_{k_2,f} = \sum_{i \in \mathcal{D}} \sum_{r \in \mathcal{R}} R_s(i,k_2)X_{i,r,f} + \sum_{\substack{k' \in \mathcal{D}' \\ k' \neq k}} R(k'_1,k_2)Y_{k',f} \tag{8}$$

$$Int''''_{k_1,f} = \sum_{i \in \mathcal{D}} \sum_{r \in \mathcal{R}} R(r,k_1)X_{i,r,f} + \sum_{\substack{k' \in \mathcal{D}' \\ k' \neq k}} R(k'_2,k_1)Y_{k',f} \tag{9}$$

Similarly, linear inequalities in (10) and (11) ensure SINR value for the D2D pair k communicating using frequency f is larger or equal to threshold th_k whenever $Y_{k,f} = 1$.

$$(1 - Y_{k,f})M + R(k_1,k_2) \geq (\eta_0 + Int'''_{k_2,f})th_k \tag{10}$$

$$(1 - Y_{k,f})M + R(k_2,k_1) \geq (\eta_0 + Int''''_{k_1,f})th_k \tag{11}$$

Inequality (12) ensures that a relay device can be used for at most one D2D pair and can transmit using a single frequency.

$$\sum_{i \in \mathcal{D}} \sum_{f \in \mathcal{F}} X_{i,r,f} \leq 1 \; \forall r \in \mathcal{R} \tag{12}$$

A D2D pair can have at most one relay and can transmit using a single frequency. This gives us the inequality (13). A D2D pair communicating directly also can transmit using a single frequency and gives inequality (14).

$$\sum_{r \in \mathcal{R}} \sum_{f \in \mathcal{F}} X_{i,r,f} \leq 1 \; \forall i \in \mathcal{D} \tag{13}$$

$$\sum_{f \in \mathcal{F}} Y_{k,f} \leq 1 \; \forall k \in \mathcal{D}' \tag{14}$$

We also have the integrality constraints (15) and (16).

$$X_{i,r,f} \in \{0,1\} \; \forall \, i \in \mathcal{D}, r \in \mathcal{R}, f \in \mathcal{F} \tag{15}$$

$$Y_{k,f} \in \{0,1\} \; \forall \, k \in \mathcal{D}', f \in \mathcal{F} \tag{16}$$

In order to maximize the number of links that can be activated together the following integer linear program (ILP) can be formulated.

$$\max \sum_{i \in \mathscr{D}} \sum_{r \in \mathscr{R}} \sum_{f \in \mathscr{F}} X_{i,r,f} + \sum_{k \in \mathscr{D}'} \sum_{f \in \mathscr{F}} Y_{k,f} \tag{17}$$

subject to constraints (2), (3), (6), (7) and (10) through (16).

5   Joint Relay Selection and Frequency Assignment

We begin with elimination of the allocation matrix Y by introducing a dummy virtual relay node r_k for each D2D pair $k = (k_1, k_2)$ in $\mathscr{D}'$ in order to simplify the equations. We set this virtual node r_k as the only relay candidate of this D2D pair k. While calculating SINR values, we consider position of r_k is same as transmitter k_1 for the first slot and the position is same as transmitter k_2 for the second slot. We set $\mathscr{D} = \mathscr{D} \cup \mathscr{D}'$ and $\mathscr{R} = \mathscr{R} \cup \{r_k \mid k \in \mathscr{D}'\}$. Now the purpose of Y matrix can be served with X matrix itself with updated dimensions. We also update the definition of received power for a transmit power P as follows.

$$R(a, b) = \begin{cases} \infty & \text{if } a \in \mathscr{D}' \text{ and } b = r_a \\ P \times h_{a,b} & \text{otherwise} \end{cases}$$

Interference calculations in (1), (4) and (5) thus reduces to (18), (19) and (20)

$$Int_{i,r,f} = \sum_{\substack{j \in \mathscr{D} \\ j \neq i}} \sum_{\substack{r' \in \mathscr{R} \\ r' \neq r}} [R(j_1, r) + R(j_2, r)] X_{j,r',f} \tag{18}$$

$$Int'_{i_1,r,f} = \sum_{\substack{j \in \mathscr{D} \\ j \neq i}} \sum_{\substack{r' \in \mathscr{R} \\ r' \neq r}} R(r', i_1) X_{j,r',f} \tag{19}$$

$$Int''_{i_2,r,f} = \sum_{\substack{j \in \mathscr{D} \\ j \neq i}} \sum_{\substack{r' \in \mathscr{R} \\ r' \neq r}} R(r', i_2) X_{j,r',f} \tag{20}$$

respectively and the objective function simplifies to

$$\max \sum_{i \in \mathscr{D}} \sum_{r \in \mathscr{R}} \sum_{f \in \mathscr{F}} X_{i,r,f} \tag{21}$$

We devise a linear programming relaxation based greedy algorithm to near optimally solve the problem. We start by relaxing the integrality constraints in (15) in order to allow the indicator variables to have fractional values between 0 and 1, as shown in Eq. (22).

$$X_{i,r,f} \in [0, 1] \; \forall \, i \in \mathscr{D}, r \in \mathscr{R}, f \in \mathscr{F} \tag{22}$$

We thus have an linear program (LP) with objective given in (21) subject to constraints (2), (3), (6), (7), (12), (13) and (22). Solving this relaxed LP we obtain

---

Algorithm 1: Relay Selection-Frequency Allocation

---

1   solve the relaxed LP to obtain solution vector $\tilde{X}$

2   apply rounding-off scheme on $\tilde{X}$ such that constraints (12), (13) and (22) are satisfied

3   create the frequency classes $\mathscr{C} = \{C_1, C_2, \ldots, C_{|\mathscr{F}|}\}$

4   set $\mathscr{L} = \phi$

5   **foreach** class $C_f \in \mathscr{C}$ **do**

6   **while** C_f not satisfying QoS constraints (2), (3), (6) and (7) **do**

7   **foreach** link $(i, r) \in C_f$ **do**

8   set $I_{i,r} = Int_{i,r,f} + Int'_{i_1,r,f} + Int''_{i_2,r,f}$

9   set $(\hat{i}, \hat{r}) = \arg \max_{(i,r) \in C_f} \{I_{i,r}\}$

10   set $C_f = C_f \setminus \{(\hat{i}, \hat{r})\}$ and $\mathscr{L} = \mathscr{L} \cup \{(\hat{i}, \hat{r})\}$

11   **while** $\mathscr{L} \neq \phi$ **do**

12   **foreach** link $(i, r) \in \mathscr{L}$ **do**

13   **foreach** $f \in \mathscr{F}$ **do**

14   **if** $C_f \cup \{(i, r)\}$ satisfies QoS constraint **then**

15   set $I_{i,r,f} = Int_{i,r,f} + Int'_{i_1,r,f} + Int''_{i_2,r,f}$

16   **else**

17              $I_{i,r,f} = \infty$

18   set $(\hat{i}, \hat{r}, \hat{f}) = \arg \min_{(i,r) \in \mathscr{L}, f \in \mathscr{F}} \{I_{i,r,f}\}$

19   **if** $I_{\hat{i}, \hat{r}, \hat{f}} \neq \infty$ **then**

20   update $C_{\hat{k}} = C_{\hat{k}} \cup \{(\hat{i}, \hat{r})\}$

21   update $\mathscr{L} = \mathscr{L} \setminus \{(\hat{i}, \hat{r})\}$

22   **return** $\mathscr{C}$

---

an allocation matrix X with fractional entries. We apply a simple rounding-off mechanism to change these fractional values to 0–1 integral values satisfying constraints (12) and (13). The resultant solution might not be a valid one with respect to the QoS constraints (2), (3), (6) and (7). Nevertheless, this gives us $|\mathscr{F}|$ frequency classes, $\mathscr{C} = \{C_1, C_2, \ldots, C_{|\mathscr{F}|}\}$, where C_f represents set of links are to be activated with frequency f. More precisely, we store (i, r) pairs in a C_f, denoting that i-th D2D pair is assigned relay r and transmits using frequency f. Admissibility of each such frequency class can be tested independently of other frequency classes using the QoS constraints (2), (3), (6) and (7). For each such C_f, disabling a few links might just satisfy the QoS constraints of the remaining links and thus can be activated with the same frequency f. We mark a link in C_f as *victim link* if it causes maximum interference to all other links in C_f. We remove this victim link into a common *discarded pool* of links $\mathscr{L}$ for later consideration. This removal of links is done iteratively until all links of C_f can be activated with same frequency f without violating QoS constraints. Repeating the same process for all the frequency classes, we can activate all of the remaining links in $\bigcup_{C_f \in \mathscr{C}} C_f$ together.

Now a link $l \in \mathscr{L}$ can be accommodated back into some frequency class C_f such that $C_f \cup \{l\}$ satisfies the QoS constraints. We should note that the order in which the links are reinserted has a significant impact on the number of links that can be activated together. Here again we employ a simple greedy scheme by iteratively finding the most *economical link* in $\mathscr{L}$ and inserting it into its most *economical frequency class* satisfying the QoS constraints. We call (l, f) the most economical link-class pair if link l incurs minimum interference into frequency class C_f for all such (l, f) pairs, where $l \in \mathscr{L}, C_f \in \mathscr{C}$. If for some link l no such accommodating frequency class satisfying the QoS constraints can be found, we permanently discard this link and move onto the next economical link. We continue this process until no new link can be admitted. The formal description of this proposed scheme is given in Algorithm 1.

Lemma 1. *Algorithm 1 terminates with a solution as good as any single frequency reuse algorithm.*

Proof. After the rounding-off we check for admissibility of each of the frequency classes and make necessary changes. This ensures that each frequency class must contain at least one link if not more. Thus, at this point, in terms of the number of D2D links activated, the solution obtained by our proposed method must be as large as any solution produced by any algorithm which consider only single use of a frequency channel. Furthermore, next we try to pack more links in the frequency classes which can only improve the solution and bring it closer to the optimal one. This iterative improvement process must terminate as we consider each of the remaining link only once.   □

6   Simulation Results

In this section we present the simulation results to demonstrate the performance of our proposed scheme. We have considered a single cell scenario similar to [15]. We take 5–20 D2D pairs and 200 idle D2D devices eligible for device relaying within a cell of 500 m. The maximum distance between a D2D pair is 50 m. Other channel parameters are also adapted from [15]. The maximum transmission power is 25 dBm, SINR threshold is 5 dB, thermal noise is −174 dBm/Hz and the pathloss exponent is 4.

For the comparison we choose two other algorithms namely iterative Hungarian method (IHM) [8] and uplink resource allocation (ULRA) [15] described in Sect. 2. Since both IHM and ULRA do not deal with network coding, for a fair comparison, we have considered a version of our algorithm which does not uses the network coding for slot reduction. We slightly modify our approach similar to [15] by halving the available bandwidth for a time slot in case of a relay aided communication. Since both IHM and ULRA reuse a channel allocated to a cellular user (CU) we consider the presence of 10 active CUs each using a unique orthogonal frequency channel similar to [15]. We assume the base station is placed at the center of the cells and CUs are distributed uniformly at random in the cell. For accurate measurements we ran these algorithm on 1000 random instances and took the average of them. Furthermore, to enable two-way communication we run these algorithm twice, once for the forward direction and on this result we run the algorithm a second time for the other direction. We only activate those links which are still feasible after the second round of execution. We compare the performance of our approach with these two algorithms in terms of number of links activated and total system throughput achieved with varying system load. By system load we imply the number of requesting D2D pairs. For throughput calculations we only select the links outputted by an algorithm for activation and apply the Shannon capacity formula. As depicted in Fig. 5 our proposed scheme outperforms both of these algorithms. This improvement can be attributed to the fact that we have considered the two problems jointly and allowed multiple frequency reuse.

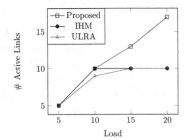 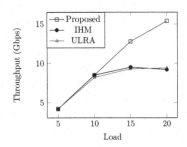

Fig. 5. Proposed vs IHM and ULRA without network coding

The true potential of our algorithm is observed when the network coding is enabled. For reference we also consider the *optimal* scheme where we directly solve the formulated ILP. Modern optimization solvers like Gurobi [10] can solve an ILP efficiently within reasonable amount of time for smaller instances. Figure 6 shows how well our proposed algorithm perform to achieve a near optimal solution in comparison to the optimal scheme.

The IHM algorithm has a running time of $O(jB^3)$, where $B = max(|\mathscr{D}|, |\mathscr{R}|, |\mathscr{F}|)$ and j is the number of iterations in IHM and the time complexity for ULRA is $O(|\mathscr{D}||\mathscr{R}||\mathscr{F}|)$. While our algorithm has a running time of $O(L)$ where L is the time complexity for solving the LP with $|\mathscr{D}||\mathscr{R}||\mathscr{F}|$ variables. Our algorithm has higher time complexity due to the fact that it allows multiple frequency reuse, while both IHM and ULRA allow only single reuse. Thus by jointly dealing the relay selection and frequency allocation problem with multiple frequency reuse our proposed algorithm results into improved system throughput. The use of network coding for slot reduction also plays a significant role in the throughput improvement.

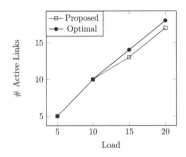
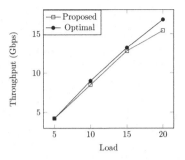

Fig. 6. Proposed vs *optimal* with network coding

7   Conclusion

We have addressed the joint relay selection and frequency allocation problem in a relay aided D2D communication and devised a LP relaxation based greedy strategy. The simulation results shows that our proposed scheme solves the problem near-optimally. Moreover, our algorithm outperforms the IHM and ULRA algorithms in terms of system throughput. This improvement can be attributed to the fact that we have jointly dealt the two problems unlike solving it in multiple stages like in IHM or ULRA algorithm. Moreover using the network coding scheme for slot reduction also contribute in throughput improvements. Lastly, instead of single reuse of frequencies, our proposed scheme allows multiple reuse to further improve the system throughput.

References

1. Chen, P., Xie, Z., Fang, Y., Chen, Z., Mumtaz, S., Rodrigues, J.J.P.C.: Physical-layer network coding: an efficient technique for wireless communications. IEEE Netw. **34**(2), 270–276 (2020). https://doi.org/10.1109/MNET.001.1900289
2. Deng, J., Tirkkonen, O., Freij-Hollanti, R., Chen, T., Nikaein, N.: Resource allocation and interference management for opportunistic relaying in integrated mmWave/sub-6 GHz 5G networks. IEEE Commun. Mag. **55**(6), 94–101 (2017). https://doi.org/10.1109/MCOM.2017.1601120
3. Feng, D., Lu, L., Yuan-Wu, Y., Li, G.Y., Feng, G., Li, S.: Device-to-device communications underlaying cellular networks. IEEE Trans. Commun. **61**(8), 3541–3551 (2013). https://doi.org/10.1109/TCOMM.2013.071013.120787
4. Gu, X., Zhao, M., Ren, L., Wu, D., Nie, S.: A two-stages relay selection and resource allocation with throughput balance scheme in relay-assisted D2D system. Mob. Netw. Appl. **22**(6), 1020–1032 (2017)
5. Hoang, T.D., Le, L.B., Le-Ngoc, T.: Joint mode selection and resource allocation for relay-based D2D communications. IEEE Commun. Lett. **21**(2), 398–401 (2017). https://doi.org/10.1109/LCOMM.2016.2617863
6. Hoymann, C., Chen, W., Montojo, J., Golitschek, A., Koutsimanis, C., Shen, X.: Relaying operation in 3GPP LTE: challenges and solutions. IEEE Commun. Lett. **50**(2), 156–162 (2012). https://doi.org/10.1109/MCOM.2012.6146495

7. Huang, J., Gharavi, H., Yan, H., Xing, C.: Network coding in relay-based device-to-device communications. IEEE Netw. **31**(4), 102–107 (2017). https://doi.org/10.1109/MNET.2017.1700063

8. Kim, T., Dong, M.: An iterative Hungarian method to joint relay selection and resource allocation for D2D communications. IEEE Wirel. Commun. Lett. **3**(6), 625–628 (2014). https://doi.org/10.1109/LWC.2014.2338318

9. Liu, M., Zhang, L.: Joint power and channel allocation for relay-assisted device-to-device communications. In: 2018 15th International Symposium on Wireless Communication Systems (ISWCS), pp. 1–5 (2018). https://doi.org/10.1109/ISWCS.2018.8491059

10. LLC, G.: Gurobi optimization LLC (2021). http://www.gurobi.com

11. Moore, S.K.: Superaccurate GPS chips coming to smartphones in 2018 (2017). https://spectrum.ieee.org/tech-talk/semiconductors/design/superaccurate-gps-chips-coming-to-smartphones-in-2018

12. Pi, Z., Khan, F.: An introduction to millimeter-wave mobile broadband systems. IEEE Commun. Mag. **49**(6), 101–107 (2011). https://doi.org/10.1109/MCOM.2011.5783993

13. Qiao, J., Shen, X.S., Mark, J.W., Shen, Q., He, Y., Lei, L.: Enabling device-to-device communications in millimeter-wave 5G cellular networks. IEEE Commun. Mag. **53**(1), 209–215 (2015). https://doi.org/10.1109/MCOM.2015.7010536

14. Sarkar, S., Ghosh, S.C.: Relay selection in millimeter wave D2D communications through obstacle learning. Ad Hoc Netw. **114**, 102419 (2021)

15. Sun, J., Zhang, Z., Xing, C., Xiao, H.: Uplink resource allocation for relay-aided device-to-device communication. IEEE Trans. Intell. Transp. Syst. **19**(12), 3883–3892 (2018). https://doi.org/10.1109/TITS.2017.2788562

16. Tehrani, M.N., Uysal, M., Yanikomeroglu, H.: Device-to-device communication in 5G cellular networks: challenges, solutions, and future directions. IEEE Commun. Mag. **52**(5), 86–92 (2014). https://doi.org/10.1109/MCOM.2014.6815897

17. Yu, G., Xu, L., Feng, D., Yin, R., Li, G.Y., Jiang, Y.: Joint mode selection and resource allocation for device-to-device communications. IEEE Trans. Commun. **62**(11), 3814–3824 (2014). https://doi.org/10.1109/TCOMM.2014.2363092

18. Zhao, Y., Li, Y., Chen, X., Ge, N.: Joint optimization of resource allocation and relay selection for network coding aided device-to-device communications. IEEE Commun. Lett. **19**(5), 807–810 (2015). https://doi.org/10.1109/LCOMM.2015.2401557

19. Zhengwen, C., Su, Z., Shixiang, S.: Research on relay selection in device-to-device communications based on maximum capacity. In: 2014 International Conference on Information Science, Electronics and Electrical Engineering, vol. 3, pp. 1429–1434, April 2014. https://doi.org/10.1109/InfoSEEE.2014.6946156

IoT Security and Lightweight Cryptography

Chaos and Logistic Map Based Key Generation Technique for AES-Driven IoT Security

· Ziaur Rahman[1(✉)], Xun Yi[1], Ibrahim Khalil[1], and Mousumi Sumi[2]

[1] RMIT University, Melbourne, VIC 3000, Australia
{rahman.ziaur,xun.yi,ibrahim.khalil}@rmit.edu.au
[2] DSI Ltd., Dhaka 1206, Bangladesh
mousumi.sumi@dsinnovators.com

Abstract. Several efforts has been seen claiming the lightweight block ciphers as a necessarily suitable substitute in securing the Internet of Things. Currently, it has been able to envisage as a pervasive frame of reference almost all across the privacy preserving of smart and sensor oriented appliances. Different approaches are likely to be inefficient, bringing desired degree of security considering the easiness and surely the process of simplicity but security. Strengthening the well-known symmetric key and block dependent algorithm using either chaos motivated logistic map or elliptic curve has shown a far reaching potentials to be a discretion in secure real-time communication. The popular feature of logistic maps, such as the un-foreseeability and randomness often expected to be used in dynamic key-propagation in sync with chaos and scheduling technique towards data integrity. As a bit alternation in keys, able to come up with oversize deviation, also would have consequence to leverage data confidentiality. Henceforth it may have proximity to time consumption, which may lead to a challenge to make sure instant data exchange between participating node entities. In consideration of delay latency required to both secure encryption and decryption, the proposed approach suggests a modification on the key-origination matrix along with S-box. It has plausibly been taken us to this point that the time required proportionate to the plain-text sent while the plain-text disproportionate to the probability happening a letter on the message made. In line with that the effort so far sought how apparent chaos escalates the desired key-initiation before message transmission.

Keywords: Internet of Things · AES modification · Key generation matrix · Logistic map

1 Introduction

Internet of Things (IoT) has its security issue which been able to pass its new born and infant stage and successfully entered into teenage stage [1,6,9]. Though

Supported by RMIT RTS Program.

X. Yuan et al. (Eds.): QShine 2021, LNICST 402, pp. 177–193, 2021.
https://doi.org/10.1007/978-3-030-91424-0_11

it was born a several decades earlier than Advance Encryption Standard (AES), enabling these two different generation strangers sitting together with a view to confluencing each other has also been just out as well [2,3]. Thus thinking that they are capable of co-aiding themselves especially through an aspect of data integrity and confidentiality has also not yet promisingly embraced with any noteworthy testament from any credible sources so forth known to us. In the face of extensive dubiety that often leads to a certain degree of perplexity among research community, Logistic Map incorporated AES has been emerged as a self-definable safe-guard to abolish the possible gap in the IoT security challenges [5,8]. It has already been able to show its potentials in particular in this field by super-setting secure smart device authentication to ensure strong communication, decentralized data formulation or even automatic data purchasing. Thus, it is conceivably estimated that an emerging phenomenon of IoT utensils would be able to equip with the internet to ease the coming security aspect of intelligible and straightforward encryption and decryption. In IoT cluster head is device on the network contributes to reliable data transmission which in response accepts information before processing and encrypting them as well. We propose this algorithm can be applied on the cluster head of simple IoT network. Though heterogeneous complex network architecture has been rapidly evolving day by day, the flexibility deserves properly concerned as more often micro-shaped sensor devices are necessarily required in this area of security and privacy [13,14]. Fig. 1 shows how Advanced Encryption Standard (AES) secures data generated from IoT sensors. However, though AES has proven security strength, its key generation technique can be broken if there is a desired computation system. Therefore, using conventional AES for critical and real-time data security brings challenges to data integrity. From the motivation of improving the AES key generation technique, the proposed paper claims contributions as follows.

1. It increases the Key generation complexity, thus reduces the chances of breaking the keys. Instead of incorporating conventional two-dimensional S-box, the proposed key generation technique uses the 3-Dimensional Key Generation Mechanism (3DKGM). To make it robust and usuable it is designed based on Chaos cryptography and Logistic Map.
2. The proposed technique can preserve the integrity of sensitive IoT data. The sensor should have the necessary computation capacity to adapt to the proposed system.
3. The coding-based empirical and extensive evaluation justifies the proposed technique's security strength compared to similar approaches.

The rest of the paper is organized as follows; Sect. 2 illustrates the background and related works. The following section includes the required technical preliminaries and the Applicability of Chaos-based key generation. Then Sect. 4 explains the proposed technique. Lastly, the paper consists of an empirical evaluation and initial cryptanalysis based on 3DKGM S-box. Finally, it concludes with the prospects of the paper.

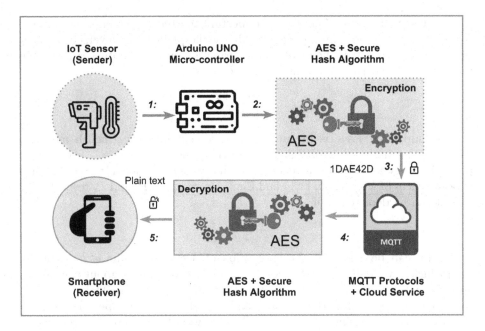

Fig. 1. How Advanced Encryption Standard (AES) is used to secure data generated from IoT sensors received by a smartphone.

2 Background and Related Works

The following portion of the paper briefly explains the issues with the Symmetric Key algorithms focusing the Latency Challenges. Applying the symmetric-key algorithm in securing Internet of Things has been encountered enormous challenges [4,13], including potentials and opportunity. For the brevity only the succinct issues have been outlined hereby.

2.1 Latency Challenges

A simple encryption algorithm can be represented as following:

$$Y = E_z X \tag{1}$$

Where X is plaintext, Y is cryptogram, Z is a secret key, and E_z is an encryption algorithm. To make any encryption algorithm workable on the devices associated, better it to simple and straightforward when we are in a time of introducing unfathomable advanced algorithms every day. In this area of secure communication certainly the principle concern should be required time to encrypt and decrypt the text messages. Long time latency during this process may slow down system thus it decreases feasibility and usability of the system. It is known that each bit of plaintext conveys information. In addition to this it is even said that probability issue may help information achieving low latency. If it is said, 'Today solar eclipse will occur', then it is an important matter, so the information of it is higher than the normal day. So, the bits of the plaintext is inversely proportional to occurring it. If the amount of information on the plaintext is I and the probability of occurrence of that event is P, then

$$I = f(x) = \begin{cases} 0 & if \quad P = 1 \\ 1 & if \quad P = 0 \end{cases} \tag{2}$$

The important issue is presuming that, almost in every English message, letters are having a low probability of occurring such as q, v, w, x, z lead to this point that they have low occurrence probability in accordance. If the probability of occurrences of letters z and r in and English message is P_z and P_r respectively, then it can be depicted as if-

$$P_r \leq P_z \tag{3}$$

It also can be said that the encryption of decryption time is much lower than which have higher probabilities. Not necessarily thinking about encryption and decryption time of letters has lower likelihood to occur. The concern of the proposed approach is those have a higher possibility to happen should have the reason for increasing the latency. Thus we would come up to introduce an algorithm that might be helping latency reduction for the letters with higher probability from a given message. We suggest that the letters have multiple occurrences may have the possibility in the text-message where maximum two letters will generate. In this situation, the popularly known $LZ78$ Algorithm [26] which will be described in the later section, has been considered to decrease the time of these types of letters.

2.2   Related Works

There are several efforts have been made in the area application of the symmetric-key encryption techniques to make sure secure data communication considering lightweight [15,32] and simplification approach [5,10]. Baptista was one those [18] applied the concept of chaos [22] in the area of cryptography [23,24]. Some other authors [27,28] proposed if he could encrypt a message using low dimensional and chaotic logistic map though it was one-dimensional [25,26]. Another work proposed to apply a single block of text message text, and it had low number of iterations and took longer time [16,21]. For data encryption algorithm, chaotic map is one of the best ways of encryption for the high sensitivity of its initial condition [6]. In the continuous-time chaotic dynamic systems, poor synchronization and high noise problems may occur [7]. So far, logistic map is a 2-D chaotic map, but, more than logistic map, discretized 2-D chaotic maps are invented such as cat map, baker map and standard map [27] But the cat map and baker map have security issues, the other one [26,28] the standard map are not thoroughly analyzed yet. LZ78 algorithm on the cryptography has been recently employed. It is used for source coding for lossless data compression [12,15]. Many more types of research have been done using LZ78 algorithm. But it is a rare case to use it as an application in the field of cryptography. Therefore, considering the chaotic properties, we have applied logistic map along with dynamic key generation matrix called 3-Dimensional Key Generation Matrix [19] to bring chaotic behavior inside. We are using it because we need faster and complex calculations to secure the algorithm and make it faster than before. The previous algorithm [19] secure with complex behavior, but we need more complex and faster procedures to cope with modern technology. So, we are dealing with chaos [20].

3   Technical Preliminaries and Applicability

In response to the challenges outlined earlier, the next portion of the paper shows how several existing approaches incorporate AES for data integrity purpose. And the following sections explains the applicability of the Chaos based technique namely *LZ78* algorithm.

3.1   Applying AES

Now thinking about the prominent algorithm, one of the most common and ever robust encryption algorithms called Advanced Encryption Standard (AES) even though it was broken many times. Day by day, new and excellent modification approaches got invented and adapted to secure AES as well as to upgrade the accuracy, intruders, and their unauthorized access of information has become a typical phenomenon with the evolution of smart technology. Chaos based security [20] has been an essential concern in security research because of its randomness and unpredictability. User may not get any prior knowledge about initial condition means to discover desired key. A small variation will change the whole result; for example, modification 1 bit on plain text or key would bring a change the result nearly 50%. Chaos-based cryptosystems are flexible for massive scale data such as audio and video in compare to the referred cryptosystems. Many authors have been trying to implement chaos in the existing cryptosystem [3,20]. Chaos is dealt with the real numbers [4], where other cryptographic methods deal with number of integers [5]. Thus, a chaos-based approach in the key-generation process could make the system much safer.

3.2   Chaos Algorithms

Chaos is fully exploited in the chaos-based cryptography. We can easily and safely transfer information using one dimensional logistic map [18,20,23]. The critical characteristics of chaos are to generate different intricate patterns and results in creating a large number of data by the mathematical model. These data can be used as secret keys [24]. The following procedures as shown in Fig. 2 are essential to stepping in the cryptographic algorithm-

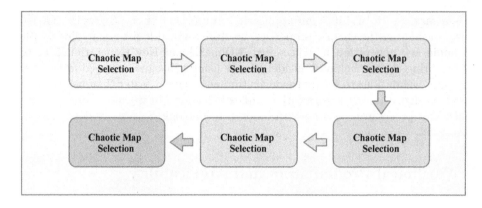

Fig. 2. A flow diagram of a generic Chaos Algorithm

3.3   LZ78 Algorithm

LZ78 is a universal lossless data compression algorithm [26]. But we are going to use here to decrease the time of decryption. Because generally, the proposed algorithm is taking time in decrypting instead encrypting. Another problem is the decrypted result is not sometimes indexed correctly on the decrypted message. So, we are going to use *LZ*78 for proper indexing. It works from finding the probability of each letter of the text-message. A percentage will be generated to find out higher occurrence of a letter and lowest occurrence of letter. So, now if the message is 'I Love to read book', then the encrypted message using *LZ*78 will be 'I Love to read bo20k'. But, in this way the bits will be too significant than the actual message's bits, which is not feasible. So, we modified this idea; rather than using *LZ*78 on letters, we are going to use it on each word of sentence. We are correctly indexing the word so that we could properly indexing the same words in a sentence. According to this concept, the above mentioned message will be the same 'I Love to read book' because no other word is identical here. If the text-message is 'Development process is a long process which helps to occur welfare development', then the message using *LZ*78 is 'Development process is a long2 process which helps to occur welfare 1development'. We have organized the remaining of this paper as follows. In Sect. 2, a brief literature review of the chaotic standard map as discussed. The properties of analyzing it and a standard map for using in this paper is presented. The logic for choosing a logistic map and the key-generation process we proposed, and its working procedure as discussed in Sect. 3. In Sect. 4, algorithm selection for correcting position of the whole message. In Sect. 4, choosing logistic map and steps of key generating is discussed, and empirical evaluation and cryptanalysis is done in Sect. 5. Finally, in Sect. 6, some conclusions are drawn.

4 Proposed Key Management Technique

Handling the security in IoT environment is a challenging thing because of low power distribution, distributed nature, and no standardization. A concern of designing a security system is to assume that all the algorithms of cryptography are known to the attackers. Kerckhoffs's principle says that 'secrecy of the key provides security.' So, a key is more comfortable to protect from attacker than keeping secret the algorithm. And it is also a wise thing to keep confidential the key as it is a small piece of information. But trying to keep the keys secret is a challenging matter because a management system exists named 'Key management.' Key management is nothing but deals with the creation, modification, alternation, storage, practice, and replacement of keys; that means has access to internal access of keys. The critical management concerns not only the essentials of user level but also for the exchanges between end users. So, an algorithm is needed to interrupt the internal mechanism of key management procedure. Instead of using one key, nowadays more keys are generated, which are entirely dependent on each other. That may damage the security breach. So, this is the headache of today's technology too. And the other one is brute force attack, which is bound in length of the key. To make the algorithm free from the brute force attack, [19] has experimented with it that may help to overcome it. This paper is concern about the increase the security breach where the key generated from the logistic map and keys are not wholly dependent on each other.

4.1 Choosing Algorithm for Accurate Positioning

Paper [1] works on AES, build a new key generation process using the 3DKGM matrix and S-box; both are three dimensional. All reduce the encrypting and decrypting time than existing AES because it tears off all the techniques that take time. But this paper uses RES method which is one of the most powerful and costing algorithms ever. Adding these operations to AES, the proposed algorithm gets additional computation to run and subsequently takes significant time. Although it has ensured about less timing, but this article aims at reducing the encrypting and decrypting the time than some other approaches. An encrypting algorithm is well-known when it concerns with both security and computational time (encrypting and decrypting time). To achieve both features, we have applied *LZ78* algorithm properties and chaos theory. However, Advanced Encryption Standard (*AES*) is one of the common block cipher algorithms, and the algorithm we propose deals with 35 bits, which is too long. After using *s-box* and *3DKGM* [19], these huge number of bits turns into 744 bits which is also long to handle with. But, we find the lowest and highest probability before applying LZ78 Algorithm on resulting plaintext. The word with the lowest probability is not created any big deal, but it will create big deal to the occurrence of highest probability. For example, if the message is 'JONNY, your public key is equivalent to your address where you will receive cryptocurrency. So, keep your public key secret not to be interrupted on cryptocurrency.' Now, the idea is that we have to find out lowest and highest probability of each word in a sentence and replace the higher probability with times of occurring in a sentence. As shown in the Table 1, the output for first sentence is $(0, JONNY,)$ $(0, your)$ $(0, public)$ $(0, key)$ $(0, is)$ $(0, equivalent)$ $(0, to)$ $(2, your)$ $(0, address)$ $(0, where)$ $(0, you)$ $(0, will)$ $(0, receive)$ $(0, cryptocurrency.)$ $(0, So,)$ $(0, keep)$ $(0, your)$ $(0, public)$ $(0, key)$ $(0, secret)$ $(0, to)$ $(0, not)$ $(7, to)$ $(0, be)$ $(0, interrupted)$ $(0, on)$ $(0, cryptocurrency)$.

Table 1. The LZ78 for the word 'JONNY, your public key is equivalent to your address where you will receive cryptocurrency'

Output	Index	String
(0, JONNY,)	1	JONNY,
(0, your)	2	your
(0, public)	3	public
(0, key)	4	key
(0, is)	5	is
(0, equivalent)	6	Equivalent
(0, to)	7	To
(2, your)	8	Your
(0, address)	9	Address
(0, where)	10	Where
(0, you)	11	You
(0, will)	12	Will
(0, receive)	13	Receive
(0, cryptocurrency)	14	cryptocurrency

Now the plaintext that is processed removing '0' is 'JONNY; your public key is equivalent to 2your address you will receive cryptocurrency'. So, 'keep your public key secret to not 7to be interrupted on cryptocurrency.' Now, it seems it taking a few bits more than real message, but it will be conducive for decrypting message.

4.2   Choosing Logistic Map and Steps of Key Generating

Different types of logistic maps have been proposed, and those are feasible. But to choose one, it must have three properties, such as-Mixing Property, Robust Chaos, Large Parameter [10]. By analyzing all the properties, we are going to use traditional logistic map. The equation is:

$$X_{n+1} = rX_n(1 - X_n) \tag{4}$$

Where X_n lies between zero and one, and the interval for r is $[0, 4]$. But, for the highly chaotic case, we are going to use $r = 3.9999$. A key is the head

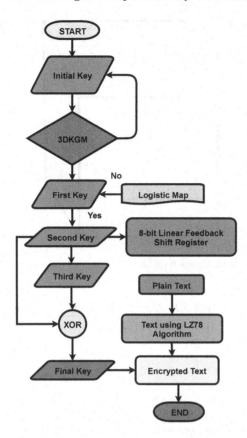

Fig. 3. Proposed key generating approach using Chaos

of any block cipher encryption algorithm. In [19], a fundamental generation matrix named *3DKGM* (3-Dimensional Key Generation Matrix), which is the combination of Latin alphabets, integers, and Greek values used. Now, we want to extend the operation by using chaos. The reason is no one can get any prior knowledge about key. We are using here three keys. The first key gives birth of 1st key using *3DKGM* [19]. The matrix looks like Fig. 4. The whole procedure of generating key is shown in Fig. 3.

4.3   First Key Generation Process

To use the matrix in the encryption algorithm is one of the tricky tasks. This type of job is building 3-Dimensional Key Generation Matrix. Let consider a secret key: '$POLY12@ + \alpha\mu$'. At first, we have to declare the position of each byte. Then by using Fig. 4, we will get the first key, k_1. The procedure of getting this value as described in [19]. But it is needed to add that if any byte is missing from the table, three zero get replaced for the corresponding byte. The First Key generation process is depicted by Listing 1.1.

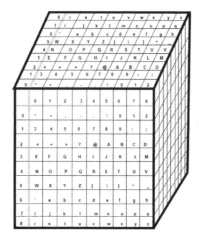

Fig. 4. 3-Dimensional Key Generation Matrix (*3DKGM*) [19]

Listing 1.1. Pseudocode foro Algorithm 1: First Key Generation Process

```
1  int cycle=0;      algorithm starts
2  for(int f=0;f<iniKey.length();f++) do
3  if(f<9) do cycle=f; end
4  if(f>=9) do cycle=0+cyy;
5          cyy++; end
6  if(f>=18) do cycle=0+cyy1;
7              cyy1++; end
8  if(f>26) do cycle=0+cyy2;
9              cyy2++; end
10 if(f>=36) do cycle=0+cyy2;cycle=0+cyy3;
11             cyy3++; end
12 for(i=0;i<9;i++) do for(k=0;k<9;k++)
13         do for(k=0;k<9;k++)
14             do if(arr1[i][j][k]==iniKey.charAt(f))
15                 do hold1 = i;
16                     hold2=j;end
17             end
18     end
19 end     algorithm ends
```

$k1 = 42, 41437C52G07U08\_24d01j000000$. Now, we have to calculate the initial condition from the logistic map.

4.4 Find the Initial Condition from Logistic Map

To find the initial condition X_0 from the logistic map, we have to choose first three blocks of first key. That is 42. And then convert it into corresponding binary number. For 4 = 00110100 (*B1*), for 2 = 00110010 (*B2*) and for , = 00101100 (*B3*). The mathematical representation of logistic map is

$$X_i = X_{i,j} \ where \ j = 1, 2$$

$$X_{01} = \frac{(B_1 + B_2 + B_3)}{2^{24}}$$

$$= (0 \times 2^0 + 0 \times 2^1 + 1 \times 2^2 + 1 \times 2^3 + 0 \times 2^4 + 1 \times 2^5 + 0 \times 2^6 + 0 \times 2^7)$$
$$+ (0 \times 2^0 + 0 \times 2^1 + 1 \times 2^2 + 1 \times 2^3 + 0 \times 2^4 + 0 \times 2^5 + 1 \times 2^6 + 0 \times 2^7)$$
$$+ (0 \times 2^0 + 0 \times 2^1 + 1 \times 2^2 + 1 \times 2^3 + 0 \times 2^4 + 0 \times 2^5 + 1 \times 2^6 + 0 \times 2^7)/2^{24}$$

$$= 1.025 \times 10^{-05} \ (decimal)$$

To calculate X_{02}, we need $4, 5, 6, 7, 8$ and 9 blocks of the first key which is $41437C$.

$$X_{02} = \frac{(B_4 + B_5 + B_6 + B_7 + B_8 + B_9)}{16 \times 6}$$

$$= \frac{(00110100 + 00110001 + 00110100 + 00110011 + 00110111 + 01000011)}{96}$$

$$= 11$$

$$= 3 \ (decimal)$$

Therefore,

$$X_0 = (X_{01} + X_{02}) \ mod \ 1$$
$$= 3 \ (decimal)$$
$$== 00000011 \ (binary)$$

For the next cycle, X_{01} will count from $B_{previous\_cycle} + 3$ to $B_{previous\_cycle} + 5$. For the next cycle, X_{02} will count from $B_{previous\_cycle} + 6$ to $B_{previous\_cycle} + 10$.

4.5 Second and Third Key Generation Process

Now, we will run several cycles to generate each byte of the second and third keys. From the above, we have found that

$$k_1 = 42, 41437C52G07U08\_24d01j000000.$$

Now, we are taking the first block of first key which is $4 \ (ASCII) = 00110100$. From X_0, we have got the value is 3, the binary value is 0000011. So, $X_0 = 0000011$. Now, adding both of these binary values, we will get new key K_2:

$$00000011$$
$$(+) \ \ 00110100$$
$$\overline{K_2 = 00110111}$$

To generate K_3, we need the help of K_2 and $8 - bit$ linear feedback shift register. The functionality of $8 - bit$ linear feedback shift register is to X-or the bits named D_0, D_4, D_5, D_6. After this operation, the answer is 0. Now, we will do left shift operation on second key, that is, 0110111. Then to put the bit on the right after $X - or$ operation: 01101110. That is our desired third key, $K_3 = 01101110$. Figure 5(a) demonstrates the process.

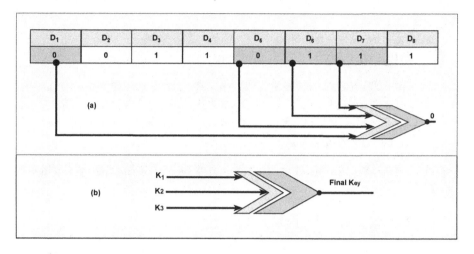

Fig. 5. (a) 8-bit linear feedback shift register (b) Generating final byte of the key

4.6 The Final Key

After doing $X - or$ operation on the first key, second key, and third key, the first byte of final key will get generated. The final result is $01101110YYYYYYYY$. So, this is the operation for one byte. Several bytes will get generated by using initial condition X_0 and the next byte of first key. Until the initial-key is covered, cycle will continue. After that plaintext and key will get into $x - or$ operation and follow the procedure from [19]. Therefore, each time, it generates bytes of key one by one. At last, It has to concatenate all the byte to build the final key which is going to the next step of encryption algorithm. Figure 5(b) illustartes the Final key building process.

5   Initial Cryptanalysis and Empirical Evaluation

The primary question of cryptography is security. The solution must be find theoretically and practically. The objectives of theoretical analysis are: increasing its randomness and computationally unpredictable. The objectives of practical analysis are to check up the above properties. In [1], we have used a key generation matrix named 3-Dimensional Key Generation Matrix. It is a static matrix which has a very similar working procedure with S-box. In [11], for every 11- round trail, it has 17 active S-boxes, so, the differential trails.

$$DP \leq (2^{-4.678})^{17} \approx 2^{-79}$$

By analyzing this, we can also get a conclusion for the key in case of differential attacks and linear-attacks, as the trail of using 3DKGM depends on the length of initial key. As we use here the key is $POLY12@ + \alpha\mu$, we have to use

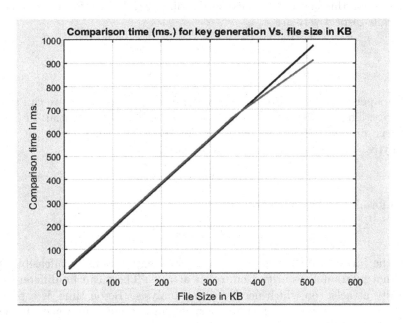

Fig. 6. Time-comparison of 2 Key generation techniques based on Table 2.

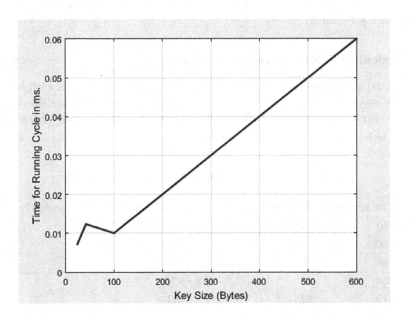

Fig. 7. Key size vs time for the cycle running based on Table 3.

the matrix for this key is 10 times, so the differential trails for 10 rounds and linear trails respectively are -

$$DP \leq (2^{-4.678})^{15} \approx 2^{-70}$$
$$LP \leq (2^{-4})^{15} \approx 2^{-60}$$

The paper [19] used 26 rounds to gain ciphertext. Using [10], we can answer its security. The standard security attacks are linear and differential. In [10], 18 round has minimum 27 active bytes, so, for these 26 rounds in [19], it has 24 active bytes. Therefore, 26 rounds of differential trails.

$$DP \leq (2^{-4.678})^{24} \approx 2^{-112}$$

And for all 26 rounds linear trails

$$LP \leq (2^{-4})^{24} \approx 2^{-96}$$

So, the linear and differential attacks are computationally infeasible. But it does not guarantee security from other attacks. There can be different type of security attacks too which needs further analysis. 'Be on time' is a popular quote today. So, timing is a fact to encrypt and decrypt a message. As key is an essential and unavoidable part, so, it is needed to keep in mind to generate it at the lowest time. But, if it is taking a short time, then there may exist risk and can be broken by brute force process. Chaos is the best with the existing algorithm [19] to secure from all kinds of approaches. For experimental analysis, we use java for coding.

5.1 Calculating Key Generation Time

In this part, a comparison result of our proposed approach is shown with existing one. We have performed with different sizes of files and calculate the time of computation that shows the performance before and after adding chaos in the existing algorithm's essential Generation process.

Table 2. Key generation time vs. file size based on [19]

File size (KB)	3DKGM key gen. (ms)	Proposed chaos (ms) approach
10	19	26
30	57	67
155	295	301
350	665	671
512	973	911

Table 3. Time for running cycle for a specific key size

Key size (bytes)	Time for running cycle (ms)
24	0.0072
41	0.0123
100	0.01
255	0.02555
300	0.003
600	0.006

Here from Table 2, we have taken file size of $10, 30, 155, 350$ and 512. And for $10, 30, 155, 350, 512$ kb we get the corresponding time $26, 67, 301, 671, 911$. Figure 5 demonstrates the further illustrations. So, the chaos-based approach decreases the computational time for long messages than the referenced one. So, it is giving two benefits, and it is giving strength and allows to encrypt the message within a little time. The respective Fig. 6 represents the time comparison between key generation process.

5.2   Evaluating Time for Each Cycle

In this part, in Table 3, we have shown a delay time corresponding to other cycles. If cycles are more, then it will take more time. But a reasonable time will be applicable. To note that, the period is entirely dependent on the length of key. Figure 7 is showing a close view of delay of cycle for above mentioned. The x axis indicates number of bytes of key and y axis showing time in millisecond. For better visualization, the following Fig. 6 is displayed.

6   Future Perspective and Conclusion

IoT sensors needs a security layer but has to be trusted enough for data integrity. Conventional AES has been proven to be insecure in several IoT cases. As known, AES security depends on S-box and key-scheduling which has significant impact on encryption and decryption. The proposed technique as demonstrated needs suitable chaotic map which lower the chances to break it. Based on chaos concept aligned with Logistic map, we have designed and demonstrated this novel key-scheduling process that has been designed to encrypt large volumes of data. Besides we have analyzed either it is secure against different vulnerabilities. The future scope includes justifying the further applicability of the proposed scheme. As evaluated so far, the proposed technique is safer for the IoT data integrity.

References

1. Song, T., Li, R., Mei, B., Yu, J., Xing, X., Cheng, X.: A privacy preserving communication protocol for IoT applications in smart homes. IEEE Internet Things J. 4(6), 1844–1852 (2017)

2. Moosavi, S.R., et al.: End-to-end security scheme for mobility enabled healthcare Internet of Things. Future Gener. Comput. Syst. **64**, 108–124 (2016)
3. Sehgal, A., Perelman, V., Kuryla, S., Schonwalder, J.: Management of resource constrained devices in the internet of things. IEEE Commun. Mag. **50**(12) (2012)
4. Mukhopadhyay, S.C., Suryadevara, N.K.: Internet of Things: challenges and opportunities. In: Mukhopadhyay, S.C. (ed.) Internet of Things. SSMI, vol. 9, pp. 1–17. Springer, Cham (2014). https://doi.org/10.1007/978-3-319-04223-7_1
5. Lee, I., Lee, K.: The Internet of Things (IoT): applications, investments, and challenges for enterprises. Bus. Horiz. **58**(4), 431–440 (2015)
6. Yang, J., He, S., Lin, Y., Lv, Z.: Multimedia cloud transmission and storage system based on internet of things. Multimed. Tools Appli. **76**(17), 17735–17750 (2015). https://doi.org/10.1007/s11042-015-2967-9
7. Farash, M.S., Turkanović, M., Kumari, S.: An efficient user authentication and key agreement scheme for heterogeneous wireless sensor network tailored for the Internet of Things environment. Ad Hoc Netw. **36**, 152–176 (2016)
8. Saied, Y.B., Olivereau, A., Zeghlache, D., Laurent, M.: Lightweight collaborative key establishment scheme for the Internet of Things. Comput. Netw. **64**, 273–295 (2014)
9. Jing, Q., Vasilakos, A.V., Wan, J., Lu, J., Qiu, D.: Security of the Internet of Things: perspectives and challenges. Wirel. Netw. **20**(8), 2481–2501 (2014). https://doi.org/10.1007/s11276-014-0761-7
10. Yao, X., Chen, Z., Tian, Y.: A lightweight attribute-based encryption scheme for the Internet of Things. Future Gener. Comput. Syst. **49**, 104–112 (2015)
11. Turkanović, M., Brumen, B., Hölbl, M.: A novel user authentication and key agreement scheme for heterogeneous ad hoc wireless sensor networks, based on the Internet of Things notion. Ad Hoc Netw. **20**, 96–112 (2014)
12. Sicari, S., Rizzardi, A., Grieco, L.A., Coen-Porisini, A.: Security, privacy and trust in Internet of Things: the road ahead. Comput. Netw. **76**, 146–164 (2015)
13. Ion, M., Zhang, J., Schooler, E.M.: Toward content-centric privacy in ICN: attribute-based encryption and routing. In Proceedings of the 3rd ACM SIG-COMM Workshop on Information-Centric Networking, pp. 39–40. ACM. (2013)
14. Doukas, C., Maglogiannis, I.: Bringing IoT and cloud computing towards pervasive healthcare. In: Sixth International Conference on Innovative Mobile and Internet Services in Ubiquitous Computing (IMIS), pp. 922–926. IEEE (2012)
15. Beaulieu, R., Treatman-Clark, S., Shors, D., Weeks, B., Smith, J., Wingers, L.: The SIMON and SPECK lightweight block ciphers. In: Design Automation Conference (DAC), 2015 52nd ACM/EDAC/IEEE, pp. 1–6. IEEE (2015)
16. Rahulamathavan, Y., Phan, R.C.W., Rajarajan, M., Misra, S., Kondoz, A.: Privacy-preserving blockchain based IoT ecosystem using attribute-based encryption. In: 2017 IEEE International Conference on Advanced Networks and Telecommunications Systems (ANTS), pp. 1–6. IEEE. December (2017)
17. Babar, S., Stango, A., Prasad, N., Sen, J., Prasad, R.: Proposed embedded security framework for internet of things (IoT). In: 2011 2nd International Conference on Wireless Communication, Vehicular Technology, Information Theory and Aerospace & Electronic Systems Technology (Wireless VITAE), pp. 1–5. IEEE. February 2011
18. Baptista, M.S.: Cryptography with chaos. Phys. Lett. A **240**(1–2), 50–54 (1998)
19. Rahaman, Z., Corraya, A.D., Sumi, M.A., Bahar, A.N.: A novel structure of advance encryption standard with 3-dimensional dynamic S-box and key generation matrix. Int. J. Adv. Comput. Sci. Appl. **8**(2), 314–320 (2017)

20. Kocarev, L.: Chaos-based cryptography: a brief overview. IEEE Circuits Syst. Mag. **1**(3), 6–21 (2001)
21. Guckenheimer, J., Holmes, P.: Nonlinear Oscillations, Dynamical Systems, and Bifurcations of Vector Fields. AMS, vol. 42. Springer, New York (1983). https://doi.org/10.1007/978-1-4612-1140-2
22. Schneier, B.: Applied cryptography-protocols, algorithms, and source code in C (1996)
23. Kotulski, Z., Szczepański, J., Górski, K., Paszkiewicz, A., Zugaj, A..: Application of discrete chaotic dynamical systems in cryptography–DCC method. Int. J. Bifurcation Chaos **9**(06), 1121–1135 (1999)
24. Alvarez, G., Montoya, F., Romera, M., Pastor, G.: Breaking parameter modulated chaotic secure communication system. Chaos Solitons Fractals **21**(4), 783–787 (2004)
25. Fridrich, J.: Symmetric ciphers based on two-dimensional chaotic maps. Int. J. Bifurcation Chaos **8**(06), 1259–1284 (1998)
26. Ziv, J., Lempel, A.: A universal algorithm for sequential data compression. IEEE Trans. Inf. Theory **23**(3), 337–343 (1977)
27. Lian, S., Sun, J., Wang, Z.: A block cipher based on a suitable use of the chaotic standard map. Chaos Solitons Fractals **26**(1), 117–129 (2005)
28. Kocarev, L., Jakimoski, G.: Logistic map as a block encryption algorithm. Phys. Lett. A **289**(4–5), 199–206 (2001)
29. Jakimoski, G., Kocarev, L.: Differential and linear probabilities of a block-encryption cipher. IEEE Trans. Circuits Syst. I Fundam. Theory Appl. **50**(1), 121–123 (2003)
30. Doukas, C., Maglogiannis, I.: Bringing IoT and cloud computing towards pervasive healthcare. In: 2012 Sixth International Conference on Innovative Mobile and Internet Services in Ubiquitous Computing (IMIS), pp. 922–926. IEEE, July 2012
31. He, D., Zeadally, S.: An analysis of RFID authentication schemes for internet of things in healthcare environment using elliptic curve cryptography. IEEE Internet Things J. **2**(1), 72–83 (2015)
32. Aziz, A., Singh, K.: Lightweight security scheme for Internet of Things. Wirel. Pers. Commun. **104**(2), 577–593 (2018). https://doi.org/10.1007/s11277-018-6035-4
33. Author, F.: Article title. Journal **2**(5), 99–110 (2016)
34. Author, F., Author, S.: Title of a proceedings paper. In: Editor, F., Editor, S. (eds.) CONFERENCE 2016, LNCS, vol. 9999, pp. 1–13. Springer, Heidelberg (2016). https://doi.org/10.10007/1234567890
35. Author, F., Author, S., Author, T.: Book title, 2nd edn. Publisher, Location (1999)
36. Author, A.-B.: Contribution title. In: 9th International Proceedings on Proceedings, pp. 1–2. Publisher, Location (2010)
37. LNCS Homepage. http://www.springer.com/lncs. Accessed 4 Oct 2017

A Usability Study of Cryptographic API Design

Junwei Luo[✉], Xun Yi, Fengling Han, and Xuechao Yang

School of Computing Technologies, RMIT University, Melbourne,
VIC 3000, Australia
{junwei.luo,xun.yi,fengling.han,xuechao.yang}@rmit.edu.au

Abstract. Software developers interact with cryptographic components via APIs provided by a cryptographic library to protect sensitive information such as passwords and files. While cryptographic algorithms have been standardised for over a decade, with variety of crypto libraries that implemented the algorithm, many developers struggle to use the library correctly. This paper evaluates 6 different cryptographic libraries written in 3 different programming languages to find out what factors affect usability. We analyse the usability of surveyed libraries with regards to its API call sequence, number of parameters, exception handling mechanism and documentation. In the end, several recommendations are provided to help developers choose which library to use and more importantly, this paper showcases a few common pitfalls for library designers to prevent common misuses when designing a cryptographic library.

Keywords: Cryptography · Usability analysis · Cryptographic APIs

1 Introduction

Cryptography is one of the most effective ways to protect private data in today's Internet, ranging from private and public key encryption schemes, message authentications, key exchanges, certificates and so on. Software developers employ different cryptographic components into their software to defend against malicious parties who attempt to compromise the software and steal sensitive information. Nowadays, most online services such as communications, bankings and others utilise different cryptographic components to strengthen the security and prevent attacks. While the practices for securing applications have been around for over a decade, many developers struggle to identify the correct way of deploying cryptography into their software. According to a survey [5] conducted by Egele et al., over three-fourth of surveyed application are vulnerable to various attacks, this is due to the fact that developers deployed cryptographic components into their software products incorrectly. Egele et al. refers such incorrect use of security-related components in production as cryptographic misuses.

Cryptographic misuses refer to incorrect implementations of cryptographic APIs in a product during the development process that potentially leads to security vulnerabilities. Incorrect use of cryptographic APIs, such as weak ciphers

© ICST Institute for Computer Sciences, Social Informatics and Telecommunications Engineering 2021
Published by Springer Nature Switzerland AG 2021. All Rights Reserved
X. Yuan et al. (Eds.): QShine 2021, LNICST 402, pp. 194–213, 2021.
https://doi.org/10.1007/978-3-030-91424-0_12

and key, can jeopardise the product and allow sensitive information to be stolen by adversaries. As a developer, it is essential to interact with APIs provided by the library to accomplish a specific task. While in many cases, APIs should be designed in a way that gives freedom to developers to achieve what they want to, it poses security issues as a poorly chosen parameter can potentially compromise the system entirely. Many developers found that using cryptography is challenging [14,15], due to the complexity of the cryptography and the design of the API being too complicating for non cryptographic experts to use it properly. Recent works have identified the problem of cryptographic misuses and its potential impacts to the industry, and come up with solution [3] that hides unnecessary complexity away from developers. While simplicity seems to improve the usability, no proper usability evaluation has been conducted as reports of cryptographic misuses continue to grow.

Therefore, it is necessary to conduct a series of case studies to evaluate the usability of different cryptographic APIs written in different languages. This paper will study 6 cryptographic libraries from 3 different programming languages to empirically evaluate their usability, a series of tasks is designed to simulate how cryptographic primitives are used by the developers. We evaluate symmetric encryption schemes provided by the library to study what factors hinder usability. While similar works [1,13,15] have been proposed previously that compares the usability of different cryptographic libraries, these works are specific to one particular programming language and did not discuss about API designs.

In the end, this paper aims to find out what affects the usability of a cryptographic library, and serves as a starting point for developers to choose which cryptographic library to use for their work. Moreover, we offer a list of recommendations for cryptographic library developers to improve the usability of libraries. To summarise, our contributions include the following:

1. We formally study the usability of cryptographic libraries written in 3 different languages, we choose 6 different cryptographic libraries to compare the usability.
2. We design a series of tasks to simulate the use of cryptography in reality and analyse the result in terms of their usability. How does the design of APIs affect the usability of a cryptographic library.
3. We compose a list of recommendations that help mitigate the issue when designing a new cryptographic library.

2   Related Work

Cryptographic misuses have become an issue for security researchers for more than a decade, this section covers the previous works for cryptographic misuses, such as detection mechanisms, mitigation mechanisms and the development of easy-to-use cryptographic libraries.

2.1   Evaluation of Cryptographic Misuses

Egele et al. [5] stated that over 11,000 applications downloaded from Google Play Store was surveyed, the team found that over 88% of them contained cryptographic misuses, ranging from the use of weak cipher, incorrect cipher settings and certificate verification. Fahl et al. [6] studied 13,500 applications on Android platform, and found that over 1000 app contained incorrect certificate verification code that can be exploited using Man-In-The-Middle (MITM) attack. Similar work [7] that analyses certificate verification on commercial grade development kit provided by company such as Amazon, also lacked usability due to API design being too confusing. Patnaik et al. [15] analysed over 2,400 questions related to cryptography on developer community such as Stack Overflow and found several common pitfalls that developers might face when using a crypto library, including poor documentation, lack of example code and bad API design with poorly chosen default settings. Similarly, [17] analysed around 1,500 reports from 5 different repositories and found that one fourth of the reports were posted due to the poor documentation as the developer cannot find appropriate answers from the document to accomplish the job, indicating that a well-written document can potentially improve usability of a library.

2.2   Mitigation Against Cryptographic Misuses

Approaches that utilise code analysis techniques to mitigate cryptographic misuses have also been proposed, CogniCrypt [10] is a code analysis framework that assists the use of cryptographic primitives in Java, CogniCrypt automatically scans for insecure cryptographic code and makes secure suggestions for developers to improve security. CogniCrypt also supports code generation based on use case scenarios chosen by the developers, these mechanisms mitigate the problem of crypto misuses. CrySL [11] is a definition language framework that allows developers to customise filtering rules for malicious code detection. CrySL allows the filtering rules to be exported as a template and shared across the community so that people can benefit from it without requiring deep understanding of writing complicating rules to detect code misuses. Other approaches such as CDRep [12] that enables automatic code detection and repair without accessing the source code for Android application have also been used extensively to mitigate the issue. CDRep is built on top of CRYPTOLINT [5] for its code detection, with added features to improve accuracy and reduce false-positive rate. As the source code of surveyed application is not available, decompilation is used to recover the code from Java Bytecode and patch incorrect cryptographic implementations. However, CDRep is limited to JCA only and has no support for third parties cryptographic libraries.

2.3   Toward Usable Cryptographic Libraries

The confusion around cryptographic misuses traces back to the creation of the library, with over complicating APIs and poor documentation, developers found that using cryptography is challenging. Lots of efforts have been put into researching cryptographic libraries that focus on usability and simplicity. NaCl [3] is one of the earliest cryptographic implementation that adopts the idea of simplicity and usability by reducing the complexity and the number of secure choices that developers need to make in order to achieve security. To do that, NaCl removes the complicating API call sequence by wrapping several functions, such as key generation, cipher initialisation and encryption/decryption, in one function, where developers are not required to make secure choices about what cipher, mode of encryption and other parameters that are crucial to overall security. Since then, NaCl has inspired lots of researchers who work in designing usable cryptographic libraries, and many of its successors such as Libsodium and HACL* [18] are compatible with NaCl, with added primitives for signature and message authentication to provide more features, without requiring developers to change the code to adapt these libraries.

3   Preliminary

3.1   AES

Advanced Encryption Standard (AES) is a symmetric encryption specification established by NIST in 2001 [16], designed to replace its predecessor Data Encryption Standard (DES) published in 1977. AES is a block cipher where each block is 128 bits with different key lengths from 128, 192 to 256 bits. AES by itself is a block cipher that denote cryptographic transformation to scramble the data, and the mode of operation indicates how the block cipher is applied to the actual data for transformation. Depending on different cipher modes, additional parameters might be introduced to the cipher. Cipher Block Chaining (CBC) mode and Galois Counter Mode (GCM) are two commonly used modes for block ciphers. Both CBC and GCM mode utilise an extra parameter initialisation Vector (IV) to add randomisation to the ciphertext. Cryptographic randomisation refers to a mechanism where the message being encrypted more than once with the same cryptographic key results in different ciphertexts. This property is known as Indistinguishability of Chosen Plaintext Attack (IND-CPA). IND-CPA ensures that the probability of learning secret information from encrypted messages is negligible. CBC mode divides data into one or multiple blocks with a fixed size of 128 bits before the transformation, while the actual data might not meet such requirement. Therefore, padding is introduced to fulfil the block to ensure the last block is of the same size. Some CBC implementations might suffer padding oracle attack, where the adversary exploits the feedback mechanism of the padding implementation to deduce plaintext without having access to the key. On top of that, encrypted data in CBC mode is not authenticated, which means that the receiver cannot identify whether the ciphertext has been tampered by adversaries.

While mitigations have been proposed to address these attacks, CBC mode is later replaced by GCM mode, and is now considered obsolete in the latest TLS revisions due to its lack of message authentication. On the other hand, GCM is a counter mode that fixes these issues presented in CBC mode. GCM requires two parameters called Nonce and counter, where Nonce is similar to IV to ensure the cipher is IND-CPA secure, and counter is used to append to the Nonce before the transformation. Difference between CBC and GCM is that CBC performs transformation on plaintext, whereas GCM transforms Nonce and the counter, and XOR the result with plaintext. Galois Message Authentication Code (GMAC) is the message authentication scheme in GCM that authenticates the ciphertext to ensure its validity.

4   Case Study

4.1   Task Design

To empirically evaluate the usability, a basic understanding of how developers usually use cryptography in their works needs to be established. A survey [14] indicates that over 30% of the questions related to cryptography posted on developer community is about symmetric encryption. This makes sense as many developers only need symmetric encryption for encrypting data such as a file or text.

We design two tasks that are common for developers, the first task is to generate a secret key corresponding to the cipher, followed by the second task: encrypt a text message with the secret key. Both tasks are designed to be simple to implement as most cryptographic libraries do support symmetric key cryptography. Our designed tasks did not involve in public key cryptography as these tend to be complicating for developers and more importantly, public key cryptography itself cannot provide security guarantee without the help of Certificate Authority to validate the identity of an entity and its related public key.

As for the experiment, we evaluate each library by completing the tasks described above and denote everything we found during the implementation of each task. On completion of implementing each task, we evaluate the usability based on common API design principles proposed by Green M [9] and Bloch J [4].

4.2   Language of Choices

C, Java and JavaScript are chosen for the experiment, as these languages have been widely used for many years. As for the cryptographic library itself, the following libraries are chosen. For C/C++, OpenSSL and Libsodium are chosen as the candidate, JCA, ACC and Tink are chosen as the candidate for Java, and lastly Crypto and SJCL are chosen as the candidate for JavaScript. OpenSSL is a commercial-grade cryptographic toolkit in C and C++ and is often considered the industry standard for applied cryptography as it provides a wide range of ciphers, along with other utilities such as key exchange, public key cryptograhy, message digest, X.509 and so on. OpenSSL is still in active development where more and more features are added to the repository and fixing security vulnerabilities. However, it is also infamous for its bad usability and poor document that bring confusion to the community and is difficult to use correctly. Libsodium is one of the successor of NaCl that brings modern features such as password hashing, key exchange and various hashing functions that are all missing from NaCl, while maintaining backward compatibility with NaCl, as NaCl is no longer in active development.

For Java, Java Cryptography Architecture (JCA) is a built-in cryptographic toolkit introduced by Oracle. JCA offers different cryptographic primitives, message digest schemes, digital signature and so on. Apache Commons Crypto (ACC) is a lightweight cryptographic library that takes advantages of Intel AES-NI instruction to provide hardware acceleration for Java. The main advantage of ACC is to offer fast hardware AES transformation for better performance, its underlying cryptographic provider is a port of OpenSSL in C. Tink is a cross-platform cryptographic library introduced by Google, it claims to have better usability than the built-in JCA and have supports for modern cryptographic primitives that are missing from both JCA and ACC.

For JavaScript, Crypto is a cryptographic module from Node.js that covers a wide range of crypto primitives and utilities for hashing and certificate verification, Crypto in Node.js is essentially a port of OpenSSL into JavaScript. SJCL is a self-contained cryptographic library developed by a group of researchers at Stanford University and has supports for symmetric cipher, hashing and digital signature scheme.

Table 1 denotes the feature of each cryptographic library that we surveyed. While some libraries offer variety of ciphers, only the most commonly used ciphers are listed for simplicity. While some libraries only offer AEAD constructions, these implementations will be treated as if they were AE by ignoring the additional messages, as they are optional. For AES, Galois Counter Mode (GCM) is the mode of operation chosen to evaluate the libraries that support it.

Table 1. Features that are supported by corresponding cryptographic libraries that we chose for the experiment. •: requires input from developers. ○: requires no input from developers

	Symmetric cipher					
	Key generation	Mode	Size	IV/Nonce	Default	Usability
OpenSSL	PRG	•	•	•	?	
Libsodium	PRG	○	○	•	?	✓
JCA	Keygen	•	•	•	AES ECB	
ACC	Keygen	•	•	•	?	
Tink	Keygen	○	○	○	?	✓
Crypto	PRG/KDF	•	•	•	?	
SJCL	PRG/KDF	○	○	○	AES CCM	✓

4.3   Evaluating the Solutions

We use the solutions as a starting point to find out the usability of these cryptographic libraries on the basis of the design principles proposed by Green M

[9] and Bloch J [4] for usable API designs. Among these design principles, we chose the following principles to evaluate the usability of these libraries as they made up the vast majority of cryptographic misuses and struggles found by other studies [14,15]. These principles are:

1. Make the APIs easy to use.
2. Make the APIs hard to misuses, with visible messages when used incorrectly.
3. Defaults should be safe and secure.
4. A well-written document with example code.

These usability principles are in line with a study on usability of cryptographic library [14], where the study found that over one-third of developers they surveyed struggled to identify the correct way of using cryptography, common obstacles include identifying the API call sequence, parameters required for the cipher and basic understanding of cryptographic implementation. The second design principle describes the error-handling mechanism of the library, some libraries do not give warning about potential security issues, such as incorrect key size and mismatched tag. The third design principle suggests that a secure default value should always be preferred if developers did not specify about what value to use. Lastly, documentation of the library also plays a critical rule to improve usability as it provides an official guideline for developers to look for features, tutorials and so on, a good API design without documentation might introduce confusion to developers, which could potentially lead to insecure implementation of a cryptographic component.

To evaluate each principle, the following criteria will be applied:

Design Principle 1: Usability of APIs is evaluated based on whether or not the APIs can address the common obstacles listed in [14]. These obstacles are: API call sequence, identifying parameters and understanding API implementation. To do that, we evaluate the solution based on the number of lines of code and parameters. Logical Lines of code (LLoC) is used to measure API call sequence, whereas the Number of Parameters (NoP) is used to measure the complexity of a cryptographic API and its implementation. For symmetric encryption, the minimum required parameters should be at least 2, which will be the key and message respectively, the more parameters involved, the less usable the library is considered to be. The exact same principle will be applied to other tasks as suggested in [15] that the library designers should make an effort to minimise the number of choices that developers have to make.

Design Principle 2: We pay our attention to the exception handling mechanism of each library. Specifically, how does the library respond to common cryptographic misuses such as weak cipher, incorrect parameters and key size as these issues make up most of the common misuses [5]. The team also suggests that the issues could have been mitigated if either the compiler or cryptographic providers sent out warnings about the potential misuses.

Design Principle 3: We investigate default configuration used by the library. Egele et al. [5] stated that over 50% of surveyed applications relied on the default cipher provided by cryptographic providers. We analyse the following three questions: Does the API provide a default option, If so, what is the default cipher provided by the API? Is the default cipher secure?

Design Principle 4: We evaluate the usability of a document in a cryptographic library. Documentation plays a critical rule [4] in usability as it provides a standard guideline for developers to get started. To do that, the following questions will be asked to each library: Does the library include a document? Is the desired function easy to locate? Did the document record all exported functions, methods, parameters and so on? Does the library provide example code for common use cases to mitigate development?

5 Study Results

AES has become industry standard for symmetric encryption, this paper will focus on analysing AES implementation of each library, all libraries support AES as part of their encryption engines. We choose GCM as the mode of operation for evaluating AES as it is considered the most widely used mode among the others. Although Libsodium has supports for AES-GCM, its supports are platform-dependent as it takes advantages of hardware-assisted AES instructions for security reason. Thus the evaluation excludes Libsodium.

5.1 API Call Sequence

API call sequence or initialisation sequence refers to the code that requires to be executed in sequence to achieve any functionality. A study [14] found that over one-third of surveyed targets believe that such API call sequence is difficult to identify, due to the lack of cryptographic background and practice. To find out if a library outperforms others with regards to the first design principle, Logical Lines of Code (LLoC) is used to measure the amount of work required for implementing a feature.

Key Generation. The first task of evaluation is to generate the symmetric key corresponding to the cipher. In this case, a symmetric key with the length of 16 bytes. Key generation typically falls into these categories: Pseudorandom Generator (PRG), Key Generator (KeyGen) or Key Derivation Functions (KDFs). All 6 libraries have a relatively simple interface for key generation, regardless of which key generation method was implemented aforementioned.

However, the differences between these libraries emerge on the second task, which is to encrypt a message using the key from task 1. To better understand call sequence, we divided it into three stages: Initialisation, Update and Finalisation.

Init. Libraries with no usability designs tend to require prior knowledge of initialisation sequence in order to initialise it properly. OpenSSL scores the lowest due to the fact that developers are responsible for identifying the API call

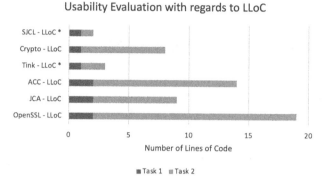

Fig. 1. Assessment criteria based on the number Logical Lines of Code (LLoC), LLoC describes the amount of efforts to complete a task. *: Usability claims

sequence and memory allocation. Followed by the ACC in Java, which also has similar pattern and requires input from developers. While JCA shares many similarity with ACC as they are both written in Java, JCA facilitates the initialisation sequence by making a parameter optional. Specifically, JCA has a default crypto provider where developers can choose from to achieve better performance or functionality whereas ACC explicitly requires it in order to initialise the cipher. Tink uses a template to store settings for different cipher, thus the need of manually initialising the cipher no longer exists. Lastly, Crypto in Node.js is also similar with regards to initialisation, while facilitating usability by adopting language-specific features such as loosely typed objects, anonymous functions and so on. Finally, SJCL does not require initialisation to be done.

Update. Cryptographic update is rather straightforward once the initialisation is done, as most mistakes occur during the initialisation. To achieve that, developers make one function call to inform the library to perform cryptographic transformation. While different libraries handle the interaction differently, we observe two patterns during the update. Specifically, how data is exchanged between the user and the library. Both OpenSSL and ACC require an extra parameter in the update function for receiving the ciphertext, whereas other libraries take advantage of the return instruction to send back ciphertexts to the user.

Final. Lastly, finalisation verifies ciphertext and generates authentication tag as an extra layer of security, as GCM mode computes the auth tag by computing the GMAC of the ciphertext for tampering prevention. OpenSSL and Crypto require developers to make two function calls to compute and retrieve the tag respectively. On the other, JCA and ACC only require one function call and the tag will be appended to the end of ciphertexts. Libraries with usability claims eliminates the need of finalisation as they are done during the update stage.

Figure 1 denotes the corresponding LLoC for both tasks across all libraries with AES supports. It is clear that initialisation stage usually results in higher number of LLoC due to the additional codes for setting up, while this is beneficial for experts who understand cryptography in practices, it exposes too much risk for those who do not have cryptographic background.

5.2   Identifying Required Parameters

Key Generation. The first task involves the generation of a cryptographic key, which is commonly done using either PRG, KeyGen or KDF. In most cases, KeyGen is implemented as a wrapper of PRG with the length of the key pre-filled to the PRG. As different ciphers might require keys in different sizes, having a KeyGen function as supposed to a general PRG might improve the usability as developers do not need to know the correct key length. Among 6 libraries, half of these libraries, namely OpenSSL, Crypto and SJCL use PRG for key generation, whereas KeyGen is utilised in the other half of the libraries for key generation. The result is obvious, all PRG functions require input of key length from developers in order to generate the key for encryption, whereas KeyGens simply return the newly generated key without requiring input from developers.

Init. Similar to call sequence where we categorise the process into stages, we divide the process of analysing parameters into different stages for better comparison. Typically the parameter needed includes the following: cipher, mode, key, Initialisation Vector (IV) or nonce, plaintext, ciphertext, and auth tag. During the initialisation, cipher, mode, IV or nonce are typically required before the encryption can occur, whereas plaintext and ciphertext are required in update and finally auth tag is retrieved in finalisation.

During initialisation, OpenSSL introduces an optional parameter that can be used for switching to a different crypto engine, similar to the crypto provider in JCA and ACC. ACC scores the lowest among other 5 libraries due to the fact that developers are required to explicitly set up crypto provider for the library to realise the backend used for actual encryption. Apart from the crypto provider which is required to be set explicitly, ACC and JCA share lots of similarities as parameters necessary for both libraries to set up are identical. Tink uses a template with pre-defined settings for every primitive supported by the library to facilitate the initialisation. On the other, Crypto requires the length of the auth tag to be set explicitly, the only library we surveyed requires this, and the rest is identical to the others with regards to the number of required parameters. Finally, SJCL only requires the key to be set whereas others are optional and the library will handle it if it is not explicitly set.

Update. As for the update, we observe there exists several pattern across different libraries for handling actual cryptographic transformation. OpenSSL requires both plaintext and ciphertext to be passed as parameters to the function that executes the transformation. On top of that, the size of the plaintext is also

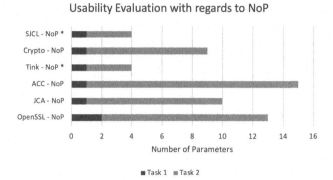

Fig. 2. Number of Parameters (NoP) used for completing task 1 and 2. NoP describes the minimum numbers of parameters required for completing a task. *: Usability claims

required for the function to work correctly. In Java, ACC follows the same pattern as the OpenSSL, it is not surprising since ACC is essentially a wrapper of OpenSSL, and the team kept the same workflow as its backend to minimise discrepancy. JCA on the other hand, eliminates such complexity and only the plaintext is required for the cipher object to perform encryption, and the ciphertext is returned upon function completion. Similarly, Tink, Crypto and SJCL follow the same idea where only the plaintext is needed for the job to be done.

Finalisation. To handle authentication tag, users of OpenSSL require to allocate free memory for holding the tag, as OpenSSL does not use return instruction to facilitate usability. In Java, ACC complicates the operation by requiring lots of parameters for computing the tag. It is surprising that 5 parameters are involved in the process of finalisation and more importantly, none of the parameters are actually required as they are integers such as the length of the plaintext and ciphertext, offsets and so on. As an OO language, we believe it could have been done better like JCA where it requires no input from developers and be able to compute the tag automatically. Tink on the other does not require involvement of the end users for finalisation as it was done in update stage. Lastly for the library in JavaScript, Crypto simplifies the process by making one function call with no parameter and the auth tag can be retrieved. SJCL follows the same design pattern as Tink and does not require any action to be taken for retrieving the tag. Figure 2 concludes the usability of API sequence with regards to the number of parameters for surveyed libraries.

5.3   Exception Handling for Incorrect Use

Exception handling describes the mechanism that informs developers about any potential issues that might arise due to incorrect inputs. In applied cryptography, common cryptographic misuses such as weak cipher, incorrect key and parameters, are found in many applications [5]. Most libraries do not have a exception handling mechanism for key generation, or the mechanism is not documented. OpenSSL exceptionally provides a function for inspecting the last error. Some key generation functions in these libraries are OS-dependent. For example, a common source of pseudorandom generator is the system device in Unix-like OS called /dev/urandom. Such device is not available in earlier version of the OS, which might cause problems generating a cryptographically secure values that can be used as a symmetric key.

For the second task, OpenSSL once again scores the lowest among other 5 libraries due to its lack of secure checks for weak ciphers, incorrect key length and related parameters. OpenSSL developers state that the user should be responsible for ensuring the correctness of all parameters. Crypto in Node.js and SJCL score similarly where both libraries are capable of identifying incorrect length of key, while ignoring other checks such as weak ciphers and incorrect parameters that are also critical to the security. JCA and ACC also have similar results where both libraries are able to identify not only the incorrect length of key, but also the incorrect size of parameters. Lastly, Tink is perhaps the best out of 6 libraries, as we have no way of mistakenly generating incorrect parameters due to its design that relies on pre-defined templates, which denote the initialisation sequence, generations of key, corresponding parameters and cipher objects.

Overall, none of the library that supports for weak ciphers has a mechanism to remind developers about the use of weak ciphers, albeit this feature is fairly trivial to implement. JCA and ACC send warnings to some extent, Crypto in Node.js and SJCL are similar regarding to the error handling mechanism as well. In the meantime, Tink does not suffer from potential incorrect use due to its pre-defined template that automatically takes care of everything.

Table 2 denotes the finding in exception handling mechanisms from libraries that support AES. Ideally, the developers of a cryptographic library should either ensure that these issues are not present, or to design an exception handling system that tells the users about any potential issues that might lead to security incidents if it is left without proper handling. Libraries that have one or more criteria labelled as "N/A" are considered a pass as the criteria is not applicable to the library.

5.4   Default Cipher

Some libraries offer default values if developers do not specify explicitly, while such feature is beneficial, some default options are considered insecure while the default option is still being used extensively [5] and the developers are unaware of the situation which can lead to security incidents. As task 1 is not applicable for the criteria, we pay our attention to the task 2, which uses newly generated key to encrypt a message.

Table 2. Exception handling of each library, sorted by the type of warning. ✓: indicates that the library is capable of identifying the potential issues. ✗: indicates that the library is not capable of identifying potential issues. N/A: Criteria is not applicable to the library.

	Weak cipher	Incorrect key size	Incorrect parameters	Constant parameters
OpenSSL	✗	✗	✗	✗
JCA	✗	✓	✓	✗
ACC	✗	✓	✓	✗
Tink	N/A	N/A	N/A	N/A
Crypto	✗	✓	✗	✗
SJCL	N/A	✓	✗	✗

Among 6 libraries, JCA allows a cipher object to be retrieved by specifying the string "AES" during the initialisation. SunJCE provider, which is by default the cryptographic provider in JCA, returns "AES/ECB/PKCS5Padding" to the developers. Electronic Code Block (ECB) mode is insecure due to the lack of the following: ECB is not IND-CPA secure, while it might consider secure if the key is used only once and the size of message is less than or equal to exact one block, it is not feasible as plaintexts are typically larger than 16 bytes in most cases. On top of that, ECB lacks randomness, which explains why the key can only be used once per message of size 16 bytes. Absence of authentication code for ciphertext in ECB mode makes it difficult for a receiver to identify if the ciphertext is valid. JCA reference guide states that ECB is the easiest mode to use, whereas it should be avoided if the message is larger than a single block. A study [5] pointed out that around 40% of all surveyed applications written in Java used the string "AES" to retrieve cipher object. It is unclear as to how such design was adopted in SunJCE, but it is clear that it makes up a portion of weak cipher misuses.

Another library that offers default cipher is SJCL in JavaScript, it returns CCM mode as the default mode of operation. CCM mode is a counter mode with combination of CBC-MAC for message authentication. CBC-MAC is deterministic and uses AES with CBC mode to compute Message Authentication Code with a fixed Initialisation Vector. While such mode is provably secure and part of the latest TLS revision, its performance is not comparable to GCM mode as CBC-MAC is not parallelisable. On top of that, AES-CCM is a MAC-then-encrypt diagram [2], which has no guarantee of ciphertext integrity until it is decrypted and more importantly, CCM mode has a lower adoption rates compared to GCM mode which has been widely used for years.

As the third design principle evaluates the default cipher and its security, only the library with supports for secure default cipher receives a pass. In the case of libraries with AES supports, SJCL in JavaScript passes the test while others fail to do so, due to either insecure default cipher or no supports for default cipher.

5.5 Documentation

The fourth design principle describes the importance of documentation in usability. To evaluate, the following questions are asked: Is the document available for a library? Is the desired function easy to locate? Did the document denote exported functions and explain the functions and parameters? Did the document have a example code for all exported functions. As documentation is available for all 6 libraries, we move our attention to evaluate the second and third criteria using task 1 and 2.

Task 1 involves the generation of a symmetric key, OpenSSL scores the lowest among others, as its documentation is very confusing, with all functions exported in one place without categorising the methods based on functionalities. Searching for a keyword "random" results in over 25 matches and only a handful of functions are what the task 1 is after. With all the confusion among locating the desired function to use, explanation of the function is clear and easy to understand, example code of this function is not available, or it might be available but not in the same page, we consider this a fail as developers should not be redirected to other places looking for the same function.

Compared to OpenSSL, JCA and ACC have a relatively simple document where it categories functions based on functionalities, while trying to explain everything in one page, both JCA and ACC fail to provide example codes for key generation, where the example code in JCA for key generation was not made for AES, a minor modification of that example code can make it compatible with AES, given the developers had prior knowledge of identifying the place to change. ACC's key generation example is absent but is documented.

Crypto in Node.js meets all 4 criteria, where every function exported is easy to locate, and receives a clear explanation and example code. For other two libraries with usability claims, Tink offers a document where the example code can be used with little modification, due to its usability designs where the interface is minimal. On top of that, Tink offers several key management mechanisms where a key can be exported as a file, or uploading to offshore Key Management System (KMS) run by third parties. Lastly, SJCL has a document where it explains the process of key generation with PBKDF2 and PRG. PBKDF2 derives a symmetric key from a passphrase by appending a random salt to HMAC and iterates multiple times to reduce the possibility of attacks. It is unclear how many iterations are used for PBKDF2 as it is directly related to the security, and the documentation of PBKDF2 is absent as of the time of writing this survey. Albeit an alternative solution namely PRG is also available and documented.

Task 2 uses the key generated in task 1 to encrypt a message. OpenSSL once again scores the lowest due to the envelope design that standardises the interface for different crypto primitives. By searching "aes" in the document, it returns the name of the cipher used in the EVP cipher routines, where the EVP cipher routines are the functions responsible for the actual cryptographic transformation. Example code for symmetric encryption is available inside a function that initialises the envelope, though the example code is not made for AES, the code can be used as to demonstrate the initialisation sequence of the cipher. The inconsistency across OpenSSL's document leads to many confusions in the community, as denoted by a study [15] where OpenSSL is considered the worst among other surveyed libraries regarding its documentation.

Documentation for Symmetric encryption in JCA is largely facilitated as the document is categorised by features, the provided example code presents the usage of GCM mode to encrypt data. ACC on the other hand, offers several example codes for the use of AES, while the example code is made for CBC mode only. As ACC is a port of OpenSSL in C, it requires the length of the ciphertext to be known for the cipher to operate. Internally, it uses the last 16 bytes to store authenticated tag, while data before the last 16 bytes are considered ciphertext. Decryption might fail if the array that stores the encrypted data contains empty bytes in between the auth tag and ciphertext, this is difficult to debug as such behaviour is not documented, the cipher will throw a warning about the tag being mismatched, as it mistakenly includes the empty bytes as part of ciphertext and computes the auth tag.

Crypto in Node.js provides example code in the document that demonstrates the use of CBC mode with scrypt as KDF to derive a 192 bits key from a passphrase. scrypt is a KDF that is designed to be computationally intensive to prevent against hardware attacks. While it is recommended to use KDF to derive a cryptographic key from a passphrase with low entropy, the example code fails to clarify some important aspects of using KDF and its parameters. In the example code, a fixed salt is applied to the KDF, whereas it is recommended to ensure the uniqueness of each salt and only use it with a unique password. The example code also fails to clarify that scrypt is memory intensive, which might be problematic if the application is deployed in an environment with limited memory. Although the document mentions about the uniqueness of salt, notices should be given at all places where the scrypt is used as developers might not be aware of the issue if the example code works.

Tink documents features such as symmetric encryptions with example code to facilitate the development, while it has supports for multiple symmetric encryption schemes, the name of these templates (used in Tink in order to initialise cipher object) is difficult to locate, as they are only written in the API documentation. SJCL on the other hand, while the mode of encryption is optional, lists the supported modes in the example code. Similar to Crypto in Node.js, SJCL provides PBKDF2 as the KDF for deriving passphrases. However, SJCL also fails to clarity important aspects of using PBKDF2, namely its iterations. PBKDF2 is computationally intensive in terms of computational time, whereas scrypt is computationally intensive in terms of memory usage, which means that the number of iterations is directly related to the cost of computation. By default, the iteration is set to 10,000, which was considered enough back then when the library is introduced to the public in 2009, it is recommended to use iterations over 50,000 or even 100,000 as the computational power of modern hardware continues to increase. On top of that, no documentation about changing the iteration is found in the page where the example code for symmetric crypto is presented.

6   Discussion and Recommendation

While it is true that OpenSSL is undeniably the industry standard for all crypto-graphic algorithms, results show that it is by far the worst among other 5 libraries with regards to usability. On top of that, the lack of detailed explanation in its official document and its cumbersome error handling mechanism result in many confusions to the community. Experiments show that users require to manually check for the correctness of each function call, one can completely bypass checks for authenticated tag by ignoring return value from **EVP_DecryptFinal**. It is unclear why developers of OpenSSL have decided to make plaintexts available to the user, given the fact that the authenticity of the text might be susceptible due to the failure of verifying the tag. After encryption, users are responsible for handling ciphertext, Initialisation Vector (IV) and authentication tag for storage or network transmission as they are the minimum required for decryption. While it is true that one can bypass checks for authentication tag in OpenSSL, such check is mandatory in most other libraries, and cannot be bypassed in such a way as OpenSSL did.

Although OpenSSL is not suitable for people who are unfamiliar with applied cryptography, it does offer greater flexibility and functionality for different secu-rity purposes. It is unfortunate that there are only a few libraries written in C that offer greater usability, and for these libraries, only one of them has supports for AES and this feature is limited to supported processors only due to several security considerations around AES.

Unlike C programming language which does not have an official cryptographic library built-in to the standard SDK, Java on the other hand receives an official cryptographic framework (JCA). JCA has quickly become the default crypto-graphic library in Java, due to its popularity and part of the standard Java SDK. It was also the default crypto library for Android until 2018 when Google has replaced it with its own cryptographic providers. One biggest issue with JCA is the default option provided by SunJCE provider when using AES. In JCA, a cipher object can be retrieved by calling crypto factory with a string parame-ter indicating what cipher to use. To facilitate usability, SunJCE allows cipher name to be simplified, which is where the issue occurs. By default, it uses the pat-tern similar to **AES/GCM/NoPadding** for the crypto factory to realise what cipher and its mode to use. However, one might simply pass in a simplified string **AES** and the crypto provider will response with **AES/ECB/PKCS5Padding**, which is the least secure mode among all other modes for AES. This simplified crypto name makes up over one-third of common cryptographic misuses in Java [5]. It remains unclear as to why such decision is made in the first place, the development team behind JCA clearly understands the issue as they also inform users about potential risks of using such simplified string in JCA documentation. One thing for sure is that many users did not read the warning as it has become one of the most common crypto misuses in JCA.

ACC uses designs similar to JCA where users might choose which crypto provider to use, and ACC is backed by OpenSSL to take advantages of hardware-assisted AES encryption for better performance and security. While the design of ACC is similar to JCA in terms of API call sequence, it requires more parameters to handle cryptographic operation. More specifically, it is similar to what OpenSSL does, with regards to the number of parameters required for **Update** and **Final**. It is less common for Java to handle low level operations such as manipulating byte array in a similar fashion to C. Such drawback is mitigated by using ByteBuffer object, a facilitated way to manage binary data, and both JCA and ACC support it. Inconsistency between encryption and decryption in ACC is also found. Particularly, it is found in the **Update** method during encryption where it takes as input plaintext, size and offset value and produces ciphertext stored in a given byte array at the starting offset value. During decryption, **Update** can be eliminated and one can call **Final** to complete both decryption and verification. It is worth noting that by default, ACC treats the last 16 bytes as authentication tag and everything above is ciphertext. A successful decryption requires both the size of ciphertext and its offset in the byte array, if a byte array contains information other than the ciphertext and authentication tag.

Lastly, Tink is a cryptographic library that offers implementations from different languages, such as Java and Python, developed by a group of security researchers at Google. The purpose of Tink is to reduce the possible cryptographic misuses that could potentially result in a security incident. In our experiments, Tink does seem to improve usability quite a lot, a concept of key template is introduced by Tink, which denotes settings such as key size, IV and other parameters that one usually finds when initialising a crypto object. A typical crypto implementation requires inputs about crypto, mode, key and other parameters from developers, whereas Tink hides such hassle by wrapping all settings necessary within one object. A crypo object can then be retrieved on basis of the key template, which defines what cipher to use and its parameters. With Tink, the only way to use its underlying crypto is to specify a key template, and the library handles the rest of them including generation of keys and IVs, setting up crypto engine and so on. Upon completing initialising the crypto engine, one simply calls encrypt to retrieve ciphertext and decrypt to verify the tag and reveal plaintext. As both IV and tag are appended to the ciphertext itself, it facilitates both storage and network transmission as users are no longer required to come up with a protocol to handle transmission over the network and disassemble the chunk of data for decryption.

In regards to JavaScript, a language that has gained attention in recent years, we analyse two libraries, Crypto Node.js has a relatively simple interface and is backed by OpenSSL in C. Therefore, both Crypto Node.js and OpenSSL are somewhat similar with regards to API call sequence, while Crypto Node.js has a much clearer interface due to adoption of language-specific features from JavaScript to simplify the work. Although at the end of encryption users also get ciphertext, IV and tag, one can serialise data easily as demonstrated in the official document and is recommended for users to follow the instruction to reduce unnecessary misuses.

SJCL is the last candidate among all 6 libraries and the design shares a lot of similarity with Tink. In particular, it eliminates the need of initialising cipher object due to the fact that the library supports AES only. On top of that, SJCL implements AES-CCM as the default cipher and all additional parameters will be generated if not explicitly specified. One notable feature is that SJCL implements PBKDF2 for deriving passphrase keys, as supposed to the keys generated at random and more importantly. In many cases, Key Derivation Function (KDF) is more preferable as it is difficult for users to memorise continuous random bytes.

Recommendation. In C, OpenSSL is still the must-go option for better versatility. Otherwise, NaCl or Libsodium are better choices than OpenSSL with regards to usability as they were designed specifically to mitigate such issues. For Java users, JCA guarantees its compatibility across different platforms and architectures, whereas Tink should offer a better experience due to its user-centred design that facilitates cryptographic usages. For JavaScript, Crypto module in Node.js is a better choice for versatility, whereas SJCL offers a clean user interface, along with better compatibility across different browsers.

As C does not have a exception handling mechanism built-in to the language itself, it is perhaps worth conducting researches on how a better error handling system can be designed, as supposed to manually check for error code by the end users. We demonstrate that OpenSSL does not have a rigorous error handling mechanism, when it is misused, one might continue to decrypt a file without knowing its validity due to the way OpenSSL was designed.

On the other hand, both Java and javaScript offer a better exception handling scheme, as the scheme has always been a part of the design of the language. Tink's implementation shows that cryptographic library can be easy for people without cryptographic background to use it properly, without worrying about potential misuses.

Furthermore, we give recommendations for library designers to prevent misuses. We observe that many libraries require two function calls for initialisation to be done, whereas libraries with usability claims reduce that to one function call. We suggest that initialisation can be simplified as many libraries have achieved that goal without issues. Same goes for finalisation where the auth tag is computed and attached to the ciphertext. While some might argue that there are reasons for not combining the tag to the ciphertext as they should be stored in different places in some cases, we recommend that the library can optionally include an interface that simplifies the process, while retaining the original design for advanced users.

For the second principle, libraries should take advantage of built-in exception handling mechanism wherever possible. Although many libraries utilise that to report issues to the end users, the error message is rather unintuitive as developers could not make sense of the message produced by the library when errors occur [8,15]. For languages that have no built-in supports for error handling, we believe that more researches can be done to investigate a better way to overcome such limitation.

For the third principle, we discourage the use of default values, this is because it could either break backward compatibility or open up a security vulnerability, whenever the default value becomes insecure. To mitigate the issue, we suggest that libraries can optionally introduce a mitigation tool that allows one to migrate to another cipher without introducing too many breaking changes.

7 Conclusion

This paper presents a study about the usability of cryptographic APIs from 6 libraries written in 3 programming languages. We set up a series of tasks as to simulate what developers use cryptography and analyse the usability with regards of their API call sequence, parameters, exception handling mechanisms and documentation. Experiments show that many libraries are designed under an assumption that developers understood cryptography to some extent, whereas the situation is the exact opposite. Many cryptographic misuses arise because of bad API designs. Libraries such as Tink and SJCL do seem to improve usability as users are no longer required to understand cryptography before using it correctly. Given the presence of issues with regards to cryptographic issues, further research is needed to improve API designs, documentation and the way that libraries interact with users as these factors affect usability. In our future work, we will focus on analysing libraries in a source code level, to have a better understanding of how decisions were made to the library, and categories these findings as to provide a guideline for cryptographic researchers when designing a cryptographic library.

References

1. Acar, Y., et al.: Comparing the Usability of Cryptographic APIs. In: 2017 IEEE Symposium on Security and Privacy (SP), pp. 154–171. IEEE (2017)
2. Bellare, M., Namprempre, C.: Authenticated encryption: relations among notions and analysis of the generic composition paradigm. In: Okamoto, T. (ed.) ASIACRYPT 2000. LNCS, vol. 1976, pp. 531–545. Springer, Heidelberg (2000). https://doi.org/10.1007/3-540-44448-3_41
3. Bernstein, D.J., Lange, T., Schwabe, P.: The security impact of a new cryptographic library. In: Hevia, A., Neven, G. (eds.) LATINCRYPT 2012. LNCS, vol. 7533, pp. 159–176. Springer, Heidelberg (2012). https://doi.org/10.1007/978-3-642-33481-8_9
4. Bloch, J.: How to design a good API and why it matters. In: Companion to the 21st ACM SIGPLAN Symposium on Object-Oriented Programming Systems, Languages, and Applications, pp. 506–507 (2006)
5. Egele, M., Brumley, D., Fratantonio, Y., Kruegel, C.: An empirical study of cryptographic misuse in android applications. In: Proceedings of the 2013 ACM SIGSAC Conference on Computer & Communications Security, pp. 73–84 (2013)
6. Fahl, S., Harbach, M., Muders, T., Baumgärtner, L., Freisleben, B., Smith, M.: Why eve and mallory love android: an analysis of android SSL (in) security. In: Proceedings of the 2012 ACM Conference on Computer and Communications Security, pp. 50–61 (2012)

7. Georgiev, M., Iyengar, S., Jana, S., Anubhai, R., Boneh, D., Shmatikov, V.: The most dangerous code in the world: validating SSL certificates in non-browser software. In: Proceedings of the 2012 ACM Conference on Computer and Communications Security, pp. 38–49 (2012)
8. Gorski, P.L., et al.: Developers deserve security warnings, too: on the effect of integrated security advice on cryptographic {API} misuse. In: Fourteenth Symposium on Usable Privacy and Security ({SOUPS} 2018), pp. 265–281 (2018)
9. Green, M., Smith, M.: Developers are not the enemy!: the need for usable security APIs. IEEE Secur. Priv. **14**(5), 40–46 (2016)
10. Krüger, S., et al.: CogniCrypt: supporting developers in using cryptography. In: 2017 32nd IEEE/ACM International Conference on Automated Software Engineering (ASE), pp. 931–936. IEEE (2017)
11. Krüger, S., Späth, J., Ali, K., Bodden, E., Mezini, M.: CrySL: an extensible approach to validating the correct usage of cryptographic APIs. IEEE Trans. Softw. Eng. (2019)
12. Ma, S., Lo, D., Li, T., Deng, R.H.: CDRep: automatic repair of cryptographic misuses in android applications. In: Proceedings of the 11th ACM on Asia Conference on Computer and Communications Security, pp. 711–722 (2016)
13. Mindermann, K., Keck, P., Wagner, S.: How usable are rust cryptography APIs? In: 2018 IEEE International Conference on Software Quality, Reliability and Security (QRS), pp. 143–154. IEEE (2018)
14. Nadi, S., Krüger, S., Mezini, M., Bodden, E.: Jumping through hoops: why do java developers struggle with cryptography APIs? In: Proceedings of the 38th International Conference on Software Engineering, pp. 935–946 (2016)
15. Patnaik, N., Hallett, J., Rashid, A.: Usability smells: an analysis of developers' struggle with crypto libraries. In: Fifteenth Symposium on Usable Privacy and Security ({SOUPS} 2019) (2019)
16. Standard, N.F.: Announcing the advanced encryption standard (AES). Federal Information Processing Standards Publication **197**(1–51), 3–3 (2001)
17. Zibran, M.F., Eishita, F.Z., Roy, C.K.: Useful, but usable? Factors affecting the usability of APIs. In: 2011 18th Working Conference on Reverse Engineering, pp. 151–155. IEEE (2011)
18. Zinzindohoué, J.K., Bhargavan, K., Protzenko, J., Beurdouche, B.: HACL*: a verified modern cryptographic library. In: Proceedings of the 2017 ACM SIGSAC Conference on Computer and Communications Security, pp. 1789–1806 (2017)

An S-box Design Using Irreducible Polynomial with Affine Transformation for Lightweight Cipher

Muhammad Rana[(⊠)], Quazi Mamun, and Rafiqul Islam

Charles Sturt University, Bathurst, NSW 2678, Australia
{mrana,qmamun,mislam}@csu.edu.au

Abstract. Traditional cryptographic block cipher algorithms are often unsuitable for low-resource profiled IoT (Internet of Things) devices. A lightweight cryptographic algorithm is thus mandated. The S boxes are often called the heart of a cryptographic protocol, as a considerable amount of resource and time complexities are associated with the design of an S box. A lightweight S box will consume less memory, less power and less time, ensuring a high-level Shanon's property of confusion. This paper proposes a lightweight S box design to meet all the requirements of lightweight cryptographic ciphers. The proposed method applies a couple of transformations- the multiplicative inverse in the Galois field (2^4) and affine transformations on selected irreducible polynomials to create 4×4 S-boxes. Several cryptanalyses such as balance test, bijection property, difference distribution table test, and Boomerang Connectivity were performed to demonstrate the robust characteristics of the proposed method.

Keywords: Block cipher · Cryptanalysis · Internet of Things (IoT) · Irreducible polynomial · S-box

1 Introduction

Block cipher is one of the most popular symmetric algorithms use to encrypt the plaintext to ensure secure data transfer by providing confusion and diffusion properties. The substitution box (S-box) provide Shanon's confusion property to hide the relationship between plaintext, ciphertext and key [1]. Henceforth, designing a robust S-box is essential for a reliable and robust cipher [2]. However, for example, the Advanced Encryption System (AES) S-box consume more time and memory. Subsequently, an S-box needs to design for low resource IoT devices.

An S-box can be split into two categories such as dynamic and static. In the case of dynamic, the S-box changes regularly in each session, making the cipher harder to break. However, the same S-box uses in every session in the static state, which is less secure but require less memory and computational power [3]. Latin Square S-box method [4] provide the increased level of security of the block cipher and requires more memory which IoT devices cannot effort. On the contrary, it is easy to identify the

© ICST Institute for Computer Sciences, Social Informatics and Telecommunications Engineering 2021
Published by Springer Nature Switzerland AG 2021. All Rights Reserved
X. Yuan et al. (Eds.): QShine 2021, LNICST 402, pp. 214–227, 2021.
https://doi.org/10.1007/978-3-030-91424-0_13

relationship between plaintext, key, and ciphertext from a static S-box cipher; thus, data communication is less secure.

Therefore, it is challenging to trade-off between security and memory consumption of S-box to secure communication between the resource-constrained IoT devices. This paper considers constructing an S-box using the algebraic method according to specific techniques, likewise Boolean functions, affine transformations, and nonlinear equations. This method involves an S-box generation is based on the selected irreducible polynomial. In this technique, S-box production includes a 4-bit multiplicative inverse from a four-degree irreducible polynomial followed by 4×4 binary affine transformations.

Several approaches have been initiated to generate an S-box such as Algebraic techniques [5], Analytical approach [6], Chaos-based [7], Cellular Automata [8], Dynamic key-dependent [9], the Heuristic method [10], Neural networks [11] Pomaranch [12], and Zhongtang system [13]. Atani et al. [14] describe the Cellular automata-based S-boxes. In [15], the Hyperchaotic system describes generating the S-box. Chaotic maps and cuckoo search algorithm based S-box propose by Wang et al. [16]. However, most methods are energy-consuming and may not be appropriate for low resourced IoT devices. This paper demonstrates the S-boxes generation applying an algebraic method that uses nonlinear irreducible polynomials $m_1(x) = 1 + x + x^4$, $m_2(x) = 1 + x^3 + x^4$, and $m_3(x) = 1 + x + x^2 + x^3 + x^4$. Based on these polynomials, multiplicative inverse tables are created. Nonlinear based block cipher algorithms secure the round transformation [17]. An affine transformation is applied to each component in the multiplicative inverse table to produce a robust S-box. This method introduces a compact S-box derived from the algebraic design and shows strong defiance against linear and dynamic analysis.

Sahoo et al. [19] use the affine matrix and reduce the time complexity of AES. Likewise, Affine matrix transformation decreases the time complexity of the S-box of AES cipher [3]. AES hardware requirement is significantly high, which resource-constrained devices may not effort, implemented in an 8-bit S-box as a 6*16 table. Unfortunately, an 8-bit S-box necessitates a relatively larger hardware area and memory than 4-bit S-box. Therefore 8-bit S-box is impractical for the lightweight block cipher [18]. The 4-bit S-box has typically used a much more cost-effective hardware area than an 8-bit S-box. Consequently, most lightweight block ciphers use a 4-bit substitution box such as RECTANGLE, PRESENT, LED, and GiFT [19].

In this paper, we design an S-box which will be suitable for resource-constrained devices. We suggested an S-box creation process based on 4×4 bits to fit the best in a lightweight cipher. We use the irreducible polynomial equation and affine matrix in this construction method. Three steps are involved in this process. Firstly, find out the irreducible polynomial equation from the four-degree polynomial and create S-box from them. Secondly, take the best affine matrix. Finally, crate the S-boxes with the combination of multiplicative inverse and affine matrix. Empirical results show the suggested S-box offers robust defiance to statical and differential cryptanalysis.

Rest of the paper is arranged as follows: Sect. 2 explains the proposed method with detailed descriptions and the steps of the design process. In Sect. 3, we discuss the efficiency of the proposed S-box design with balanced, bijection, difference distribution tables and boomerang connectivity table. Finally, the conclusion is illustrated in Sect. 4.

2 The Proposed S-box

This section demonstrates the proposed technique to create a cryptographically strong S-box with nominated irreducible polynomials. The three steps involved in the method:

1. Create a multiplicative inverse table from a hexadecimal table.
2. Generate S-box by transforming the affine matrix.
3. Select irreducible polynomial equation and generate the hexadecimal table.

2.1 Select Irreducible Polynomial Equation and Generate the Hexadecimal Table

Figure 1 indicates the selection technique of the irreducible polynomials. The irreducible polynomial has a diffusion property and makes a nonlinear premutation function. This system allocates input bits to output bits in a nonlinear way.

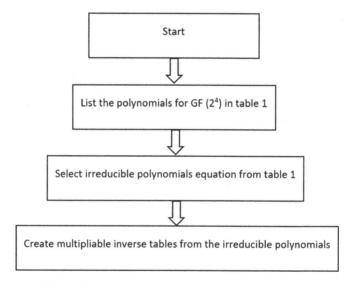

Fig. 1. Flowchart to create a multiplicative inverse table

We found three irreducible polynomials from $GF(2^4)$ such as $m_1(x) = x^4 + 1$, $m_2(x) = x^4 + x^3 + 1$, and $m_3(x) = x^4 + x^3 + x^2 + x + 1$. Galois field $GF(2^4)$, also noted as F_2^4 contains $2^4 = 16$ elements. F_2^4 is the quotient ring $F_2[X]/(x^4 = x + 1)$ of the polynomial ring generated by $(x^4 = x + 1)$ in the field of order 2^4. $GF(2^4)$ elements list can be produced on the polynomial with the defining primitive polynomial.

$a_3\alpha^3 + a_2\alpha^2 + a_1\alpha + a_0$, where $a_i \in$ for $i = 0, 1, 2, 3$ and α is the primitive root of this field.

Table 1. The elements for $x^4 + x + 1$ irreducible polynomial of Galois field $GF(2^4)$

GF (2^4) elements for $x^4 + x + 1$				
$\alpha^4 + \alpha + 1 = 0$	$\alpha^4 = \alpha + 1$			
$\alpha^5 = \alpha^4.\alpha$	$\alpha^5 = (\alpha + 1).\alpha$	$\alpha^5 = \alpha^2 + \alpha$		
$\alpha^6 = \alpha^5.\alpha$	$\alpha^6 = (\alpha^2 + \alpha).\alpha$	$\alpha^6 = \alpha^3 + \alpha^2$		
$\alpha^7 = \alpha^6.\alpha$	$\alpha^7 = (\alpha^3 + \alpha^2).\alpha$	$\alpha^7 = \alpha^4 + \alpha^3$	$\alpha^7 = \alpha^3 + \alpha + 1$	
$\alpha^8 = \alpha^7.\alpha$	$\alpha^8 = (\alpha^3 + \alpha + 1).\alpha$	$\alpha^8 = \alpha^4 + \alpha^2 + \alpha$	$\alpha^8 = \alpha + 1 + \alpha^2 + \alpha$	$\alpha^8 = \alpha^2 + 1$
$\alpha^9 = \alpha^8.\alpha$	$\alpha^9 = (\alpha^2 + 1).\alpha$	$\alpha^9 = \alpha^3 + \alpha$		
$\alpha^{10} = \alpha^9.\alpha$	$\alpha^{10} = (\alpha^3 + \alpha).\alpha$	$\alpha^{10} = \alpha^4 + \alpha^2$	$\alpha^{10} = (\alpha + 1) + \alpha^2$	$\alpha^{10} = \alpha^2 + \alpha + 1$
$\alpha^{11} = \alpha^{10}.\alpha$	$\alpha^{11} = (\alpha^2 + \alpha + 1).\alpha$	$\alpha^{11} = (\alpha^2 + \alpha + 1).A$	$\alpha^{11} = \alpha^3 + \alpha^2 + \alpha$	
$\alpha^{12} = \alpha^{11}.\alpha$	$\alpha^{12} = (\alpha^3 + \alpha^2 + \alpha).\alpha$	$\alpha^{12} = \alpha^4 + \alpha^3 + \alpha^2$	$\alpha^{12} = \alpha + 1 + \alpha^3 + \alpha^2$	$\alpha^{12} = \alpha^3 + \alpha^2 + \alpha + 1$
$\alpha^{13} = \alpha^{12}.\alpha$	$\alpha^{13} = (\alpha^3 + \alpha^2 + \alpha + 1).\alpha$	$\alpha^{13} = \alpha^4 + \alpha^3 + \alpha^2 + \alpha$	$\alpha^{13} = \alpha + 1 + \alpha^3 + \alpha^2 + \alpha$	$\alpha^{13} = \alpha^3 + \alpha^2 + 1$
$\alpha^{14} = \alpha^{13}.\alpha$	$\alpha^{14} = (\alpha^3 + \alpha^2 + 1).\alpha$	$\alpha^{14} = \alpha^4 + \alpha^3 + \alpha$	$\alpha^{14} = \alpha + 1 + \alpha^3 + \alpha$	$\alpha^{14} = \alpha^3 + 1$
$\alpha^{15} = \alpha^{14}.\alpha$	$\alpha^{15} = (\alpha^3 + 1).\alpha$	$\alpha^{15} = \alpha^4 + \alpha$	$\alpha^{15} = \alpha + 1 + \alpha$	$\alpha^{15} = 1$

$GF(2^4)$ is a field; therefore, every component has a unique multiplicative inverse, except the zero. Based on these chosen irreducible polynomials, their elements, binary representation, and multiplicative inverse tables are created and are given in Tables 1, 2, and 3.

The non-zero elements of the field are typically denoted by adding a star sign on the upper right $F_{2^4}^* = F_{2^4} - \{0\}$ form a multiplicative cycle group. $F_{2^4}^*$ can be generated by x i.e. $F_{2^4}^* = (x)$.

2.2   Generating the Multiplicative Inverse Table

The S-Box is considered with the multiplicative inverse over the Galois Field $GF(2^4)$ using an irreducible polynomial. The multiplicative inverses m_1, m_2 and m_3 are created from irreducible polynomials $m_1(x)$, $m_3(x)$, and $m_3(x)$. Three S-boxes have been produced from the multiplicative inverse of four-degree irreducible polynomials presented in Tables 4, 5 and 6.() 10, 11 and 12.

Table 2. Binary and hexadecimal representation of $m_1(x) = x^4 + x + 1$ irreducible polynomial

Power representation	Polynomial representation				4-Tuple representation				Hexadecimal
	α^3	α^2	α	1	α^3	α^2	α	1	
0					0	0	0	0	0
1				1	0	0	0	1	1
α			α		0	0	1	0	2
α^2		α^2			0	1	0	0	4
α^3	α^3				1	0	0	0	8
α^4			α	1	0	0	1	1	3
α^5		α^2	α		0	1	1	0	6
α^6	α^3	α^2			1	1	0	0	C
α^7	α^3		α	1	1	0	1	1	B
α^8		α^2		1	0	1	0	1	5
α^9	α^3		α		1	0	1	0	A
α^{10}		α^2	α	1	0	1	1	1	7
α^{11}	α^3	α^2	α		1	1	1	0	E
α^{12}	α^3	α^2	α	1	1	1	1	1	F
α^{13}	α^3	α^2		1	1	1	0	1	D
α^{14}	α^3			1	1	0	0	1	9

2.3 Affine Transformation and S-box Creation

An affine transformation is used to obtain a robust S-box. This transformation relocates the elements of the S-box. However, the resultant S-box properties remain unchanged. This technique improves the complexity of the algebraic expression of an S-box, which transform the S-box stronger against interpolation attacks and foundation for the protection against differential attacks [20].

Affine mapping is defined in $GF(2^4)$ as $\beta_i = \alpha\,\beta_i' + \gamma\,_{I,}$ where, $\gamma\,_I$ is the addition of a 4-bit vector constant, α is an invertible 4×4 (nxn) matrix [21]. Here($\beta_3', \beta_2', \ldots, \beta_0'$) are the multiplicative inverse of the byte at the input of the S-box and ($\beta_3, \beta_2, \ldots, \beta_0$) are the byte at the output of the S-box. In a matrix, an affine matrix is formulated in Eq. 1.

$$\begin{bmatrix} \beta_0 \\ \beta_1 \\ \beta_2 \\ \beta_3 \end{bmatrix} = \begin{bmatrix} 0 & 1 & 1 & 1 \\ 1 & 0 & 1 & 1 \\ 1 & 1 & 0 & 1 \\ 1 & 1 & 1 & 0 \end{bmatrix} \begin{bmatrix} \beta_0' \\ \beta_1' \\ \beta_2' \\ \beta_3' \end{bmatrix} + \begin{bmatrix} 1 \\ 1 \\ 0 \\ 1 \end{bmatrix} \tag{1}$$

The following three affine transformations to assemble in $GF(2^4)$ [22].

Table 3. The power generator and proposed multiplicative inverse for $m_1(x) = x^4 + x + 1$ irreducible polynomial

I	$P(\alpha) \in GF(2^4)$	$P(\alpha) \in GF\left(2^4\right)$ bin	Multiplicative Inverse	Multiplicative Inv. bin	Hexadecimal
α^0	1	0001	1	0001	1
α^1	α	0010	$\alpha^3 + 1$	1001	9
α^2	α^2	0100	$\alpha^3 + \alpha^2 + 1$	1101	D
α^3	α^3	1000	$\alpha^3 + \alpha^2 + \alpha + 1$	1111	F
α^4	$\alpha + 1$	0011	$\alpha^3 + \alpha^2 + \alpha$	1110	E
α^5	$\alpha^2 + \alpha$	0110	$\alpha^2 + \alpha + 1$	0111	7
α^6	$\alpha^3 + \alpha^2$	1100	$\alpha^3 + \alpha$	1010	A
α^7	$\alpha^3 + \alpha + 1$	1011	$\alpha^2 + 1$	0101	5
α^8	$\alpha^2 + 1$	0101	$\alpha^3 + \alpha + 1$	1011	B
α^9	$\alpha^3 + \alpha$	1010	$\alpha^3 + \alpha^2$	1100	C
α^{10}	$\alpha^2 + \alpha + 1$	0111	$\alpha^2 + \alpha$	0110	6
α^{11}	$\alpha^3 + \alpha^2 + \alpha$	1110	$\alpha + 1$	0011	3
α^{12}	$\alpha^3 + \alpha^2 + \alpha + 1$	1111	α^3	1000	8
α^{13}	$\alpha^3 + \alpha^2 + 1$	1101	α^2	0100	4
α^{14}	$\alpha^3 + 1$	1001	α	0010	2

Affine matrix 1 **Affine matrix 2**

$$\begin{bmatrix} \beta_0 \\ \beta_1 \\ \beta_2 \\ \beta_3 \end{bmatrix} = \begin{bmatrix} 0\ 1\ 1\ 1 \\ 1\ 0\ 1\ 1 \\ 1\ 1\ 0\ 1 \\ 1\ 1\ 1\ 0 \end{bmatrix} \begin{bmatrix} \beta_0' \\ \beta_1' \\ \beta_2' \\ \beta_3' \end{bmatrix} + \begin{bmatrix} 1 \\ 1 \\ 0 \\ 0 \end{bmatrix} \qquad \begin{bmatrix} \beta_0 \\ \beta_1 \\ \beta_2 \\ \beta_3 \end{bmatrix} = \begin{bmatrix} 1\ 0\ 1\ 1 \\ 1\ 1\ 0\ 1 \\ 1\ 1\ 1\ 0 \\ 0\ 1\ 1\ 1 \end{bmatrix} \begin{bmatrix} \beta_0' \\ \beta_1' \\ \beta_2' \\ \beta_3' \end{bmatrix} + \begin{bmatrix} 1 \\ 0 \\ 0 \\ 1 \end{bmatrix}$$

Affine matrix 3

$$\begin{bmatrix} \beta_0 \\ \beta_1 \\ \beta_2 \\ \beta_3 \end{bmatrix} = \begin{bmatrix} 1\ 1\ 0\ 1 \\ 1\ 1\ 1\ 0 \\ 0\ 1\ 1\ 1 \\ 1\ 0\ 1\ 1 \end{bmatrix} \begin{bmatrix} \beta_0' \\ \beta_1' \\ \beta_2' \\ \beta_3' \end{bmatrix} + \begin{bmatrix} 0 \\ 0 \\ 1 \\ 1 \end{bmatrix}$$

We are transforming irreducible polynomial $x^4 + x + 1$ using affine matrix 1, irreducible polynomial $x^4 + x^3 + 1$ using affine matrix 2 and irreducible polynomial

Table 4. S-Box created from $x^4 + x + 1$ multiplicative inverse at $GF(2^4)$

4-bit value at $GF(2^4)$	Multiplicative inverse	x	$m_1(x)$
0000	0000	0	0
0001	0001	1	1
0010	1001	2	9
0011	1110	3	E
0100	1101	4	D
0101	1011	5	B
0110	0111	6	7
0111	0110	7	6
1000	1111	8	F
1001	0010	9	2
1010	1100	A	C
1011	0101	B	5
1100	1010	C	A
1101	0100	D	4
1110	0011	E	3
1111	1000	F	8

$x^4 + x^3 + x^2 + x + 1$ using affine matrix 3. Table 7 shows the three new S-boxes using three affine matrixes by three irreducible polynomials.

3   Performance Analysis of Proposed S-box

The nonlinear transformation is an essential criterion in modern cipher. It should provide a robust cryptographic character against different cryptanalyses such as Balance, Bijection, Difference Distribution Table (DDT), and Boomerang Connectivity Table (BCT), which will be discussed in this chapter.

3.1   Balance and Bijective

A Boolean function $S : GF(2^n) \rightarrow GF(2)$ is called balanced when the number of ones and zeros are equal in the output set in the corresponding truth table. Two Boolean functions XOR and AND defined as follows:

$$S_1 = \oplus : GF\left(2^2\right) \rightarrow GF(2)$$

$$S_2 = . : GF\left(2^2\right) \rightarrow GF(2)$$

Table 5. S-box created from $x^4 + x^3 + 1$ multiplicative inverse at $GF\left(2^4\right)$

4-bit value at $GF\left(2^4\right)$	Multiplicative inverse	x	$m_2(x)$
0000	0000	0	0
0001	0001	1	1
0010	1100	2	C
0011	1000	3	8
0100	0110	4	6
0101	1111	5	F
0110	0100	6	4
0111	1110	7	E
1000	0011	8	3
1001	1101	9	D
1010	1011	A	B
1011	1010	B	A
1100	0010	C	2
1101	1001	D	9
1110	0111	E	7
1111	0101	F	5

The following truth table with two variables x_1 and x_2 can define this (Table 8)

The *XOR* function has an equal number of zeros and ones; thus, this is balanced. On the other hand, the fourth column denotes *AND* function, which is not balanced.

If all linear combinations of columns are balanced, then a Boolean function S : $GF\left(2^2\right) \rightarrow GF(2)$ is called bijective. According to Tang et al. [23], the bijective property is satisfied with an (nxn) S-box if the Boolean functions f_i (for $1 \leq i \leq n$) of S-box can be represented, where $c_i \in \{0.1\}$ for $(c_1, c_2, ...c_3) \neq (0, 0, ..., 0)$ and the Hamming weight is *Hwt* [24]

$$Hwt\left(\sum_{i=1}^{n} c_i f_i\right) = 2^{n-1}$$

According to the above calculation, sage math [25], a free and open-source mathematics software, can calculate the balance for different S-boxes by the following command. The analysis shows the S-box$_1$, S-box$_2$, and S-box$_3$ are balanced and bijective.

Table 6. S-box created from $x^4 + x^3 + x^2 + x + 1$ multiplicative inverse at $GF\left(2^4\right)$

4-bit value at $GF\left(2^4\right)$	Multiplicative inverse	x	$m_3(x)$
0000	0000	0	0
0001	0001	1	1
0010	1111	2	F
0011	1010	3	A
0100	1000	4	8
0101	0110	5	6
0110	0101	6	5
0111	1001	7	9
1000	0100	8	4
1001	0111	9	7
1010	0011	A	3
1011	1110	B	E
1100	1101	C	D
1101	1100	D	C
1110	1011	E	B
1111	0010	F	2

```
sage: S1 = SBox(3,0xd,0xa,2,1,7,0xb,5,0xc,0xe,0xf,6,9,8,0,4)
sage: S1.is_balanced()
True

sage: S2 = SBox(9,0xe,0xf,2,0xa,6,4,1,0,8,0xb,0xc,7,5,0xd,3)
sage: S2.is_balanced()
True
sage: S3 = SBox(0xc,7,3,6,1,5,9,0xa,2,0xe,0,8,4,0xf,0xd,0xb)
sage: S3.is_balanced()
True
```

3.2   Difference Distribution Table and Boomerang Connectivity Table

Differential cryptanalysis is one of the essential cryptographical methods for evaluating the security of block ciphers. The defiance against differential cryptanalysis is highly reliant on the non-linearity structures of the predefined S-box.

$S : \{0, 1\}^n \rightarrow \{0, 1\}^n$, n-bit S-box, the differential propagations of S are typically represented in the $2^n x 2^n$ Difference Distribution table (DDT)τ, value for any pair (Δ_i, Δ_0)

Table 7. Three S-boxes after an affine transformation

4-bit value at $GF(2^4)$	S-box$_1$ binary	S-box$_1$ hex	S-box$_2$ binary	S-box$_2$ hex	S-box$_3$ binary	S-box$_3$ hex
0000	0011	3	1001	9	1100	C
0001	1101	D	1110	E	0111	7
0010	1010	A	1111	F	0011	3
0011	0010	2	0010	2	0110	6
0100	0001	1	1010	A	0001	1
0101	0111	7	0110	6	0101	5
0110	1011	B	0100	4	1001	9
0111	0101	5	0001	1	1010	A
1000	1100	C	0000	0	0010	2
1001	1110	E	1000	8	1110	E
1010	1111	F	1011	B	0000	0
1011	0110	6	1100	C	1000	8
1100	1001	9	0111	7	0100	4
1101	1000	8	0101	5	1111	F
1110	0000	0	1101	D	1101	D
1111	0100	4	0011	3	1011	B

Table 8. The truth table shows *XOR, AND*

x_1	x_2	$x_1 \oplus x_2$	$x_1 \cdot x_2$
0	0	0	0
0	1	1	0
1	0	1	0
1	1	0	1

is stored in the corresponding entry $\tau(\Delta_i, \Delta_0)$ of DDT, which denotes the input difference Δ_i propagates to the output difference Δ_0 with the likelihood, the highest entry in the table is named the differential uniformity of S [26].

$$\#\{x \in \{0, 1\}^n | S_{(x)} S(x\Delta_i) = \Delta_0$$

$$\tau(\Delta_i, \Delta_o)\backslash 2^n$$

The DDT for S-box$_1$ is shown in Table 9; We can observe the differential uniformity of the S-box is 4. The Boomerang Connectivity table may exploit the differential properties of diverse sections of the cipher. In the boomerang attack, E is the target cipher

Table 9. Difference Distribution Table (DDT) of S-box$_1$

Output Difference S-box$_1$

Input Difference S-box$_1$		0	1	2	3	4	5	6	7	8	9	A	B	C	D	E	F
	0	16	0	0	0	0	0	0	0	0	0	0	0	0	0	0	0
	1	0	2	2	0	2	0	2	0	2	2	0	0	0	0	4	0
	2	0	0	2	2	0	0	0	0	2	4	2	0	2	0	0	2
	3	0	4	0	0	2	0	0	2	2	0	2	0	2	2	0	0
	4	0	2	4	0	0	2	2	2	0	0	2	0	0	0	0	2
	5	0	0	0	0	4	0	2	2	0	2	0	2	2	0	0	2
	6	0	0	0	0	0	2	2	0	4	0	2	2	2	0	2	0
	7	0	0	0	2	0	0	4	2	2	0	0	0	0	2	2	2
	8	0	2	0	2	2	2	0	0	2	0	0	2	0	0	0	4
	9	0	2	0	0	0	2	0	0	0	2	0	0	2	4	2	2
	A	0	2	2	2	0	0	2	0	0	0	0	2	4	2	0	0
	B	0	0	2	2	2	4	0	2	0	0	0	0	2	0	2	0
	C	0	0	0	2	2	2	2	0	0	2	4	0	0	2	0	0
	D	0	0	2	0	2	0	0	0	0	0	2	4	0	2	2	2
	E	0	2	0	4	0	0	0	2	0	2	2	2	0	0	2	0
	F	0	0	2	0	0	2	0	4	2	2	0	2	0	2	0	0

compare to two sub-ciphers E_0 and E_1. So, $E = E_1 o E_0$. If the input difference α is propagated to the difference β by E_0 with the probability p. Then, with the probability p, the difference γ is propagated to δ by E_1. The boomerang attack can exploit the following difference with expected probability [27],

$$Pr\left[E^{-1}(E(x) \oplus \delta) \oplus E^{-1}(E(x \oplus \alpha) \oplus \delta) = \alpha\right] = q^2 p^2$$

E can be distinguished from a model cipher, on making around $(qp)^{-2}$ adaptive selected cipher/plain text requests.

The boomerang connectivity tale (BCT) is two-dimensional denoted by S can be represented by

$$BCT(\alpha, \beta) = \#\{x \in \mathbb{F}_2^n : S^{-1}(S(x) \oplus \beta) \oplus S^{-1}(S(x \oplus \alpha) \oplus \beta) = \alpha\}$$

Where $\alpha, \beta \in \mathbb{F}_2^n$. The S, the boomerang uniformity, is the highest value in the BCT except for the first row and the first column.

S-box$_1$ DDT and BCT are provided in Tables 9 and 10, respectively. The differential uniformity is 4, and boomerang uniformity is 16.

Table 10 shows the difference distribution table of our proposed S-box$_1$. The DDT has 16 rows, 16 columns, and 265 cells. The row and column represent the output

Table 10. Boomerang Connectivity Table (BCT) of S-box$_1$

∇_0 S-box$_1$																
Δ_i S-box$_1$	**0**	**1**	**2**	**3**	**4**	**5**	**6**	**7**	**8**	**9**	**A**	**B**	**C**	**D**	**E**	**F**
0	16	16	16	16	16	16	16	16	16	16	16	16	16	16	16	16
1	16	0	6	0	0	6	0	4	2	0	0	0	2	2	2	0
2	16	0	0	0	2	0	4	2	0	0	6	2	6	0	2	0
3	16	2	2	6	2	0	0	0	6	0	0	4	2	0	0	0
4	16	0	0	4	0	0	2	2	6	0	0	6	0	2	0	2
5	16	6	0	0	2	2	2	0	2	0	0	0	0	0	6	4
6	16	0	0	0	6	2	0	0	0	6	0	2	2	4	0	2
7	16	0	0	6	0	2	0	0	4	2	2	6	0	0	2	0
8	16	0	2	2	6	0	2	0	0	4	0	0	0	6	2	0
9	16	4	0	2	0	0	0	2	0	2	0	0	2	0	6	6
A	16	0	4	2	2	6	0	6	0	0	2	0	0	0	0	2
B	16	2	6	0	0	4	2	6	0	2	0	2	0	0	0	0
C	16	6	2	0	0	0	0	0	0	0	2	2	0	2	4	6
D	16	0	2	0	0	0	6	0	2	2	6	0	4	0	0	2
E	16	2	0	0	4	0	0	2	2	6	2	0	0	6	0	0
F	16	2	0	2	0	2	6	0	0	0	4	0	6	2	0	0

difference from 0 to F for each input difference. Zero represents the absence of that output difference for the following input difference. Too high or too low zero discloses more information concerning output difference [28]. S-box$_1$ difference distribution table indicates that it has three values 0, 2, and 4. Only one 4 find in each row and column. Consequently, S-box$_1$ can offer robust defiance alongside differential cryptoanalysis.

4 Conclusion

In this paper, we proposed a lightweight S-box design that uses algebraic methods to fulfil all of the requirements of lightweight cryptographic ciphers. This algebraic technique employs three irreducible polynomials from the Galois field $GF(2^4)$. Three multiplicative matrices, $m_1(x)$, $m_2(x)$, and $m_3(x)$ give rise to three multiplicative inverses, $m_1, m_2,$ and m_3. Then, using affine transformations, three S-boxes, S-boxe1, S-box2, and S-box3, are constructed. The cryptographic analysis demonstrates strong resistance to differential and boomerang cryptanalysis. In the future, produced S-boxes should be subjected to further testing and utilized for lightweight block ciphers to protect network interactions between IoT resource-constrained devices. This approach creates S-boxes that are suitable for resource end devices. S-boxes can also be used to provide a lightweight block cipher for IoT network communications.

References

1. Gao, W., et al.: Construction of nonlinear component of block cipher by action of modular group PSL(2, Z) on projective line PL(GF(28)). IEEE Access **8**, 136736–136749 (2020)
2. Wang, X., et al.: A chaotic system with infinite equilibria and its S-Box constructing application. Appl. Sci. **8**(11), 2132 (2018)
3. Ibrahim, S., Abbas, A.M.: A novel optimization method for constructing cryptographically strong dynamic s-boxes. IEEE Access **8**, 225004–225017 (2020)
4. Mohamed, K., et al.: Study of S-box Properties in Block Cipher. In: International Conference on Computer, Communications, and Control Technology (I4CT) (2014)
5. Jamal, S.S., Shah, T.: A novel algebraic technique for the construction of strong substitution box. Wireless Pers. Commun. **99**(1), 213–226 (2018)
6. Radhakrishnan, S.V., Subramanian, S.: An analytical approach to S-Box generation. Comput. Electr. Eng. **39**(3), 1006–1015 (2013)
7. Özkaynak, F.: On the effect of a chaotic system in performance characteristics of chaos based s-box designs. Physica A: Stat. Mech. Appl. **550**, 124072 (2020)
8. Mariot, L., et al.: Cellular automata based S-boxes. Crypt. Commun. **11**, 41–62 (2018)
9. Partheeban, P., Kavitha, V.: Dynamic key dependent AES S-box generation with optimized quality analysis. Clust. Comput. **22**(6), 14731–14741 (2018). https://doi.org/10.1007/s10586-018-2386-6
10. Lineham, A., Gulliver, T.A.: Heuristic S-box Design. Contemporary. Eng. Sci. **1**, 147–168 (2008)
11. Noughabi, M.N.A., Sadeghiyan, B.:Design of S-boxes based on neural networks. In: 2010 International Conference on Electronics and Information Engineering (2010)
12. Isa, H., Jamil, N., Z'aba, M.R.: S-box construction from non-permutation power functions. In: 6th International Conference on Security of Information and Networks (2013)
13. Çavuṣoğlu, Ü., et al.: A novel approach for strong S-Box generation algorithm design based on chaotic scaled Zhongtang system. Nonlinear Dyn. **87**(2), 1081–1094 (2017)
14. Atani, R.E., Mirzakuchaki, S., Atani, S.E.:Low cost implementation of Pomaranch S-Box. In: 1st International Conference on Wireless Communication. (2009)
15. Islam, F.U., Liu, G.: Designing S-Box Based on 4D-4Wing Hyperchaotic System (2017)
16. Alhadawi, H.S., Majid, M.A., Lambić, D., Ahmad, M.: A novel method of S-box design based on discrete chaotic maps and cuckoo search algorithm. Multimedia Tools Appl. **80**(5), 7333–7350 (2020). https://doi.org/10.1007/s11042-020-10048-8
17. Dey, S., Ghosh, R.: A Review of Cryptographic Properties of 4-Bit S-Boxes with Generation and Analysis of Crypto Secure S-Boxes. Taylor & Francis Group (2019)
18. Wong, M.M., Wong, M.L.D.: New lightweight AES S-box using LFSR. In: International Symposium on Intelligent Signal Processing and Communication Systems (ISPACS), Kuching, Malaysia (2014)
19. Zhang, W., Bao, Z., Rijmen, V., Liu, M.: A New Classification of 4-bit Optimal S-boxes and Its Application to PRESENT, RECTANGLE and SPONGENT. In: Leander, G. (ed.) FSE 2015. LNCS, vol. 9054, pp. 494–515. Springer, Heidelberg (2015). https://doi.org/10.1007/978-3-662-48116-5_24
20. Dawood, O.A., et al.: Design a compact non-linear S-Box with multiple-affine transformations. In: Khalaf, M., Al-Jumeily, D., Lisitsa, A. (eds.) Applied Computing to Support Industry: Innovation and Technology, ACRIT 2019, Communications in Computer and Information Science, vol 1174. Springer, Cham (2020)
21. Waqas, U., et al.: Generation of AES-Like S-Boxes by Replacing Affine Matrix. In: 12th International Conference on Frontiers of Information Technology (2014)

22. Zhang, X., et al.: Hardware Implementation of Compact AES S-box. Int. J. Comput. Sci. **42**, 125–131 (2015)
23. Tang, G., Liao, X., Chen, Y.: A novel method for designing S-boxes based on chaotic maps. Chaos, Solitons Fractals **23**(2), 413–419 (2005)
24. Song, L., Qin, X., Hu, L.: Boomerang connectivity table revisited. application to SKINNY and AES. IACR Trans. Symmetric Crypt. **1**, 118–141 (2019)
25. Stein, W.A.: S-Boxes and their algebraic representations. Sage 9.3 Reference Manual: Cryptography (2021)
26. Cid, C., et al.: Boomerang Connectivity Table: A New Cryptanalysis Tool. In: Annual International Conference on the Theory and Applications of Cryptographic Techniques (2018)
27. Boura, C., Canteaut, A.: On the Boomerang Uniformity of Cryptographic Sboxes. IACR Trans. Symmetric Crypt. **3**, 290–310 (2018)
28. Dey, S., Ghosh, R.: A review of existing 4-bit crypto S-Box cryptanalysis techniques and two new techniques with 4-bit boolean functions for cryptanalysis of 4-bit crypto S-Boxes. Adv. Pure Math. **8**(3), 273 (2018)

The Phantom Gradient Attack: A Study of Replacement Functions for the XOR Function

Åvald Åslaugson Sommervoll$^{(\boxtimes)}$ ⓘ

University of Oslo, Problemveien 7, 0315 Oslo, Norway
aavalds@ifi.uio.no
https://www.mn.uio.no/ifi/english/people/aca/aavalds/

Abstract. We build on the phantom gradient attack by introducing some new replacement function candidates for XOR. In this work, we put forward four new candidates' replacement functions and investigate the impact of different learning rates. We also extend and investigate the new replacement functions power on bitwise rotation XOR, of which previous phantom gradient attack works have struggled.

Keywords: Phantom gradient attack · Replacement function · Neural network · Neuro-cryptanalysis

1 Introduction

The recent publication in ICISSP 2021, *Dreaming of keys: introducing the phantom gradient attack* by Sommervoll [12], showed a new cryptanalytical approach. This work tries to unite the usually disjoint fields of algorithmic level of cryptanalysis with the heavily researched neural network training. The initial results for simple cryptographic functions were promising, but the attacks on the more complex XOR functions were not encouraging. In this paper, we present attacks on the XOR function using the *phantom gradient attack*.

As almost modern communication is done using bits, modern cryptographic functions typically work on a bitwise level. Moreover, cryptographic algorithms can be represented as a sequence of bitwise operations. That is, a symmetric key cryptographic encryption can be viewed as a function f can be broken down into multiple subfunctions $f_0, f_1, ..., f_n$ making an encryption:

$$f_{enc}(k, p) = f_0^\circ f_1^\circ ...^\circ f_n(k, p) = c, \tag{1}$$

where k is the symmetric key, p is the plaintext and c is the resulting ciphertext. This disjoint processing of information can be viewed as different layers of a neural network. However, a challenge is that these f_i's are typically discrete operations that do not have any gradient. The *phantom gradient attack* therefore works by replacing them with piecewise continuous ones. By replacing the subfunctions with, *replacement functions* allow our neural network representation of the

X. Yuan et al. (Eds.): QShine 2021, LNICST 402, pp. 228–238, 2021.
https://doi.org/10.1007/978-3-030-91424-0_14

cryptographic algorithm to have *gradients*. Part of the challenge that Sommervoll [12] put forward in his paper was to find good such *replacement functions*, of which will be the focus of this paper. In Sommervoll's network, he assumed that the plaintext was fixed and tried to recover the unknown key k, we abstract away from such problems and focus exclusively on finding good replacement functions for the XOR function. Moreover, we aim to find a better replacement function than the one presented in Sommervoll's paper. An improved replacement function is a key ingredient to more successful phantom gradient attacks.

The remaining paper is organized as follows: Sect. 2 discusses related work. Next, Sect. 3 discusses replacement functions, their most important qualities, and which replacement functions we will be looking at in this paper. In Sect. 3.1, we analyze the replacement functions' performance on XOR between 3 inputs. Section 3.2 increases the complexity by analyzing their performance on XOR between three bitwise rotated inputs. A more complicated example, ASCONS Σ_1 permutation, is tested in Sect. 3.3. Finally, Sect. 4 concludes and provides a short security discussion.

2   Related Work

The phantom gradient attack introduced by Sommervoll in *Dreaming of keys: introducing the phantom gradient attack* [12], is a recent addition to the field of neuro-cryptology. A field that has seen limited growth since Dourlens introduced it in 1996 [4]. Especially the field of neuro-cryptography has had limited contributions since Kinzel and Kanter in 2002 introduced a neural cryptosystem [7], which was quickly broken by Klimov et al. [8] the same year. On the other hand, neuro-cryptanalysis has been catching some wind in recent years, with Alini successfully applying an attack on DES and Triple-DES using neuro-Cryptanalysis in 2012s [1], and So applying a deep learning-based attack on simplified DES, and round reduced Simon and Speck [11]. While the works by Alani, So, and Sommervoll are all instances of neuro-cryptanalysis, they all differ in their approach. All three works assume to be in the known plaintext case; in contrast to the others, Alani does not try to recover the key. Instead, he tries to simulate the decryption under an unknown key by feeding a neural network the ciphertext as input and assigning loss based on how close the output is to the expected plaintext. On the other hand, So's attack tries to train a deep network to guess the key by giving both the ciphertext and the plaintext as inputs and having the key as the desired output. By training the network like this, he uses this trained network to predict a possible key given the input-ed cipher- and plaintext pair. Sommervoll, with his phantom gradient attack, defines the network to be trained in that the known plaintext is integrated as part of the network's fixed weights, and the desired target is the ciphertext. While the input is initially a guessed key, which is "trained" and permuted in a similar manner to how adversarial examples are created for image recognition. A weakness to this approach is that since the gradients are only given by the replacement functions, there is the possibility of choosing bad phantom gradients, which may lead the attack astray. However, we may draw from the field of adversarial examples; Goodfellow et al.

found that "linear models lack the capacity to resist adversarial perturbation" in their work *Explaining and Harnessing Adversarial Examples* [5]. Thereby, if we have the freedom to choose linear functions as replacement functions, this may be favorable in our endeavor to find candidate keys. On the note of adversarial examples, some works only alter parts of an image like Su et al., which introduce adversarial examples that only alter one pixel [13] and Gritsenko et al. with briar patches that only affect a portion of the image [6]. This is especially interesting as some portions of cryptographic functions' initial state is known, like in the ASCON cryptosystem [3]. Therefore, a phantom gradient attack on such a cryptosystem should make sure not to alter the initial state's known parts.

3   Replacement Functions XOR

The most important quality for a replacement function is that the function and its discrete counterpart should have the same output given the same input. For the XOR function this means that inputs [1,1] and [0,0], should result in 0 and the inputs [1,0] and [0,1] should result in 1. This operation can be viewed as addition under modulo 2, which naturally gives us our first replacement function:

$$f(x,y) = x + y \ (mod \ 2). \tag{xori0}$$

We will call this replacement function *xori0*, as it is the most natural replacement function for *xor* between *indexes*. Furthermore, its derivatives are quite simple:

$$\frac{\partial f}{\partial x} = 1 \tag{2}$$

$$\frac{\partial f}{\partial y} = 1, \tag{3}$$

This representation is also linear, which is be favorable for generating adversarial examples [5]. Sommervoll also mentioned that XOR can be viewed as an addition under *mod2* but did not consider it as a possible replacement function [12]. He did however consider what we will refer to as xori1:

$$f(x,y) = x + y - 2xy, \tag{xori1}$$

which had the unfavorable quality of having derivatives that are 0 for 0.5, midway between the bitshift from 0 and 1, namely:

$$\frac{\partial f}{\partial x} = 1 - 2y \tag{4}$$

$$\frac{\partial f}{\partial y} = 1 - 2x, \tag{5}$$

Our third candidate is a natural extension of xori1, without the weakness of having a fixed zero gradient between 0 and 1:

$$f(x,y) = (x - y)^2 = x^2 + y^2 - 2xy, \tag{xori2}$$

which has gradients that are 0 for x = y, which will be rare especially given a random initial guess. Our 4th replacement function *xori3* views the second index as a constant and splits the output into two separate cases, where the input x is either bitflipped or not depending on y:

$$f(x,y) = \begin{cases} x \text{ for } y \leq 0.5 \\ 1 - x \text{ for } y > 0.5 \end{cases} \tag{xori3}$$

This gives us our second linear replacement function, also making it especially vulnerable to adversarial examples [5]. Our 5th and final replacement function is xori4 which again is simple addition, but switches out the activation function mod2 which xori0 uses, and instead utilizes a sine-based activation function: $g(x) = \frac{1+sin(\pi x - \frac{\pi}{2})}{2}$, so we have:

$$f(x,y) = \frac{1 + sin(\pi(x + y) - \frac{\pi}{2})}{2} \tag{xori4}$$

This variation of xori0 is differentiable everywhere, which is favorable from a mathematical perspective. However, in the context of neural networks, this property seems to hold little significance as many state-of-the-art activation functions are not differentiable everywhere, for example, ReLU [10]. To visualize these activation functions Fig. 1 shows how the different XOR functions behave in the interval from −1 to 2. All these replacement functions look quite different apart from all of them sharing the same final output for the binary inputs 1 and 0. Eq. (xori0) and Eq. (xori4) look similar since they both just use addition and some form of activation function to restrict the output. Similarly, Eq. (xori1) and Eq. (xori2) are similar as they are include the interaction term xy, and have no activation function. The odd one out in the group is definetly Eq. (xori3) as it takes a more discrete approach treating y as either a 1 in xor or a 0 in xor. These five xori functions differ in mathematical complexity, and there are no apriori reasons for the supremacy of one over the others. We use the same simplified model as used in Sommervoll's paper [12], Fig. 2: where FFNN stands for feed-forward neural network. For the network, we have four[1]. possible outputs and potentially infinitely many different starting values. We choose 1000 different starting values and try to recover all four of the different states from each of these 1000 different starting values. Table 1 shows the pct success rate of the different xor replacement functions for different learning rates, when run for 1000 generations.

We see that all the replacement functions perform reasonably well for this simple example, especially with a learning rate of 0.2, where all of them get 100% recovery across all 4000 trials. Moreover, we see that a learning rate of 0.001 is a bit low for only 1000 iterations[2]. Aside from this, we see that both the linear replacement functions xori0 and xori3 perform extraordinarily well with

---

[1] The four possible 2 bit inputs are (0,0), (0,1), (1,0), and (1,1).
[2] For more intricate problems, we may need more iterations and perhaps an even lower learning rate.

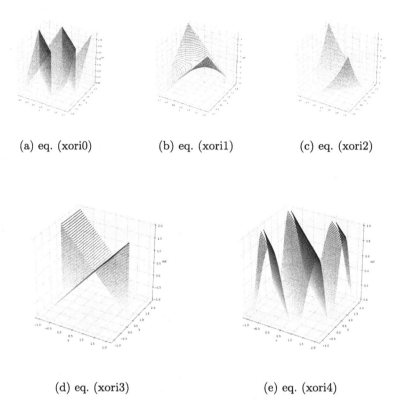

(a) eq. (xori0)   (b) eq. (xori1)   (c) eq. (xori2)

(d) eq. (xori3)   (e) eq. (xori4)

Fig. 1. View of the behaviour of the different XOR implementations in the range -1 to 2

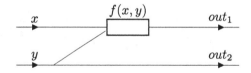

Fig. 2. Example FFNN for XOR between two inputs

Table 1. Percentage success rate of the the different XOR replacement functions across 1000 trials for each of the possible 2 bit outputs.

lr $\rightarrow$	0.001	0.01	0.1	0.2	0.5	1.0
xori0	0.00	99.88	100.00	100.00	100.00	100.00
xori1	0.05	75.47	96.08	100.00	97.12	0.08
xori2	0.48	31.08	100.00	100.00	49.65	30.90
xori3	0.00	100.00	100.00	100.00	100.00	100.00
xori4	0.08	7.68	100.00	100.00	100.00	100.00

the higher learning rates with almost 100% recovery rate for every instance. Also, in contrast to what Parascandolo et al. [9] found, we see that the sine activation function used in *xori4* performs very well in this example, outperforming both xori1 and xori2, in all learning rates except for 0.01. Perhaps surprisingly, we also observe that Sommervoll's xori1 performs reasonably well with a learning rate between 0.1 and 0.5; however, we will see how this strength holds up as we increase the complexity of the problem.

3.1   XOR Between Three Inputs

Some cryptographic functions include a three-way XOR between indices; these indices can be complicated and, as is evident from Sommervoll's limited success with such functions [12]. We can illustrate this three-way XOR problem as a FFNN in the way shown in Fig. 3. This construction is straightforward and does

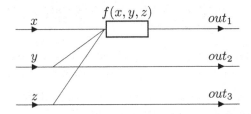

Fig. 3. Example FFNN for XOR between three inputs

not pose a much more significant challenge than XOR between two inputs. So we will not be looking at the phantom gradient attack on this network but instead, use it as an example to extend our pre-existing xori-functions, Eqs. (xori0) to (xori4). Extending xori0 is very simple we let:

$$f(x,y,z) = xori0(xori0(x,y),z) = x + y + z \ (mod \ 2), \qquad \text{(xorti0)}$$

we call this xorti0, because it is the natural extension of xori0 and it is an *XOR* between *three inputs*. For Eq. (xori1) we will use Sommervoll's [12] extension:

$$f(x,y,z) = x + y + z - 2xy - 2xz - 2yz + 4xyz, \qquad \text{(xorti1)}$$

of which is the same as
$xori1(xori1(x,y),z) = xori1(xori1(x,z),y) = xori1(xori1(y,z),x)$. For xori2, on the other hand, it is a little bit more complicated. We have four natural candidates:

$$f(x,y,z) = x^2 + y^2 + z^2 - 2xy - 2xz - 2yz + 4xyz \qquad \text{(xorti2)}$$

$$f(x, y, z) = f(f(x, y), z) = ((x - y)^2 - z)^2$$
$$= x^4 + y^4 + z^2 + 2x^2y^2 - 4x^3y - 4xy^3 + 4x^2y^2 - 2x^2z + y^2z - 2xyz$$
$$\text{(xorti2z)}$$

$$f(x, y, z) = f(f(x, z), y) = ((x - z)^2 - y)^2$$
$$= x^4 + z^4 + y^2 + 2x^2z^2 - 4x^3z - 4xz^3 + 4x^2z^2 - 2x^2y + z^2y - 2xzy$$
$$\text{(xorti2y)}$$

$$f(x, y, z) = f(f(y, z), x) = ((z - y)^2 - x)^2$$
$$= z^4 + y^4 + x^2 + 2z^2y^2 - 4z^3y - 4zy^3 + 4z^2y^2 - 2z^2x + y^2x - 2zyx,$$
$$\text{(xorti2x)}$$

where Eq. (xorti2) is based on Eq. (xorti1) and symmetric across the three inputs we are XOR-ing, while Eqs. (xorti2z) to (xorti2x) the natural extention of Eq. (xori2), but vary with respect two which index is XOR-ed last. For Eq. (xori3) we treated the second index as an external index from the start; we extend this by doing the same with the third index.

$$f(x, y, z) = \begin{cases} x \text{ for } (y \le 0.5 \wedge z \le 0.5) \vee (y > 0.5 \wedge z > 0.5) \\ 1 - x \text{ for } (y > 0.5 \wedge z \le 0.5) \vee (y \le 0.5 \wedge z > 0.5) \end{cases} \quad \text{(xorti3)}$$

Equation (xori4) we extend the same way we extended Eq. (xori0) as they are both based on addition and an activation function.

$$f(x, y, z) = \frac{1 + sin(\pi * (x + y + z) - \frac{\pi}{2})}{2} \quad \text{(xorti4)}$$

With these xorti functions in mind, let us move on to XOR between three bitwise rotated instances of the input.

3.2   XOR with Bitwise Rotation

To ensure no loss of information in this three way bitwise rotated XOR we construct a network with 4 inputs as shown in Fig. 4. where we have 4 inputs and xor between rotations 0, 1 and 2, in other words it defines an XOR on the form:

$$x_i \oplus x_{i+1(mod4)} \oplus x_{i+2(mod4)}.$$

This setup means that we have 16 different inputs, moreover, the recovered bit sequence will be unique if recovered. So if we want to check each xorti's performance 250 times per target, we get 4000 trials per xorti. Furthermore, as we are working with bitwise rotation the three replacement functions Eqs. (xorti2z) to (xorti2x) are equivalent so we only check eq. (xorti2z). The resulting performance is shown in Table 2. We see clearly that with XOR between three indices, the learning quickly becomes more complex. Note that the main xorti1 previously used by Sommervoll performs poorly and never has a success rate above 0.2. Of the proposed replacement functions, the clear winner among the candidates is

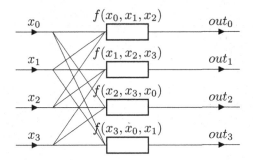

Fig. 4. XOR between three round rotated instances of a four-bit input

Table 2. Percentage success rate of the different XOR replacement functions on Fig. 4

lr →	0.01	0.1	0.2	0.5	1.0
xorti0	0.00	0.02	0.00	0.00	99.95
xorti1	16.98	17.10	16.58	9.93	0.00
xorti2z	4.70	29.88	17.00	7.80	2.92
xorti2	25.48	31.82	11.40	4.68	4.58
xorti3	21.38	19.85	18.60	100.00	100.00
xorti4	0.00	0.02	0.75	22.35	7.85

xorti3, which gets a 100% success rate for both learning rate 0.5 and learning rate 1. Also, note that xorti0 gets almost a 100% recovery rate for learning rate 1. It is quite surprising that such high learning rates are the ones that perform the best, which in contrast to the general case in neural network training. For example, for stochastic gradient descent in KERAS, the default value is 0.01 [2], it is even lower for some of the more fine-tuned optimizers. Also, perhaps surprisingly, we see that the xorti's based on addition and an activation function (XORITR0 and XORITR4) both seem to favor higher learning rates. In contrast, the continuous ones such as XORITR1, XORITR2, and XORITR2z seem to favor more midrange learning rates such as 0.1. Maybe with more iterations and better optimizers, they can perform even better.

3.3 ASCON's Σ_1 permutation

The cryptosystem ASCON has some instances of XOR between three bitwise rotated instances of inputs [3]. One of which is the Σ_1 permutation:

$$x_i \oplus x_{i+61(modn)} \oplus x_{i+39(modn)}, \tag{6}$$

where n is the input size, which in ASCON's case is 64. However, in our analysis, we will vary this input size to study our replacement functions' effectiveness. We

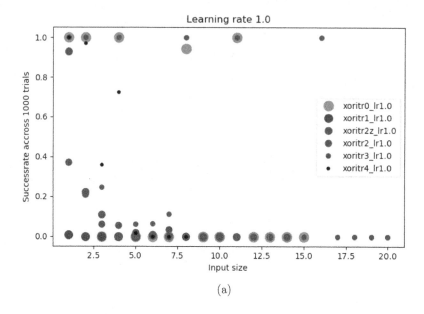

(a)

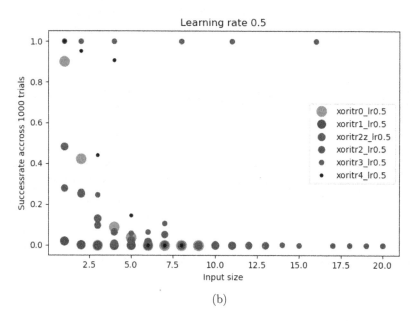

(b)

Fig. 5. Comparison of the different xorti's under the learning rates 0.5 and 1.0

wish to test input sizes from 1 up to 64, where input size four will be similar to the case we studied in Fig. 4 this time, it will be (i+1) and (i+3) instead. Similar to earlier trials, we run a 1000 iterations and a 1000 trials per input size. However, we do not test all input sizes from 1 to 64; if all 1000 trials fail for four incrementally larger input sizes, we terminate the run and assume that it will also fail for larger block sizes. We do this for learning rates 1 and 0.5, and the results are shown in Fig. 5. We see that, like in Sommervoll's paper, they all perform rather poorly as we increase the number of bits. Sommervoll's earlier suggestions xoritr1 performs exceptionally bad, having no successes when dealing with more than 2 bits. Among the others, we see that xorti3 generally performs the best. This may be because of its semidiscrete nature. Also, it is influenced by fewer gradients simultaneously as y and z are treated as constants; however, this is not the entire story as xori0 performs similarly with a learning rate of 1.0. Some final tests with learning rates 0.2, 0.1 and 0.01, showed that xorti3 was successful in recovering the full 64 bits $\frac{25}{1000}$ trials with a learning rate of 0.2. This is still only a recovery rate of 2.5%. However, it shows that the phantom gradient attack can be successful on the full 64 bits.

4   Conclusion

In this work, we have put forward a series of candidate replacement functions for the XOR function. All of which performed well for a simple XOR between two indices. However, in the more complex case of XOR between three bitwise rotated instances of the input, the replacement functions perform considerably worse. Perhaps most interesting was that a considerably high learning rate was the best performing and that the more simplistic replacement functions also performed best. The piecewise differentiable xori3 and xorti3 performed the best, clearly outperforming Sommervoll's previous xori1 and xorti1. We also found some merit in attempting to use linear representations as it is easier to find adversarial examples in these cases.

The phantom gradient attack introduced by Sommervoll in 2021 does not yet pose any threat to state-of-the-art cryptosystems. The phantom gradient attack is heavily based on the training of neural networks, of which current state-of-the-art works best with deep networks, so any cryptosystem that employs a particularly wide network should be more robust. In this paper, we did show that we could recover 64 bits of a permutation 2.5% of the time. This is not enough to threaten most modern cryptosystems yet but can provide a building block for future attacks.

We iteratively run 1000 trials per xorti on the different input sizes 1 through 64 for the permutation shown in eq. (6). If the success rate is 0% for four input sizes in a row, then the run terminates, and we assume the larger input sizes also to achieve roughly 0% success.

Acknowledgement. The author wishes to give special thanks to Audun Jøsang and Thomas Gregersen for valuable discussion and words of encouragement.

References

1. Alani, M.M.: Neuro-cryptanalysis of DES and triple-DES. In: Huang, T., Zeng, Z., Li, C., Leung, C.S. (eds.) ICONIP 2012. LNCS, vol. 7667, pp. 637–646. Springer, Heidelberg (2012). https://doi.org/10.1007/978-3-642-34500-5_75
2. Chollet, F.: Keras (2015).https://github.com/fchollet/keras
3. Dobraunig, C., Eichlseder, M., Mendel, F., Schläffer, M.: Ascon v1.2. submission to round 3 of the CAESAR competition (2016). https://competitions.cr.yp.to/round3/asconv12.pdf
4. Dourlens, S.: Applied neuro-cryptography and neuro-cryptanalysis of des. Master Thesis (1996). https://doi.org/10.13140/RG.2.2.35476.24960
5. Goodfellow, I.J., Shlens, J., Szegedy, C.: Explaining and harnessing adversarial examples. arXiv preprint arXiv:1412.6572 (2014)
6. Gritsenko, A.A., D'Amour, A., Atwood, J., Halpern, Y., Sculley, D.: Briarpatches: Pixel-space interventions for inducing demographic parity. arXiv preprint arXiv:1812.06869 (2018)
7. Kinzel, W., Kanter, I.: Neural cryptography. In: Proceedings of the 9th International Conference on Neural Information Processing 2002, ICONIP 2002, vol. 3, pp. 1351–1354. IEEE (2002)
8. Klimov, A., Mityagin, A., Shamir, A.: Analysis of neural cryptography. In: Zheng, Y. (ed.) ASIACRYPT 2002. LNCS, vol. 2501, pp. 288–298. Springer, Heidelberg (2002). https://doi.org/10.1007/3-540-36178-2_18
9. Parascandolo, G., Huttunen, H., Virtanen, T.: Taming the waves: sine as activation function in deep neural networks (2016)
10. Ramachandran, P., Zoph, B., Le, Q.V.: Searching for activation functions. arXiv preprint arXiv:1710.05941 (2017)
11. So, J.: Deep learning-based cryptanalysis of lightweight block ciphers. Secur. Commun. Netw. **2020** (2020)
12. Sommervoll, Å.: Dreaming of keys: Introducing the phantom gradient attack. In: 7th International Conference on Information Systems Security and Privacy, ICISSP 2021, 11 February 2021 through 13 February 2021, SciTePress (2021)
13. Su, J., Vargas, D.V., Sakurai, K.: One pixel attack for fooling deep neural networks. IEEE Trans. Evol. Comput. **23**(5), 828–841 (2019)

Network Security

Topology Validator - Defense Against Topology Poisoning Attack in SDN

Abhay Kumar$^{(\boxtimes)}$ and Sandeep Shukla

Department of CSE, IIT Kanpur, Kanpur 208016, India
{abhkum,sandeeps}@iitk.ac.in

Abstract. SDN controller in the SDN (Software Defined Network) environment needs to know the topology of the whole network under its control to ensure successful delivery and routing of packets to their respective destinations and paths. SDN Controller uses OFDP to learn the topology, for which it uses a variant of LLDP packets used in the legacy network. The current implementations of OFDP in popular SDN controllers suffer mainly two categories of attacks, namely Topology Poisoning by LLDP packet injection and Topology Poisoning by LLDP packet relay. Several solutions have been proposed to deal with these two categories of attacks. Our study found that, while most of these proposed solutions successfully prevented the LLDP packet injection-based attack, none could defend the relay-based attack with promising accuracy. In this paper, we have proposed a solution, namely Topology Validator, along with its implementation as a module of Flood-Light SDN controller, which, apart from preventing LLDP injection-based attack, was also able to detect and thwart the LLDP relay-based attack successfully.

Keywords: Software Defined Network · SDN · SDN security · Topology attack

1 Introduction

SDN is a novel networking paradigm that has gained momentum during the last decade. It decouples the data plane and control plane against the standard networking concept, where the control plane and data plane are tightly coupled and present on each device. SDN makes the network programmable allowing it to be more dynamic, cost-effective and controllable. While it has added many features, being an evolving concept, it is also open to several explored and unexplored vulnerabilities. Many of such attacks have been discovered by multiple researchers [11, 14, 15, 17, 18, 21, 25] distributed across control plane, data plane and applications connected to the SDN eco-system via different APIs. Further countermeasures corresponding to each discovered attack has been proposed by researchers [1, 12, 13, 21] with various degree of success.

In this paper, we have explored an attack related to how topology is learned and maintained in the SDN environment. We further have proposed a countermeasure, namely Topology Validator, against the relay-based ghost link creation attack that not just defends against the attack completely but also requires minimal overhead compared to prior

The original version of this chapter was revised: an error in the name of one of the authors has been corrected. The correction to this chapter is available at https://doi.org/10.1007/978-3-030-91424-0_21

© ICST Institute for Computer Sciences, Social Informatics and Telecommunications Engineering 2021, corrected publication 2021
Published by Springer Nature Switzerland AG 2021. All Rights Reserved
X. Yuan et al. (Eds.): QShine 2021, LNICST 402, pp. 241–260, 2021.
https://doi.org/10.1007/978-3-030-91424-0_15

solutions for this type of attack. In this work, we have assumed that only hosts can be compromised, switches and controller remain immune.

This paper further is organized as below. Section 2 is about the background of the topic, where we have briefed about SDN (Software Defined Network) and methods used for learning topology in SDN. Section 3 explores topology poisoning attacks and their experimental verifications. Section 4 discusses some of the previously proposed state-of-art works. Section 5 details our proposed solution, experimental observations and related works. Section 6 discusses the result and analyze different parameters that may be affecting our solution adaptation. Section 7 concludes this paper.

2   Background

SDN is a novel networking paradigm that has gained momentum during the last decade. It decouples the data plane and control plane against the standard networking concept, where the control plane and data plane are tightly coupled and present on each device. SDN makes the network programmable allowing it to be more dynamic, cost-effective and controllable. While it has added many features, being an evolving concept, it is also open to several explored and unexplored vulnerabilities. Many of such attacks have been discovered by multiple researchers [11, 14, 15, 17, 18, 21, 25] distributed across control plane, data plane and applications connected to the SDN eco-system via different APIs. Further countermeasures corresponding to each discovered attack has been proposed by researchers [1, 12, 13, 21] with various degree of success.

In this paper, we have explored an attack related to how topology is learned and maintained in the SDN environment. We further have proposed a countermeasure, namely Topology Validator, to the said attack that not just defends against the attack but also requires minimal overhead compared with prior solutions for this category of attacks. In this work, we have assumed that only hosts can be compromised, switches and controller remained immune.

2.1   Software Defined Network

Software Defined Network is a growing architecture that is dynamic, programmable, cost-effective and versatile, making it perfect for the high data transfer capacity networking. The thought behind SDN is to isolate the control plane and the data plane of the networking devices. The primary distinction between SDN and traditional systems is that in the conventional systems, the data plane and the control plane are integrated inside the networking devices, i.e. each networking device has its controlling functions and switching functions. As packets enter the networking device, the networking device itself decides the further activity. However, in the case of SDN, the control plane is logically centralized. The control plane contains controllers that offer guidance to the data plane about how to act whenever a packet arrives. The data plane is included only in forwarding devices where they simply forward the arrived packet as per the flow rules present in the forwarding table.

2.2   Topology Learning in SDN

SDN networks have their intelligence put inside the SDN Controller, which keeps the network functional by commanding switches to route/forward packets to their respective destinations. To function appropriately, SDN controllers need to learn a lot of information from the network. One such important piece of information is the network's topology. Contrary to a legacy network where each switch requires to learn the topology, SDN requires only the controller to know the complete topology of the network. Though the process of learning the topology under both forms of networking is different, SDN OFDP (OpenFlow Discovery Protocol) also uses LLDP (Link Layer Discovery Protocol) packets to learn the topology. The SDN controller for each connected switch generates number of LLDP packets equal to the number of active ports on that switch and sends these to the switches via the controller-switch links at regular intervals. The information about the number of active ports and other details of the switch are learned by the controller at the time the switch registers with the controller and keeps it updated by its host tracking service.

2.2.1 LLDP Packet Format
Figure 1 describes the standard LLDP packet format, while Fig. 2 is an LLDP packet capture from our experimental setup. Apart from common fields such as Preamble, Destination MAC address, Source MAC address, Ethernet type (which describes the link-layer protocol, here 0x88cc) and Frame checksum, it contains four compulsory TLV (Type-Length-Values)s and variable numbers of optional TLVs. DPID and Port ID TLVs are set with Data-Path-ID and port number of the switch respectively, for which the SDN controller has generated that particular LLDP packet.

Preamble	Dst MAC	Src MAC	EthType 0x88CC	DPID of Switch TLV	PORTID Switch TLV	Time to Live TLV	Optional TLV	End TLV	Frame Check Seq.

Fig. 1. LLDP packet format

This further generalizes to the fact that all LLDP packets sent to a specific switch will have the same DPID TLV but different PORT ID TLV corresponding to each port. TTL (Time-To-Live) TLV decides the lifespan of the LLDP packet, after which it will be discarded.

In Fig. 2, the captured LLDP packet has four optional TLVs put in for multiple purposes; the last optional TLV, however, will be of our interest which has been discussed in Sect. 4. From the DPID and Port ID TLVs, it can be learned that this LLDP packet was sent to port number 2 of the switch with DPID - 00:00:00:00:00:02.

```
▶ Frame 1: 77 bytes on wire (616 bits), 77 bytes captured
▶ Linux cooked capture
▼ Link Layer Discovery Protocol
    ▼ Chassis Subtype = MAC address, Id: 00:00:00:00:00:02
        0000 001. .... .... = TLV Type: Chassis Id (1)
        .... ...0 0000 0111 = TLV Length: 7
        Chassis Id Subtype: MAC address (4)
        Chassis Id: 00:00:00_00:00:02 (00:00:00:00:00:02)
    ▶ Port Subtype = Port component, Id: 0002
    ▶ Time To Live = 120 sec
    ▶ Stanford University, OpenFlow Group - Unknown (0)
    ▶ Unknown TLV
    ▶ Unknown TLV
    ▶ Stanford University, OpenFlow Group - Unknown (1)
    ▶ End of LLDPDU
```

Fig. 2. Wireshark capture of LLDP packet

2.2.2 Link Discovery Service (LDS)

LDS is accomplished by OFDP (OpenFlow Discovery Protocol), which uses LLDP packets to learn the network's topology and keeps it updated as and when new links are added, existing links fail or are removed. LDS in the SDN controller can do so by sending LLDP packets to switches corresponding to each active port on respective switches at regular interval. Intervals after which LLDP packets are sent may be SDN controller dependent. However, in our experimental setup where we had used FloodLight [7, 8] SDN controller, it sends LLDP packets at an interval of 15 s which can be seen in Fig. 3 which is a capture of the FloodLight console output.

```
14:48:14.168 INFO [n.f.l.i.LinkDiscoveryManager:Scheduled-1] Sending LLDP packets out of all the enabled ports
14:48:29.171 INFO [n.f.l.i.LinkDiscoveryManager:Scheduled-2] Sending LLDP packets out of all the enabled ports
14:48:44.175 INFO [n.f.l.i.LinkDiscoveryManager:Scheduled-2] Sending LLDP packets out of all the enabled ports
14:48:59.179 INFO [n.f.l.i.LinkDiscoveryManager:Scheduled-3] Sending LLDP packets out of all the enabled ports
14:49:14.184 INFO [n.f.l.i.LinkDiscoveryManager:Scheduled-0] Sending LLDP packets out of all the enabled ports
14:49:29.188 INFO [n.f.l.i.LinkDiscoveryManager:Scheduled-3] Sending LLDP packets out of all the enabled ports
```

Fig. 3. FloodLight console output LLDP frequency

As illustrated in Fig. 4, let's consider a topology with one controller, two switches and two hosts connected to each switch making the total number of active ports three on each switch. SDN controller will send three (corresponding to each active port on each switch) LLDP packets to each switch embedded inside individual OFPT PACKET OUT messages. Switch extracts out the LLDP packets and forwards them to their respective destination ports. Ports connecting hosts will ignore these LLDP packets. However, ports connecting to other switches will make the LLDP packet marked for that particular port forwarded to other connected switches; in Fig. 4, the LLDP packet sent to switch S1 and port number 3 (S1,3) will reach the switch S2 on port number 1 (S2,1). On arrival at S2, these packets are embedded inside an OFPT PACKET IN message and forwarded to the controller. We found some authors [30] attributed this action of switch S2 to some pre-set rule inside the switch Flow Table or some firmware. However, our observation differed from that.

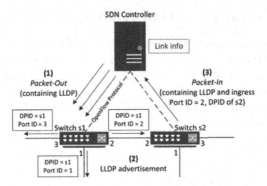

Fig. 4. Working of link discovery service

We could not see any specific flow rules for handling LLDP packet in particular, ref. Fig. 5, instead they got forwarded to the controller following the primary/default rule (which exists in the flow table of all switches all the time, Fig. 5), which says when a switch does not find a match for some arrived packet; it forwards it to the controller after embedding it inside an OFPT PACKET IN message.

```
mininet> dpctl dump-flows
*** s2 ------------------------------------------------
------------------------------
 cookie=0x0, duration=81258.874s, table=0, n_packets=61
47, n_bytes=481648, priority=0 actions=CONTROLLER:65535
*** s1 ------------------------------------------------
------------------------------
 cookie=0x0, duration=81258.889s, table=0, n_packets=61
44, n_bytes=481391, priority=0 actions=CONTROLLER:65535
```

Fig. 5. Flow tables of S1 and S2 with LLDP traffic only

Once this forwarded packet arrives at the controller, the controller can learn that the LLDP packet it has sent to (S1,3) is being received at (S2,1) confirms a unidirectional link between S1 and S2 via port number 3 and 1, respectively. Similarly, the LLDP packet sent by the controller to Switch S2 on port number 1 will be received via (S1,3), confirming another unidirectional link between (S2,1) and (S1,3). As both unidirectional links will be processed in one round, this will result in the discovery of the bi-directional link between S1 and S2. Accordingly, the controller will update the overall topology of the network.

3 Topology Poisoning Attacks in SDN

Poisoning the system's topology isn't altogether new in SDN. A compromised host or a compromised switch can start poisoning the topology. Our paper mainly focuses on the attack started by a compromised host.

3.1 Topology Poisoning by Fake LLDP Packet Injection

Assumption 1: To keep it simple, let us assume that all LLDP packets sent by a controller all the time have all Optional TLVs same (This assumption is not very much leveraged, as we have found an old version of FloodLight, the controller under our study doing the same). We further assume that any one host on any of switches, say h1 (connected on port number 1) on S1, is under an attacker's control, using which attacker can inject some packet to the switch.

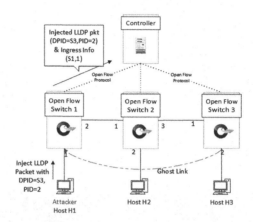

Fig. 6. Ghost link creation by fake LLDP packet

On receiving a genuine LLDP packet, this compromised host injects an LLDP packet with DPID switch S3 and port number 2. When this injected LLDP packet reaches switch S1, unaware of any malicious activity in the network, switch S1 will treat this packet as if it is coming from some switch connected on port 1 of switch S1 and will forward it to the controller after embedding it inside PACKET IN message with source information as (S1,1). This will lead the controller to assume that there exists a link between (S3,2) & (S1,1) and update the overall topology of the network accordingly. Post this topology update, when a host on S3 will try to communicate with a host on S1, the controller will route it through just discovered non-existent link resulting in communication failure.

Assumption 2: Restricting Assumption 1 to cases from all optional TLVs same in all round for all switches, to at least one Optional TLV unique in each round but same for all switches, will not make any difference on the ease of attack and attacker will be able to create a fake link without any new cost.

Assumption 3: On further restricting our Assumption 2 to have at least one unique Optional TLV corresponding to each switch will force the attacker to change its strategy. It will be no longer the same easy task using this approach to create a fake link as it was earlier. For creating a fake link between S3 and S1 under this updated assumption with the compromised host on (S1,1), the attacker on (S1,1) will need to learn the unique Optional TLV sent to S3, and then only it can inject an LLDP packet with learned unique optional TLV to succeed in creating the fake link. The attacker may learn it by going through the controller's source code if it is open-source or listening to the traffic and making a guess about it (unless it is some random value each time). It is evident that the latest added restriction will rule out the possibility of an attack of nature discussed in this subsection to a larger extent; however, this will not rule out the kind of attack we have discussed in Subsect. 3.2.

We were able to execute the attack under the first assumption by deploying a C executable on host h1. Executable actively listened for the LLDP packet multicast and injects it to S1 after making changes as illustrated in the Fig. 6. With this setup, we were not just able to create the fake link for once, but maintain it in a controlled manner also. The same setup as able to execute the attack under second assumption as well.

3.2 Topology Poisoning by LLDP Packet Relay

The first assumption for the attack under this category remains the same as what we had after adding the second restriction (all rounds of topology discovery will have at least one optional TLV unique to each switch in every round) to our basic assumption (only hosts can be compromised, switches and controllers remain immune). We further assume that we have at least one host compromised on each switch between which attacker wishes to create the fake link. In our example topology illustrated in Fig. 7, we assume hosts on (S1,1) and (S3,2) are under attacker control.

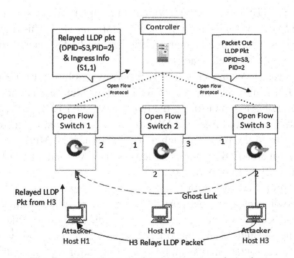

Fig. 7. Ghost link creation by LLDP packet relay

For the execution of the attack, on receiving LLDP packet from the controller, compromised host on (S3,2) uses already existing connectivity between S1 and S3 to relay received LLDP packet to (S1,1). A host connected to (S1,1) on receiving this relayed packet, injects it to the switch S1, which will get forwarded to the controller (as this will not match any of existing flow-table rules), making the controller assume that there exists a unidirectional link from (S3,1) to (S1,1). This unidirectional link can easily be converted to bidirectional by making the host on (S1,1) to relay the received LLDP packet to host at (S3,2) and host on (S3,2) later injecting it to S3.

We must note here that, restricting our first assumption even to the extent that the LLDP packet corresponding to each port has some unique Optional TLV, this type of attack cannot be prevented.

We were able to execute this attack even with the latest version of FloodLight. SDN controller under our experimental setup. We installed a C program executable on both compromised hosts; each of these C programs had two threads. One thread was used for listening for LLDP packets, while the other one for creating a UDP server. First thread on each compromised host, when receives an LLDP packet relays it to UDP server running on another compromised host. The second thread used for running the UDP server on receipt of relayed LLDP packet was injecting it to the network via the switch they were connected to. In this case, as well we were just not able to create the fake link but were able to maintain it as well.

4 Existing Solutions and Analysis

In this section, we give a concise review of applicable state-of-the-art endeavours that are accomplished for the relief of topology poisoning attacks in SDN. Mostly, these methodologies depend on the consideration of hash or static functions.

1. Adding Unique TLV (Type Length Value) to each LLDP packet: This solution we found in the SDN controller Floodlight V2.3 implemented. This method can defend the attack cases where an adversary fabricates the LLDP packet to be injected. It fails to counter relay-based attacks.
2. S. Hong, L. Xu, H. Wang, G. Gu [33] proposes a solution to the link fabrication attack, which distinguishes the reason for LLDP packet-based attacks as a failure in identifying the origin and ensuring the integrity of the LLDP packet. It additionally states that no host should inject LLDP packet to the switch, i.e. it stops injection of LLDP packet from the port to which a host is connected. Moreover, to prevent the Link fabrication attack, the authors added one HMAC to the LLDP packet through one extra TLV (Type Length Value).

    Defense proposed by Hong et al. [33] relies heavily on the categorization of the port as switch-port or host-port. However, there is no promising way to find the same has been described in their work. Any assumption like the amount of traffic flowing through a switch-port is higher when compared with host-port, to do the port categorization may not work in situations where intra-switch traffic on a switch is higher than inter-switch traffic and will result in a high number of false-positive and negative cases. Labelling of hosts based on pre-condition and post-condition validation too will not be an effective solution when multiple virtual hosts are connected to the same physical port in bridge mode.
3. Skowyra et al. [12] discovered and demonstrated two topology attacks called port amnesia and port probing in Topoguard proposed by Hong et al. They later proposed and implemented Topoguard+, a modified version of Topoguard after fixing the

cause for attacks they discovered. A module named Link Latency Inspector (LLI) was used to differentiate between genuine and fake switch links. Eduard Marin et al. [1], in their work, discovered two attacks involving TopoGuard and TopoGuard+. In the first, they were able to remove a genuine link, while in the second, a fake link was established, taking advantage of the way LLI works. They proposed that overloading a genuine switch link by overloading two involved switches will end in LLI computing a latency which can cause a genuine link removed. Shrivastava et al. were able to successfully create fake link even in the presence of Topoguard+ by increasing the overall latency of the network such that it becomes comparable to that of the out-of-band link that the attacker is using to relay the packets to create fake links.

4. SPHINX [31] utilizes a form of flow graphs, which is created by PACKET-IN and FEATURES-REPLY messages. Flow graphs are utilized to approve all the updates done in networks and the given requirements. To prevent Link fabrication attack, SPHINX utilizes static switchport binding. Hence it doesn't support the SDN Dynamic evolution.

5. SPV proposed by Alimohammadifar et al. [7] attempted to detect link fabrication attack by sending probing packets indistinguishable from standard packets. While most of the work assumed the switch be trusted, this work claimed to work even with few switches compromised.

   Authors in their work itself have acknowledged that SPV will not work when the compromised relay host is forwarding all packets using out-of-band channels. Their solution worked with an assumption that the attacker is using low bandwidth out-of-band channel for relaying packet, which we consider a very impractical consideration as the attacker may use one of the already existing links to relay the packets.

6. OFDP [8], unlike the previous methods here, the HMAC TLV (Type Length Value), which is being added, provides both authentication and integrity. The HMAC is nothing but a hash function that is appended in every LLDP packets. Here the key which is generated for LLDP packets is dynamic, i.e. a key value is calculated for every LLDP packets. Hence it prevents LLDP Replay attacks.

Although It is better than previous TLV based methods, it utilizes more resources as it calculates HMAC for every LLDP packets; further, it adds no defense against relay-based attacks.

5 Proposed Solution and Implementation

In this section, we provide the details of our proposed solution, which we found not just prevents topology learning based attack more robustly but also with minimum overhead compared to existing solutions.

Before we go into further details, we define here the two terminologies link and switch-port (or port). Link represents the presence of physical connectivity on a particular switch-port to an end-user device/host or some other switch. Port is an administratively controllable entity utilizing the software. It may seem that the status of a link and the status of a port is tightly coupled in both directions, i.e. according to the status of a port as UP or DOWN, the corresponding link will be UP or DOWN or vice-versa; in real they are not. Table 1 describes the relation between port status and link status. When the link status is down, the port status will be down implicitly. However, if the link is UP, a switch port can be kept administratively UP or DOWN. The administrative controllability of a port plays a vital role in our proposed solution.

Table 1. Port and link status relation

Port status	Link status	Effective port status	Effective link status
UP	UP	UP	UP
UP	DOWN	DOWN	DOWN
DOWN	UP	DOWN	DOWN
DOWN	DOWN	DOWN	DOWN

5.1 Motivation

The real challenge in mitigating LLDP based topology poisoning attacks is identifying if the end device connected to a particular switch-port is an end-user device/host or some other switch. Had there been an accurate way of distinguishing between a switch and end-user device/host, LLDP based topology poisoning attack could have been thwarted easily by simply dropping any LLDP packet coming from any device but switches, as switches are the only device which are supposed to forward the LLDP packets. As discussed in Sect. 4, some efforts were made in this direction using Machine Learning techniques, but they were not accurate enough. Without handling false positive and false negative cases, it may end up collapsing the whole network topology. Other heuristics-based approaches such as traffic on a switch-port to switch-port link should, in general, be higher compared to traffic on switch-port and host link, will not have promising accuracy either as there can be genuine cases where intra-switch communication has more traffic than inter-switch communication. Distinguishing between a switch and a host based on MAC Address will equally be a bad idea, as it is effortless for an attacker to tamper the MAC address of a compromised host to present itself as some switch. Hence our prime focus is to develop a way to decide if the device connected on a switch-port is another switch or some end-user device/host with no false-positive or false-negative cases.

Figure 8(a) describes the cases when all links are good, Fig. 8(b) when a link between one switch and a host goes down, and Fig. 8(c) when a link between two switches goes down. Link *down* activity in Fig. 8(b) will cause the Host 1 and connecting port on switch S1 to go down as well. While there will be no reporting by the Host H1, the involved switch, i.e. S1, will report this new status change to the controller. Similarly, the Link *down*, as shown in Fig. 8(c), will make both the involved switch-ports at respective switches status change to DOWN owing to link failure, and the same will be reported by both the switched to the controller.

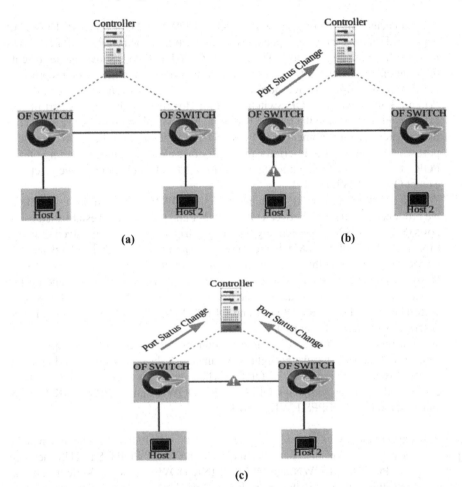

Fig. 8. (a) Topology under normal scenario. (b) Switch to host link failure. (c) Switch to switch link failure

We can summarize the above observation as Switch Port status change are reported by switches and recorded by the controller, while port status change at hosts are not reported. This observation can further be used to identify if the other device connected on a switch port is a host or some other switch by the controller.

5.2 Experimental Observations

Experimental topology used for recording the observation was as illustrated in Fig. 10.

1. When a link between an OF-Switch and End-Host is brought DOWN: As part of this experiment, we brought down the link between OF-Switch S1 and Host h1 in our experimental topology. This link down action triggered the switch to send two OFPT PORT STATUS messages corresponding to the switch-port on which host h1

was connected, the first one with OFPC PORT DOWN and OFPPS LINK DOWN of config and state descriptors respectively set to 0, while second OFPT PORT STATUS message has both flags set to 1. The first OFPT PORT STATUS message represents the state of the switch-port before the link down event, while the second represents the current state of the switch-port, i.e. after the link down event was recorded.

2. When a link between an OF-Switch and End-Host is brought UP: As part of this experiment, we restored the link we had brought down in step 1 above. This resulted in the switch sending another OFPT PORT STATUS message for the involved switch-port where it has config descriptor in which other element values including OFPC PORT DOWN reset to 0, while state descriptor has all its elements value reset to 0 except OFPPS LIVE set to 1.

3. When a link between two OF-Switch is brought DOWN: As part of this experiment, we brought down the link between OF-Switch-1 and OF-Switch-2 established using ports (S1,3) and (S2,1), respectively. This action triggered both the involved switches to send OFPT PORT STATUS message corresponding to each involved port on respective switches with values for flags OFPC PORT DOWN and OFPPS LINK DOWN of config and state descriptors respectively set to 1. Before sending the updated values post-event, each switch first sends OFPT PORT STATUS messages with flags of OFPC PORT DOWN and OFPPS LINK DOWN of config and state descriptors respectively set to 0.

4. When a link between two OF-Switch is brought UP: As part of this experiment, we restored the link that we brought down in step 3 above. This triggered both the involved switches to send OFPT PORT STATUS messages to the controller for their corresponding ports with flags OFPC PORT DOWN and OFPPS LINK DOWN values set to 0 and OFPPS LIVE set to 1.

With experimental verification, we can conclude that if a link that connects a switch-port to a host goes down, the controller receives one OFPT PORT STATUS message with flags OFPC PORT DOWN and OFPPS LINK DOWN set to 1. While a link that connects one switch-port to another switch-port goes down, the controller receives two OFPT PORT STATUS message with flags OFPC PORT DOWN and OFPPS LINK DOWN set to 1, one OFPT PORT STATUS message corresponding to each involved switch. Similarly, when a link is restored for each involved switch-port, the controller receives an OFPT PORT STATUS message with OFPPS LIVE set to 1.

5.3 Algorithm

Algorithm 1 describes the steps involved in validating the topology.

Lemma 1. Algorithm 1, if it detects a new link, always ensure that it is not a ghost link.

Proof: Suppose the algorithm considers a ghost link as the genuine one. To validate its consideration, it will make any of the involved ports on the link connecting switches administratively down. As per the algorithm and assumption, it should result in only one PORT DOWN message. However, in actual it will result in two PORT DOWN messages, making our initial consideration incorrect.

Algorithm 1: Topology Validator Algorithm

while a new link discovered do

    Get the details of switches and ports involved;

    Controller sends ofp port config to any of participating switch with OFPPC PORT DOWN set to 1;

    if ofp port state with OFPP PORT DOWN set to 1 is generated by both involved ports then

        Discovered Link is a genuine one;

    Else

        Discovered Link is an attack attempt;

    end

end

Lemma 2. Algorithm 1 ensures a genuine link is never declared a ghost link.

Proof: We assume that the algorithm considers a newly discovered genuine link a ghost link. For validation as per the stated algorithm, any of the involved ports on link connecting switches will be made down administratively. As this has been considered a ghost link, it should result in only one PORT DOWN message. However, it will result in two PORT DOWN message making our assumption incorrect.

5.4 Implementation

Figure 9 describes the port presentation of ports in the SDN environment as per the latest implemented specification of OpenFlow protocol V1.3.0. From the list of descriptors in Fig. 9, config and state are the ones we are interested in.

The config descriptor as defined above records the administrative setting of the port. OFPPC PORT DOWN field tells about the administrative status of the port, which takes a binary value, where 0 represents the port being administratively DOWN while 1 represents the port as administratively UP. Further specification demands this field to be set/reset by the controller, and the switch should not change it. However, if some external interface or activity causes a change of this field value, the switch must convey this change to the controller using the OFPT PORT STATUS message.

The state descriptor as defined above records the physical link state of the port. OFPP LINK DOWN value is set to 1 when a physical link is present and reset to 0 when there is no physical link present. This descriptor's value cannot be changed by the controller. The switch sends an OFPT PORT STATUS message to update the controller if there is any change in the physical state of the port. Our proposed solution exploits the above two discussed descriptors for thwarting topology poisoning attack, described in Sect. 1 (Table 2).

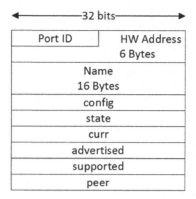

Fig. 9. Switch port representation in SDN

Table 2. Config and state descriptor

Config Descriptor	State Descriptor

enum ofp_port_config {
    OFPPC_PORT_DOWN = 1 << 0 ,
    OFPPC_NO_RECV = 1 << 2 ,
    OFPPC_NO_FWD = 1 << 5 ,
    OFPPC_NO_PACKET_IN = 1 << 6
} ;
	enum ofp_port_state {
	    OFPPS_LINK_DOWN = 1 << 0 ,
	    OFPPS_BLOCKED = 1 << 1 ,
	    OFPPS_LIVE = 1 << 2 ,
	} ;

Case 1: The Normal Scenario: We assume that the initial topology is depicted in Fig. 10, and a new link between (S1,3) and (S2,1) is being made live by connecting a physical wire. This activity will trigger two OFPT PORT STATUS messages from each of switches s1 and s2 for the ports (S1,3) and (S2,1). Following algorithm 1, a controller will make any of the randomly chosen switch port, say (S2,1) administratively DOWN by sending a port down message. As per Table 1, this will cause the link between (S1,3) and (s2,1) to down, and it should follow events as in experiment no 4, and the controller will receive one port status change message for each involved port on both switches. This will confirm to the controller that the newly discovered link is a genuine one and will make the port (S2,1) from administratively DOWN to UP which will re-enable the link between (S1,3) and (S2,1). As the newly discovered link has been verified between two switches, it can now be incorporated in the topology, and topology routing may be updated accordingly.

We achieved this scenario under our experimental setup by first disabling the link between switches S1 & S2 and enabling them again. Enabling action of the link between two switches can be considered equivalent to connecting the two switched with a physical wire.

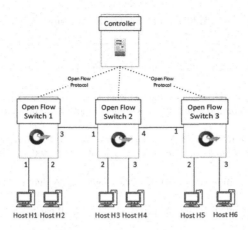

Fig. 10. Experimental topology

Case 2: The Attack scenario: We assume that in one round of LLDP discovery message sent and received. On analysis, it discovered a link between (S1,2) and (S3,2), and this link is an attack attempt by compromised hosts at (S1,2) and (S3,2) where host at (S1,2) relaying the copy of LLDP packet received by it to host (S3,2) by using the existing link (out-of-band) that connects switches S1 and S3 as depicted in Fig. 10. On discovery of the new link, going by the algorithm, the controller will turn any of the ports (S1,2) and (S3,2) chosen at random, say (S3,2) administratively DOWN by sending port down message to the switch S3. On receipt of this message going by the Table 1 link between host h3 and (S3,2) will go down too, which will make switch S3 send one status change message to the controller corresponding to (S3,2). However, turning DOWN will have no effect on the link between (S1,2) and host h2; hence no activity will be recorded by the controller against switch S1. Had this newly discovered link been a genuine one, failure of the link would have triggered status messages from switch S1. As the controller did not receive two status messages from both allegedly involved switches, it will ignore the newly discovered link, and no update will be made to the existing topology of the network. Moreover, the port connecting to the link may administratively be turned down depending upon the network's policy to avoid further poisoning attack by these machines.

This case under our experimental setup was achieved in the same fashion it was used for verifying relay-based topology poisoning attack as mentioned in Sect. 3.2. We implemented our proposed solution as a separate module of floodlight. We did not change the normal functioning of the topology manager; instead, we confirmed if we can detect the attack attempt. Table 3 captures floodlight console output, where activities corresponding to our implementation can be seen.

Table 3. Floodlight console output

01.240 INFO [n.f.l.i.LinkDiscoveryManager] Sending LLDP packets out of all the enabled ports

13.605 INFO [n.f.l.i.LinkDiscoveryManager] Interswitch link removed: Link [src=00:00:00:00:00:00:00:02 outPort=1, dst=00:00:00:00:00:00:00:01, inPort=1, latency=2]

13.605 INFO [n.f.l.i.LinkDiscoveryManager] Interswitch link removed: Link [src=00:00:00:00:00:00:00:01 outPort=1, dst=00:00:00:00:00:00:00:02, inPort=1, latency=2]

13.925 INFO [n.f.t.TopologyManager] Recomputing topology due to: link-discovery-updates

16.243 INFO [n.f.l.i.LinkDiscoveryManager] Sending LLDP packets out of all the enabled ports

31.434 INFO [n.f.t.TopologyManager] Recomputing topology due to: link-discovery-updates

31.503 INFO [TopologyValidator] Discovered a new link [src=00:00:00:00:00:00:00:01 outPort=1, dst=00:00:00:00:00:00:00:02, inPort=1, latency=2]

31.620 INFO [TopologyValidator] About to issue Administrative Down to [src=00:00:00:00:00:00:00:01 outPort=1]

31.987 INFO [TopologyValidator] Port down recorded from [src=00:00:00:00:00:00:00:01 outPort=1]

32.105 INFO [TopologyValidator] Waiting for port down from [src=00:00:00:00:00:00:00:02 outPort=1]

32.995 INFO [TopologyValidator] Port Down recorded from [src=00:00:00:00:00:00:00:02 outPort=1]

33.204 INFO [TopologyValidator] Validation Success

33.379 INFO [TopologyValidator] About to issue Administrative UP to [src=00:00:00:00:00:00:00:01 outPort=1]

33.834 INFO [TopologyValidator] Port UP event recorded for [src=00:00:00:00:00:00:00:01 outPort=1]

34.367 INFO [TopologyValidator] Port UP event recorded for [src=00:00:00:00:00:00:00:02 outPort=2]

01.254 INFO [n.f.l.i.LinkDiscoveryManager] Sending LLDP packets out of all the enabled ports

01.447 INFO [n.f.t.TopologyManager] Recomputing topology due to: link-discovery-updates

16.257 INFO [n.f.l.i.LinkDiscoveryManager] Sending LLDP packets out of all the enabled ports

6   Result and Analysis

Our solution was able to mitigate the LLDP relay-based topology poisoning attack with minimal overhead. However, we evaluated it further on the parameters of time taken to update the topology and its effect on the availability of the network. As the update is not being made to the topology immediately after discovering an LLDP packet sent/receive round, in the non-attack scenario, it will take more time than the typical scenario.

Effect on Availability: As the link discovered will be new, it will in no way affect the availability of existing topology, as all the administrative port DOWN/UP activity will be restricted to the port involved in forming a new link. Hence our solution will not have any impact on the existing topology without incorporating a new link.

Delay in the Incorporation of New Link: New link validity check will consume some time. We measured the time lag between the intercept of the new link and final validation by the java (programming language used in Floodlight) logging feature. Figure 11 depicts the time consumed over ten experimental attempts. Mean time delay was found to be 3301.9 ms. The average time elapsed can be considered acceptable, considering the fact that the LLDP round runs every 15 s.

Comparison with Existing Solutions: A parametric comparison is not possible with existing works, as different authors have proposed solutions using different approaches. It is the end result, i.e. if the proposed solution could prevent topology poisoning attack with no false positive and false negative cases, is the only measuring criteria. We have discussed it in Sect. 4 to conclude that all of the already proposed state-of-art works fail to prevent *topology poisoning by relay*-based attacks on some of all cases. However, we have found our solution preventing topology learning based poisoning attacks with no false-positive or false-negative cases.

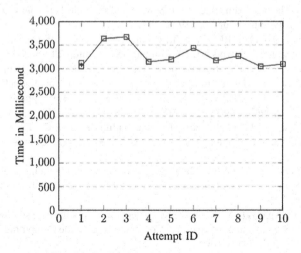

Fig. 11. Validation time consumption plot

7 Conclusion

This paper presented a novel defense method against relay-based poisoning attack in the the SDN environment. The described solution was able to defend the relay-based topology poisoning attack with no false positive or false negative cases. We also were able to keep the overhead minimal as it does not require any additional headers added to the standard LLDP packets, all that it takes is an average of 3301 ms delay in incorporating new topology changes.

Acknowledgements. This research was partially funded by the c3i center (Interdisciplinary Center for Cyber Security and Cyber Defense of Critical Infrastructures, IIT Kanpur) funding SERB, Government of India.

References

1. Popic, S., Vuleta, M., Cvjetkovic, P., Todorović, B.M.: Secure topology detection in software-defined networking with network configuration protocol and link layer discovery protocol. In: 2020 International Symposium on Industrial Electronics and Applications (INDEL), pp. 1–5 (2020). https://doi.org/10.1109/INDEL50386.2020.9266137

2. Chou, L.-D., et al.: Behavior anomaly detection in SDN control plane: a case study of topology discovery attacks. Wirel. Commun. Mobile Comput. (2020). http://dxp.doi.org/10.1155/2020/8898949

3. Huang, X., Shi, P., Liu, Y., Xu, F.: Towards trusted and efficient SDN topology discovery: a lightweight topology verification scheme. Comput. Netw. **170**, 107119 (2020). ISSN 1389-1286

4. Marin, E., Conti, M.: An in-depth look into SDN topology discovery mechanisms: novel attacks and practical countermeasures. In: CCS 2019, London, United Kingdom (2019)

5. Cao, J., et al.: The crosspath attack: disrupting the SDN control channel via shared links. In: USENIX Security Symposium, pp. 19–36 (2019)

6. Abdou, A., van Oorschot, P.C., Wan, T.: Comparative analysis of control plane security of SDN and conventional networks. IEEE Commun. Surv. Tutor. **20**, 3542–3559 (2018)

7. Alimohammadifar, A., et al.: Stealthy probing-based verification (SPV): an active approach to defending software defined networks against topology poisoning attacks. In: Lopez, J., Zhou, J., Soriano, M. (eds.) ESORICS 2018. LNCS, vol. 11099, pp. 463–484. Springer, Cham (2018). https://doi.org/10.1007/978-3-319-98989-1_23

8. Nehra, A., Tripathi, M., Singh Gaur, M., Babu Battula, R., Lal, C.: TILAK: a token based prevention approach for topology discovery threats in SDN. Int. J. Commun. Syst. **32**, e3781 (2018)

9. Big Switch Networks. Floodlight (2020). http://www.projectfloodlight.org/floodlight/

10. Big Switch Networks. Floodlight Git repository (2020). https://github.com/floodlight/floodlight

11. Shrivastava, P., Agarwal, A., Kataoka, K.: Detection of topology poisoning by silent relay attacker in SDN. In: Annual International Conference on Mobile Computing and Networking (MobiCom), pp. 792–794 (2018)

12. Skowyra, R., et al.: Effective topology tampering attacks and defenses in software-defined networks. In: International Conference on Dependable Systems and Networks (DSN), pp. 374–385 (2018)

13. Mininet Team. Mininet (2020). http://mininet.org
14. Ujcich, B.E., et al.: Cross-app poisoning in software-defined networking. In: ACM SIGSAC Conference on Computer and Communications Security (CCS), pp. 648–663 (2018)
15. Wang, H., Yang, G., Chinprutthiwong, P., Xu, L., Zhang, Y., Gu, G.: Towards fine-grained network security forensics and diagnosis in the SDN era. In: ACM SIGSAC Conference on Computer and Communications Security (CCS), pp. 3–16 (2018)
16. Xue, L., Ma, X., Luo, X., Chan, E.W.W., Miu, T.T.N., Gu, G.: LinkScope: towards detecting target link flooding attacks. IEEE Trans. Inf. Forensics Secur. (TIFS) **13**, 2423–2438 (2018)
17. Zhang, M., Li, G., Xu, L., Bi, J., Gu, G., Bai, J.: Control plane reflection attacks in SDNs: new attacks and countermeasures. In: Symposium on Research in Attacks, Intrusions and Defenses (RAID) (2018)
18. Lee, S., Yoon, C., Lee, C., Shin, S., Yegneswaran, V., Porras, P.A.: DELTA: a security assessment framework for software-defined networks. In: Network and Distributed System Security Symposium (NDSS) (2017)
19. Lin, P.P., Li, P., Nguyen, V.L.: Inferring OpenFlow rules by active probing in software-defined networks. In: International Conference on Advanced Communication Technology (ICACT), pp. 415–420 (2017)
20. Thimmaraju, K., Schiff, L., Schmid, S.: Outsmarting network security with SDN teleportation. In: IEEE European Symposium on Security and Privacy (EuroS\&P), pp. 563–578 (2017)
21. Xu, L., Huang, J., Hong, S., Zhang, J., Gu, G.: Attacking the brain: races in the SDN control plane. In: USENIX Security Symposium, pp. 451–468 (2017)
22. Zhang, P.: Towards rule enforcement verification for software defined networks. In: IEEE Conference on Computer Communications (INFOCOM), pp. 1–9 (2017)
23. Jero, S., Koch, W., Skowyra, R., Okhravi, H., Nita-Rotaru, C., Bigelow, D.: Identifier binding attacks and defenses in software-defined networks. In: USENIX Security Symposium, pp. 415–432 (2017)
24. Jero, S., Bu, X., NitaRotaru, C., Okhravi, H., Skowyra, R., Fahmy, S.: BEADS: automated attack discovery in OpenFlow-based SDN systems. In: Dacier, M., Bailey, M., Polychronakis, M., Antonakakis, M. (eds.) RAID 2017. LNCS, vol. 10453, pp. 311–333. Springer, Cham (2017). https://doi.org/10.1007/978-3-319-66332-6_14
25. Chen, H., Benson, T.: The case for making tight control plane latency guarantees in SDN switches. In: Symposium on SDN Research (SOSR), pp. 150–156 (2017)
26. Ambrosin, M., Conti, M., De Gaspari, F., Poovendran, R.: Lineswitch: tackling control plane saturation attacks in software-defined networking. IEEE/ACM Trans. Netw. (TON) **25**(2), 1206–1219 (2017)
27. Katta, N., Alipourfard, O., Rexford, J., Walker, D.: CacheFlow: dependency aware rule-caching for software-defined networks. In: Symposium on SDN Research (SOSR), pp. 6:1–6:12 (2016)
28. Sonchack, J., Dubey, A., Aviv, A.J., Smith, J.M., Keller, E.: Timing-based reconnaissance and defense in software-defined networks. In: Annual Conference on Computer Security Applications (ACSAC), pp. 89–100 (2016)
29. Xu, H., Yu, Z., Yang Li, X., Qian, C., Huang, L., Jung, T.: Real-time update with joint optimization of route selection and update scheduling for SDNs. In: International Conference on Network Protocols (ICNP), pp. 1–10 (2016)
30. Alharbi, T., Portmann, M., Pakzad, F.: The (in)security of topology discovery in software defined networks. In: Local Computer Networks (LCN), pp. 502–505 (2015)
31. Dhawan, M., Poddar, R., Mahajan, K., Mann, V.: SPHINX: detecting security attacks in software-defined networks. In: Network and Distributed System Security Symposium (NDSS), pp. 8–11 (2015)
32. He, K., et al.: Measuring control plane latency in SDN-enabled switches. In: Symposium on SDN Research (SOSR), pp. 25:1–25:6 (2015)

33. Hong, S., Xu, L., Wang, H., Gu, G.: Poisoning network visibility in software defined networks: new attacks and countermeasures. In: Network and Distributed System Security Symposium (NDSS), pp. 8–11 (2015)

34. Kreutz, D., Ramos, F., Verissimo, P., Esteve Rothenberg, C., Azodolmolky, S., Uhlig, S.: Software-defined networking: a comprehensive survey. ArXive-prints (2014). https://doi.org/10.1109/JPROC.2014.2371999

Towards an Attention-Based Accurate Intrusion Detection Approach

Arunavo Dey[1], Md. Shohrab Hossain[2], Md. Nazmul Hoq[3],
and Suryadipta Majumdar[3]($\boxtimes$)

[1] Department of Computer Science and Engineering, Bangladesh University
of Business and Technology, Dhaka, Bangladesh
`aronava.d@bubt.edu.bd`
[2] Department of Computer Science and Engineering, Bangladesh University
of Engineering and Technology, Dhaka, Bangladesh
`mshohrabhossain@cse.buet.ac.bd`
[3] Concordia Institute for Information Systems Engineering (CIISE),
Concordia University, Montreal, Canada
`md_oq@encs.concordia.ca, suryadipta.majumdar@concordia.ca`

Abstract. With the advancement of 5G and IoT, the volume of network traffic is growing in a tremendous rate (e.g., 235.7 Exabytes (EB) in Internet traffic, a 3.2-fold increase from 2016), leading to an alarming rise in different types of attacks. As a result, the requirements of an intrusion detection system (IDS) are also evolving. In addition to having a large number of flow-based intrusion detection systems powered by machine learning techniques, achieving higher accuracy including higher recall and precision has become equally important. While most of the existing works successfully achieve accuracy, they still strive to achieve a good recall score or minimize the False Negative Rate (FNR) as well as the False Positive Rate (FPR). In this paper, we investigate the potential of combining the state-of-the-art neural network models (i.e., CNN, LSTM, and GRU) with attention mechanisms (where attention helps the model to selectively concentrate on more relevant factors) for improving the accuracy of intrusion detection systems. We evaluate our model with the most recent and state-of-the-art benchmark datasets (e.g., CSE-CIC-IDS-2018, and NSL-KDD) and compare the obtained results with the existing works. Empirical results show that our proposed model outperforms the existing works in terms of accuracy while achieving a higher recall score (e.g., a maximum recall of 100%, 99.91% for CSE-CIC-IDS-2018, and NSL-KDD datasets, respectively) and higher F1-Score (e.g., a maximum F-1 score of 100%, 99.22% for CSE-CIC-IDS-2018, and NSL-KDD datasets, respectively).

Keywords: Network security · Intrusion detection · Attention · Neural network

© ICST Institute for Computer Sciences, Social Informatics and Telecommunications Engineering 2021
Published by Springer Nature Switzerland AG 2021. All Rights Reserved
X. Yuan et al. (Eds.): QShine 2021, LNICST 402, pp. 261–279, 2021.
https://doi.org/10.1007/978-3-030-91424-0_16

1   Introduction

In the modern era, network traffic is a growing entity, which is only getting bigger with each new addition of technologies (e.g., IoT, 5G). According to the global reports by CISCO, Internet traffic will rise to 7.7 Exabytes per day and 235.7 Exabytes (EB) per month in 2021 [1]. In addition, the growing traffic due to 5G and IoT is adding huge volume to the already existing load in the network (e.g., estimated to rise by three-fold within 2025 [2]). With this increase in the network traffic and data, the number of security breaches and total records exposed per breach continue to grow as there was 776% growth in network attacks from 2018 to 2019 [3]. To detect such security breaches, the intrusion detection is gaining a fair share of its importance and on the way to gain more.

Being a widely-studied topics of cybersecurity, intrusion detection has been experimented with a lot of techniques, including neural network based approaches (e.g., [4–9]); where all of those recent works show the effectiveness (in terms of accuracy) of the detection approach. However, most of them are not focused on improving recall score, False Negative Rate (FNR), and False Positive Rate (FPR), which are also equally important for an intrusion detection system. Moreover, most of those works are not based on the most recent benchmark datasets (e.g., NSL-KDD [10], CSE-CIC-IDS-2018 [11]). Even though LuNet [12] shows comparatively better accuracy and recall score for the NSL-KDD dataset, it is still burdened with a large architecture (later we will compare our proposed method with LuNet). Moreover, apart from achieving accuracy, what matters most for an intrusion detection system is achieving a low false-positive rate (FPR) and low false-negative rate (FNR) by achieving high recall and precision values [13,14]. As recall and FNR are related, we can get the value of FNR simply by calculating recall. While accuracy is a good metric for a balanced datasets that contain almost the same amount of false positive and false negative data, F-score is better suited for unbalanced datasets like intrusion detection data. Most of the existing works focused on the accuracy measure more than other metrics i.e., recall, F-Score, etc. None of the existing works achieves a good recall score nor evaluates their performance on all the state-of-the-art benchmark datasets (including the latest CSE-CIC-IDS-2018 dataset [11]). Additionally, most of the existing models are comprised of several layers which renders computational overhead.

To overcome this limitation, in this paper, we investigate the potential to leverage the advantages of both Convolutional Neural Network (CNN) for extracting features from input and Recurrent Neural Network (RNN) for extracting sequential features together with the advantage of attention mechanism for better performance in sequential features (which is mostly used in NLP tasks including similar problem like ours). This proposed method is evaluated with both NSL-KDD [10] and CSE-CIC-IDS-2018 datasets [11]. Our obtained results show that our proposed model outperforms all the state-of-the-art models in terms of F1-Score as well as recall score. Particularly, our results indicate that our model can achieve a higher F1-Score with the highest recall score amongst all of the existing neural network models used in intrusion detection with a simpleton architecture that is faster to train and can perform on raw data, excluding any need for scaling or normalization. Thus, this work can help to detect almost all the latest variations of Web, DDos, Botnet, HeartBleed, and Infiltration attacks (exploited in the CSE-CIC-IDS-2018 datasets [11]) while achieving a higher F1-score, and hence shows its potential for the networks where recall score is given priority over accuracy.

The main contributions of this paper are as follows.

- As per our knowledge, we are the first to investigate the potential of combining the CNN, LSTM, and GRU models with attention mechanisms for improving different aspects of accuracy metrics (including recall, F1-score, etc.) of intrusion detection systems.
- We utilize state-of-the-art benchmark network traffic datasets (including NSL-KDD [10] and CSE-CIC-IDS-2018 [11] comprising various network attacks to evaluate our proposed model.
- Through experimental results, we demonstrate that our proposed model can improve the accuracy (including F1-Score and recall Score) in comparison to the existing neural network-based models (e.g., an average F1-Score value of 95.41% by our model vs. 81.87% for CNN and 83.50% for CNN-LSTM using CSE-CIC-IDS-2018 [11] dataset).

The rest of the paper is organized as follows. Section 2 reviews existing works. In Sect. 3, the proposed approach is presented. Section 4 describes the dataset as well as experimental setup and model details. Section 5 presents our experimental results with the comparison of the performance of the proposed model with existing works. Finally, Sect. 6 provides concluding remarks including future directions.

2   Related Work

There are several works (e.g., [4–9]) applying deep neural networks for intrusion detection, where different deep learning mechanisms, e.g., CNN, RNN, and LSTM, are leveraged. Recently, attention-based approaches [15–17] are also being popular in intrusion detection systems. In the following, we further discuss the related works and analysis the current gaps in the intrusion detection system.

2.1   Neural Network Based Intrusion Detection Systems

Neural Network (NN) and Deep Neural Network (DNN) have been used in intrusion detection for a long time. Botros et al. [8] study the methods and apparatus for training a neural network model to apply for intrusion detection. They outline a model workflow for leveraging neural network algorithms in intrusion detection without evaluating the model with any particular dataset. Shun et al. [18] study the application of neural network on DARPA dataset [19] with the simplest configuration consisting of input and output layers coupled with a few hidden layers and demonstrate the potential of neural networks in this domain without applying their model on various datasets or specifying other evaluation details such as recall and FPR. Chiba et al. [20] propose a neural network with back propagation for intrusion detection and exhibit the neural network performance on the KDD-99 Cup dataset [21] by achieving a lower FPR and higher recall score than the others. Mahalingam et al. [22] propose an intelligent intrusion detection system based on the combination of signature analysis and anomaly analysis using a neural network. However, this model lags behind others in terms of accuracy, which provides only 70% accurate results. Su et al. [23] use an improved version of the rough set-particle swarm optimization algorithm for improving intrusion detection systems where they cluster similar data and reduce the difficulty in the identification of data. They use an open dataset with a simple SVM-based approach and show that their proposed model could achieve a 98% recall score.

Recently, different variations of DNN, such as CNN, LSTM, RNN, etc., and different combinations among them are being used in detecting intrusion. The most recent work with CNN on IDS has been demonstrated by Mendon et al. [24]. They use a Tri-CNN model with a soft-sign activation function to detect intrusion and get a good accuracy of 98% while reducing the training time significantly by 36%. However, they use the CSE-CIC-IDS-2017 dataset [25] instead of the most recent one. Kim et al. [26] use a CNN-based approach for intrusion detection focusing on only DoS attacks. They use the KDD-99 and CSE-CIC-IDS-2018 datasets to evaluate the performance and show that their CNN-based approach is better than any RNN-based approach. Nonetheless, as mentioned earlier, this works is only focused on a single attack. Whereas Wang et al. [27] develop a CNN-based approach and show the performance only on the NSL-KDD dataset. Bandyopadhyay et al. [28] recently propose an optimized deep CNN model with evaluation results based on experiments only on the KDD-99 dataset, but many of the recent works mentioned above already outperform their work (84% accuracy) in terms of accuracy and other evaluation metrics.

A combination of CNN with LSTM model (CNN-LSTM) is also popular in IDS. Sun et al. [29] apply a category weight optimization method on a CNN-LSTM based method to detect intrusion. They use the CSE-CIC-IDS-2017 dataset instead of the most recent one and show that the overall accuracy is 98.67% and F1-Score is 93.32%. However, for specific attack types (i.e., Heartbleed and SSHPatator attacks), they obtain a low detection accuracy. Kim et al. [30] use LSTM cells with recurrent neural network for intrusion detection though not surpassing the higher accuracy and recall achieved by the previous works. Kuang et al. [31] propose an one dimensional (1-D) CNN-LSTM model and show its accuracy on CSIC-2010 dataset [32]. Where Hsu et al. [9] propose almost similar CNN-LSTM model and show its effectiveness on NSL-KDD dataset. Hsu et al. [33] show the performance of the LSTM model and the combination of CNN with the LSTM model (CNN-LSTM). Using the NSL-KDD dataset, they show that both the proposed methods achieve a better accuracy than the RNN based models.

2.2   Attention and Encoder-Decoder Based IDS

In recent times, attention mechanism incorporated with neural networks have become widely available. Most of them use the auto encoder-decoder structure or neural machine translation approach. In the following, we will elaborate on the works regarding attention based model.

Several recent works incorporated attention-based mechanisms in neural networks. For example, Liu et al. [15] use an attention-based bi-directional GRU model for IDS and show the model performance on UNSW-NB-15 [34], NSL-KDD [10], and KDD-99 [21] datasets instead of using the most recent dataset. Liu et al. [17] use the payload information for web attack detection with their attention based neural network but additional payload analysis before classification adds up to already existing workload occupying much time. Although they achieve a higher accuracy and lower FPR, they evaluate their model performance only on CSIC-2010 dataset instead of the most recent one.

Moreover, the latest encoder decoder based approaches also show promising performance. Basati et al. [35] propose an IDS named APAE specifically for IoT networks where they use two parallel encoder-decoder. They measure the efficiency of the system using UNSW-NB-15, KDD-99, and CSE-CIC-IDS-2017 datasets, instead of the most recent dataset. Sekhar et al. [36] also use a deep autoencoder with fruitfly-Optimization-based IDS and measure the performance on UNSW-NB-15 and NSL-KDD datasets instead of using the most recent dataset. Nathan et al. [37] propose a non-symmetric autoencoder based intrusion detection system and evaluate the performance using the KDD-99 Cup and NSL-KDD datasets showing accuracy's for each of the attacks separately. Tang et al. [38] use an encoder-decoder network for detecting zero day attack by applying neural machine translation converting http requests through encoder and converting them back using decoder and detecting attacks based on the similarity (BLEU score) between original and translations. However, instead of showing their performance on any benchmark dataset they evaluated their performance on a simulated environment. Moradi et al. [39] use stacked autoencoder for detecting web attacks on the CSIC-2010 dataset though not surpassing the previous achieved performance. Mac et al. [40] follow an unsupervised approach and study the performance of autoencoder on CSIC-2010 dataset detecting web attacks; ending up with regularized autoencoder outperforming eleven other encoder-decoder with an AUC score of 98.23% and recall score of 94.62%. Yan et al. [16] use neural machine translation with NLP techniques for web attack detection on CSIC-2010 dataset. However, they perform their technique separately on the dataset for each type of the attack individually achieving a highest recall of 98.29% and lowest recall of 43.98%.

2.3   Gap Analysis

Most of the models achieve better accuracy without achieving better recall scores and F1-Scores. Moreover, the better accuracy and better recall score achieving model LuNet [12] involve a batch normalization between model layers with a huge architecture. Thus, achieving better performance with a light-weight model is what has driven us, and nevertheless, our model surpasses them all on the benchmark datasets by detection rate achieving higher recall and higher F1-score from almost all of them, and its performance is also elaborated on the latest dataset (i.e., CSE-CIC-IDS-2018 [11] and NSL-KDD [10]).

Unlike others, in this paper, we follow a straightforward approach by combining the NLP aspect with CNN and LSTM networks by enriching them with attention mechanism. Instead of dealing with each attack separately, we generalize all of the attacks in an anomaly class and perform a binary classification.

3   Proposed Approach

Generally, attention-based models regarding IDS, use autoencoder-decoder or stacked layers that make the model heavy and computationally expensive. To keep our model simple, we combine CNN and LSTM models together with the attention mechanism. As LSTM in spite of being proven worthy, fails to capture long-term dependencies, thus we combine GRU with the above-mentioned combination and further combine an attention layer to focus on the important parts. The detailed structure of our model is shown in Fig. 1, which shows that the model is constructed with an embedding layer following an input layer, followed by a single 1D convolution layer (best suited for models dealing with textual classifications), and as usual followed by a max-pooling layer. We combine the LSTM with GRU as well as with an attention layer, later concatenating those two-fed layers before the final output layer. A detailed description of these layers is given below.

3.1   Input Pre-processing

Tokenization. We treat the HTTP requests as text sequences. If the request is in the format:

$$X : x_1, x_2, ..., x_n$$

containing n columns, where the n columns are converted as string entries and concatenated and then tokens are generated according to punctuation marks. Tokens are the smallest part of a string or sentence. A token could be a word, number, or punctuation. In the tokenization process, the words are converted into integer numbers so that it would be efficient to feed them into the neural network. Below example, shows a sample sentence with its tokens converted to an integer sequence: Sample Sentence: *"Hello, this one sentence!"* and its corresponding integer Sequence: **125, 778, 3, 63.**

Vocabulary. All the sentences are used to generate the vocabulary, and the tokens exceeding a certain threshold are being selected. The vocabulary consists of all unique tokens in the datasets. This vocabulary is also a mapping of the words and integer numbers. It has been used in encoding the sentences into number sequences and also does the reverse.

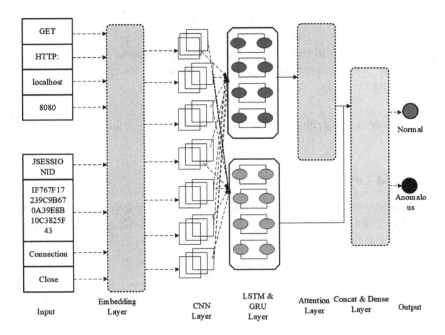

Fig. 1. Structure of our model

Padding and Truncating the Sequence. After the sequences are tokenized, formed into number sequences, they are padded and fed to the embedding layer. Padding is just adding zero, either the beginning or end of the integer or number sequence. The padding ensures that all the sentence lengths are equal. Sometimes instead of padding, truncating is also used. Truncating means removing some tokens from the beginning or end to make all the sentence lengths equal.

Embedding. After processing, these sequences are fed into the embedding layer, where these sequences are formed as embedded vectors. Embedding layers vectors holds the relationship among the words. Also, the corpus of the embedded vectors is previously built on the vocabulary, and the dimension is fixed after a number of observations.

3.2   Input Layer

The input layer receives an embedded vector array of fixed length and simply passes this to the convolution layer after inspecting the specified input dimensions. The input layer consists of the pre-processed data, which has been described in the previous section.

3.3   CNN Layer

The Convolution layer performs the convolution operation on the input fed from the input layer. If the convolution operation is performed upon m word vectors with weight matrix $W \in R^{l*m}$ then

$$O_i = f(X_{i+m-1} * W_i + b_i).$$

This layers works to find the features from the input sequences by operating with several filters. After completing convolution operation, max pooling is performed upon the output:

$$M_i = maxO_i.$$

This max pooling contributes to finding more important features from the collected ones.

3.4 LSTM Layer

LSTM is one of the stronger variants of RNN, capturing long-term dependencies successfully. Here we use the context learned from the CNN as input to this layer to generate the final feature map:

$$h_i = lstm(M_i).$$

As we are dealing with inputs as sequences and some features may remain co-related sequentially; we use LSTM to capture these specifically. For example, some specific sources may be the sources of repeated attacks, and extracting sequential information may be helpful. LSTM cell calculates and saves the information it finds relevant in cell state and saves the previous information in hidden states. We pass the outputs and hidden state to the next layer to calculate the attention score.

3.5 Attention Layer

We feed the output of the maxpooling layer to our attention layer through a LSTM layer. The LSTM layer gives us the outputs as well as forward (hidden) states and back (cell) states. We feed the forward states along with outputs to our own implemented Bahdanau Attention layer. Bahdanau Attention layer calculates the score as

$$score(F, O) = v_a{}^T tanh(W_1F + W_2O).$$

where F and O are the forward states and output of the previous layer, respectively, and the C is the context vector or Output of attention layer and W is the attention states or attention weights.

According to the Bahdanau [41] Attention layer, we compute the attention weights and context vector using the following formula:

$$\alpha_{ts} = \frac{exp(score(F, O_s))}{\sum_{i=1}^{S} exp(score(F, O_i))},$$

$$c_t = \sum \alpha_{ts}O_s.$$

The attention mechanism focuses on the more important parts by calculating scores from the forward states and outputs and generating context vectors from them using attention weights. These context vectors work as the summarized output, which is being fed to the Concatenation Layer.

3.6 GRU Layer

The output from Maxpooling layer is also fed to a GRU layer. GRU is the variation of RNN which uses update gate and reset gate to calculate the output

$$z_i = \sigma(WM_i + Uh_{t-1}),$$
$$r_i = \sigma(WM_i + Uh_{t-1}),$$
$$h_i = tanh(WM_i + r_i \odot Uh_{t-1}).$$

GRU is another variant of RNN which is good at extracting sequential information. We leverage this to keep the important features that may be missed by the attention layer and used afterward together with attention layers output.

3.7 Concatenation Layer

The concatenation layer concatenates the outputs from the attention layer and GRU layer to generates output for the next layer. This layer takes inputs from the attention layer and from the GRU layer which should have the same dimensions except for concatenation axes. The concatenated output then feed to the dense layer. If W_1 and W_2 be the wight matrices and x and y are the feature matrices, then the contention could be expressed as:

$$W[x, y] = W_1 x + W_2 y.$$

3.8 Dense Layer

Lastly, the output layer performs sentiment classification where we use sigmoid activation function the mostly used in the neural network. The sigmoid activation function converts the matrix of numeric values into non-linear binary values of 0 and 1. As the loss function, Cross-Entropy has been used.

4 Experimental Setup

We build our model using the TensorFlow [42] backend, Keras [43], and sci-kit learn packages [44], and we conduct the training on a personal computer (pc) with Intel(R) Xeon(R) Haswell CPU @ 2.30 GHz processor and 12.0 GB RAM with a T4 GPU. For comparison, we also implement other state-of-the-art machine learning algorithms. We use the Nadam optimizer [45] to adjust weights and the categorical cross-entropy as the cost function during the training. In addition, the configuration of the hyper-parameter that is being used is described in Table 1.

Table 1. Hyper-parameter configuration

Hyper parameter	Value
CNN layers	1
CNN filters	256
LSTM layer	1
LSTM nodes	20
GRU layer	1
GRU nodes	20

4.1 Datasets

Performance evaluation of a neural network design is highly dependent on the dataset used. Many datasets collected for IDS contain a significant amount of redundant data [46,47], making the experiment questionable where on the other hand using the latest available dataset proves the models performance in dealing with the latest types of attacks. To ensure the effectiveness of the evaluation, we perform our experiment on four different datasets: CSE-CIC-IDS-2018 [11] (which is one of the most recent benchmarking datasets), NSL-KDD [10], Original KDD-99 Cup [21], and CSIC-2010 [32].

Table 2. Attack distribution in KDD-99 [21] and NSL-KDD datasets [10]

Attack types	KDD-99	NSL-KDD
DoS	3883370	45927
Probe	41102	11656
R2L	1126	995
U2R	52	52
Normal	972781	67343

Among these, KDD-99 Cup [21] is the oldest one used for benchmarking. After that the NSL-KDD [10] dataset was developed and since then it has been utilized in almost every work as a benchmark for the intrusion detection system. The NSL-KDD [10] dataset is an updated version of the KDD-99 Cup dataset which has some drawbacks [48] that can affect the accuracy of the model. In addition, unlike the original KDD-99, NSL-KDD doesn't contain the redundancy in the training set, and neither has duplicate records in the test set. This dataset contains 41 features and an additional feature as the label for each record. In this paper, as we concentrate our model on binary classification, We divide the data into two categories normal and anomalous data. Table 2 provides attack distribution that has been used in the KDD-99 and NSL-KDD datasets.

The CSIC 2010 dataset is another widely used dataset, which is divided into two subsets. The first subset contains 36,000 normal requests, and the second subset contains 36,000 normal and more than 25,000 abnormal requests. Basically, this data set is used to train unsupervised machine learning models where the first set is used for training. The second subset is used to measure the models accuracy in detecting the unknown attacks. We use it to compare with how the model performs on this data set if used in a supervised way.

Table 3. Attack types and durations in CSE-CIC-IDS-2018 datasets [11]

Attack types	Tools	Attack duration
Bruteforce	FTP – Patator, SSH – Patator	One day
DoS	Heartleech	One day
DoS	Slowloris, Slowhttptest, and others.	One day
Web	DVWA, XSS, and others	Two days
Infiltration	Nmap and portscan	Two days
Botnet	Keylogging and others	One day
DDoS+PortScan	LOIC	Two days

Canadian Institute for Cybersecurity (CIC) generated IDS datasets in 2012, 2017, and 2018 among which CSE-CIC-IDS-2018 [11] is the most up-to-date dataset for IDS evaluation with more recent network traffic with/without attacks. CSE-CIC-IDS-2018 dataset was generated by collecting ten days of network traffic, and system logs in ten subsets with different types of attacks using CICFlowMeter-V3 [49] and contains about 80 features for each record, including forward and backward directions of network flow and packets. Table 3 listed different types of attacks used in preparing the CIC-IDS-2018 dataset and the tools it used to generate the attack and attack duration. Qianru [50] analyzes the CSE-CIC-IDS-2018 dataset and pre-processes the dataset by eliminating normal and noisy ones and removing unnecessary values after the decimal point. After applying these techniques, the size of CSE-CIC-IDS-2018 decreased by 4MB, still 400GB way bigger than that of CSE-CIC-IDS-2017.

4.2   Data Pre-possessing

We pre-process each record into a string and fill up the NaN values with a default string. Afterwards, we generate tokens from the vocabulary and tokenize each input string by punctuation. To realize the large non-redundant data for training and verification, we employ a Stratified K-Fold Cross Validation strategy [51], which is also commonly used in machine learning. The scheme splits the dataset into k groups and from them, $k-1$ groups as a whole are used for training and the rest one group is used for validation and the strategy is also called *Leave One Out Strategy*.

One-hot-encoding technique is employed to convert labels into numerical forms. One-hot-encoding is a process in which categorical variables are converted into a form that could be provided to machine learning or deep learning algorithms to predict performance better.

5   Results and Performance Evaluation

In this section, we first compare the performance of our proposed model with different benchmark datasets. Then, we compare the performance of our model with the existing variations of our model. We mainly compare our work with the two most common variations which are CNN [24, 26–28] and LSTM-CNN [9, 12, 29–31, 33] based models. We also compare our works with the works [12] that obtained the highest accuracy among existing works.

5.1   Evaluation Metrics

While we value the accuracy most, it has some serious flaws for imbalanced datasets like intrusion detection data. Accuracy is mainly used with a balanced dataset when a true positive and true negative is more important than identifying false positives (normal traffic predicted as anomalous traffic) and false negatives (anomalous traffic predicted as normal traffic). However, in an intrusion detection system, where the data is imbalanced, false positive and false negative count is also equally important to true positive and true negative count. In this scenario, calculating recall and F1-Score is more important than accuracy where F1-Score consider both the false positive and false negative count.

We evaluate our model in terms of the F1-Score and Recall score. We calculate standard machine learning algorithm performance metrics precision, recall, and F1-score with respect to True Positives (TP), False Positives (FP), True Negatives (TN) and False Negatives (FN) values as follows using Eqs. (1), (2) and (3):

Precision (ρ) [52]: It measures the proportion of the predicted attack that is actually an attack. Precision is calculated using the following equation.

$$\rho = \frac{TP}{TP + FP} \tag{1}$$

Recall (γ) [53]: It measures the proportion of actual attacks that are correctly identified and are computed as follows. We can also get the value of FNR simply by calculating recall.

$$\gamma = \frac{TP}{TP + FN}. = 1 - FNR \tag{2}$$

F1-Score (F1-Score) [54]: F1-Score is the harmonic mean of precision and recall. Validation accuracy is computed as the following equation.

$$F1 - Score = \frac{2 * \rho * \gamma}{\rho + \gamma} \tag{3}$$

5.2   Performance Analysis with Different Benchmark Datasets

We measure the performance against four different datasets, which are CSE-CIC-IDS-2018 [11], NSL-KDD [10], CSIC-2010 [32], and KDD-99 [21]. Table 4 summarizes our model's performance in terms of both F1-score and recall score.

The table also shows the comparison with other variants on the CSE-CIC-IDS-2018 dataset. In almost all cases, we operate on the whole dataset following 10-fold validation except 22-02-2018 and 23-02-2018, where the anomaly data is less than 0.0001% of the total data, and we have to work with a balanced dataset. It is evident from the table that we got 100% accuracy and recall scores from a few datasets, and for most of the datasets, the results are very promising.

In Table 5, the performance of our model on NSL-KDD data has been elaborated. We tested with different values of K-folds cross-validation for NSL-KDD data. We get a maximum F1-Score of 99.22% for 10-fold cross-validation, with a maximum recall of 99.97% for 8-fold cross-validation. Overall, 10-fold cross-validation provides a better result than others. Table 6 shows KDD-99 & CSIC-2010 data performance. Here our model clearly outperforms the LSTM-CNN based model [33] by a significant margin where they achieved the highest 94% accuracy by their proposed methods on the CSIC-2010 dataset. We obtain a low recall for the CSIC-2010 dataset because the dataset was primarily built for unsupervised learning while our approach is supervised. We also get a satisfactory result with the KDD-99 dataset and this outperforms all the existing works in terms of F1-Score (99.74%) and recall score (100%).

Table 4. Performance comparison of our proposed model using CSE-CIC-IDS-2018 dataset [11]

Dataset	Models					
	F1-Score			Recall		
	CNN	*CNN-LSTM*	*Proposed model*	*CNN*	*CNN-LSTM*	*Proposed model*
14-02-18	99.88	85.35	100.0	99.96	99.88	100.0
15-02-18	67.07	92.65	99.96	55.09	96.47	99.94
16-02-18	99.11	98.72	99.99	99.95	98.38	100.0
21-02-18	99.66	93.10	100.0	99.45	90.25	100.0
22-02-18	80.65	74.19	93.10	68.88	97.22	94.44
23-02-18	62.65	71.91	81.61	64.10	60.20	69.23
28-02-18	71.07	70.67	95.91	56.13	59.39	98.01
01-03-18	56.28	65.52	88.19	39.40	52.99	95.23
02-03-18	99.74	99.33	99.97	99.77	99.40	99.98

Table 5. Performance of the proposed model on NSL-KDD dataset [10]

Dataset	Metrics					
	F1-Score	*Precision*	*Recall*	*TNR*	*FPR*	*FNR*
2 fold	98.19	97.86	98.53	98.01	1.98	1.46
4 fold	96.00	92.37	99.94	96.51	3.49	0.05
6 fold	98.72	97.82	99.63	96.36	3.63	0.37
8 fold	99.12	98.30	99.97	97.1	2.89	0.22
10 fold	99.22	98.55	99.91	97.5	2.49	0.08

Table 6. Performance on CSIC-2010 [32] and KDD-99 [21] dataset

Dataset	Metrics		
	F1-Score	Precision	Recall
KDD-99	99.74	99.5	1.00
CSIC 2010	36.12	72.74	24.03

5.3 Performance Comparison with State-of-the-Art Works

In this section, we compare the performance of our proposed model with existing variations. We mainly compare our work with the two most common variations, which are CNN [24,26–28], and LSTM-CNN [9,12,29–31,33] based models. For comparing the performance of our model, we implement the state-of-the-art machine learning algorithms and use the most recent benchmark dataset CSE-CIC-IDS-2018 [11]. We also compare our works with the latest proposed model LuNet [12] which encompasses the highest proclaimed accuracy using the NSL-KDD dataset [10].

Figure 2 shows that our proposed model outperforms the nearest variants in terms of F1-Score using the CSE-CIC-IDS-2018 dataset [11]. At the same time, our model achieves a higher recall score which is nearly optimum, as shown in Fig. 3. From the results, it is also evident that normal CNN performs better than the CNN-LSTM models. We get comparatively poor results on the dataset of 22-02-2018 and 23-2018 because there were less anomalous or attacked data on the dataset, and we had to use a balanced dataset. But the overall performance of our model is superior to the nearest variations, and our model provides nearly optimal results. Thus, it easily proves the efficiency of our model for detecting known attacks with a higher F1-Score and Recall value.

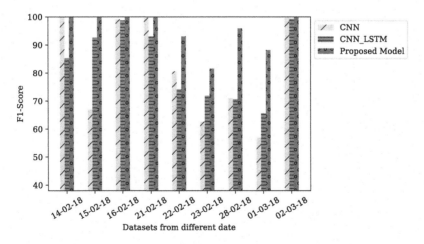

Fig. 2. Comparing F1-Score between our model and State-of-the-art CNN [24,26–28], and CNN-LSTM [9,12,29–31,33] models using CSE-CIC-IDS-2018 dataset [11]

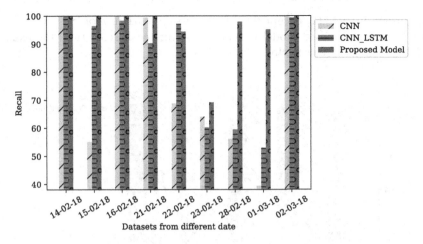

Fig. 3. Comparing recall between our proposed model and State-of-the-art CNN [24, 26–28], and CNN-LSTM [9,12,29–31,33] model using CSE-CIC-IDS-2018 dataset [11]

We compare the performance of our model with LuNet [12] using the NSL-KDD dataset [10] as LuNet does not use the latest CSE-CIC-IDS-2018 dataset [11]. From Fig. 4, it can be seen that our model closely follows LuNet by the F1-Score, achieving almost similar or even better in the 10-fold dataset. It is also worth mentioning that our proposed model is a lightweight model with a few layers compared to LuNet.

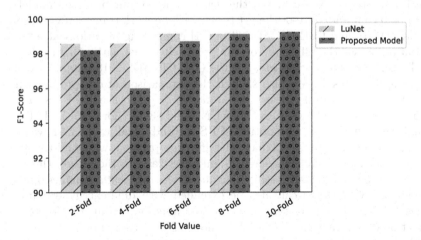

Fig. 4. Performance comparison based on F1-Score between LuNet [12] and our model

Figure 5 shows the comparison of Recall score between our proposed model and LuNet [12]. It is very prominent from the figure that our proposed model outperforms LuNet [12] except for 2-fold cross-validation data. So, we can conclude that our proposed model provides a better recall score than the existing models, which ensures the efficiency of IDS.

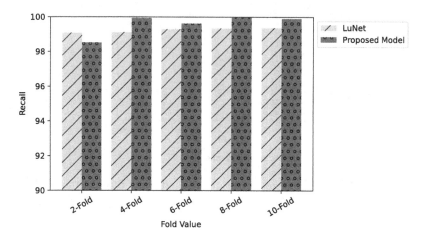

Fig. 5. Performance comparison based on Recall between LuNet [12] and our model

6   Conclusion

In this paper, we investigated the potential of combining the CNN, LSTM, and GRU models with attention mechanisms for improving the accuracy of intrusion detection systems. We evaluated the performance of our proposed model with the most recent and state-of-the-art benchmark network traffic datasets, such as NSL-KDD [10] and CSE-CIC-IDS-2018 [11] comprising of various attacks. The evaluation shows the efficiency of our proposed model with a higher F1-score and Recall score for all datasets. For the CSE-CIC-IDS-2018 dataset, we get an almost optimal result. We also showed the comparison of our proposed model with the existing neural network based models (e.g., an average F1-Score value of 95.41% by our model vs. 81.87% for CNN and 83.50% for CNN-LSTM). Even though we built a model with optimal F1-Score and Recall value, we have considered anomaly detection as a binary classification problem where all the anomalous data or attacks are considered in only one class. In the future, this can be generalized for multi-class classification and detect different anomalies or attacks individually. Our works can also be extended with different hyper-parameter values of CNN (i.e., activation function, loss function, learning rate, etc.). The impact of adding more layers to CNN and LSTM or using bi-directional LSTM could also be investigated in the future. Currently, the detection is offline, it could be make online as an application to deal with online data.

Acknowledgment. The authors thank the anonymous reviewers for their comments. This material is based upon work partially supported by the Natural Sciences and Engineering Research Council of Canada under Discovery Grant N02815.

References

1. CISCO: Global 2021 forecast highlights (2021). https://www.cisco.com/c/dam/m/en_us/solutions/service-provider/vni-forecast-highlights/pdf/Global_2021_Forecast_Highlights.pdf. Accessed 30 June 2021
2. IoT Business News: Global IoT roaming data traffic to increase by 300% to reach 500pb in 2025 (2021). https://iotbusinessnews.com/2020/10/15/70310-global-iot-roaming-data-traffic-to-increase-by-300-to-reach-500pb-in-2025/. Accessed 30 June 2021
3. CISCO: Cisco annual internet report (2018–2023) white paper (2021). https://www.cisco.com/c/en/us/solutions/collateral/executive-perspectives/annual-internet-report/white-paper-c11-741490.html. Accessed 30 June 2021
4. Biermann, E., Cloete, E., Venter, L.M.: A comparison of intrusion detection systems. Comput. Secur. **20**(8), 676–683 (2001)
5. Tsai, C.-F., Hsu, Y.-F., Lin, C.-Y., Lin, W.-Y.: Intrusion detection by machine learning: a review. Expert Syst. Appl. **36**(10), 11994–12000 (2009)
6. Zhang, Z., Li, J., Manikopoulos, C.N., Jorgenson, J., Ucles, J.: HIDE: a hierarchical network intrusion detection system using statistical preprocessing and neural network classification. In: Proceedings of the IEEE Workshop on Information Assurance and Security, vol. 85, p. 90 (2001)
7. Vinayakumar, R., Soman, K.P., Poornachandran, P.: Applying convolutional neural network for network intrusion detection. In: ICACCI. IEEE (2017)
8. Botros, S.M., Diep, T.A., Izenson, M.D.: Method and apparatus for training a neural network model for use in computer network intrusion detection. US Patent 6,769,066, 27 July 2004
9. Hsu, C.-M., Azhari, M.Z., Hsieh, H.-Y., Prakosa, S.W., Leu, J.-S.: Robust network intrusion detection scheme using long-short term memory based convolutional neural networks. Mob. Netw. Appl. **26**(3), 1137–1144 (2020). https://doi.org/10.1007/s11036-020-01623-2
10. Canadian Institute for Cybersecurity (CIC): NSL-KDD dataset (2009). https://www.unb.ca/cic/datasets/nsl.html. Accessed 30 June 2021
11. Canadian Institute for Cybersecurity (CIC): CSE-CIC-IDS2018 on AWS (2018). https://www.unb.ca/cic/datasets/ids-2018.html. Accessed 30 June 2021
12. Wu, P., Guo, H.: LuNET: a deep neural network for network intrusion detection. In: SSCI. IEEE (2019)
13. Tjhai, G.C., Papadaki, M., Furnell, S.M., Clarke, N.L.: Investigating the problem of IDS false alarms: an experimental study using snort. In: Jajodia, S., Samarati, P., Cimato, S. (eds.) SEC 2008. ITIFIP, vol. 278, pp. 253–267. Springer, Boston, MA (2008). https://doi.org/10.1007/978-0-387-09699-5_17
14. KirstenS, Wichers, Jkurucar, kingthorin: Intrusion detection control-OWASP (2021). https://owasp.org/www-community/controls/Intrusion_Detection. Accessed 30 June 2021
15. Liu, C., Liu, Y., Yan, Y., Wang, J.: An intrusion detection model with hierarchical attention mechanism. IEEE Access **8**, 67542–67554 (2020)
16. Yan, L., Xiong, J.: Web-APT-Detect: a framework for web-based advanced persistent threat detection using self-translation machine with attention. IEEE Lett. Comput. Soc. **3**(2), 66–69 (2020)
17. Liu, T., Qi, Y., Shi, L., Yan, J.: Locate-then-detect: real-time web attack detection via attention-based deep neural networks. In: IJCAI, pp. 4725–4731 (2019)

18. Shun, J., Malki, H.A.: Network intrusion detection system using neural networks. In: ICNC, vol. 5, pp. 242–246. IEEE (2008)
19. MIT: 1999 DARPA intrusion detection evaluation dataset (1999). https://www.ll.mit.edu/r-d/datasets/1999-darpa-intrusion-detection-evaluation-dataset. Accessed 30 June 2021
20. Chiba, Z., Abghour, N., Moussaid, K., El Omri, A., Rida, M.: A novel architecture combined with optimal parameters for back propagation neural networks applied to anomaly network intrusion detection. Comput. Secur. **75**, 36–58 (2018)
21. KDD 1999: KDD cup 1999 data (2021). http://kdd.ics.uci.edu/databases/kddcup99/kddcup99.html. Accessed 30 June 2021
22. Mahalingam, P.R.: Intelligent network-based intrusion detection system (iNIDS). In: Meghanathan, N., Nagamalai, D., Chaki, N. (eds.) Advances in Computing and Information Technology. Advances in Intelligent Systems and Computing, vol. 176, pp. 1–9. Springer, Heidelberg (2012). https://doi.org/10.1007/978-3-642-31513-8_1
23. Su, L., Yu, L., Li, T., Liu, X.: Research on network data security based on RS-PS Support Vector Machine (SVM). J. Phys: Conf. Ser. **1748**(3), 032057 (2020). IOP Publishing
24. Mendonça, R.V., et al.: Intrusion detection system based on fast hierarchical deep convolutional neural network. IEEE Access **9**, 61024–61034 (2021)
25. Canadian Institute for Cybersecurity (CIC): Intrusion detection evaluation dataset (CIC-IDS2017) (2017). https://www.unb.ca/cic/datasets/ids-2017.html. Accessed 30 June 2021
26. Kim, J., Kim, J., Kim, H., Shim, M., Choi, E.: CNN-based network intrusion detection against denial-of-service attacks. Electronics **9**(6), 916 (2020)
27. Wang, H., Cao, Z., Hong, B.: A network intrusion detection system based on convolutional neural network. J. Intell. Fuzzy Syst. **38**(6), 7623–7637 (2020)
28. Bandyopadhyay, S., Chowdhury, R., Roy, A., Saha, B.: A step forward to revolutionise intrusiondetection system using deep convolution neural network. Preprints (2020)
29. Sun, P., et al.: DL-IDS: extracting features using CNN-LSTM hybrid network for intrusion detection system. Secur. Commun. Netw. **2020**, Article ID: 8890306, 11 (2020). https://doi.org/10.1155/2020/8890306
30. Kim, J., Kim, J., Thu, H.L.T., Kim, H.: Long short term memory recurrent neural network classifier for intrusion detection. In: PlatCon, pp. 1–5. IEEE (2016)
31. Kuang, X., et al.: DeepWAF: detecting web attacks based on CNN and LSTM models. In: Vaidya, J., Zhang, X., Li, J. (eds.) CSS 2019. LNCS, vol. 11983, pp. 121–136. Springer, Cham (2019). https://doi.org/10.1007/978-3-030-37352-8_11
32. CSIC: HTTP dataset CSIC 2010 (2010). https://www.tic.itefi.csic.es/dataset/. Accessed 30 June 2021
33. Hsu, C.-M., Hsieh, H.-Y., Prakosa, S.W., Azhari, M.Z., Leu, J.-S.: Using long-short-term memory based convolutional neural networks for network intrusion detection. In: Chen, J.-L., Pang, A.-C., Deng, D.-J., Lin, C.-C. (eds.) WICON 2018. LNICST, vol. 264, pp. 86–94. Springer, Cham (2019). https://doi.org/10.1007/978-3-030-06158-6_9
34. UNSW: The UNSW-NB15 dataset (2015). https://research.unsw.edu.au/projects/unsw-nb15-dataset. Accessed 30 June 2021
35. Basati, A., Faghih, M.M.: APAE: an IoT intrusion detection system using asymmetric parallel auto-encoder. Neural Comput. Appl. 1–21 (2021). https://doi.org/10.1007/s00521-021-06011-9

36. Sekhar, R., Sasirekha, K., Raja, P.S., Thangavel, K.: A novel GPU based intrusion detection system using deep autoencoder with Fruitfly optimization. SN Appl. Sci. **3**(6), 1–16 (2021)
37. Shone, N., Ngoc, T.N., Phai, V.D., Shi, Q.: A deep learning approach to network intrusion detection. IEEE Trans. Emerg. Top. Comput. Intell. **2**(1), 41–50 (2018)
38. Tang, R., et al.: ZeroWall: detecting zero-day web attacks through encoder-decoder recurrent neural networks. In: IEEE INFOCOM 2020-IEEE Conference on Computer Communications, pp. 2479–2488. IEEE (2020)
39. Vartouni, A.M., Kashi, S.S., Teshnehlab, M.: An anomaly detection method to detect web attacks using stacked auto-encoder. In: 2018 6th Iranian Joint Congress on Fuzzy and Intelligent Systems (CFIS), pp. 131–134. IEEE (2018)
40. Mac, H., Truong, D., Nguyen, L., Nguyen, H., Tran, H.A., Tran, D.: Detecting attacks on web applications using autoencoder. In: Proceedings of the Ninth International Symposium on Information and Communication Technology, pp. 416–421 (2018)
41. Bahdanau, D., Cho, K., Bengio, Y.: Neural machine translation by jointly learning to align and translate. arXiv preprint arXiv:1409.0473 (2014)
42. Abadi, M., et al.: TensorFlow: large-scale machine learning on heterogeneous systems (2015)
43. Keras: Keras (2020). https://keras.io/. Accessed 30 June 2021
44. Pedregosa, F., et al.: Scikit-learn: machine learning in Python. J. Mach. Learn. Res. **12**, 2825–2830 (2011)
45. Keras: Nadam (2015). https://keras.io/api/optimizers/Nadam/. Accessed 30 June 2021
46. Lippmann, R.P., et al.: Evaluating intrusion detection systems: the 1998 DARPA off-line intrusion detection evaluation. In: Proceedings of the DARPA Information Survivability Conference and Exposition, DISCEX 2000, vol. 2, pp. 12–26. IEEE (2000)
47. McHugh, J.: Testing intrusion detection systems: a critique of the 1998 and 1999 DARPA intrusion detection system evaluations as performed by Lincoln laboratory. ACM Trans. Inf. Syst. Secur. (TISSEC) **3**(4), 262–294 (2000)
48. Kaushik, S.S., Deshmukh, P.R.: Detection of attacks in an intrusion detection system. Int. J. Comput. Sci. Inf. Technol. (IJCSIT) **2**(3), 982–986 (2011)
49. The Communications Security Establishment (CSE) & the Canadian Institute for Cybersecurity (CIC): Cicflowmeter (formerly iscxflowmeter) (2021). https://www.unb.ca/cic/research/applications.html. Accessed 30 June 2021
50. Zhou, Q., Pezaros, D.: Evaluation of machine learning classifiers for zero-day intrusion detection-an analysis on CIC-AWS-2018 dataset. arXiv preprint arXiv:1905.03685 (2019)
51. scikit-learn.org: sklearn.model_selection.stratifiedkfold (2020). https://scikit-learn.org/stable/. Accessed 30 June 2021
52. scikit-learn.org: sklearn.metrics.precision_score (2021). https://scikit-learn.org/stable/modules/generated/sklearn.metrics.precision_score.html. Accessed 30 June 2021
53. scikit-learn.org: sklearn.metrics.recall_score (2021). https://scikit-learn.org/stable/modules/generated/sklearn.metrics.recall_score.html. Accessed 30 June 2021
54. scikit-learn.org: sklearn.metrics.f1_score (2021). https://scikit-learn.org/stable/modules/generated/sklearn.metrics.f1_score.html. Accessed 30 June 2021

Avoiding VPN Bottlenecks: Exploring Network-Level Client Identity Validation Options

Yu Liu$^{(\boxtimes)}$ and Craig A. Shue

Worcester Polytechnic Institute, Worcester, MA 10609, USA
{yliu25,cshue}@cs.wpi.edu

Abstract. Virtual private networks (VPNs) allow organizations to support their remote employees by creating tunnels that ensure confidentiality, integrity and authenticity of communicated packets. However, these same services are often provided by the application, in protocols such as TLS. As a result, the historical driving force for VPNs may be in decline. Instead, VPNs are often used to determine whether a communicating host is a legitimate member of the network to simplify filtering and access control. However, this comes with a cost: VPN implementations often introduce performance bottlenecks that affect the user experience.

To preserve straightforward filtering without the limitations of VPN deployments, we explore a simple network-level identifier that allows remote users to provide evidence that they have previously been vetted. This approach uniquely identifies each user, even if they are behind Carrier-Grade Network Address Translation, which causes widespread IP address sharing. Such identifiers remove the redundant cryptography, packet header overheads, and need for dedicated servers to implement VPNs. This lightweight approach can achieve access control goals with minimal performance overheads.

Keywords: Virtual private networks · Access control · Software-defined networking · Residential networks · Carrier-grade NAT

1 Introduction

Virtual private network (VPN) protocols are often used by organizations to allow remote users to access the organization's network as if they were on-site. These protocols have been used for decades [3] and were designed for an Internet that needed cryptography to protect the confidentiality, integrity, and authenticity of communication payload. In essence, VPNs allow organizations to treat the traffic from a remote worker the same as that from a local worker.

In recent years, the deployment of end-to-end cryptography has grown substantially, with over 90% of web servers supporting the TLS/SSL application-layer protocol [41]. When remote users access an HTTPS server through a VPN,

X. Yuan et al. (Eds.): QShine 2021, LNICST 402, pp. 280–300, 2021.
https://doi.org/10.1007/978-3-030-91424-0_17

the traffic is encrypted and authenticated by TLS between the application-layer endpoints and is again encrypted and authenticated between the VPN termination points. Since confidentiality, integrity, and authenticity can be reasonably assured by either of the protocols, having both is redundant. Further, VPN deployments often come with performance overheads since 1) VPN servers are usually an aggregation point for network traffic and their limited resources can cause network congestion [22,45], 2) redundant protocol headers use more space in each packet, and 3) VPN licenses, which cost more than $2 million annually for a large company, can be expensive [47].

The traditional motivations for deploying a VPN [36,38,39] are to 1) provide data with confidentiality and authenticity, 2) manage network activities at the remote endpoint, and 3) simplify access control. Application-layer security achieves the first goal. We address the second goal in Sect. 2.5, where we discuss better management through endpoint filtering. We explore the third goal, access control, throughout this work. Importantly, 67% of organizations are exploring VPN alternatives for security, maintenance, and fiscal reasons [54].

Organizations often implicitly use a host's position within a network perimeter as a factor in determining whether to trust the host or not. As examples, the configuration instructions for web servers [37,40], email servers [12,33,34], and firewalls [9] often describe how administrators can configure the systems to permit only traffic within an organization's IP prefix. Organizations may also use network address translation (NAT) to assign private, unroutable addresses to hosts and devices so that the infrastructure cannot be reached by outsiders without traversing NAT devices that could enforce policy [5].

While organizations can employ such address filtering within their networks, it may be impractical to do so with remote users. Internet Service Providers (ISPs) often use dynamic addresses for their customers, with lease times that vary greatly [6]. Residential users often deploy NAT in their home networks to share addresses, so authorizing a particular user's IP address would allow others at the same residence access to the organization's resources. Even worse, some ISPs have adopted a competing technology called carrier-grade network address translation ("carrier-grade NAT" or CGN). CGN is used in 92% of cellular networks [1]. Some of these carriers plan to use 5G cellular networks to provide residential network connectivity, with some providers estimating 30 million home networks will be connected in this fashion [11]. In some cases, hundreds of users share an IP address [2] and in others, a single customer's traffic may be simultaneously associated with multiple public IP addresses.

Organizations may use VPNs to mitigate the problems that accompany address sharing. The VPN tunneling approach allows an organization to provide remote access to systems that are highly sensitive or have weaker protections, such as printers, Supervisory Control and Data Acquisition (SCADA) or Internet of Things (IoT) infrastructure, or other embedded devices. However, a heavyweight VPNs approach may not be necessary to achieve these goals.

Organizations need a quick and simple way for a network-level identifier to validate a remote end user. This validation can be a quick, "first-factor" authenticator that provides evidence that the connecting machine or network is likely legitimate. This factor can work with other authentication factors, such as application-layer credentials, on the server endpoint. It must be cooperatively used by both the end-user and the organization to avoid abuse by malicious parties. While identifiers have been used by network providers to identify clients in the past, such as "super cookie" deployments in cellular networks [13], the use of the factor in authentication requires it to be cross-application, dynamic, and under the associated user's control.

With a "less may be more" perspective, we explore a practical and deployable approach to allow end-users to create dynamic network-level factors for access control. Our contributions include:

- **Dynamic Identifier Insertion:** Our software-defined networking (SDN) approach leverages endpoint programs and modified residential routers to insert application-agnostic identifiers into network flows. This approach allows organizations to determine if a user is connecting from a known device or network location while introducing minimal latency overheads that affect only the first packet in each network flow.
- **Gateway and Endpoint Validation:** Using our implementation, built using the popular `iptables` tool, organizations can validate clients at either a gateway or endpoint, providing functionality similar to a VPN without unnecessary performance overhead. This method can verify each flow in around 90 ms (of which only around 0.8 ms is spent at the validator). Unlike a VPN, it adds no overhead after the handshake. We eliminate the need for a VPN server and its associated CPU bottleneck, resulting in a 2.5–2.9 times increase in throughput for clients.

2   Background and Related Work

This section discusses background and related work on CGN, software-defined networking, user identity, and techniques to encode and transmit identifiers.

2.1   Carrier-Grade NAT (CGN) and Address Sharing

As IPv4 addresses availability became scarce, Internet Service Providers (ISPs) started deploying CGN to share IPv4 addresses among subscribers and to minimize disruption during the transition from IPv4 to IPv6. CGN utilizes both network-level addresses and transport-layer port numbers to map traffic to the appropriate end-user. The number of public addresses needed for a given number of end-users can be estimated with formulas. Some guides suggest sharing 30,517 public IP address among 1,000,000 subscribers [2]. In measuring CGN behavior, Richter et al. [1] observed that some CGNs used the same public IP address and varying transport layer ports for subsequent TCP sessions from the same subscriber. In Netalyzr [6], the authors found that more than 60% of the TCP sessions for a given subscriber used different public IP addresses. These guides and measurements show that providers use highly dynamic, and widely shared, public IP addresses for their subscribers.

With their Revelio tool, Mandalari et al. [7] performed Internet measurements and found around 10% of ISPs deployed CGN. With web server logs and multiple measurement points, Livadariu et al. [8] estimated that around 4.1k of the 17.4k ASes they measured deployed CGNs. Richter et al. [1] found that while only 13.3% of non-cellular ASes use CGNs, 92% of cellular networks use them [1]. In their plans to deploy 5G cellular connectivity, some providers estimate they will serve 30 million residential networks through 5G [11].

2.2 Software-Defined Networking (SDN)

The software-defined networking approach separates the data plane and control plane for network traffic, often using a centralized network controller. The OpenFlow protocol [30] allows a network controller to alter data structures in switches and routers to enable inspection and arbitrary forwarding of packets. The Open vSwitch [19] tool can be used to enable the OpenFlow protocol on a router. In OpenFlow, a controller can intercept packets from a network device via a PACKET_IN message. To authorize a packet, with possible alteration, the controller replies with a PACKET_OUT message. A controller can also command switches to cache certain rules through FLOW_MOD messages, allowing switches to process subsequent packets without controller involvement. This avoids causing performance overheads in subsequent packets in a flow.

2.3 Host Identity and Reputation Systems

Address sharing introduces challenges for a wide range of applications relying on public IP addresses. For example, enterprise-grade firewalls often utilize public IP addresses in policies [20]. Efforts to mitigate DNS amplification attacks use IP addresses in response rate limiting [29]. IP reputation systems, which are used by major email providers, are often used to determine the threat associated with incoming email messages [12], such as Microsoft's SmartScreen technology in Outlook [33] or Gmail's delivery rate throttling [34]. For websites, Cloudflare identifies users with a bad IP reputation and challenges them with CAPTCHAs [35]. Such tools may mistakenly assume that IP addresses change infrequently and are unlikely to be shared. This leads to false negatives when attackers move across IP addresses and false positives when innocent people happen to use an IP address previously involved in an attack [10].

Komu et al. [31] investigated methods to separate the functionalities of "locator" and "identifier" from network addresses. The locator can be used to find a host while a separate long-term identifier is associated with the system. This separation is important for mobile hosts or for times when addresses change. HIP is a protocol to maintain persistent identity even with dynamic IP addresses [27]. HIP uses a public key to identify end-hosts and uses IPSec for packet tunneling. Since HIP requires HIP-aware gateways to forward packets to the correct destination, the deployment of HIP requires infrastructure changes.

DeCusatis et al. [56] introduce a TCP-based access control mechanism using first packet authentication. That work uses an ephemeral four-byte value in the TCP protocol that is used for access control and must be established for each interaction. That work only evaluates token evaluation. In contrast to our work, it does not explore token creation, insertion, storage, or protocols for conveying these values in a way that allows longer-term, cross-protocol use. Other work has proposed persistent identifier, but provided only an abbreviated analysis of performance impacts in limited deployment scenarios [46]. Our work provides the necessary information and analysis for a practical implementation.

At the application layer, web applications can track user identities with cookies, supported by browsers. Unfortunately, cookies are application-specific and only work with web traffic. In some cases, network providers create persistent identifiers, called "super cookies," to identify systems at the device-level [28]. These super cookies are outside the end-user's control. They enable tracking that could violate end-user privacy. These deployments resulted in fines for some ISPs [13]. Our approach is mindful of these potential privacy concerns. A key design goal is to allow end-users to have control over persistent identifiers while supporting multiple applications, which we discuss in Sect. 3.4.

Organizations often use virtual private network (VPN) protocols, such as IPSec [3], to authenticate remote users and then leverage the VPN server's position inside a local area network (LAN) to provide access to LAN resources. As aggregation points, VPN servers can become throughput bottlenecks since they must be involved in the entire network flow and use cryptography to encrypt and authenticate traffic, even if the application-layer already offers that support (e.g., in HTTPS or SSH). Application-layer software typically lacks options to configure IPSec tunnels for specific flows or destinations. Instead, current VPN software works across all applications on a device-wide basis. Often, all network traffic from a host in a VPN is forwarded to the VPN server, which increases overhead and decreases throughput. Hauser et al. [57] propose an SDN extension to IPSec for programmable data planes. In practice, VPNs can increase organization costs [47], reduce performance [22], create single points of failure [21], and add complexity [44]. In our approach, we avoid these limitations.

2.4   Mechanisms to Encode Application-Agnostic Identifiers

Protocols such as TCP and IP support options for communicating information, such as identifiers and authenticators. Options in the IP header can be used for all transport layer protocols, rather than just TCP. However, intermediary routers may drop packets with IP options they do not support [17,18].

Prior work has examined using "shim" layers between the IP header and transport layer headers to encode data [26]. IPSec does so using the ESP or AH headers to encapsulate protected traffic [24,25]. Special-purpose shims have the downside of requiring support from endpoints and the risk that they will be discarded by firewalls or routers that do not understand the shim layer headers. However, the IP-in-IP tunneling technique, standardized in RFC 1853 [15], essentially provides a second IP header as a shim layer. The use of an IP-in-IP shim gives us a straightforward way to add options in a backwards-compatible manner. We can insert a second IP header in front of the original transport layer header using the standardized approach. Mobile IP [14] uses this same technique.

2.5 Motivations and Perspectives with VPN Deployments

Commonly cited reasons for organizations to use VPNs with their employees include [38,39]: 1) to build a communication tunnel with confidentiality, integrity, and authenticity via cryptography, 2) to control communication to remote systems, and 3) to provide authentication to achieve simplified access control. In this section, we explore these techniques and describe how they may be affected by changing Internet trends. We also note recent changes in VPN planning.

Confidentiality, Integrity, and Authenticity. Web traffic comprises a majority of Internet communication. Currently, 90% of HTTP traffic is protected by TLS [4,41]. TLS supports common business applications, such as remote desktop, file transfer, and remote terminals. Further, studies show that over 98% of printers support Internet Printing Protocol (which supports encryption and authentication) [42]. Most network traffic is protected by application-layer cryptography, which achieves confidentiality, integrity and authenticity.

Some legacy protocols or devices may not support cryptography. However, organizations may use the reverse proxy model [43] to protect such devices by creating application-specific security tunnels without requiring VPNs.

Organizations Pursuing VPN Alternatives. In a recent report [54], Zscaler indicates that 67% of companies are seeking alternatives to VPNs. In addition to performance issues, companies expressed concerned about 1) the changing role of VPNs with pandemic-related work-from-home patterns, 2) increased VPN infrastructure's impact on organizational architecture, which makes maintenance more complex and expensive, and 3) attackers who are increasingly using VPNs to gain access to corporate networks via social engineering and malware. Given this context, 77% of companies have indicated an interest in using a zero-trust model to manage remote access for their employees instead. Our approach aligns with these corporate goals.

3 Approach: Indicating Authenticity Validation

Inspired by Kerberos and HTTP cookies, we explore a token-based identity approach. A remote authenticator distinguishes legitimate and unauthenticated users via a token provided by the user and device. We describe the goals of such a system and how they differ from the robust authentication present in end-to-end applications. We then describe our threat model and the techniques we use.

3.1   Design Goal: Evidence Supporting Legitimacy

VPN servers can robustly authenticate their remote VPN gateways. For gateway-to-gateway VPNs that interconnect two LANs, this approach may not uniquely identify the connecting end-user. The VPN server may be able to uniquely identify the connecting end-user if the remote VPN gateway runs on the remote user's endpoint. However, the VPN server does not share that identification with the endpoints that the user then connects to through the VPN server. The VPN server often performs NAT to proxy the connection between the remote user and server, but the IP addresses may be randomly selected from the available IPs. The server endpoint may be able to infer that the end-user authenticated with the VPN server by determining if the remote IP belongs to an IP address associated with the VPN server's pool. This is a useful, but relatively weak authenticator because it lacks a unique identifier or strong authenticity guarantees.

Our approach aims to re-build the authentication between a remote user and an organization network and the weak authenticator available to a remote server.

3.2   Threat Model

Our approach enables clients to provide an application-agnostic device-level authenticator. This authenticator is not designed to be authoritative about the identity of a client. Instead, it is a quick "first-pass" authenticator that can be used to separate out "likely legitimate" traffic from completely unknown traffic. It can be used in combination with application-layer authentication (e.g., as a mechanism to address brute-force guessing on SSH servers). Enterprises can also calculate reputation based upon these identifiers, with better reputation leading to better services, as incentives.

Our approach is designed to effectively defend against "on-the-side" attackers, such as a user who is not on the network path, but who might share IP address with a client (e.g., behind the same CGN). We deploy identifiers that protect against any brute-force guessing. However, "on-path" adversaries can inspect the inner IP header, observe the identifiers, and misuse the identifier information. We rely on the application layer to provide robust authentication to defeat such powerful on-path adversaries.

3.3   Leveraging Authentication Servers

In our approach, we create a mechanism that allows an organization to authenticate its remote users using a lightweight device-level authentication factor. The end user can authenticate to the organization using a pre-existing authentication system, such as a web-based authentication page. This authentication system can use multi-factor authentication to robustly verify the end-user. Upon successful verification, the authentication system provides a token that can be used by the user's device as an authentication factor. If verification is unsuccessful, the server simply does not provide a token.

Our approach requires both the device and authentication server to automatically determine each others' support for the protocol, as well as for the other systems that are able to support the device-level authenticator. We enable automated deployment discovery using specially-crafted DNS records. When a client requests certain DNS records associated with the organization's domain (e.g., A records for www.example.com), the DNS server provides a TXT record in the Additional Records section of the response indicating the authentication server that is authorized to create authentication tokens for the domain. The TXT record also indicates which servers at the organization support the authentication scheme by listing public-facing IP address or CIDR prefixes.

3.4   Using OpenFlow to Manage Tokens

To avoid requiring support for the authentication mechanism in each application, we use an SDN technique to engage in the protocol on the client's behalf. An OpenFlow agent in the client's network, which could be on the client endpoint device itself (e.g., via Open vSwitch) or on a network gateway (e.g., a residential router), intercepts new flow requests and directs them to a SDN controller. The controller examines the related DNS responses for any TXT records that indicate support for the protocol. It also manages the authentication factors on behalf of the end-user on the device or on multiple devices in the network.

Our approach is designed to grant users full control over their identifiers. Unlike the "super cookies" approach [28], our system allows users to configure their identifies and choose when to use tokens with a remote party. The OpenFlow controller can allow users to manage the entries (e.g., via a web page). Based on the user's configuration and the destination of each flow, the controller determines whether to insert identifiers.

We use the standardized IP-in-IP tunneling approach [15] to create a "shim" layer. This creates two IP headers, allowing the outer IP header to be processed normally by routers while the inner IP header contains options that might otherwise result in the packet being dropped. We use those IP options to communicate the token that provides evidence of authentication.

When a client first interacts with an authorized authentication server, the OpenFlow agent intercepts the initial packet in the flow and sends it to the OpenFlow controller. The controller modifies the packet to signal that the client supports the scheme and sends it back to the OpenFlow agent, which then transmits it to the authentication server. Since the DNS records signal the server's support for the approach, we can construct packets that require the server to engage in custom parsing. The controller alters the packet to insert the IP shim layer, resulting in an IP-in-IP packet. In the inner IP header, the controller includes an option indicating that the client supports the protocol. Upon successful login, the authentication server replies with its own IP-in-IP packet, with the authentication data contained in an option field in the inner IP header. The OpenFlow agent elevates this response to the OpenFlow controller, which extracts the authentication factor, removes the IP shim header, and orders the OpenFlow agent to send the decapsulated packet to the client application.

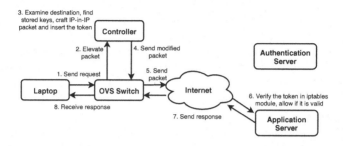

Fig. 1. The process for the client to authenticate to the application server.

When a client subsequently creates a new network flow to a server that supports the scheme, the OpenFlow agent intercepts the request and elevates it to the controller (Fig. 1). The controller again performs the necessary alteration of the packet to create the IP-in-IP shim that contains the pre-determined authentication data. The controller then returns the modified packet to the OpenFlow agent for transmission to the server. The server, or a gateway or middlebox on the path to the server, processes any packets containing the IP-in-IP shim to verify and strip the authentication data. In doing so, the server or middlebox can record that the flow is verified and, depending on policy, allow the flow where unverified flows may be denied.

Importantly, the inner IP header addresses can be used by a gateway or middlebox validator to implement NAT translations that allow a remote user to have local IP addresses in the same manner as VPN servers. However, unlike VPN servers, the inner IP header only needs to appear in the initial exchange to create the appropriate NAT mapping to translate the remote machine's address.

4   Implementation

We implement our system in a home network to allow us to evaluate its security and performance. As shown in Fig. 2, we explore the modifications that would be needed to include a regular client, an authentication server (e.g., a single sign-on identity provider), an application server (e.g., a relying party), and an SDN controller to coordinate it all.

We run our client in a virtual machine (VM) hosted on a Thinkpad S3 laptop with four cores and 8 GBytes RAM. We create two other VMs on a Macbook Pro laptop, with four cores and 16 GBytes RAM, for applications and authentication servers respectively. Each VM has one core and 4 GBytes memory. We configure a physical TP-Link Archer C7 router with OpenWrt and the Open vSwitch module as our SDN switch. The VMs are bridged through laptop interfaces and get DHCP services from the router. All the physical devices are located in the same home network. However, we configure our Floodlight SDN controller on a remote network machine with two cores and 4 GBytes memory.

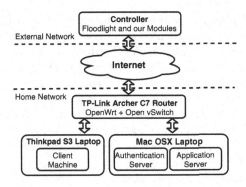

Fig. 2. Our experiment architecture.

4.1 Identity Provider Interactions

In Sect. 3.4, we described how the OpenFlow switch and controller cooperate to detect that the application and authentication servers support the approach. The Kerberos approach provides a shared-key architecture for identity providers to construct keys for relying parties [16].

The SDN controller learns about the authentication server through DNS records and signals the client's support via an IP-in-IP shim. When the authentication server replies, it includes a shared secret that the client can use to authenticate itself.

As with Kerberos, each application server pre-shares a unique key with the authentication server [55]. The authentication server uses that `applicationServerSecretKey`, along with a unique identifier for the user and a nonce value it generates, to produce a shared secret that is a one-way hash of these values (i.e., `clientKey=SHA224(uniqueIdentifier || nonce1 || applicationServerSecretKey)`). The authentication server then sends both the `clientKey` value and the concatenation of the `uniqueIdentifier` and `nonce1` value to the client.

The authentication server communicates the key and identifier by crafting an IP-in-IP packet. The inner IP header includes an option field in which both the `clientKey` and `uniqueIdentifier` are encoded. The protocol field differs between the two IP headers (the outer header indicates the protocol is another IP header, while the inner header indicates the transport protocol used), but otherwise the two headers contain identical values.

The OpenFlow switch elevates packets with IP-in-IP shims to the controller, allowing the controller to obtain the `clientKey` and the `uniqueIdentifier`.

4.2 Application Server Interactions

In our implementation, when the client initiates a connection to the application server, the OpenFlow switch elevates the request to the OpenFlow controller. The controller consults its database, determines that a token is needed, and creates an IP-in-IP shim. In the inner header, it creates an IP option that contains the user identity, the authentication server's nonce (nonce1), the client's own nonce value (nonce2), and a SHA224 value constructed from the concatenation of the identity, nonce2, and clientKey (i.e., SHA224(uniqueIdentifier || nonce2 || clientKey)). The token we construct is 37 bytes total (5 bytes for the user ID, 2 bytes for the nonce1, 2 bytes for nonce2, and 28 bytes for the SHA224 output). The controller sends this modified packet back to the switch for transmission using an OpenFlow PACKET_OUT message.

The application server must parse the IP-in-IP message, validate the token, and then remove it before delivering it to the actual destination application. To do this, we develop an open source iptables module using the Xtables-Addons framework [32]. This module efficiently performs the interception and validation before the packet reaches the destination application.

Our functionality is divided into an iptables match module that specifies user-defined conditions. It passes any matching packets on to a target module for processing. We configure our match module to examine any IP-in-IP packets. For all such packets, it searches for our specific IP option type inside the inner IP header. If found, it parses the option to obtain the unique identifier and nonces. The match module then uses the client-supplied information and the key shared by the application server with the authentication server to calculate the corresponding clientKey (i.e., clientKey=SHA224(uniqueIdentifier || nonce1 || applicationServerSecretKey)). The application server then constructs a SHA224 digest using this clientKey, the uniqueIdentifier, and the client's nonce (i.e., SHA224(uniqueIdentifier || nonce2 || clientKey)) and compares it with the SHA224 value that is contained within the IP option. If the digests match, it knows the client interacted with the authentication server to obtain the clientKey. The match module only returns true if a match is found.

We next implement a target module that is used if the match module successfully validates a packet. Our target module modifies the skb buffer, which is the data structure used in Linux for packet processing. The target module must decapsulate the packet to remove the shim. It does so by removing the inner IP header and IP options, updating the protocol field in the outer IP header and recalculating the checksum. It then sends the packet to the application for processing. This allows the destination to validate the communication across applications. Importantly, the iptables tool can be run on a middlebox or on the application server itself to avoid bottlenecks.

5   Evaluation: Security and Performance

We evaluate our approach from both a security and performance perspective using the configuration depicted in Fig. 2. We focus on the performance of the token validation and shim layer operations between the client and application server, since these same operations are used in the interaction between the client and authentication server.

5.1   Security Evaluation

To assess our approach, we simulate the authentication process by issuing new network requests to the organization network, where our `iptables` modules are deployed on the servers. The application servers deny packets without validation by default. Only the packets approved by our match module can pass through `iptables` rules and be received by the services that run on the server.

Table 1. Result of effectiveness evaluation. We performed experiments 20 times for three scenarios: 1) network request without a token, 2) network request with an invalid token, and 3) network request with a valid token.

Result	No token	Invalid token	Valid token
Access allowed	0	0	20
Access denied	20	20	0

The first experiment setup simulates network queries without providing a token. As shown in Table 1, all 20 requests were successfully blocked by the default deny rule set up on the application server. In our second scenario, we enable the OpenFlow and `iptables` modules we implemented. We craft client request packets that contain invalid tokens. As shown in Table 1, all 20 requests failed to reach the applications. In our third scenario, we also enable our Open-Flow and `iptables` modules on both client and server side. We craft proper packet headers and the first packets of these flows contain valid tokens. As shown in Table 1, all such requests were approved by our `iptables` module.

5.2   Network Delay Overhead Evaluation

Our approach affects only the first exchange in each flow. The controller elevation to insert the shim, and the `iptables` processing to validate and remove the shim, are only needed on the initial message from the client to the server. Subsequent packets in the flow are not modified and or inspected by our custom `iptables` module. Those packets will proceed through standard packet processing. Therefore, the only significant overhead in our approach is incurred in the initial round-trip, so we focus our measurements accordingly.

During key transfer, the client initiates a TCP connection to the authentication server. Since the authentication server program is essentially unchanged, we use a simple echo reply to omit its overhead. For our measurements, we transmit a TCP `SYN` packet to a port without an associated application server, resulting in a TCP `RST` packet that refuses the connection. This simple exchange allows us to monitor any overheads at the OpenFlow controller and `iptables` modules to signal support for the protocol, encode keys into packets, and extract those keys. The client sends 1,000 TCP requests and measures the round-trip time (RTT) that includes all the overheads.

Our evaluation examines two deployment scenarios: 1) where the OpenFlow agent runs on a separate, physical router for a local network deployment and 2) where the OpenFlow agent runs on the client machine itself, in which the endpoint natively supports the use of a controller for persistent identity. Our router-based experiment uses a TP-Link Archer C7 router (see Fig. 2).

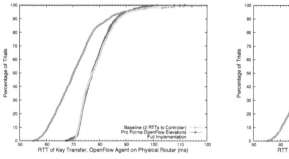
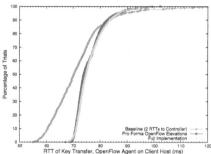

(a) Key Transfer via SDN Router Agent   (b) Key Transfer via SDN Client Agent

Fig. 3. Round trip time for key transfer (1,000 trials) (Color figure online)

During the key transfer between the authentication server and client SDN controller, two elevations to the OpenFlow controller are required. Since this includes significant propagation delay to and from the controller, we measure that RTT and refer to it as the baseline in our method. In Fig. 3a, we explore the scenario where the OpenFlow agent runs on a physical router. In the diagram, the leftmost (green) line indicates the baseline case of two RTTs with the controller. The 90th percentile is 83 ms. The middle (blue) line shows a control experiment measuring end-to-end RTT for the client to the server using *pro forma* OpenFlow elevations, where the OpenFlow agent is configured to elevate each packet for approval, but the controller simply approves each packet without changes (i.e., the controller simply approves packets using `PACKET_OUT` messages without using `FLOW_MOD` rules). In the pro forma exchanges, no packet encapsulation or `iptables` verification occurs. In this scenario, the 90th percentile of the RTT is 86 ms. In our full key transfer implementation (the rightmost, red line), the 90th percentile is 87 ms. The similarity of the results of the pro forma and full implementations indicate that the overheads for encapsulation, `iptables`, and the OpenFlow controller are not significant.

We show the results where the OpenFlow agent runs on the client host in Fig. 3b. The baseline remains same. In the pro forma scenario, the 90th percentile is 82 ms. When we enable the full key transfer functions, the 90th percentile is 83 ms. The OpenFlow overheads are lower when the client runs the OpenFlow agent rather than a router. However, the overheads of encapsulation, `iptables`, and controller processing remain similar.

Next, we evaluate the overhead introduced by the key validation functionality between the client and the application server. In this experiment, our client

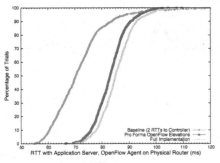
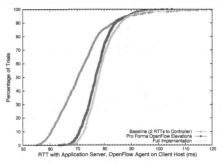

(a) Verification via SDN Router Agent   (b) Verification via SDN Client Agent

Fig. 4. RTT for application server validation (1,000 trials) (Color figure online)

sends 1,000 UDP packets to the server. We measure the end-to-end delay from transmission to response, so each trial contains two packet elevations: 1) the elevation to the SDN controller for IP-in-IP encapsulation and 2) for the SDN controller to processes the UDP response.

In Fig. 4a, the green line (leftmost) again shows the baseline of two RTTs where the 90th percentile RTT is 82 ms. The blue line (middle) shows the overhead of the pro forma scenario in which 90% of the results have less than 90 ms delay. The red line (rightmost) shows our full implementation, which introduces 93 ms of delay or less for 90% of the trials. When we move the OpenFlow agent to the client machine, the pro forma 90th percentile drops to 84 ms and the full implementation drops to 86 ms, as shown in Fig. 4b. We again see that the full implementation has only modest overheads over a basic OpenFlow elevation approach. Further, the time spent at the validator in the full implementation was around 0.8 ms, indicating the verification overheads are low.

Importantly, the latency overheads incurred here occur only on the first round-trip between the client and the application server for each flow. Since they do not affect ongoing flows, they are unlikely to have a major impact on the end-user's experience. A subsequent optimization, to insert a FLOW_MOD during the first encapsulation, would cut the propagation time in half, reducing the RTT by roughly 40 ms in these experiments. End-users could further reduce their delay by hosting the controller closer to the client, such as in the LAN or in nearby ISP-hosted data centers.

5.3   VPN Server Throughput Comparison

As we will discuss in Sect. 6.2, our approach aims to improve bandwidth performance when an enterprise deploys its VPN server on a general-purpose machine. In this section, we simulate real environments and design experiments to create that bottleneck. We demonstrate the extent to which our approach can remove the bandwidth bottleneck associated with many VPN deployments. We explore five scenarios with some employing TLS, VPNs, and our approach.

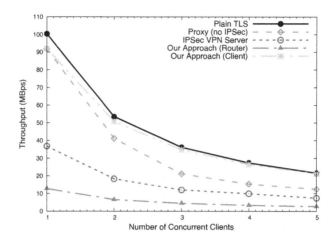

Fig. 5. Median client throughput in different security tool deployment scenarios.

In these experiments, we use `Strongswan` as our VPN software and `apache2` to host a large file for download via HTTPS. For each case, we run a varying number of clients concurrently to determine the per client throughput in each scenario. We measure the time used for downloading for each client, as well as CPU usage on the servers. In the experiments, we explore up to five clients since this degree of parallelism is sufficient to expose bottlenecks and demonstrate trends. Except as noted, we transfer a 1 GByte file in our trials. Each data point is the result of 30 trials.

In Fig. 5, we show the results of these scenarios. The first scenario, `Plain TLS`, represents a baseline in which the enterprise network has a TLS server that clients directly access for file transfer. This essentially represents an upper-bound on performance capabilities of the system. The traffic is constrained by the web server's ability to send traffic. In the second scenario, `Proxy (no IPSec)`, we forward the network traffic through an Ubuntu server VM that simply proxies traffic (i.e., forwards it using IP addresses) without any additional services (like IPSec). The throughput decreases in this scenario since the gateway host starts to constrain throughput and the CPU on the gateway vary from 35.41% to 95.83% utilization as we increase number of concurrent clients. In the `IPSec VPN Server` scenario, we enable IPSec on the Ubuntu proxy server and clients use the IPSec tunnel to reach the web server. This scenario represents an enterprise configuration in which organizations host their VPN services on a generic server. The CPU use climbs on the VPN server to around 100% usage and the result is a decrease in bandwidth from the baseline by around 65%. Compared to the 21.6 MBps in the baseline, the VPN server is only able to provide 7.4 MBps throughput per client during a five concurrent client scenario.

Next, we explore our approach using SDN support in either a consumer-grade router or in the endpoint itself. We first enable our approach in a consumer-grade router in the `Our Approach (Router)` scenario. This scenario does not require the gateway server from the second or third scenarios and reflects the architecture as described in Sect. 3. The residential router scenario results show the challenges of repurposing hardware with limited computational capabilities. While it can deliver 12.8 MBps for a single client our tests of a 100 MByte file, it exhausts the router's computational resources (since it uses the general purpose CPU for OpenFlow forwarding lookups). While we explore up to five concurrent clients for a consistent presentation of results, these client-side routers would likely only service a single user at a time and do not act as an aggregation point, unlike the VPN server. With more capable residential routers, the computational limits would be less likely to constrain performance.

In our final scenario, Our Approach (Client), we explore the approach where the SDN agent runs in software on the client, allowing us to characterize the performance implications of running the SDN agent on the residential router. When running on the client, the SDN functions no longer serve as a performance bottleneck (CPU usage at the client does not exceed 31%). This approach yields a performance improvement of roughly 2.5 to 2.9 times the throughput of an IPSec VPN. The performance decrease of the SDN approach verses the baseline ranges from 1% to 8%. Accordingly, with endpoint software, clients can attain far better throughput than VPNs and approximate the baseline.

5.4   Packet Header Overhead

VPNs may have to combine multiple protocols together to support some clients. A standardized implementation for this combines IPSec with L2TP [23]. When used with ESP and preshared secrets, the combined packet headers and trailers for the two protocols amounts to around 92 bytes (40 bytes for L2TP with UDP, 20 bytes for an encapsulated IP header, 16 bytes for the ESP header, 2 bytes for padding, and 14 bytes for the ESP trailer and authentication data). This can reduce the maximum transmission unit (MTU) for payload in many networks from 1500 to 1408, which is around a 6.1% reduction in payload per packet. This overhead occurs in each packet in the flow.

In our approach, we use packet encapsulation on the first packet sent from a client to an application server. Our IP-in-IP shim uses 20 bytes for the inner IP header, with an additional 40 bytes for our IP option, for a total of 60 bytes of overhead. Unlike VPN traffic, this overhead only applies to the first packet in a flow. For applications using TCP, this overhead would apply to the TCP SYN packet. Since those packets do not carry payload, our approach would often avoid the MTU complications present in VPN protocols.

6   Discussion

Our approach focuses on mechanisms that eliminate the need for VPN software by providing application servers with evidence that a client has been successfully authenticated. We now explore how a similar concept could be used with other kinds of services. We also explore scenarios in which we compare our system with VPN deployments and the role it can play in addressing bandwidth bottlenecks.

6.1 A Second-Factor Service for Public Infrastructure

For sensitive transactions, organizations with public-facing services can minimize risk by using multiple sources of evidence. For example, financial institutions may authenticate an end-user in multiple ways to minimize the risk in financial transactions. These forms of validation can include username and password, browser cookies, the use of one-time passcodes via SMS messaging or applications, or answers to secret questions.

Some organizations try to reduce risk by identifying a user's location. They may leverage databases that map IP addresses to geographical location and thereby prevent authentication attempts, or require more robust verification, when a user's location changes by a configured distance. Unfortunately, such mechanisms may be less effective when CGN is widely deployed.

Our approach can offer a lightweight, secondary factor that simply indicates if a client is located within a given source network (e.g., inside the LAN serviced by a given residential router) or if it is the same physical device (e.g., for a laptop or mobile device that changes networks). In such circumstances, the SDN controller can effectively act like a password manager by tracking secondary factors for a user across infrastructure.

6.2 Impact of VPN Server Provisioning

Enterprise networks may apply different architectures to deploy their VPN services. Enterprise networks may deploy their VPN services on their network gateways or devices that handle all the network's traffic. These devices can be purpose-built for VPNs. For example, the Cisco AST 1000 Series Embedded Processors achieves IPSec throughput up to 78 Gbit/s [48,49]. The downside associated with in-line hardware is that the service subscription for VPNs and the system's capital costs can be considerable [47].

Enterprises can also host VPN servers inside their networks using existing server infrastructure or other physical machines. Most commodity servers lack the hardware designed for VPN services. Pudelko et al. [53] indicate open source VPN servers on commodity servers have poor throughput compared to dedicated hardware. A Windows 2008 server can achieve gigabit throughput [50]. Other servers can achieve higher throughput [51] and a multi-core Linux machine can achieve 6.1 Gbps [52].

Our in-lab environment experiments in Sect. 5.3 show the potential bottlenecks associated with VPN gateways on general purpose systems. These results demonstrate the ability of our approach to remove such bottlenecks.

7 Conclusion

This work explores the roles that VPNs play in organizational security. With the rise of application-layer encryption and authentication, the secure tunneling features of VPNs are increasingly redundant. However, VPN tunnels are still useful in simplifying perimeter-based access control by allowing authenticated remote users to bypass perimeter policies and interact with insider infrastructure.

We analyze the access control capabilities of VPNs and propose a new lightweight method. It requires no additional network infrastructure and removes the performance bottleneck on a VPN server, as well as eliminating redundant encryption and unnecessary packet header overheads. Our method is based on the SDN paradigm and gives clients the choice to implement a persistent identity on a per-application basis. We create `iptables` modules, which are required on the server side, to support our protocol. Our evaluation results show the method to be effective and lightweight.

Acknowledgements. This material is based upon work supported by the National Science Foundation under Grant No. 1651540.

References

1. Richter, P., et al.: A multi-perspective analysis of carrier-grade NAT deployment. In: ACM Internet Measurement Conference, pp. 215–29 (2016). https://doi.org/10.1145/2987443.2987474
2. Carrier-Grade-NAT (CGN) Deployment Considerations (2021). https://tools.ietf.org/id/draft-nishizuka-cgn-deployment-considerations-00.html
3. Atkinson, R.: Security Architecture for the Internet Protocol. RFC 1825, Internet Engineering Task Force (1995)
4. Sandvine Releases 2019 Global Internet Phenomena Report (2019). https://www.sandvine.com/press-releases/sandvine-releases-2019-global-internet-phenomena-report
5. Rekhter, Y., Moskowitz, B., De Groot, G.: Address Allocation for Private Internets. RFC 1597, Internet Engineering Task Force (1994)
6. Kreibich, C., Weaver, N., Nechaev, B.: Netalyzr: illuminating the edge network. In: ACM Internet Measurement Conference, p. 246 (2010). https://doi.org/10.1145/1879141.1879173
7. Mandalari, A., Lutu, A., Dhamdhere, A., Bagnulo, M., Claffy K.: Tracking the Big NAT across Europe and the U.S. ArXiv:1704.01296 (2017). arXiv.org, http://arxiv.org/abs/1704.01296
8. Livadariu, I., Benson, K., Elmokashfi, A., Dhamdhere, A., Dainotti, A.: Inferring carrier-grade NAT deployment in the wild. In: IEEE Conference on Computer Communications, pp. 2249–2257 (2018). https://doi.org/10.1109/INFOCOM.2018.8486223
9. Global Security Appliance Market Share 2012–2020 (2021). https://www.statista.com/statistics/235347/global-security-appliance-revenue-market-share-by-vendors/
10. Cloudflare Blocking My IP? (2021). https://community.cloudflare.com/t/cloudflare-blocking-my-ip/65453
11. Verizon to Launch 5G Residential Broadband Services in up to 5 Markets in 2018 (2021). https://www.verizon.com/about/news/verizon-launch-5g-residential-broadband-services-5-markets-2018

12. Amazon Simple Email Service Classic (2021). https://docs.aws.amazon.com/ses/latest/DeveloperGuide/
13. FCC Fines Verizon $1.35 Million over 'Supercookie' Tracking. https://www.theverge.com/2016/3/7/11173010/verizon-supercookie-fine-1-3-million-fcc
14. Perkins, C.E.: Mobile IP. IEEE Commun. Mag. **35**(5), 84–99 (1997). https://doi.org/10.1109/35.592101
15. Simpson, W.: IP in IP Tunneling. Request for Comments, RFC 1853, Internet Engineering Task Force (1995)
16. Neuman, C., Ts'o, T.: The Kerberos Network Authentication Service (V5). RFC 1510, Internet Engineering Task Force (1993)
17. Craven, R., Beverly, R., Allman, M.: A middlebox-cooperative TCP for a non end-to-end internet. In: ACM SIGCOMM Conference, pp. 151–162 (2014). https://doi.org/10.1145/2619239.2626321
18. Gont, F., Atkinson, R., Pignataro, C.: Recommendations on Filtering of IPv4 Packets Containing IPv4 Options. Request for Comments, RFC 7126, Internet Engineering Task Force (2014)
19. Open VSwitch (2021). https://www.openvswitch.org/
20. Cisco-Security-Manager-4-1 (2021). https://www.cisco.com/c/en/us/obsolete/security/cisco-security-manager-4-1.html
21. Bommareddy, S., Kale, M., Chaganty, S.: VPN Device Clustering Using a Network Flow Switch and a Different Mac Address for Each VPN Device in the Cluster. US6772226B1 (2004). https://patents.google.com/patent/US6772226B1/en
22. Coronavirus Challenges Remote Networking (2021). https://www.networkworld.com/article/3532440/coronavirus-challenges-remote-networking.html
23. Booth, S., Zorn, G., Patel, B., Aboba, B., Dixon, W.: Securing L2TP Using IPsec. Request for Comments, RFC 3193, Internet Engineering Task Force (2001)
24. Atkinson, R., Kent S.: IP Authentication Header. RFC 2402, Internet Engineering Task Force (1998)
25. Kent, S., Atkinson R.: IP Encapsulating Security Payload (ESP). RFC 2406, Internet Engineering Task Force (1998)
26. Nordmark, E, Bagnulo, M.: Shim6: Level 3 Multihoming Shim Protocol for IPv6. RFC 5533, Internet Engineering Task Force (2009)
27. Moskowitz, R., Nikander P.: Host Identity Protocol (HIP) Architecture. RFC 4423, Internet Engineering Task Force (2006)
28. Estes, A.: The Dangers of Supercookies (2011). https://www.theatlantic.com/technology/archive/2011/08/dangers-supercookies/354297/
29. MacFarland, D., Shue, C, Kalafut, A.: Characterizing optimal DNS amplification attacks and effective mitigation. In: Passive and Active Measurement Conference, pp. 15–27 (2015). https://doi.org/10.1007/978-3-319-15509-8_2
30. McKeown, N., et al.: OpenFlow: enabling innovation in campus networks. ACM SIGCOMM Comput. Commun. Rev. **38**(2), 69–74 (2008). https://doi.org/10.1145/1355734.1355746
31. Komu, M., Sethi, M., Beijar, N.: A survey of identifier-locator split addressing architectures. Comput. Sci. Rev. **17**, 25–42 (2015). https://doi.org/10.1016/j.cosrev.2015.04.002
32. Netfilter/Iptables Project Homepage - The "Xtables-Addons" Project (2021). https://www.netfilter.org/projects/xtables-addons/index.html
33. Troubleshooting (2021). https://sendersupport.olc.protection.outlook.com/pm/troubleshooting.aspx
34. Prevent Mail to Gmail Users from Being Blocked or Sent to Spam - Gmail Help (2021). https://support.google.com/mail/answer/81126

35. Understanding the Cloudflare Security Level (2021). https://support.cloudflare. com/hc/en-us/articles/200170056-Understanding-the-Cloudflare-Security-Level
36. Malis, A., Lin, A., Heinanen, J., Gleeson, B., Armitage, G.: A Framework for IP Based Virtual Private Networks. RFC 2764, Internet Engineering Task Force (2000)
37. Access Control - Apache HTTP Server Version 2.4 (2021). https://httpd.apache. org/docs/2.4/howto/access.html
38. Benefits Of A VPN (2021). https://www.forbes.com/sites/tjmccue/2019/06/20/ benefits-of-a-vpn/
39. Benefits of a VPN You Might Not Know About (2021). https://us.norton.com/ internetsecurity-privacy-benefits-of-vpn.html
40. Dynamic IP Denylisting with NGINX Plus and Fail2ban (2021). https://www. nginx.com/blog/dynamic-ip-denylisting-with-nginx-plus-and-fail2ban/
41. Google Transparency Report (2021). https://transparencyreport.google.com/ https/overview?hl=en
42. CUPS Plenary (2021). https://ftp.pwg.org/pub/pwg/liaison/openprinting/ presentations/cups-plenary-may-18.pdf
43. What Is a Reverse Proxy Server? (2021). https://www.nginx.com/resources/ glossary/reverse-proxy-server/
44. Francisco, Shaun Nichols in San. Corporate VPN Huffing and Puffing While Everyone Works from Home over COVID-19? You're Not Alone, Admins (2021). https:// www.theregister.com/2020/03/11/corporate_vpn_coronavirus_crunch/
45. Comparing TCP performance of tunneled and non-tunneled traffic using OpenVPN (2021). https://www.os3.nl/_media/2010-2011/courses/rp2/p09_report.pdf
46. Liu, Y., Shue, C.: Beyond the VPN: practical client identity in an internet with widespread IP address sharing. In: IEEE Conference on Local Computer Networks, pp. 425–428 (2020). https://doi.org/10.1109/LCN48667.2020.9314846
47. Savings Calculator, Pulse Secure (2021). https://www.pulsesecure.net/savings-calculator/
48. Raumer, D., Gallenmuller S., Emmerich, P., Mardian L., Carle, G.: Efficient serving of VPN endpoints on COTS server hardware. In: IEEE International Conference on Cloud Networking (Cloudnet), pp. 164–169 (2016). https://doi.org/10.1109/ CloudNet.2016.25
49. Cisco ASR 1000 Series Embedded Services Processors Data Sheet (2021). https:// www.cisco.com/c/en/us/products/collateral/routers/asr-1000-series-aggregation-services-routers/asr-1000-series-embedded-services-ds.html
50. IP Security Features. Intel Ethernet Server Adapters (2021). https://docplayer. net/20618334-Ip-security-features-intel-ethernet-server-adapters.html
51. Han, S., Jang, K., Park, K, Moon, S.: PacketShader: A GPU-Accelerated software router. In: ACM SIGCOMM Conference, p. 195 (2010). https://doi.org/10.1145/ 1851182.1851207
52. Dobrescu, M., et al.: RouteBricks: exploiting parallelism to scale software routers. In: ACM Symposium on Operating Systems Principles, p. 15 (2009). https://doi. org/10.1145/1629575.1629578
53. Pudelko M., Emmerich, P.: Performance analysis of VPN gateways. In: IFIP Networking Conference (Networking), pp. 325–333 (2020)
54. VPN Risk Report - Cybersecurity Insiders|Industry Report (2021). https://info. zscaler.com/resources-industry-reports-vpn-risk-report-cybersecurity-insiders

55. Initial Credentials - MIT Kerberos Documentation (2021). https://web.mit.edu/kerberos/krb5-latest/doc/appdev/init_creds.html

56. DeCusatis, C., Liengtiraphan, P., Sager, A., Pinelli, M.: Implementing zero trust cloud networks with transport access control and first packet authentication. In: IEEE International Conference on Smart Cloud (SmartCloud), pp. 5–10 (2016). https://doi.org/10.1109/SmartCloud.2016.22

57. Hauser, F., Haberle, M., Schmidt, M., Menth, M.: P4-IPsec: site-to-site and host-to-site VPN With IPsec in P4-Based SDN. IEEE Access **8**, 139567–139586 (2020). https://doi.org/10.1109/ACCESS.2020.3012738

Privacy-Preserving Emerging Networked Applications

Puncturable Search: Enabling Authorized Search in Cross-data Federation

Lin Mei, Chungen Xu$^{(\boxtimes)}$, and Qianmu Li

Nanjing University of Science and Technology, Nanjing 210094, JS, China
{meilin,xuchung,qianmu}@njust.edu.cn

Abstract. Recently, most popular cloud storage solutions offer data syncing and federation, but it also brings security risks. Generally, users can deploy encryption technology to dispel data privacy concerns, but the usability of data will be hindered, e.g., searchability. Multi-user searchable encryption (MUSE) scheme is a paradigm that enables search over encrypted data federated from different users. However, to the best of our knowledge, most of the existing MUSEs are vulnerable to the insider keyword guessing attack (IKGA). Besides, therein real-time team collaboration incurs significant communication and computation costs, leading to high latency. To this end, in this paper, we focus on developing a secure and efficient encrypted search scheme with little cost. Specifically, we first propose a dual-server Public-key Puncturable Encryption with Keyword Search (dPPEKS) scheme in a cross data federation scenario by extending the Puncturable Encryption (PE) and searchable encryption (SE) technologies. Our scheme realizes the efficient and dynamic update of teammates, including user joining and exiting. Through analysis, we prove that our scheme can achieve IND-CKA2 security and resist IKGA. In addition, the performance analysis demonstrates that our scheme gains a better balance in security and efficiency.

Keywords: Cloud storage · Data federation · Searchable encryption · Puncturable encryption · Keyword guessing attack

1 Introduction

Working remotely against the COVID-19 pandemic has become the norm since 2020. Many enterprises are requiring their employees to use applications like Dropbox, Google Drive to facilitate office collaboration on the cross-data from various team members [1]. Take Dropbox as an example, a manager creates the file on the Dropbox server, together with the detailed access policy to regulate other teammates' authority on this file, namely which user can read or write these files. However, these files generally involve some sensitive information of the company like financial budget, federating and storing them on the thirty-party may bring potential privacy challenges. Untrusted server and unauthorized users can be free to fetch and abuse these files, which may bring enterprises significant economic damages.

© ICST Institute for Computer Sciences, Social Informatics and Telecommunications Engineering 2021
Published by Springer Nature Switzerland AG 2021. All Rights Reserved
X. Yuan et al. (Eds.): QShine 2021, LNICST 402, pp. 303–322, 2021.
https://doi.org/10.1007/978-3-030-91424-0_18

Preventing unauthorized access with encryption mechanism is the key to mitigating above privacy issues, however, directly encrypting them will incur many practical issues. One of the most fundamental problem is how to search on the encrypted data. It is clear that traditional plaintext search methods on plaintext data will fail naturally unless the user downloads and decrypts all outsourced ciphertexts. Moreover, the encrypted files should also be amenable to fine-grained access control. That is, the data owner can set access barriers on some teammates transferred out of the current project team to prevent them from retrieving files.

To achieve the goal for secure multi-client search, multi-user searchable encryption (MUSE) [2,9] is proposed, which enables data users to securely search and selectively share files according to user's privilege friendly. In early stages, a straightforward but expensive approach is to leverage the broadcast encryption [9] to revoke the key of all users and assign the new key to authorized ones. Some other works propose to introduce the attribute-based encryption (ABE) [13,14,16,20,23], but doing so will suffer from a high overhead for data authorization. In addition, there are some works propose to integrate a proxy server to authorize legal teammates to access the outsourced files, which burdens the communication costs of data owner [12,21].

In addition to above performance issues, another problem that hinders the development of MUSEs is its security issue. Specifically, most of MUSE schemes [13,14,16,20] are designed under the public-key framework, in this case, the cloud server (i.e., the insider attacker) can use the public key to generate the ciphertexts of all keywords freely. For a token space with low entropy, the keyword corresponding to each token can be gradually identified by performing test with the generated ciphertexts. The above attack is called the insider keyword guessing attack (IKGA), which has been demonstrated can destroy the security of most MUSE schemes.

To tackle with the above challenges, in this paper, our first goal is to develop an efficient authorized encrypted keyword search scheme, with the hope of realizing fine-grained authorization in team collaboration. We achieve this goal by adopting the philosophy of puncturable encryption (PE) [10]. Specifically, we use the tags of unauthorized users to update the access policy of ciphertexts. Compared to directly applying PE to SE schemes for updating secret keys repeatedly, doing so can reduce the communication cost between data owners and users. And when the total number of users remains unchanged and the number of authorized users increases, the communication cost between data owners and cloud server and the computation cost of the encryption will be further reduced.

Based on the above construction, we further study how to harden it to against IKGA. In prior arts, researchers try to address this problem by using authentication encryption [11,17,18]. Specifically, the data owner and the user use their own secret key and the other party's public key to encrypt keyword and generate token, respectively. As a result, given the token, the cloud server can only search over the ciphertexts generated by the specific owner whose public key is used in the token. However, such a solution is only feasible to the single-user scenario because the authentication process is performed one-to-one between the data owner and the user. In this work, we propose to leverage the dual-server [6,7] technology, which generally requires two servers to cooperate to complete the test algorithm.

In the following, we summarize our contributions:

- We motivate the need of MUSE in achieving authorized search in cloud-based team cooperation. Specifically, we devise a multi-user public-key puncturable encryption with keyword search scheme and optimize it to support IKGA-resistance.
- Compared with existing MUSE schemes, our scheme has the following two merits: 1) Efficient update. Any teammate can efficiently update the access policy when some users exit or join without affecting the unchanged user. 2) Non-interactive. There is no need for any third-party agencies to intervene in the authorization or revocation process.
- Our scheme is proved to be secure to resist IKGA, which is missing in most existing MUSE schemes. In addition, it also has better performance than existing works. More specifically, the size of ciphertexts in our scheme is about 6 times smaller than that of [8,15], and the computation time of ciphertexts is about 6 and 12 times less than that in [8,15], respectively.

Organization. The rest of this paper is organized as follows. Section 2 introduces related works. In Sect. 3, we give the system overview and the threat model of our scheme. Then the notations used throughout this paper, the bilinear pairing used in the scheme construction, and the hardness assumptions applied in security proof are all presented in Sect. 4. In Sect. 5, we define the dual-server Public-key Puncturable Encryption with Keyword Search (dPPEKS) scheme and its security model. Section 6 describes the dPPEKS scheme in detail, and Sect. 7 gives strict security proof. We analyze the performance of our scheme through experiments in Sect. 8. Finally, we present a brief conclusion in Sect. 9.

2 Related Work

The first PEKS scheme was proposed to enable one to search over encrypted data generated by public key system from different writers [3]. Following the work of Boneh et al. [3], researchers paid a number of efforts on this research direction and developed versatile PEKS schemes. MUSE is one of them which focuses on meeting the requirement of data sharing among multiple users. Zheng et al. [27] first introduced attribute-based keyword search (ABKS) to enable the data owner to encrypt the keyword with access control policy so that multiple users with proper cryptographic credentials can launch valid queries. Later, in order to delegate heavy system update workload to the cloud server, Sun et al. [20] incorporated proxy re-encryption and lazy re-encryption techniques to their ABKS scheme. Moreover, considering the requirement of multi-keyword search, Yang et al. [24] developed a multi-keyword rank search system which supports flexible search authorization and time-controlled revocation for multiple users. Closely-related to the above mentioned schemes, some MUSE works based on symmetric SE are proposed as well. Curtmola et al. [9] used broadcast encryption to naturally extend the symmetric SE to support multiple users in keyword queries as long as they are authorized. In [2,25], a trusted third-party is introduced to manage the key for user authorization and revocation.

In addition to the achievement in enriching search functionality, there are some works focused on the investigation of PEKS security, particularly the potential risk from keyword guessing attack (KGA). The main reason KGA can work is aforementioned limited size of keyword space in real life. And with the follow-up to the investigation, the KGA has led to the launch of three research directions: 1) Off-line KGA from the external adversary, which means anyone other than the server can continuously generate the ciphertext and test its correspondence with eavesdropping token [5]; 2) On-line KGA from the external adversary, a unique attack method, which requires the server to be on-line during the attack. In another word, the adversary computes the ciphertexts for his choice of candidate keywords and sends the crafted ciphertexts to the server [26]. Finally, upon observing the returning ciphertexts, including one of the crafted ciphertext, the adversary can determine which keyword is relate to the token [26]. 3) IKGA, namely the KGA from the internal adversary, where the cloud server generates the keyword ciphertext of its choice and then performs the test operation to find out the keyword of the search token [5].

To mitigate the potential risk of these three IKGAs, many efforts have been made, yet, most solutions are concentrated on PEKS with single user [6,7,11, 17,18] and few on MUSE schemes. Li et al. [15] discussed how to defeat off-line KGA for MUSE from the external adversary, while the influence of the internal adversary is not mentioned. Regarding IKGA, two typical solutions are: 1) authentication encryption [11,17,18], which enables only legitimate senders can generate the keyword ciphertext; and 2) dual-server technology [6,7], which makes sure that only two servers cooperate to complete the test operation. Most recently, Chen et al. [8] proposed an IKGA secure MUSE scheme. They first introduced one server to generate the temporary search results, which later be transformed into the final results by another server. In this way, neither server can independently perform the test algorithm, and hence resisting the IKGA. However, the empirical result shows that their scheme comes with expensive computation and communication cost. To this end, in this paper, we concentrate on addressing how to realize IKGA secure in an efficient manner.

3 Problem Statement

In this section, we first describe different parties involved in the proposed system and provide a high-level description of our system. Then, to capture the capability of each participant, we define the threat model and make the information each one holds and the behaviors they act explicit.

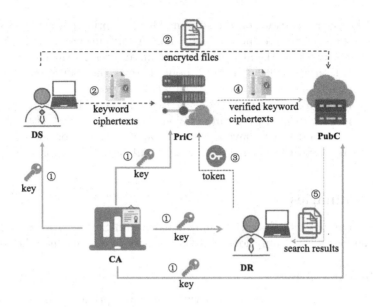

Fig. 1. The system model of the dPPEKS scheme

3.1 System Model

Figure 1 illustrates the architecture of the encrypted file search in cloud storage system. The data hosting service we consider to design involves four entities: central authority, users, private cloud, and public cloud.

1. Central authority (CA). CA plays the role of a key generator, who is in charge of generating system parameters and master secret key for the whole system. Generating secret keys for the server and team members is the responsibility of CA as well.
2. Users. Each user in our model has dual roles: the data sender (DS) and the data receiver (DR). When a user acts as the DS, he generates and sends the keyword ciphertext to the private cloud. Meanwhile, the file is encrypted and sent to the public cloud. In another case, when a user plays the role of DR, he will generate the token of the wanted keyword and send it to the private cloud.
3. Private cloud (PriC). PriC is responsible for storing the encrypted files with the keyword ciphertext and performing the access policy verification with the token submitted by users.
4. Public cloud (PubC). PubC conducts the keyword test operation on the authenticated ciphertext sent from the PriC.

3.2 Threat Model

Being consistent with most previous MUSE schemes, CA is supposed to be wholly trusted in our model, who knows the secret key of the whole system but never launches an attack on the system. Then, we primarily stress that both servers in our model behave entirely in an "honest-but-curious" fashion. Namely, they will honestly follow the algorithm we set up and return the correct results. However, both servers will be curious about the files the user searches for and try to extract additional information from what they own, e.g., conducting the IKGA. Furthermore, we assume that the two servers will never collude with each other, in other words, they will not share their secret key. Lastly, the team members in our model, who have the search capability, are considered reliable. Yet, once they leave the current team, they will be regarded as the external adversary.

4 Preliminaries

In this section, we introduce the bilinear pairing in Sect. 4.1. In Sect. 4.2, we present the hardness assumptions that the security of our scheme relies on.

4.1 Bilinear Pairing

Let $\mathbb{G}$ and $\mathbb{G}_T$ be two cyclic groups with the same prime order p. A map e: $\mathbb{G} \times \mathbb{G} \to \mathbb{G}_T$ is bilinear if it satisfies the following three conditions [4]:

1. Bilinear: $\forall\, u, v \in \mathbb{G}$ and $x, y \in Z_p^*$, we have $e(u^x, v^y) = e(u, v)^{xy}$;
2. Non-degeneracy: If g is a generator of $\mathbb{G}$, then we have $e(g, g) \neq 1$;
3. Computability: For any group elements $x, y \in Z_p^*$, there is a polynomial time algorithm to compute the value of $e(g^x, g^y)$.

4.2 Hardness Assumption

Given a tuple $(g,\ g^a, g^b)$, where $g, g^a, g^b \in \mathbb{G}_1$. The Computational Diffie-Hellman (CDH) problem in $\mathbb{G}_1$ is to compute g^{ab}. The advantage for a probabilistic polynomial-time (PPT) adversary $\mathcal{A}$ to solve the above problem is: $Adv_{CDH}(\mathcal{A}) = |\Pr[\mathcal{A}(g, g^a, g^b) = g^{ab}]|$.

Definition 1. *(CDH assumption) We say that the CDH assumption holds if $Adv_{CDH}(\mathcal{A})$ is negligible for $\mathcal{A}$.*

Given a tuple $(g,\ g^a, g^b, g^c, g')$, where $g, g^a, g^b, g^c \in \mathbb{G}_1$ and $g' \in \mathbb{G}_2$. The Decisional Bilinear Diffie-Hellman (DBDH) problem [22] in $(\mathbb{G}_1, \mathbb{G}_2)$ is to decide if $g' = e(g, g)^{abc}$. The advantage for a PPT adversary $\mathcal{A}$ to solve the problem is: $Adv_{DBDH}(\mathcal{A}) = |\Pr[\mathcal{A}(g, g^a, g^b, g^c, e(g, g)^{abc}) = 1] - \Pr[\mathcal{A}(g, g^a, g^b, g^c, g') = 1]|$.

Definition 2. *(DBDH assumption) We say that the DBDH assumption [22] holds if $Adv_{DBDH}(\mathcal{A})$ is negligible for $\mathcal{A}$.*

Given a tuple (g, g^a), where $g, g^a \in \mathbb{G}_1$. The Discrete Logarithms (DL) problem in $\mathbb{G}_1$ is to compute the value of a. The advantage for a PPT adversary $\mathcal{A}$ to solve the above problem is: $Adv_{DL}(\mathcal{A}) = |\Pr[\mathcal{A}(g, g^a) = a]|$.

Definition 3. *(DL assumption) We say that the DL assumption holds if $Adv_{DL}(\mathcal{A})$ is negligible for $\mathcal{A}$.*

5   Definition and Security

Definition 4. *A dPPEKS scheme can be constructed from the following six algorithms:*

- **Setup**$(1^k, d)$. This probabilistic algorithm is run by the CA to setup the system. It inputs a security parameter k, the threshold d and returns the system parameter SP, the master secret key MSK, PubC's secret key SK_{PubC}, PriC's secret key SK_{PriC} and servers' joint public key PK_{js}.
- **Derive**(SP, MSK, τ_i). This probabilistic algorithm is run by the CA to derive keys for users. It inputs the system parameter SP, the master secret key MSK and the user's tag τ_i, and returns the authentication secret key $SK_{au}^{\tau_i}$, public key pk_{τ_i} and identity secret key $SK_{id}^{\tau_i}$ to the user.
- **PunEnc**(SP, $SK_{au}^{\tau_i}$, PK_{js}, w, $T^\dagger$). This probabilistic algorithm is run by DS to generate the keyword ciphertext. It inputs the system parameter SP, authentication secret key $SK_{au}^{\tau_i}$, servers' joint public key PK_{js}, keyword w and access policy $T^\dagger$, and returns the keyword ciphertext CT_w.
- **TokGen**(SP, w^*, $SK_{id}^{\tau_j}$). This probabilistic algorithm is run by DR whenever he wants to search for some files containing the specific keyword w^*. It inputs the system parameter SP, the keyword w^* and DR's identity secret key $SK_{id}^{\tau_j}$, and finally returns the search token ST_{w^*}.
- **PolicyTest**(SK_{PriC}, ST_{w^*}, CT_w). This algorithm is run by the PriC to verify if the ST_{w^*} satisfies the access policy contained in CT_w. It inputs the PriC's secret key SK_{PriC}, the search token ST_{w^*} and the keyword ciphertext CT_w, and returns authenticated ciphertexts C, whose tag satisfies $\tau \notin T^\dagger$.
- **KeywordTest**(SK_{PubC},C). This algorithm is run by PubC to test if the authenticated ciphertexts C contains the same keyword in ST_{w^*}. It inputs the PubC's secret key SK_{PubC} and the authenticated keyword ciphertext C, and returns 1 if $w = w^*$, otherwise returns 0.

For clarity, hereafter we consider the two algorithms **PolicyTest**(SK_{PriC}, ST_{w^*}, CT_w) and **KeywordTest**(SK_{PubC},C) as one algorithm **Test**(SK_{PriC}, SK_{PubC}, ST_{w^*}, CT_w) in all security game and proof, which will not influence the security proof. It is reasonable as we assume that the challenger holds the ability of both policy test and keyword with the secret key of PriC and PubC.

Definition 5. *(CT-IND-CKA game) Given the security parameter k and the threshold parameter d, let $\mathcal{A}$ be the adversary, $\mathcal{B}$ be the challenger, and W be the keyword space.*

- **Setup.** $\mathcal{B}$ *runs the setup algorithm* **Setup**$(1^k, d)$, *gives the system parameters* SP *to the $\mathcal{A}$, and keeps the master secret key* MSK *and the secret key of both two servers* SK_{PriC}, SK_{PubC}.
- **Query phase 1.** $\mathcal{A}$ *is allowed to adaptively makes the following four queries:*
  - ⋆ *Key query* $\langle \tau_i \rangle$: $\mathcal{A}$ *can adaptively ask $\mathcal{B}$ the secret key for any tag $\tau_i \in \{0,1\}^*$ of his choice. $\mathcal{B}$ generates the secret key following the algorithm* **Derive**(SP, MSK, τ_i) *and returns it to $\mathcal{A}$.*

⋆ *Ciphertext query ⟨w⟩: $\mathcal{A}$ can adaptively choose a random keyword w from W, and ask $\mathcal{B}$ the ciphertext of w. After receiving the request, $\mathcal{B}$ calls the algorithm* **PunEnc** *to generate the keyword ciphertext $CT_w = $* **PunEnc**$(SP, SK_{au}^{\tau_i}, PK_{js}, w, T^{\dagger})$ *and finally returns it to $\mathcal{A}$.*

⋆ *Token query ⟨w⟩ : $\mathcal{A}$ can adaptively choose a random keyword w from W, and ask $\mathcal{B}$ the search token of keyword w. After receiving the request, $\mathcal{B}$ calls the algorithm* **TokGen** *to generate the search token of keyword $ST_w = $* **Tok-Gen**$(SP, w^*, SK_{id}^{\tau_j})$ *and finally returns it to $\mathcal{A}$.*

⋆ *Test query ⟨$CT_w, ST_{w'}$⟩ : $\mathcal{A}$ can adaptively test if the CT_w and $ST_{w'}$ containing the same keyword by asking $\mathcal{B}$. After receiving the test request from $\mathcal{A}$, $\mathcal{B}$ runs the* **Test**$(SK_{PriC}, SK_{PubC}, ST_{w^*}, CT_w)$. *$\mathcal{B}$ returns 1 to $\mathcal{A}$ if ST_w and CT_{w_i} containing the same keyword and the tag in ST_w does not exist in the access policy of CT_{w_i} or 0 otherwise.*

– **Challenge.** *Once $\mathcal{A}$ decides to finish the phase 1, he will choose two different keywords w_0 and w_1 from W and a tag τ^*, which are then sent to $\mathcal{B}$ as $\mathcal{A}'s$ challenge. The only restriction is that $\mathcal{A}$ cannot query the ciphertext of w_0 and w_1 in phase 1. After receiving the two challenge keywords, $\mathcal{B}$ selects a random bit $b \in \{0, 1\}$ and sends a challenge ciphertext CT_{w_b} to $\mathcal{A}$.*

– **Query phase 2.** *$\mathcal{A}$ continues to adaptively query to oracles as in phase 1. The only restriction is that $\mathcal{A}$ cannot query the keyword ciphertexts of w_0 and w_1 in query phase 1.*

– **Guess.** *$\mathcal{A}$ outputs his guess $b' \in \{0, 1\}$. If $b' = b$, we say $\mathcal{A}$ wins the game.*

We define the advantage of $\mathcal{A}$ in CT-IND-CKA game is $Adv_{\mathcal{A}}^{CT}(k) = |Pr[b' = b] - 1/2|$.

Definition 6. *A dPPEKS scheme is assumed to be CT-IND-CKA secure if for all sufficiently large k and PPT adversary $\mathcal{A}$, there exists a negligible function negl such that $Adv_{\mathcal{A}}^{CT}(k) \leq negl(k)$.*

Definition 7. *(ST-IND-CKA game) Given the security parameter k and the threshold parameter d, and let $\mathcal{A}$ be the adversary, $\mathcal{B}$ be the challenger, and W be the keyword space.*

– **Setup.** *$\mathcal{B}$ runs the setup algorithm* **Setup**$(1^k, d)$, *gives the system parameters SP to $\mathcal{A}$, and keeps the master secret key MSK and the secret key of both two servers SK_{PriC}, SK_{PubC}.*

– **Query phase 1.** *$\mathcal{A}$ is allowed to adaptively makes four queries as in Definition 5.*

– **Challenge.** *Once $\mathcal{A}$ decides to finish the phase 1, he will choose two different keywords w_0 and w_1 from W and a tag τ^* as his challenge. The only restriction is that $\mathcal{A}$ cannot query the secret key of τ^* and the search token of w_0 and w_1 in query phase 1. After receiving the two challenge keywords, $\mathcal{B}$ selects a random bit $b \in \{0, 1\}$ and sends a challenge search token $ST_{w_b} = $* **TokGen**$(w_b, SK_{\tau^*}, SP)$ *to $\mathcal{A}$.*

– **Query phase 2.** *$\mathcal{A}$ continues to adaptively query to oracles as in phase 1. There are two restrictions here. The first is that no secret key query is* *allowed on tag τ^*, and the second is that both keywords w_0 and w_1 should not be queried to the **TokGen** oracle.*

- **Guess.** $\mathcal{A}$ *outputs the guess* $b' \in \{0, 1\}$. *If* $b' = b$, *we say* $\mathcal{A}$ *wins the game.*

We define the advantage of $\mathcal{A}$ *in ST-IND-CKA game is* $Adv_{\mathcal{A}}^{ST}(k) = |Pr[b' = b] - 1/2|$.

Definition 8. *A dPPEKS scheme is assumed to be ST-IND-CKA secure if for all sufficiently large k and PPT adversary $\mathcal{A}$, there exists a negligible function negl such that $Adv_{\mathcal{A}}^{ST}(k) \leq negl(k)$.*

Definition 9. *A dPPEKS scheme is assumed to be semantically secure against insider keyword guessing attack if for any PPT adversary $\mathcal{A}$, both $Adv_{\mathcal{A}}^{ST}(k)$ and $Adv_{\mathcal{A}}^{CT}(k)$ are negligible in the security parameter k.*

6 Our dPPEKS Scheme

As introduced in Sect. 4, our scheme is composed of six algorithms. In this section, we will describe the dPPEKS scheme algorithm by algorithm.

6.1 Construction

First of all, the tag of each user in our paper is randomly chosen from $\{0, 1\}^*$, and each user is required to submit his tag before the whole process. The tag set of all team members is denoted by T. The threshold d represents the number of unauthorized users (i.e., leaving users). The access policy $T^\dagger$ is consisted in the tags of all leaving members and the random strings if the number of leaving members is less than the threshold d. Then our design details are given as follows.

System Setup. The **Setup** algorithm, performed by CA, with inputs security parameter k and the threshold d, first generates the system parameters for the whole system, and then outputs the master secret key for key derivation. When generating the master secret key, the most important point is that choosing a tag t_0, which should be different with all tags in T. As for server's key, it chooses two random elements y, z from Z_p as the secret key of the PriC and PubC, respectively. Then, computing g^{yz} as the joint public key of these two servers, where g is an element of the system parameters. In this paper, we assume that system parameters and the joint public key are shared for all participants within the system, while the master secret key is only known to the CA. Given part of the system parameters $(g_2, V(1), \ldots, V(d))$, it's easy for any participants to compute $V(\cdot)$ by interpolating in the exponent. The **Setup** algorithm is formulated in Algorithm 1.

Key Derivation. The **Derive** algorithm, performed by CA, is responsible for computing the secret and public key pairs for each member in the team. Without loss of generality, here we take the ith user as an example. First, a random number chosen from the group Z_p is set to be the authentication secret key

---

Algorithm 1. Setup

Require: Security parameter k; the threshold value d.

Ensure: System parameters SP; master secret key MSK; PubC's secret key SK_{PubC}; PriC's secret key SK_{PriC}; the server's joint public key PK_{js};.

1: Choose a group $\mathbb{G}$ of prime order p, a generator g and a hash function $H:\{0,1\}^* \rightarrow Z_p$

2: $(a_d, a_{d-1}, \ldots, a_1, a_0) \xleftarrow{R} Z_p^{d+1}, q(x) \leftarrow a_d x^d + a_{d-1} x^{d-1} + \ldots + a_1 x + a_0$

3: $r, \alpha \xleftarrow{R} Z_p, t_0 \xleftarrow{R} \{0,1\}^*, g_1 \leftarrow g^\alpha, g_2 \leftarrow g^{a_0}, V(x) \leftarrow g^{q(x)}$

4: $\text{SP} \leftarrow (g, g_1, g_2, V(1), \ldots, V(d)), sk_0^{(1)} \leftarrow g_2^{\alpha+r}, sk_0^{(2)} \leftarrow V(H(t_0))^r$

5: $sk_0^{(3)} \leftarrow g^r, sk_0^{(4)} \leftarrow V(H(t_0)), sk_0^{(5)} \leftarrow t_0$

6: $\text{MSK} \leftarrow (sk_0^{(1)}, sk_0^{(2)}, sk_0^{(3)}, sk_0^{(4)}, sk_0^{(5)})$

7: $y, z \xleftarrow{R} Z_p, SK_{PubC} \leftarrow y, SK_{PriC} \leftarrow z, PK_{js} \leftarrow g^{yz}$

Algorithm 2. Derive

Require: System parameters SP; master secret key MSK; the ith user's tag τ_i.

Ensure: The ith user's authentication secret key $SK_{au}^{\tau_i}$; public key $PK_{au}^{\tau_i}$; identity secret key $SK_{id}^{\tau_i}$.

1: $x \xleftarrow{R} Z_p, SK_{au}^{\tau_i} \leftarrow x, PK_{au}^{\tau_i} \leftarrow g^x, r_0, r_1, \lambda' \xleftarrow{R} Z_p$

2: $sk_{i0} \leftarrow (sk_0^{(1)} \cdot g_2^{r_0-\lambda'}, sk_0^{(2)} \cdot (sk_0^{(5)})^{r_0}, sk_0^{(3)} \cdot g^{r_0}, sk_0^{(4)}, sk_0^{(5)})$

3: $sk_{i1} \leftarrow (g_2^{\lambda'+r_1}, V(H(\tau_i))^{r_1}, g^{r_1}, \tau_i, V(H(\tau_i))), SK_{id}^{\tau_i} \leftarrow [sk_{i0}, sk_{i1}]$

---

of the ith user. Then, the public key of the ith user can be derived from the authentication secret key (line 3 in Algorithm 2). Taking the system parameters, master secret key and the tag of the ith user as inputs, this algorithm computes the identity secret key and sends it with the authentication secret key to the ith user through a secure channel. The public key of the ith user will be sent to the user publicly. The detailed generation process is described in Algorithm 2.

Keyword Encryption. Given a keyword w, the **PunEnc** algorithm will first choose a bilinear paring map and a hash function (line 1 in Algorithm 3), with which it can compute the keyword ciphertext. Only the tags of unauthorized users will be added into the access policy $T^\dagger$ (line 3 in Algorithm 3). If the number of leaving users is smaller than the threshold, some random bit string will be chosen to fill the gap. More succinctly, once someone's tag, usually the tag of leaving members, belongs to the access policy, he cannot pass the Algorithm 5 and get the DS's ciphertext. Except for the access policy, system parameters and authentication secret key are used to generate the keyword ciphertext as well. Algorithm 3 displays the details of **PunEnc**.

Token Generation. For the purpose of searching the encrypted files containing specific keyword w^*, DR will run the **TokGen** algorithm to obtain the token with his identity secret key. Without loss of generality, we take the jth user as an example in this algorithm. Input the identity secret key of the jth user, this algorithm outputs the search token, a tuple (st_{j0}, st_{j1}), where st_{j0} and st_{j1} are both consisted of four parts. Note that, the random number r' (line 1 in

---

Algorithm 3. PunEnc

Require: System parameters SP; the server's joint public key PK_{js}; the ith user's authentication secret key $SK_{au}^{\tau_i}$; keyword w; access policy $T^\dagger$.

Ensure: Ciphertext CT_w.

1: Choose a bilinear pairing map e: $\mathbb{G} \times \mathbb{G} \rightarrow \mathbb{G}_T$ and a hash function H_1: $G \rightarrow G_T$

2: $s \xleftarrow{R} Z_p, ct^{(1)} \leftarrow e(g_1, g_2)^{sH(w)} \cdot H_1(g^{xyz}), ct^{(2)} \leftarrow g^s, ct^{(3)} \leftarrow g^x$

3: $ct^{(3,1)} \leftarrow V(H(t_1))^s, \ldots, ct^{(3,d)} \leftarrow V(H(t_d))^s$

4: $CT_w \leftarrow (ct^{(1)}, ct^{(2)}, ct^{(3)}, ct^{(3,1)}, \ldots, ct^{(3,d)}, T^\dagger)$

Algorithm 4. TokGen

Require: System parameters SP; user's identity secret key $SK_{id}^{\tau_j}$; keyword w^*

Ensure: Token ST_{w^*}.

1: $r' \xleftarrow{R} Z_p, st_{j0}^{(1)} \leftarrow (sk_{j0}^{(1)})^{H(w^*)} \cdot g_2^{r'}, st_{j0}^{(2)} \leftarrow (sk_{j0}^{(2)})^{H(w^*)} \cdot (sk_{j0}^{(5)})^{r'}$

2: $st_{j0}^{(3)} \leftarrow (sk_{j0}^{(3)})^{H(w^*)} \cdot g^{r'}, st_{j0}^{(4)} \leftarrow sk_{j0}^{(4)}, st_{j0} \leftarrow (st_{j0}^{(1)}, st_{j0}^{(2)}, st_{j0}^{(3)}, st_{j0}^{(4)})$

3: $st_{j1}^{(1)} \leftarrow (sk_{j1}^{(1)})^{H(w^*)} \cdot g_2^{r'}, st_{j1}^{(2)} \leftarrow (sk_{j1}^{(2)})^{H(w^*)} \cdot (sk_{j1}^{(5)})^{r'}$

4: $st_{j1}^{(3)} \leftarrow (sk_{j1}^{(3)})^{H(w^*)} \cdot g^{r'}, st_{j1}^{(4)} \leftarrow sk_{j1}^{(4)}, st_{j1} \leftarrow (st_{j1}^{(1)}, st_{j1}^{(2)}, st_{j1}^{(3)}, st_{j1}^{(4)})$

5: $ST_{w^*} \leftarrow (st_{j0}, st_{j1})$

Algorithm 4) ensures the indistinguishability of the token. Algorithm 4 displays the details of **TokGen**.

Policy Test. Upon receiving the search token (st_{j0}, st_{j1}) from the jth user, PriC searches the keyword ciphertexts sent from different DS. Here we take the keyword ciphertext generated by the ith user as an example. Note that, the pseudo-code showed below ignores a step that the PriC will first verify the validity of ciphertext by comparing the $ct^{(3)}$ with the public key set of the whole team. If the $ct^{(3)}$ is not contained in the public key set of the team, the subsequent test process of this ciphertext will be terminated. This step is added to prevent malicious external users from uploading illegal ciphertexts. Then, based on the Lagrange interpolation polynomial, it calculates the coefficients by exploiting the access policy, a part of the search token (lines 7 to 11 in Algorithm 5). The results make an explanation to the fact that once the DR's tag is contained in the access policy, then he cannot get corresponding ciphertexts. If the jth user is authorized to the keyword, this algorithm will continue with PriC's secret key. Finally, PriC sends the verified keyword ciphertext to PubC. The detail of **PolicyTest** is described by the Algorithm 5.

Keyword Test. In this algorithm, the relationship between the ciphertexts and the search token will be test. PubC will conduct the keyword test with its secret key to obtain all ciphertext containing the queried keyword. The detailed process of **KeywordTest** is shown in Algorithm 6.

Algorithm 5. PolicyTest

Require: Token ST_{w^*}; ciphertext CT_w; PriC's secret key SK_{PriC}.
Ensure: Output: Authenticated ciphertext.
1: **for** i=0 to 1 **do**
2:    $T_i^\dagger \leftarrow (st_{ji}^{(4)}, t_1, t_2, \ldots, t_d), u_i^* \leftarrow \prod_{t_m \in T_i^\dagger \setminus \{st_{ji}^{(4)}\}} \frac{-H(t_m)}{H(st_{ji}^{(4)}) - H(t_m)}$
3:    **for** k=1 to d **do**
4:       $u_{ki} \leftarrow \prod_{t_m \in T_i^\dagger \setminus \{t_k\}} \frac{-H(t_m)}{H(t_k) - H(t_m)}$
5:    **end for**
6:    $z_{i1} \leftarrow e(st_{ji}^{(1)}, ct^{(2)}), z_{i2} \leftarrow e(st_{ji}^{(2)}, ct^{(2)})^{u_i^*}$
7:    $z_{i3} \leftarrow e(st_{ji}^{(3)}, \prod_{k=1}^d (ct^{(3,k)})^{u_{ki}}), Z_i \leftarrow \frac{z_{i1}}{z_{i2} \cdot z_{i3}}$
8: **end for**
9: $C \leftarrow (ct^{(1)}, ct^{(3)^z}, \prod_{i=0}^1 Z_i)$

Algorithm 6. KeywordTest

Require: Authenticated ciphertext C; PubC's secret key SK_{PubC}.
Ensure: Authenticated ciphertext.
1: $c \leftarrow \frac{C(1)}{H_1(C(2)^y) \cdot C(3)}$

Correctness. Let $SK_{au}^{\tau_i}$, pk_{τ_i} be the authentication secret key and public key of the ith user, $SK_{id}^{\tau_j}$ be the identity secret key of the jth user, whose tag is τ_j. Let CT_w be the ciphertext that contains the keyword w and access policy $T^\dagger$ sent from the ith user, ST_{w^*} be the search token of keyword w^* that generated by the jth user. Then we can verify the correctness of our scheme as follow:

- First of all, find a tuple $(u_0^*, u_{10}, \ldots, u_{d0})$ that meets $q(0) = u_0^* \cdot q(H(st_{j0}^{(4)})) + \sum_{k=1}^d (u_{k0} \cdot q(H(t_k)))$. In this step, since $st_{j0}^{(4)} = t_0$ and t_0 is a tag that does not belong to T, we can work out the correct coefficient value $u_0^*, u_{10}, \ldots, u_{d0}$ and compute as following:

$$u_{k0} = \prod_{t_i \in T_0^\dagger \setminus \{t_k\}} \frac{-H(t_i)}{H(t_k) - H(t_i)}, u_0^* = \prod_{t_i \in T_0^\dagger \setminus \{st_{j0}^{(4)}\}} \frac{-H(t_i)}{H(st_{j0}^{(4)}) - H(t_i)},$$

$$z_{01} = e(st_{j0}^{(1)}, ct^{(2)}), z_{02} = e(st_{j0}^{(2)}, ct^{(2)})^{u_0^*}, z_{03} = e(st_{j0}^{(3)} \prod_{k=1}^d (ct^{(3,k)})^{u_{k0}}),$$

$$z_{02} \cdot z_{03} = e(g^{(r+r_0)H(w^*)+r'}, g^{sa_0}), Z_0 = \frac{z_{01}}{z_{02} \cdot z_{03}} = e(g^{(\alpha-\lambda')H(w^*)}, g^{sa_0}).$$

- Second, find a tuple $(u_1^*, u_{11}, \ldots, u_{d1})$ that meets $q(0) = u_1^* \cdot q(H(st_{j1}^{(4)})) + \sum_{k=1}^d (u_{k1} \cdot q(H(t_k)))$. In this step, the value of $st_{j1}^{(4)}$ is the tag of the receiver τ_j. Once the receiver's tag does not belong to the access policy $T^\dagger$, the coefficient can be properly computed. This characteristic is determined by the properties of the Lagrange interpolation polynomial. Now we suppose that the receiver is authorized by sender for the keyword w, then we can work out the correct coefficient value $u_1^*, u_{11}, \ldots, u_{d1}$ and compute as following:

$$u_{k1} = \prod_{t_i \in T_1^\dagger \backslash \{t_k\}} \frac{-H(t_i)}{H(t_k) - H(t_i)}, u_1^* = \prod_{t_i \in T_1^\dagger \backslash \{st_{j1}^{(4)}\}} \frac{-H(t_i)}{H(st_{j1}^{(4)}) - H(t_i)}$$

$$z_{11} = e(st_{j1}^{(1)}, ct^{(2)}), z_{12} = e(st_{j1}^{(2)}, ct^{(2)})^{u_1^*}, z_{13} = e(st_{j1}^{(3)}, \prod_{k=1}^d (ct^{(3,k)})^{u_{k1}}),$$

$$z_{12} \cdot z_{13} = e(g^{r_1 \cdot H(w^*) + r'}, g^{sa_0}), Z_1 = \frac{z_{11}}{z_{12} \cdot z_{13}} = e(g^{\lambda' H(w^*)}, g^{sa_0}).$$

- Finally, set $C = (ct^{(1)}, ct^{(3)^z}, \prod_{i=0}^1 Z_i)$, and test the relationship between the ciphertext CT_w and the search token ST_{w^*} as follows:

$$c = \frac{C(1)}{H_1(C(2)^y) \cdot C(3)} = \frac{e(g_1, g_2)^{sH(w)} \cdot H_1(g^{xyz})}{H_1(g^{xyz}) \cdot e\left(g^{(\alpha - \lambda')H(w^*)}, g^{sa_0}\right) \cdot e(g^{\lambda' H(w^*)}, g^{sa_0})}$$

$$= \frac{e(g_1, g_2)^{sH(w)}}{e(g^{\alpha H(w^*)}, g^{sa_0})} = \frac{e(g_1, g_2)^{sH(w)}}{e(g_1, g_2)^{sH(w^*)}}.$$

Then it can be discussed from the following two cases: if $w = w^*$ holds, then set the value of c to 1; otherwise, set the value of c to 0. In summary, the correctness of our scheme has been proved.

7   Security Analysis

We evaluate the security of our dPPEKS scheme by analyzing its achievement of the definitions in Sect. 5. The dPPEKS scheme that can resist KGA defined in this paper needs to simultaneously satisfy the ciphertext indistinguishability and the search token indistinguishability under adaptively chosen keyword attack [19]. In the game described in this section, the adversary can access the key oracle, the ciphertext oracle, the token oracle and the test oracle arbitrarily. In the following, we give the security proof of our proposed scheme.

Theorem 1. *Under the DBDH and DL assumptions in the standard model, our dPPEKS scheme is secure against the off-line keyword guessing attack from internal attackers.*

This theorem will be proved through Lemmas 1 and 2 stated as follows.

Lemma 1. *Our dPPEKS scheme satisfies the CT-IND-CKA security under the DBDH assumption in the standard model.*

Proof. Here we will show that if there is an adversary $\mathcal{A}_{CT}$ that can break the CT-IND-CKA security of our dPPEKS scheme with a non-negligible advantage ε, it is equivalent to the existence of an algorithm $\mathcal{A}_{DBDH}$ that can solve the DBDH problem with the same advantage.

Let $(p, \mathbb{G}_1, \mathbb{G}_2, e, g, A = g^a, B = g^b, C = g^c, X)$ be an instance of the DBDH problem. $\mathcal{A}_{DBDH}$ tries to distinguish X and $e(g, g)^{abc}$, then it interacts with the adversary $\mathcal{A}_{CT}$ as follows:

Setup. The algorithm $\mathcal{A}_{DBDH}$ randomly chooses a d-degree polynomial $q(\cdot)$ whose constant term is equal to a_0, sets $V(x) = g^{q(x)}$ and $g_2 = g^{a_0}$. Then it selects one hash function $H : \{0,1\}^* \to Z_p$, two random numbers $\alpha, r \in Z_p$, $t_0 \in \{0,1\}^*$, and sets $g_1 = g^\alpha$. Set the master key MSK, a five-tuple, which consists of the following five parts: $sk_0^{(1)} = g_2^{\alpha+r}, sk_0^{(2)} = V(H(t_0))^r, sk_0^{(3)} = g^r, sk_0^{(4)} = t_0, sk_0^{(5)} = V(H(t_0))$. Set the secret key and joint public key of two servers: $SK_{PubC} = y, SK_{PriC} = z, PK_{js} = g^{yz}$, where y, z is randomly chosen from Z_p. Finally, it sends $PK_{js} = g^{yz}$ and SP $= (g, A^\alpha, B^{a_0}, V(1), \ldots, V(d))$ to the adversary $\mathcal{A}_{CT}$.

Query Phase 1. The adversary $\mathcal{A}_{CT}$ adaptively makes queries to oracles. The algorithm $\mathcal{A}_{DBDH}$ responds in the following form:

Key query $\langle \tau_i \rangle$. The algorithm $\mathcal{A}_{DBDH}$ randomly samples $x, r_0, r_1, \lambda' \in Z_p$ and a tag $\tau_i \in \{0,1\}^*$ and sets authentication key pair $(SK_{au}^{\tau_i}, PK_{au}^{\tau_i}) = (x, g^x)$, identity secret key $SK_{id}^{\tau_i} = (sk_{n0}, sk_{n1})$, where

$$sk_{n0} = (g_2^{\alpha+r+r_0-\lambda'}, V(H(t_0))^{r+r_0}, g^{r+r_0}, t_0, V(H(t_0)))$$
$$sk_{n1} = (g_2^{\lambda'+r_1}, V(H(\tau_i))^{r_1}, g^{r_1}, \tau_i, V(H(\tau_i)))$$

Finally, $\mathcal{A}_{DBDH}$ returns $(SK_{au}^{\tau_i}, PK_{au}^{\tau_i})$ and $SK_{id}^{\tau_i}$ to $\mathcal{A}_{CT}$.

Ciphertext query $\langle w \rangle$. The algorithm $\mathcal{A}_{DBDH}$ samples a random number $s \in Z_p$ to generate the keyword ciphertext $CT_w = (ct^{(1)}, ct^{(2)}, ct^{(3,1)}, ct^{(3,2)}, \ldots, ct^{(3,d)}, T^\dagger)$, where $ct^{(1)} = e(A^\alpha, B^{a_0})^{sH(w)} \cdot H_1(g^{xyz})$, $ct^{(2)} = g^s$, $ct^{(3)} = g^x, ct^{(3,1)} = V(H(t_1'))^s, \ldots, ct^{(3,d)} = V(H(t_d'))^s$. Finally, $\mathcal{A}_{DBDH}$ returns CT_w to $\mathcal{A}_{CT}$.

Token query $\langle w \rangle$. The algorithm $\mathcal{A}_{DBDH}$ randomly selects a number $r' \in Z_p$, generates the search token of keyword $ST_w = (st_{n0}, st_{n1})$, where

$$st_{n0} = (st_{n0}^{(1)}, st_{n0}^{(2)}, st_{n0}^{(3)}, st_{n0}^{(4)}), st_{n0}^{(1)} = g_2^{(\alpha+r+r_0-\lambda')H(w)+r'},$$
$$st_{n0}^{(2)} = V(H(t_0))^{(r+r_0)H(w)+r'}, st_{n0}^{(3)} = g^{(r+r_0)H(w)+r'}, st_{n0}^{(4)} = t_0,$$
$$st_{n1} = (st_{n1}^{(1)}, st_{n1}^{(2)}, st_{n1}^{(3)}, st_{n1}^{(4)}), st_{n1}^{(1)} = g_2^{(\lambda'+r_1)H(w)+r'},$$
$$st_{n1}^{(2)} = V(H(t_\tau))^{r_1 H(w)+r'}, st_{n1}^{(3)} = g^{r_1 H(w)+r'}, st_{n1}^{(4)} = \tau.$$

and returns it to $\mathcal{A}_{CT}$.

Test query $\langle CT_w, ST_{w'} \rangle$. The algorithm $\mathcal{A}_{DBDH}$ runs the **Test**$(SK_{PriC}, SK_{PubC}, ST_{w^*}, CT_w)$ and returns 1 to $\mathcal{A}_{CT}$ if the keyword corresponding to ST_w and CT_{w_i} is the same and the tag in ST_w does not exist in the access policy of CT_{w_i} or 0 otherwise.

Challenge. In this step, the adversary $\mathcal{A}_{CT}$ will submit his challenge: two different keywords w_0, w_1 and a tag τ^* with the restriction that both two keywords and tag τ^* never be queried in phase 1. The algorithm $\mathcal{A}_{DBDH}$ randomly selects a bit $\beta \in \{0, 1\}$. Then it chooses a random number $s^* \in Z_p$ and computes CT_{w_β} $= (X^{\alpha a_0 s^* H(w_\beta)} \cdot H_1(g^{xyz}), g^{\alpha a_0 cs^*}, g^x, V(H(t_1))^{\alpha a_0 cs^*}, \ldots, V(H(t_d))^{\alpha a_0 cs^*})$. It should be noted that there should be one tag t_i equals to τ. Finally, it returns the challenge ciphertext CT_{w_β} to the adversary $\mathcal{A}_{CT}$.

Query Phase 2. The adversary $\mathcal{A}_{CT}$ adaptively makes the queries to oracles as in phase 1. Notice that both keywords w_0 and w_1 should not be queried to get their ciphertexts and the secret key should not be queried on the tag τ^*.

Guess. The adversary $\mathcal{A}_{CT}$ outputs the guess $\beta' \in \{0, 1\}$. If $\beta = \beta'$ which means that $X = e(g, g)^{abc}$, the algorithm $\mathcal{A}_{DBDH}$ outputs 1 or 0 otherwise.

Next, we analyze the advantage of the algorithm $\mathcal{A}_{DBDH}$ in solving the DBDH problem. In the challenge phase, if $X = e(g, g)^{abc}$, then let $s' = s^* \cdot \alpha a_0 c$. We will get $CT_{w_\beta} = (ct^{(1)}, ct^{(2)}, ct^{(3)}, ct^{(3,1)}, \ldots, ct^{(3,d)})$, where

$$ct^{(1)} = e(g, g)^{ab\alpha a_0 cs^* H(w_\beta)} \cdot H_1(g^{xyz}) = e(A, B)^{s' H(w_\beta)} \cdot H_1(g^{xyz})$$

$$ct^{(2)} = g^{\alpha a_0 cs^*} = g^{s'}, ct^{(3)} = g^x$$

$$ct^{(3,1)} = g^{\alpha a_0 cs^* q(H(t_1))} = V(H(t_1))^{s'}, \ldots, ct^{(3,d)} = g^{\alpha a_0 cs^* q(H(t_d))} = V(H(t_d))^{s'}$$

It is clear that when $X = e(g, g)^{abc}$, CT_{w_β} is a valid ciphertext of the keyword w_β. And the adversary $\mathcal{A}_{CT}$ wins the game with the probability: $|Pr[\beta' = \beta] - 1/2| = \varepsilon$. In another case, when X is a random element in the group $\mathbb{G}_2$, the adversary $\mathcal{A}_{CT}$ can obtain no additional information from the ciphertext of the keyword w_β. Therefore, the guess β' satisfies $Pr[\beta' = \beta] = 1/2$. In summary, the advantage of the algorithm $\mathcal{A}_{DBDH}$ to solve the DBDH problem satisfies the following equation: $|Pr[\mathcal{A}_{DBDH}(p, \mathbb{G}_1, \mathbb{G}_2, e, g, g^a, g^b, g^c, e(g, g)^{abc}) = 1|a, b, c \in Z_p] - Pr[\mathcal{A}_{DBDH}(p, \mathbb{G}_1, \mathbb{G}_2, e, g, g^a, g^b, g^c, X) = 1|a, b, c \in Z_p \wedge X \in \mathbb{G}_2]| = |(1/2 \pm \varepsilon) - 1/2| = \varepsilon$. This completes the proof of Lemma 1.

Lemma 2. *Our dPPEKS scheme satisfies the ST-IND-CKA security under the DL assumption in the standard model.*

Proof. Here we will show a series of games based on the Definition 8.

Game 0. This is the original game as described in Definition 7, and we can redefine the advantage that the adversary wins in **Game 0** as $Adv^{\mathbf{Game0}}(\mathcal{A}) = Adv^{ST}(\mathcal{A})$.

Game 1. Let **Game 1** be the same as **Game 0**, except for the choice of challenge token. The token of w_β, referred as $ST^*_{w_\beta} = (st^*_{n0}, st^*_{n1})$, is computed in the following way:

$$st^*_{n0} = (st^{(1)*}_{n0}, st^{(2)*}_{n0}, st^{(3)*}_{n0}, st^{(4)*}_{n0}), st^{(1)*}_{n0} = g_2^{c_1 \cdot H(w_\beta) + r'},$$

$$st^{(2)*}_{n0} = (V(H(t_0)))^{c_2 \cdot H(w_\beta) + r'}, st^{(3)*}_{n0} = g^{c_3 \cdot H(w_\beta) + r'}, st^{(4)*}_{n0} = t_0,$$

$$st^*_{n1} = (st^{(1)*}_{n1}, st^{(2)*}_{n1}, st^{(3)*}_{n1}, st^{(4)*}_{n1}), st^{(1)*}_{n1} = g_2^{c_4 \cdot H(w_\beta) + r'},$$

$$st^{(2)*}_{n1} = (V(H(t_\tau)))^{c_5 \cdot H(w_\beta) + r'}, st^{(3)*}_{n1} = g^{c_6 \cdot H(w_\beta) + r'}, st^{(4)*}_{n1} = \tau$$

where $c_1, c_2, c_3, c_4, c_5, c_6$ are chosen randomly from Z_p. We can find that it is impossible for any PPT adversary to compute the value of r' based on the DL assumption, even if SP, pk and pk_s are known to the adversary. Furthermore, due to the randomness of r', the distribution of $ST^*_{w_\beta}$ and ST_{w_β} cannot be distinguished from the perspective of adversary. Thus, we have $| Adv^{\mathbf{Game1}}(\mathcal{A}) - Adv^{\mathbf{Game0}}(\mathcal{A}) | \leq Adv_{DL}(\mathcal{A})$, and the $Adv_{DL}(\mathcal{A})$ is negligible if the DL assumption holds (Definition 3).

Game 2. Let **Game** 2 be the same as **Game** 1, except for the choice of challenge token. Randomly choose st^{**}_{n0} and st^{**}_{n1} from $\mathbb{G}_1$ as the component of $ST^{**}_{w_\beta}$. Due to the randomness of r' and the chosen approach of $ST^{**}_{w_\beta}$, it is impossible for adversary to distinguish $ST^*_{w_\beta}$ and $ST^{**}_{w_\beta}$. Thus, we have $Adv^{\mathbf{Game2}}(\mathcal{A}) = Adv^{\mathbf{Game1}}(\mathcal{A})$. Moreover, we know that the adversary wins in **Game** 2 with probability $\frac{1}{2}$ because $ST^{**}_{w_\beta}$ is independent of β. Therefore, the advantage that the adversary wins in the **Game** 2 can be presented as $Adv^{\mathbf{Game2}}(\mathcal{A}) = | \frac{1}{2} - \frac{1}{2} | = 0$.

Finally, based on the game defined above, we have $| Adv^{\mathbf{Game2}}(\mathcal{A}) - Adv^{ST}(\mathcal{A}) | \leq Adv_{DL}(\mathcal{A})$, where $Adv^{\mathbf{Game2}}(\mathcal{A}) = 0$ and $Adv_{DL}(\mathcal{A})$ is negligible. In all, the advantage $Adv^{ST}(\mathcal{A})$ is negligible.

This completes the proof of Lemma 2.

8   Performance Analysis

Comparing with the prior dual-server scheme [6] and MUSE schemes [8,15], we briefly conduct theoretical analysis and actual experiments of our dPPEKS scheme in this section. All the experiments in this section are conducted on a laptop with Windows 10 Intel (R) Core (TM) i5-5200U CPU @ 2.20 GHz and 4 GB RAM with Java language. In our implementation, the cryptographic operations are implemented with the help of source library jpbc. As for the experimental configuration, the Type A which can be constructed on the curve $y^2 = x^3 + x$ over the finite field F_p for the prime number $p = 3 \mod 4$, is chosen to do the pairing operation.

8.1   Theoretical Analysis

When conducting theoretical analysis on [6,8,15] and the proposed dPPEKS scheme, for the sake of fairness, we exclude the communication and computation cost of encrypting and decrypting steps existing in [15]. Furthermore, for attribute-based schemes [8,15], the attribute contained in their access policy is equivalent to the authorized tags in dPPEKS scheme. The number of keywords is fixed to one in conjunctive keyword search scheme [8]. Note that, only time-consuming operations like the exponential operation (E), bilinear pairing operation (P) and three kinds of hash operation $(H : \{0, 1\}^* \rightarrow \mathbb{G}_1, H_1: \mathbb{G}_T \rightarrow \{0, 1\}^k, H_T: \mathbb{G}_1 \rightarrow \mathbb{G}_T$ respectively) are considered in our theoretical computation cost analysis.

To demonstrate the efficiency of our scheme in keyword encryption intuitively, we compare the communication (comm.) and computation (comp.) costs by histogram in Fig. 2(a) and (b). In terms of communication cost, Fig. 2(a) clearly shows that with the increase of authorized users, the size of ciphertexts in $[6, 8, 15]$ increases linearly. While the proposed dPPEKS scheme is superior with the aforementioned three schemes. The difference of $[8, 15]$ and our scheme in ciphertext size is slight when n equals to 50, but when n increases to 90, the communication cost in our scheme is only 1.8 Kb, which is about 6 times smaller than that of $[8, 15]$.

The proposed dPPEKS scheme has much less computational burden than those in $[6, 8, 15]$. As shown in Fig. 2(b), the average encryption time of our scheme is far less than the other three schemes. For example, when setting $n = 90$, it only costs 0.177 s to generate the ciphertext containing 90 users in our scheme, which is about 6 and 12 times less than that in $[8, 15]$.

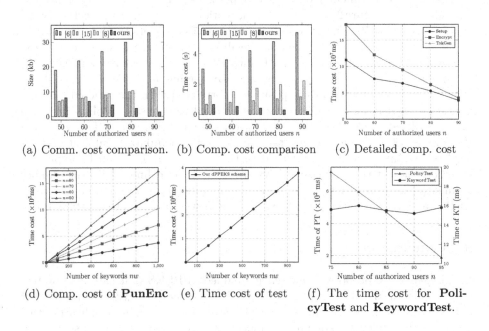

(a) Comm. cost comparison.   (b) Comp. cost comparison   (c) Detailed comp. cost

(d) Comp. cost of **PunEnc**   (e) Time cost of test   (f) The time cost for **PolicyTest** and **KeywordTest**.

Fig. 2. Demonstration of effectiveness for our dPPEKS scheme.

8.2   Experiment Analysis

As for the performance analysis, we conduct experiment simulation of our dPPEKS scheme. In our experiments, the tag and keyword space are consists of 100 and 1000 strings randomly selected in $\{0, 1\}^*$, respectively. The security parameter k is set to 128 bits. For comparison, we set $N = 100$ in the whole paper. Note that, the reason why we omit the experimental comparison between our scheme and other schemes are listed as follows: First, the scheme in $[6]$ is only suitable for single user scenario. Second, the authorization mechanism of our scheme is completely different from other MUSE schemes. Through theoretical analysis, we prove that the size of the team does not affect the time cost in our proposed scheme. Other schemes sacrifice communication costs to achieve efficient privilege matching, i.e., the authorization matrix [15] and the access tree [8].

First, we explore how n affects the time cost of the three algorithms containing in our scheme: **Setup**, **PunEnc** and **TokGen**. As shown in Fig. 2(c), the algorithm **TokGen** costs an average of 141 ms, which is independent with the value of n. Besides, Fig. 2(c) also lists the **Setup** and **PunEnc** time cost against the value of n increases, which indicates that the more users are authorized, the less is the computational cost derived by **Setup** and **PunEnc**.

To have a better understanding of the effect of n and nw on algorithm **PunEnc**, our experiment shows the total per keyword encrypting time for different values of n. Figure 2(d) shows the encryption time it takes for each keyword is 1.7 s when $n = 50$, while it only consumes 0.37 s on average when $n = 90$.

Finally, given a search token, we evaluate the performance of ciphertext retrieval in test operation including **PolicyTest** (PT) and **KeywordTest** (KT) when the number of keywords increases. By setting $n = 95$, Fig. 2(e) shows that the number of keywords is positively correlated with the time cost of test operation. Furthermore, considering the detailed time cost of **PolicyTest** and **KeywordTest**, we analyze the two algorithms separately in Fig. 2(f). By varying the number of authorized users from 75 to 95, the computational cost of **PolicyTest** is almost negatively related to the variable n. This can be explained based on the fact that the size of keyword ciphertexts is linear with the number of unauthorized users, which will decrease when the number of users n increases. At the same time, the time cost of **KeywordTest** approaches to constant 16ms.

9   Conclusion

In this paper, we propose a new scheme named dPPEKS that can be appropriately applied in the cloud storage system. This scheme deals with the problem of data sharing within a team implementing encryption strategies. The heart of this scheme is the exploration of a new perspective to realize efficient data sharing by changing the object contained in the access policy from authorized users to unauthorized users. It enables data senders to set the access policy of their encrypted files and allows other teammates to search and read the ciphertexts without the help of data owners. Besides, when teammates change, the data owner can efficiently update the user's search rights without affecting other users. The scheme has been proved to be KGA-secure against any internal adversary through thorough security proof under the standard model. Furthermore, we also analyze the communication and computational cost of our scheme in detail. Extensive results prove that our scheme is superior as compared with other schemes in efficiency and security. Last but not least, we hope our research can take a new perspective for designing the MUSE schemes and promote the research on access strategies for cloud-based data deploying encryption.

Acknowledgment. This work was supported by the National Natural Science Foundation of China (No: 62072240) and the National Key Research and Development Program of China (No. 2020YFB1804604).

References

1. Coronavirus: Six tech challenges small businesses face when working from home. https://www.stuff.co.nz/business/prosper/advice/121410081/coronavirus-six-tech-challenges-small-businesses-face-when-working-from-home. Accessed 10 June 2021

2. Bao, F., Deng, R.H., Ding, X., Yang, Y.: Private query on encrypted data in multi-user settings. In: Chen, L., Mu, Y., Susilo, W. (eds.) ISPEC 2008. LNCS, vol. 4991, pp. 71–85. Springer, Heidelberg (2008). https://doi.org/10.1007/978-3-540-79104-1_6

3. Boneh, D., Di Crescenzo, G., Ostrovsky, R., Persiano, G.: Public key encryption with keyword search. In: Cachin, C., Camenisch, J.L. (eds.) EUROCRYPT 2004. LNCS, vol. 3027, pp. 506–522. Springer, Heidelberg (2004). https://doi.org/10.1007/978-3-540-24676-3_30

4. Boneh, D., Franklin, M.: Identity-based encryption from the Weil pairing. In: Kilian, J. (ed.) CRYPTO 2001. LNCS, vol. 2139, pp. 213–229. Springer, Heidelberg (2001). https://doi.org/10.1007/3-540-44647-8_13

5. Byun, J.W., Rhee, H.S., Park, H.-A., Lee, D.H.: Off-line keyword guessing attacks on recent keyword search schemes over encrypted data. In: Jonker, W., Petković, M. (eds.) SDM 2006. LNCS, vol. 4165, pp. 75–83. Springer, Heidelberg (2006). https://doi.org/10.1007/11844662_6

6. Chen, B., Wu, L., Zeadally, S., He, D.: Dual-server public-key authenticated encryption with keyword search. IEEE Trans. Cloud Comput. (2019). https://doi.org/10.1109/TCC.2019.2945714

7. Chen, R., Mu, Y., Yang, G., Guo, F., Wang, X.: Dual-server public-key encryption with keyword search for secure cloud storage. IEEE Trans. Inf. Forensics Secur. **11**(4), 789–798 (2016)

8. Chen, Y., Li, W., Gao, F., Wen, Q., Zhang, H., Wang, H.: Practical attribute-based multi-keyword ranked search scheme in cloud computing. IEEE Trans. Serv. Comput. (2019). https://doi.org/10.1109/TSC.2019.2959306

9. Curtmola, R., Garay, J.A., Kamara, S., Ostrovsky, R.: Searchable symmetric encryption: improved definitions and efficient constructions. In: CCS, pp. 79–88. ACM, New York (2006)

10. Green, M.D., Miers, I.: Forward secure asynchronous messaging from puncturable encryption. In: S&P, pp. 305–320. IEEE Computer Society, New York (2015)

11. Huang, Q., Li, H.: An efficient public-key searchable encryption scheme secure against inside keyword guessing attacks. Inf. Sci. **403**, 1–14 (2017)

12. Jie, C., Han, Z., Hong, Z., Yan, X.: AKSER: attribute-based keyword search with efficient revocation in cloud computing. Inf. Sci. **423**, 343–352 (2017)

13. Kaushik, K., Varadharajan, V., Nallusamy, R.: Multi-user attribute based searchable encryption. In: MDM, pp. 200–205. IEEE Computer Society, New York (2013)

14. Li, J., Shi, Y., Zhang, Y.: Searchable ciphertext-policy attribute-based encryption with revocation in cloud storage. Int. J. Commun. Syst. **30**(1), 1–13 (2017)

15. Li, Z., Zhao, M., Jiang, H., Xu, Q.: Multi-user searchable encryption with a designated server. Ann. des Télécommunications **72**, 617–629 (2017)

16. Liang, K., Susilo, W.: Searchable attribute-based mechanism with efficient data sharing for secure cloud storage. IEEE Trans. Inf. Forensics Secur. **10**(9), 1981–1992 (2015)

17. Lu, Y., Wang, G., Li, J.: Keyword guessing attacks on a public key encryption with keyword search scheme without random oracle and its improvement. Inf. Sci. **479**, 270–276 (2019)

18. Miao, Y., Tong, Q., Deng, R., Choo, K.R., Liu, X., Li, H.: Verifiable searchable encryption framework against insider keyword-guessing attack in cloud storage. IEEE Trans. Cloud Comput. (2020). https://doi.org/10.1109/TCC.2020.2989296

19. Rhee, H.S., Park, J.H., Susilo, W., Lee, D.H.: Trapdoor security in a searchable public-key encryption scheme with a designated tester. J. Syst. Softw. **83**(5), 763–771 (2010)

20. Sun, W., Yu, S., Lou, W., Hou, Y.T., Li, H.: Protecting your right: verifiable attribute-based keyword search with fine-grained owner-enforced search authorization in the cloud. IEEE Trans. Parallel Distrib. Syst. **27**(4), 1187–1198 (2016)

21. Wang, S., Zhang, X., Zhang, Y.: Efficiently multi-user searchable encryption scheme with attribute revocation and grant for cloud storage. Plos One **11**(11), 1–23 (2016)

22. Waters, B.: Efficient identity-based encryption without random oracles. In: Cramer, R. (ed.) EUROCRYPT 2005. LNCS, vol. 3494, pp. 114–127. Springer, Heidelberg (2005). https://doi.org/10.1007/11426639_7

23. Xu, L., Xu, C., Liu, J.K., Zuo, C., Zhang, P.: Building a dynamic searchable encrypted medical database for multi-client. Inf. Sci. **527**, 394–405 (2020)

24. Yang, Y., Liu, X., Deng, R.H.: Multi-user multi-keyword rank search over encrypted data in arbitrary language. IEEE Trans. Dependable Secur. Comput. **17**(2), 320–334 (2020)

25. Yang, Y.: Towards multi-user private keyword search for cloud computing. In: IEEE Cloud, pp. 758–759. IEEE Computer Society, New York (2011)

26. Yau, W., Phan, R.C., Heng, S., Goi, B.: Keyword guessing attacks on secure searchable public key encryption schemes with a designated tester. Int. J. Comput. Math. **90**(12), 2581–2587 (2013)

27. Zheng, Q., Xu, S., Ateniese, G.: VABKS: verifiable attribute-based keyword search over outsourced encrypted data. In: INFOCOM, pp. 522–530. IEEE, New York (2014)

Privacy-Preserving Ranked Searchable Encryption Based on Differential Privacy

Yu Zhao, Chungen Xu$^{(\boxtimes)}$, Lin Mei, and Pan Zhang

Nanjing University of Science and Technology, Nanjing 210094, JS, China
{zy0326,xuchungen,meilin}@njust.edu.cn

Abstract. Ranked search allows the cloud server to search the top-k most relevant documents according to the relevance score between query keyword and documents, which has been recognized as the most promising way to realize secure search over encrypted database. However, recent studies show that some privacy protection methods commonly used in ranked search, like order-preserving encryption (OPE), have some security problems. In this paper, we first propose a scheme, called privacy-preserving ranked searchable encryption based on differential privacy (DP-RSE). Specifically, we add noise drawn from a Laplace distribution into the relevance score to disturb its value. In this way, no matter how much background the adversary has, he (or she) cannot obtain the true relevance score or ranked order. Moreover, our scheme ensures the correctness of search results with high probability. The experiment results show that our scheme can achieve sub-linear efficiency and the accuracy of search results can reach 94%.

Keywords: Differential privacy · Ranked search · Laplace distribution · Order-preserving encryption

1 Introduction

The huge storage capacity and economic service cost of cloud servers attract more and more clients to outsource private data to them. While in practice, cloud server is not always fully trusted. Considering the privacy of data, it is necessary to encrypt the data before uploading. But this will bring another problem, that is, some common retrieval methods such as the keyword search cannot be directly executed on ciphertexts. Ranked searchable encryption allows the cloud server to search the top-k most relevant documents according to the relevance score between query keyword and documents, which has been recognized as the most promising way to realize secure search over encrypted database. This reduces not only the computational overhead, but also the network burden.

This work was supported by the National Natural Science Foundation of China (No: 62072240) and the National Key Research and Development Program of China (No. 2020YFB1804604).

X. Yuan et al. (Eds.): QShine 2021, LNICST 402, pp. 323–339, 2021.
https://doi.org/10.1007/978-3-030-91424-0_19

Considering that relevance score may reveal the frequency information of the private data, some researchers suggest using order-preserving encryption (OPE) to hide above relevance scores. Here OPE refers to the order-preserving encryption, which can preserve the numerical order of the plaintexts even after encryption. Nevertheless, many recent studies [7,14,15,20,21,23] show that OPE is vulnerable to inference attacks which can reveal the plaintexts accurately. More specifically, the adversary can leverage order information to estimate the expected distribution of the plaintexts and then correlate it with the encrypted data based on the underlying property being preserved [12]. Therefore, it is desired to design a scheme which can disturb the ranked order while optimizing the search results. Some schemes [26,30] propose to mask the real score by adding a certain number of virtual scores to the search results under a fixed safety parameter. However, these suggested solutions are empiric and no theoretical security analysis is provided to guarantee their claims.

To this end, in this paper, our goal is to design a practical scheme to safeguard prior rank schemes while providing meaningful security guarantees. Our initial idea is to introduce the notion of differential privacy which is defined with respect to a privacy parameter ϵ. Compared to cryptographic techniques or k-anonymity, the advantage of differential privacy is that there is no need to provide special attack assumptions, i.e., even if the attacker has the greatest background knowledge, it can provide strong privacy protection [8].

In light of above observations, we summarize our methodology and contribution as follows. First, we propose a ranked search scheme over encrypted cloud data with differential privacy which masks the real relevance score through adding noise drawn from a Laplace distribution. As a result, the relevance score the server obtained is obfuscated. Thus, the server cannot combine with its known background knowledge to infer privacy information. Furthermore, to maintain the utility of the basic rank search scheme, we also investigate how to select approximate ϵ. We prove the security of the proposed scheme and conduct a series of experiments to evaluate its efficiency. The experiments show that the accuracy of search results in our scheme can reach 94% and the search efficiency of our scheme is almost the same as that of the existing schemes.

Organization. The rest of this paper is organized as follows. In Sect. 2, we introduce related work. Section 3 describes the system model, threat model, design goals and some notations used in this paper. In Sect. 4, we present some primitives used in this paper. In Sect. 5, we give the detailed structure of our scheme and give the security proof. We discuss efficiency and accuracy as well as give experimental results in Sect. 6 Finally, we give a brief conclusion in Sect. 7

2   Related Work

Searchable Encryption was first proposed by Song et al. [25], but the search efficiency of this scheme is low. In order to improve the efficiency, Goh et al. [13] proposed an index-based scheme named Z-IDX, which used bloom filter as the index. Curtmola et al. [4] proposed the inverted index, which can achieve sublinear search time. At the same time, they standardized symmetric searchable encryption and its security, and their proposed SSE-1 and SSE-2 schemes can achieve indistinguishability in non-adaptive and adaptive attack models, separately. Unfortunately, they all have to make use of generic and relatively expensive techniques to achieve dynamization. Kamara et al. [17] first proposed a dynamic SSE scheme to achieve efficient updating in ciphertext. Noted that, all the schemes above need the client decrypt all the returned documents to obtain ones most matching his (or her) interest, which will bring huge cost to the client.

Ranked SSE allows cloud server to quantify and rank-order the relevance of documents in response to any given search query. In this way, the client just needs to decrypt a small part of ciphertexts to obtain ones most matching their interest. Wang et al. [27] proposed the first ranked search scheme in cloud computing environment. In order to improve the practicability, Cao et al. [3] proposed the first multi-keyword ranked searchable encryption scheme based on the secure KNN technique. But the search efficiency of the scheme is not high, the search complexity is linear with the number of documents. To improve the search efficiency, Sun et al. [26] proposed a scheme using the MDB-tree based on the vector space model. But it is hard to support sub-linear search time and efficient updates. Liu et al. [22] proposed a verifiable and dynamic ranked search encryption scheme, which can achieve sub-linear search time. Recently, Yang et al. [31] overcame the shortcomings of KNN technology, and proposed a scheme not require a predefined keyword set and supported keywords in arbitrary languages.

Order-preserving encryption is often used to encrypt the relevance score in ranked search. It was first proposed by Agrawal et al. [1]. This technology can keep the numerical order of the ciphertext consistent with that of plaintext. Boldyreva et al. [2] first proposed order-preserving symmetric encryption (OPSE). Popa et al. [24] proposed a variable order preserving coding scheme (mutable Order Preserving Encoding, mOPE). Different from conventional order-preserving encryption, mOPE encodes sensitive data sequentially. Nevertheless, recent studies show that these commonly used OPE schemes [19,24] are vulnerable to many attacks like: inference attack, frequency analysis, sorting and cumulative attack [15,21].

Differential privacy is a new privacy protection mechanism proposed by Dwork et al. [8] in 2006. In this model, the purpose of privacy protection is achieved by adding noise to data. The advantage is that it can ignore how much background knowledge the attacker has. Traditional differential privacy schemes [9,11] centralize the original data to a center, which is called centralized differential privacy. But in practical applications, it is very difficult to find a truly trusted third-party data collection platform, which greatly limits the application of centralized differential privacy technology. In view of this, in the scenario of untrusted third-party data collectors, local differential privacy [6,18] appears. Nowadays, differential privacy has been adopted in many practical settings, especially in the field of machine learning [16,29]. Some major commercial organizations like Alibaba [28], Microsoft [5], Google [10] also use differential privacy to protect some sensitive data.

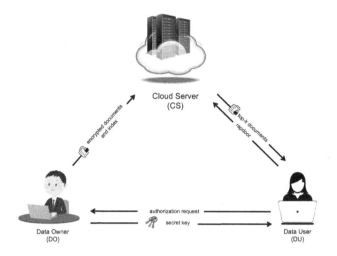

Fig. 1. System model

3   Problem Formulation

3.1   System Model

The system model involves three parties: the data owner (DO), data user (DU), and cloud server (CS), as illustrated in Fig. 1.

Data Owner: The data owner first extracts the keywords from a collection of documents $F = \{F_1, F_2, ..., F_n\}$, then calculates the relevance score between each document and its keywords. After that, he (or she) builds the secure encrypted index I and outsources I to the CS, together with the ciphertext **c** of F.

Data User: To search the document containing a specific keyword w, the data user first gets authorization from data owner and obtains the secret key, then generates the trapdoor T_w and submits it to the CS.

Cloud Server: Upon receiving the trapdoor T_w, the cloud server is responsible to search the index I and returns the top-k most relevant documents according to the relevance score between the search keyword w and each documents.

3.2   Threat Model

In this paper, we think that the data owner and user are fully trusted. We consider that the CS is honest-but-curious in our scheme. That is, the CS will execute the cryptographic protocol correctly, but it will try to learn the privacy information from the executive process.

Known Background Model. In this model, the cloud server knows more statistical information about dataset, except the ciphertext **c** and the index I. The cloud server may infer the specific content of keyword or document based on the known trapdoor ranked information of documents.

3.3 Design Goals

- **Ranked Search:** The proposed scheme should allow the CS to sort encrypted documents according to the relevance score between the search keyword and document, then return the ranked results to the user.
- **Differential Privacy:** Our scheme can achieve differential privacy, i.e., no matter how much background knowledge the attacker has, he (or she) will not infer the true ranked information according to the disturbed relevance score.
- **Efficiency:** Above goals on functionality and privacy should be achieved with low communication and computation overhead.

4 Preliminaries

In this section, we present some primitives used in this paper. Table 1 is part of the notations we use in this paper.

Table 1. Notations and descriptions

Notation	Description
F	The collection of n plaintext documents, $F = \{F_1, F_2, ..., F_n\}$
c	The collection of ciphertexts for F, $\mathbf{c} = (C_1, C_2, ..., C_n)$
$F(w_i)$	A sequence of documents containing keyword w_i
F_{ij}	The j-th document in $F(w_i)$
s_{ij}	The real relevance score of F_{ij} about w_i
S_{ij}	The disturbed s_{ij}
ES_{ij}	The encrypted S_{ij}
W	A dictionary of m keywords, $W = \{w_1, w_2, ..., w_m\}$
$\delta(F)$	The collection of distinct keywords in F
A	A search array
T	A search table
I	The encrypted index, $I = (A, T)$

4.1 Symmetric Encryption

Definition 1. *(Symmetric Encryption) A symmetric encryption scheme is a collection of three polynomial-time algorithms **SKE** = (**Gen, Enc, Dec**) such that:*

- **Gen**(1^λ): *It takes a security parameter λ as input, and returns a secret key SK.*
- **Enc**(m, SK): *It takes a plaintext m and a secret key SK as inputs, then returns a ciphertext c.*
- **Dec**(c, SK): *It takes a ciphertext c and a secret key SK as inputs, then returns plaintext m.*

Definition 2. *(Order-Preserving Function) For $A, B \subseteq \mathbb{R}$ with $|A| \leq |B|$, a function $f : A \rightarrow B$ is order-preserving if for any $i, j \in A$, $f(i) > f(j)$ iff $i > j$.*

Definition 3. *(Order-Preserving Encryption) [2] For plaintext-space $\mathcal{D}$, ciphertext-space $\mathcal{R}$ and key-space $\mathcal{K}$, we say a collection of three polynomial-time algorithms **OPE** = ($\mathcal{G}en, \mathcal{E}nc, \mathcal{D}ec$) is order-preserving if $\mathcal{E}nc$ is an order-preserving function from $\mathcal{D}$ to $\mathcal{R}$ for all K output by $\mathcal{G}en$, which can be described as follows:*

- $\mathcal{G}en(1^\lambda)$: *It takes a security parameter λ as input, and returns a secret key $K \in \mathcal{K}$.*
- $\mathcal{E}nc(K, m)$: *It takes a secret key K and a plaintext m as inputs, then returns a ciphertext c.*
- $\mathcal{D}ec(K, c)$: *It takes a secret key K and a ciphertext c as inputs, then returns plaintext m.*

4.2 Relevance Score Function

TF× IDF rule is always used to evaluate relevance score in information retrieval. Here, the term frequency (TF) refers to the number of times for a given keyword appears within a document, and the inverse document frequency (IDF) refers to the importance of keywords in the whole document collection, which can obtained through dividing the cardinality of document collection by the number of documents containing the keyword. Without losing generality, we choose the following formula to calculate the relevance score s_{ij} between a document F_i and a keyword w_j:

$$s_{ij} = Score(F_i, w_j) = \frac{1 + \ln f_{i,j}}{|F_i|} \cdot \ln(1 + \frac{n}{|F(w_j)|}) \qquad (1)$$

Here F_i denotes the document with length $|F_i|$; w_j denotes a search keyword; $f_{i,j}$ denotes the TF value of w_j in document F_i; n denotes the total number of documents in the collection and $|F(w_j)|$ denotes the number of documents that contain the keyword w_j in the collection.

4.3   Differential Privacy

Definition 4. (ϵ-*Local **Differential Privacy***) *A randomized mechanism Q satisfies ϵ-local differential privacy (ϵ-LDP) if and only if for any two inputs x_1, x_2 and any possible output y of Q, we have that*

$$Pr[Q(x_1) = y] \le e^\epsilon \cdot Pr[Q(x_2) = y] \tag{2}$$

In practice, in order to let an algorithm meet the requirement of differential privacy, there are different methods for different problems. Among them, adding the noise which corresponds to Laplace distribution, i.e., noise drawn from a Laplace distribution, to the results is a common method to protect numerical results.

Definition 5. (***Laplace Distribution***) *The distribution with following density function is called Laplace distribution:*

$$f(x|\mu, \lambda) = \frac{1}{2\lambda} e^{\frac{(-|x-\mu|)}{\lambda}} \tag{3}$$

where μ is the positional parameter and λ is the scale parameter.

4.4   Inverted Index

Inverted index [4] is widely used in information retrieval, which is an efficient indexing structure. In this paper, we use the inverted index with the same as [4], which containing a search array A and a search table T. $A[i]$ denotes the value stored at location i in A, which refers to the information about a document containing the keyword w. All nodes in A containing the same keyword w constitute a ranked linked list L_w, which defined as follows. All head node of $L_w (w \in W)$ constitute the search table T.

Definition 6. (***Ranked Linked List***) *For a dictionary $W = \{w_1, w_2, ..., w_m\}$, L_{w_i} is a linked list about keyword w_i, which containing $|F(w_i)|$ nodes $(N_{i1}, N_{i2}, ..., N_{i|F(w_i)|})$. Each node $N_{ij} = < fid_{ij}||ES_{ij}||k_{ij}||addr(N_{i,j+1}) >$ is stored in search array A, where fid_{ij} is the identifier of the j-th document in $F(w_i)$, ES_{ij} is the encrypted disturbed score of fid_{ij} using **OPE**, k_{ij} is the secret key of next node $N_{i,j+1}$ and $addr(N_{i,j+1})$ is the address of the next node $N_{i,j+1}$ in search array A. Each N_{i1} is stored in search table T.*

5   DP-RSE Scheme

In this section, we first introduce the idea of our scheme, and then give the concrete construction. Finally, we give the security proof.

5.1   Intuition Behind Our Construction

Before building the index, we first calculate the relevance score of each document and its keywords. Then we add noise drawn from a Laplace distribution to the relevance score to realize differential privacy. Specifically, let q be the query function, which inputs a query keyword w and then outputs k scores of the top-k most relevant documents in F. For example, $q(w_j) = (s_{j1}, s_{j2}, ..., s_{jk})$ is the output of the function which inputs the keyword w_j. And $s_{j1}, s_{j2}, ..., s_{jk}$ are the k relevance scores between top-k most relevant documents and w_j. Now, we set $q(w_i) = (s_{i1}, s_{i2}, ..., s_{ik})$ is the outputs of the function which inputs another keyword w_i. We define

$$\Delta q = \max_{w_i, w_j \in W} (\sum_{g=1}^{k} |s_{jg} - s_{ig}|). \tag{4}$$

Then the disturbed relevance score of document F_{ij} is

$$S_{ij} = s_{ij} + Lap(\frac{\Delta q}{\epsilon}) \tag{5}$$

where $Lap(\Delta q/\epsilon)$ is a Laplace distribution with $\mu = 0, \lambda = \Delta q/\epsilon$.

To avoid the cloud server recovering the original scores according to some statistics of disturbed relevance score, we use **OPE** to encrypt the disturbed score S_{ij} to ES_{ij} before outsourcing to cloud server. We define Q is a function, which inputs the search keyword w_i and then outputs k encrypted relevance scores after being disturbed of the top-k most relevant documents, i.e. $Q(w_i) = (ES_{i1}, ES_{i2}, ..., ES_{ik})$.

5.2   Construction

Now we give the detail of our scheme.

Let **SKE = (Gen,Enc,Dec)** be a secure symmetric encryption scheme. Let $W = (w_1, w_2, ..., w_m)$ be a dictionary of m keywords. $\delta(F)$ is the collection of distinct keywords in the document collection F. Let H be a pseudo-random function and ψ, π be two pseudo-random permutations with the following parameters:

- $H : \{0,1\}^\lambda \times \{0,1\}^l \to \{0,1\}^{\lambda + \log_2(r)}$
- $\pi : \{0,1\}^\lambda \times \{0,1\}^l \to \{0,1\}^l$
- $\psi : \{0,1\}^\lambda \times \{0,1\}^{\log_2(r)} \to \{0,1\}^{\log_2(r)}$

where l means that the keyword can be represented using at most l bits, r is the total size of the encrypted document collection in *min-units* (e.g., one byte).

As can be seen from Fig. 2, our scheme contains four algorithms, which can be described as follows:

- **KeyGen** (1^λ): The data owner simply chooses five random λ-bit strings k_e, k_o, k_1, k_2, k_3 separately. Set secret key $SK = \{k_e, k_o, k_1, k_2, k_3\}$, where k_e is the key to encrypt the document and k_o is the key used in **OPE**.

KeyGen(1^λ)

1: $k_e, k_o, k_1, k_2, k_3 \xleftarrow{R} \{0,1\}^\lambda$
2: $SK = \{k_e, k_o, k_1, k_2, k_3\}$

BuildIndex(W, F, SK)

1: Initialize $ctr = 1$
2: Calculate Δq
3: **for** $1 \leq i \leq \delta(F)$ **do**
4:      $k_{i0} \xleftarrow{R} \{0,1\}^\lambda$
5:      **for** $1 \leq j \leq |F(w_i)| - 1$ **do**
6:          $S_{ij} \leftarrow s_{ij} + Lap(\dfrac{\Delta q}{\epsilon})$
7:          $ES_{ij} \leftarrow \mathbf{OPE}.\mathcal{E}nc(k_o, S_{ij})$
8:          $k_{ij} \xleftarrow{R} \{0,1\}^\lambda$
9:          $N_{ij} = < fid_{ij} || ES_{ij} || k_{ij} || \psi_{k_1}(ctr+1) >$
10:         $A[\psi_{k_1}(ctr)] \leftarrow \mathbf{SKE}.\mathcal{E}nc(k_{i,j-1}, N_{ij})$
11:         $ctr = ctr + 1$
12:      **end for**
13:      $N_{i,|F(w_i)|} = < fid_{i|F(w_i)|} || ES_{i,|F(w_i)|} || 0^\lambda || NULL >$
14:      $A[\psi_{k_1}(ctr)] \leftarrow \mathbf{SKE}.\mathcal{E}nc(k_{i,|F(w_i)|-1}, N_{i,|F(w_i)|})$
15:      $T[\pi_{k_2}(w_i)] \leftarrow < addr(N_{i1}) || k_{i0} > \oplus H_{k_3}(w_i)$
16: **end for**
17: Padding A and T, and set $I = (A, T)$
18: **for** each F_i in F **do**
19:      Set $C_k = \mathbf{SKE}.\mathcal{E}nc(k_e, F_i)$ and $\mathbf{c} = \mathbf{c} \cup C_k$
20: **end for**
21: Output $(I, \mathbf{c})$

Trapdoor(SK, w)

1: Search token $T_w = (\pi_{k_2}(w), H_{k_3}(w))$.

Search(I, T_w)

1: Let $(\alpha, \beta) = T_w$
2: $\gamma \leftarrow T[\alpha]$
3: $< \theta || k > \leftarrow \gamma \oplus \beta$
4: **while** $\theta \neq NULL$ **do**
5:      $N_i \leftarrow \mathbf{SKE}.\mathcal{D}ec(A[\theta], k)$
6:      $< fid_i || ES_i || k' || \theta' > \leftarrow N_i$
7:      $\theta \leftarrow \theta', k \leftarrow k'$
8: **end while**
9: Sort documents according to their scores ES_i
10: Return the top-k relevant documents

Fig. 2. Our DP-RSE scheme construction

- **BuildIndex** (W, F, SK): The data owner first calculates Δq corresponding to the document set F, and then for each keyword $w_i \in \delta(F)$, randomly selects λ-bit string k_{i0} as the encryption key of N_{i1}. For each document containing w_i, the data owner generates an encrypted disturbance relevance score ES_{ij} by adding noise drawn from a Laplace distribution $Lap(\frac{\Delta q}{\epsilon})$ and using OPE to encrypt it. Next, N_{ij} is generated according to definition 6 and stored in A. Meanwhile, the secret key and the location in A of N_{ij} are stored in T. To avoid revealing the number of distinct keyword in F, we pad the remaining $|W| - |\delta(F)|$ entries in T with the random strings. Meanwhile, we set the size of A to r, and pad remaining entries in A with some random strings. Finally, the data owner generates a sequence of ciphertext $\mathbf{c}$ using the secure symmetric encryption algorithm, then sends $(I, \mathbf{c})$ to the cloud server.
- **Trapdoor** (SK, w): When a data user wants to search some documents containing the keyword w, he (or she) first gets authorization from data owner and obtains the secret key, then generates the trapdoor $T_w = (\pi_{k_2}(w), H_{k_3}(w))$ about the keyword w and sends it to the cloud server.
- **Search** (I, T_w): When receiving the trapdoor T_w, the CS first parses T_w as (α, β), then gets the address θ and decrypted key k of the head node in L_w through $T[\alpha] \oplus \beta$. Using the k, the CS can recover the head node in L_w, then get the address and decrypted key of next node. Repeating the same operation, the CS can obtain the information of all documents containing w. Finally, the CS sorts documents according to their scores ES_i, and returns the top-k documents.

5.3 Security

In this section, we analyze the security of our scheme.

Theorem 1. *The DP-RSE scheme satisfies ϵ-local differential privacy.*

Proof. We inject noise drawn from a Laplace distribution into the relevance score of each document to hide its true value before outsourcing to CS. When performing a search operation, the CS will get the encrypted disturbed relevance scores. According to formula (3), (4) and (5), we get that:

$$\frac{Pr[\mathcal{Dec}(Q(w_i)) = Y]}{Pr[\mathcal{Dec}(Q(w_j)) = Y]} = \frac{Pr[(S_{i1}, S_{i2}, ..., S_{ik}) = (y_1, y_2, ..., y_k)]}{Pr[(S_{j1}, S_{j2}, ..., S_{jk}) = (y_1, y_2, ..., y_k)]}$$

$$= \frac{Pr[(s_{i1} + n_{i1}, s_{i2} + n_{i2}, ..., s_{ik} + n_{ik}) = (y_1, y_2, ..., y_k)]}{Pr[(s_{j1} + n_{j1}, s_{j2} + n_{j2}, ..., s_{jk} + n_{jk}) = (y_1, y_2, ..., y_k)]}$$

$$= \frac{Pr[(s_{i1}, s_{i2}, ..., s_{ik}) + (n_{i1}, n_{i2}, ..., n_{ik}) = (y_1, y_2, ..., y_k)]}{Pr[(s_{j1}, s_{j2}, ..., s_{jk}) + (n_{j1}, n_{j2}, ..., n_{jk}) = (y_1, y_2, ..., y_k)]}$$

$$= \frac{Pr[(n_{i1}, n_{i2}, ..., n_{ik}) = (y_1, y_2, ..., y_k) - (s_{i1}, s_{i2}, ..., s_{ik})]}{Pr[(n_{j1}, n_{j2}, ..., n_{jk}) = (y_1, y_2, ..., y_k) - (s_{j1}, s_{j2}, ..., s_{jk})]}$$

$$= \frac{\prod_{l=1}^{k} e^{\frac{-|y_l - s_{il}|\epsilon}{\Delta q}}}{\prod_{l=1}^{k} e^{\frac{-|y_l - s_{jl}|\epsilon}{\Delta q}}} = e^{\frac{\epsilon}{\Delta q} \sum_{l=1}^{k} (|y_l - s_{jl}| - |y_l - s_{il}|)}$$

$$\leq e^{\frac{\epsilon}{\Delta q} \sum_{l=1}^{k} |s_{il} - s_{jl}|} \leq e^{\frac{\epsilon}{\Delta q} \cdot \Delta q} = e^{\epsilon}$$

According to definition 4, we know that the DP-RSE scheme satisfies ϵ-local differential privacy.

6 Performance Analysis

In this section, we mainly test the efficiency and the accuracy of the scheme. Meanwhile, we compare our scheme with two schemes proposed in [22] and [27] that have the same index construction as our scheme. We implement the scheme on a personal computer with Windows 10 64-bit operating system, 3 GHz AMD R5 CPU, and 16 GB RAM. We first generate a set of data and then use the Cryptography library in JAVA to test the efficiency and the accuracy.

6.1 Efficiency

In this subsection, we mainly discuss the efficiency of our scheme from two algorithms, **Buildindex** and **Search**. We choose SHA256 as the pseudo-random

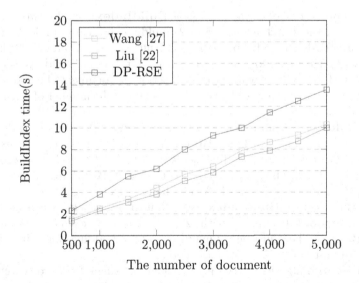

Fig. 3. Set $k = 20$, $\delta(F) = 100$, the time cost of **BuildIndex** towards different number of document for each keyword.

function and pseudo-random permutation in our scheme. Besides, we choose SM4 as the secure symmetric encryption to replace **SKE**. Similar to [27], we use the **OPE** proposed in [2], and set $|\mathcal{R}| = 2^{46}$.

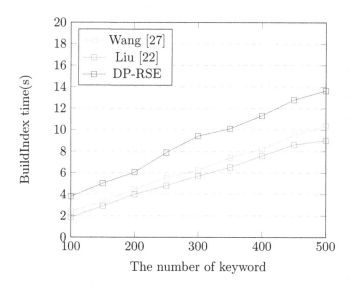

Fig. 4. Fix $k = 20$, $|F(w_i)| = 1000(w_i \in W)$, the time cost of **BuildIndex** towards different number of keyword

In the proposed scheme, the process of **BuildIndex** includes two main steps, i.e.,1) building the search array A and 2) building the search table T. The time cost of **BuildIndex** mainly comes from the number of document and keyword. So we test the time cost for these two factors. On the one hand, we set $k = 20$, the number of distinct keyword in the collection of documents be 100, then test the cost time of **BuildIndex** algorithm by changing the number of document for each keyword. As can be seen from Fig. 3, the result reveals that the time cost of **BuildIndex** algorithm in our scheme is linear with the number of document. The reason is that for each **BuildIndex** operation, there is a tuple inserted to index. On the other hand, we first set $k = 20$, and for each keyword w_i, we set $|F(w_i)| = 1000$. Then we test the cost time of **BuildIndex** algorithm by changing the number of keyword. As can be seen from Fig. 4, the result reveals that the time cost of **BuildIndex** algorithm in our scheme is linear with the number of keyword. Compared with [22] and [27], our scheme costs more time in **BuildIndex**. The difference is mainly caused by adding noise drawn from a Laplace distribution to the relevance score.

In the **Search** algorithm, we only consider the single keyword search. When a client wants to search the top-k documents containing a specified keyword, he (or she) just needs to send the trapdoor to the cloud server. Then the server search for the corresponding entries through A and T. Finally, returning the

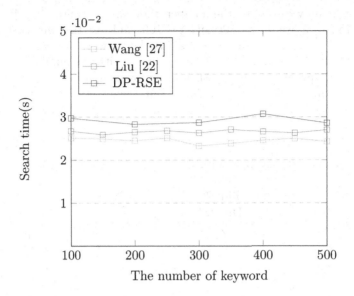

Fig. 5. Set $k = 20$, $|F(w_i)| = 1000(w_i \in W)$, the time cost of **Search** towards different number of keyword

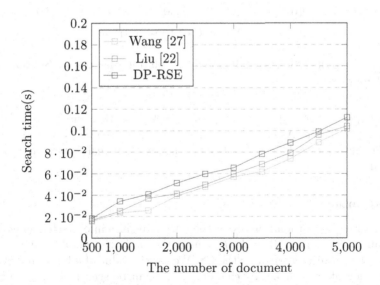

Fig. 6. Fix $k = 20$, $\delta(F) = 100$, the time cost of **Search** towards different number of document of each keyword.

top-k documents to the client. As can be seen from the Fig. 5 and Fig. 6, the time cost is mainly caused by the number of document containing the specified keyword. In Fig. 6, we set $k = 20$, $\delta(F) = 100$, and test the time cost of search for different number of document containing the keyword. We get that the time cost of **Search** algorithm in our scheme is linear with the number of document containing the specified keyword. Meanwhile, by comparison, the result reveals that the cost time of **Search** algorithm in our scheme is almost the same as [22] and [27].

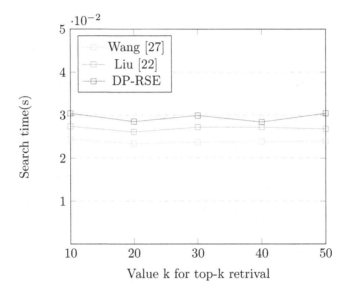

Fig. 7. Set $|F(w_i)| = 1000(w_i \in W)$, $\delta(F) = 100$, the time cost of **Search** towards different value of k

Finally, we set $|\delta(F)| = 100, |F(w_i)| = 1000(w_i \in W)$, and change the value of k for top-k search. As can be seen from Fig. 7, the search time is about 0.03s for different value of k in our scheme. The result reveals that our scheme is practical.

6.2   Accuracy

In order to measure the accuracy of the output results in our scheme, we define a measure as accuracy $P = k'/k$, where the k' is the number of real top-k documents that are returned by the CS. We set the value of k be 20 and evaluate the accuracy of the scheme by changing ϵ. As can be seen in Fig. 8, we change ϵ from 0.01 to 1.2, and when $\epsilon = 1.2$, the accuracy can reach 94%. As shown in Fig. 8, the higher value of ϵ, the higher accuracy. But from the notion of differential privacy, we can see that the higher value of ϵ, the worse privacy. So we should weigh the value of ϵ according to the demand of privacy and accuracy.

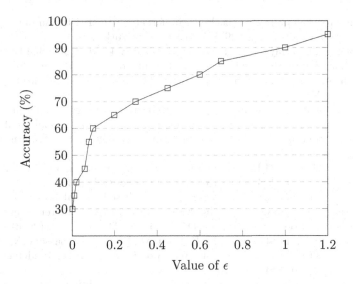

Fig. 8. Set $|F(w_i)| = 1000(w_i \in W)$, $\delta(F) = 100$, the **Accuracy** for different value of ϵ

7   Conclusion

OPE is a common means to protect privacy in ranked searchable encryption, but some studies show that **OPE** scheme will bring privacy leakage. To solve this problem, in this paper, we introduce the notion of differential privacy to the ranked searchable encryption and propose a privacy-preserving ranked searchable encryption scheme. In our scheme, we add noise drawn from a Laplace distribution to the relevance score between the search keyword and document to realize the differential privacy. In this way, no matter how much background knowledge the attacker has, he (or she) will not obtain the information of plaintext according to the relevance score. The experiments show that our scheme is efficient and practical. In the future work, we will be committed to exploring multi-keyword ranked search scheme over encrypted cloud data based on differential privacy.

References

1. Agrawal, R., Kiernan, J., Srikant, R., Xu, Y.: Order-preserving encryption for numeric data. In: Proceedings of the ACM SIGMOD International Conference on Management of Data, pp. 563–574. ACM, New York (2004)
2. Boldyreva, A., Chenette, N., Lee, Y., O'Neill, A.: Order-preserving symmetric encryption. In: Joux, A. (ed.) Advances in Cryptology - EUROCRYPT 2009, 28th Annual International Conference on the Theory and Applications of Cryptographic Techniques, 2009. LNCS, vol. 5479, pp. 224–241. Springer, Heidelberg (2009)
3. Cao, N., Wang, C., Li, M., Ren, K., Lou, W.: Privacy-preserving multi-keyword ranked search over encrypted cloud data. In: 30th IEEE International Conference

on Computer Communications, Joint Conference of the IEEE Computer and Communications Societies, pp. 829–837. IEEE, New York (2011)

4. Curtmola, R., Garay, J.A., Kamara, S., Ostrovsky, R.: Searchable symmetric encryption: improved definitions and efficient constructions. In: Proceedings of the 13th ACM Conference on Computer and Communications Security, pp. 79–88. ACM, New York (2006)

5. Ding, B., Kulkarni, J., Yekhanin, S.: Collecting telemetry data privately. In: Advances in Neural Information Processing Systems 30: Annual Conference on Neural Information Processing Systems, pp. 3571–3580. Neural Information Processing System (2017)

6. Duchi, J.C., Jordan, M.I., Wainwright, M.J.: Local privacy and statistical minimax rates. CoRR abs/1302.3203 (2013). http://arxiv.org/abs/1302.3203

7. Durak, F.B., DuBuisson, T.M., Cash, D.: What else is revealed by order-revealing encryption? In: Proceedings of the 2016 ACM SIGSAC Conference on Computer and Communications Security, pp. 1155–1166. ACM, New York (2016)

8. Dwork, C.: Differential Privacy. In: Bugliesi, M., Preneel, B., Sassone, V., Wegener, I. (eds.) ICALP 2006. LNCS, vol. 4052, pp. 1–12. Springer, Heidelberg (2006). https://doi.org/10.1007/11787006_1

9. Dwork, C., Roth, A.: The algorithmic foundations of differential privacy. Found. Trends Theor. Comput. Sci. 9(3–4), 211–407 (2014)

10. Erlingsson, Ú., Pihur, V., Korolova, A.: RAPPOR: randomized aggregable privacy-preserving ordinal response. In: Proceedings of the 2014 ACM SIGSAC Conference on Computer and Communications Security, pp. 1054–1067. ACM, New York (2014)

11. Friedman, A., Schuster, A.: Data mining with differential privacy. In: Proceedings of the 16th ACM SIGKDD International Conference on Knowledge Discovery and Data Mining, pp. 493–502. ACM, New York (2010)

12. Fuller, B., Varia, M., Yerukhimovich, A., et al.: Sok: cryptographically protected database search. In: 2017 IEEE Symposium on Security and Privacy, pp. 172–191. IEEE Computer Society, Washington (2017)

13. Goh, E.: Secure indexes. IACR Cryptol. ePrint Arch. 2003, 216 (2003). http://eprint.iacr.org/2003/216

14. Grubbs, P., Lacharité, M., Minaud, B., Paterson, K.G.: Learning to reconstruct: statistical learning theory and encrypted database attacks. In: 2019 IEEE Symposium on Security and Privacy, pp. 1067–1083. IEEE Computer Society (2019)

15. Grubbs, P., Sekniqi, K., Bindschaedler, V., Naveed, M., Ristenpart, T.: Leakage-abuse attacks against order-revealing encryption. In: 2017 IEEE Symposium on Security and Privacy, pp. 655–672. IEEE Computer Society, Washington (2017)

16. Ji, Z., Lipton, Z.C., Elkan, C.: Differential privacy and machine learning: a survey and review. CoRR abs/1412.7584 (2014). http://arxiv.org/abs/1412.7584

17. Kamara, S., Papamanthou, C., Roeder, T.: Dynamic searchable symmetric encryption. In: Proceedings of the 2012 ACM Conference on Computer and Communications Security, pp. 965–976. ACM, New York (2012)

18. Kasiviswanathan, S.P., Lee, H.K., Nissim, K., Raskhodnikova, S., Smith, A.D.: What can we learn privately? CoRR abs/0803.0924 (2008). http://arxiv.org/abs/0803.0924

19. Kerschbaum, F., Schröpfer, A.: Optimal average-complexity ideal-security order-preserving encryption. In: Proceedings of the 2014 ACM SIGSAC Conference on Computer and Communications Security, pp. 275–286. ACM, New York (2014)

20. Lacharité, M., Minaud, B., Paterson, K.G.: Improved reconstruction attacks on encrypted data using range query leakage. In: 2018 IEEE Symposium on Security and Privacy, pp. 297–314. IEEE Computer Society, Washington (2018)
21. Li, K., Zhang, W., Yang, C., Yu, N.: Security analysis on one-to-many order preserving encryption-based cloud data search. IEEE Trans. Inf. Forensics Secur. **10**(9), 1918–1926 (2015)
22. Liu, Q., Tian, Y., Wu, J., Peng, T., Wang, G.: Enabling verifiable and dynamic ranked search over outsourced data. IEEE Trans. Serv. Comput. (2019). https://doi.org/10.1109/TSC.2019.2922177
23. Onozawa, S., Kunihiro, N., Yoshino, M., Naganuma, K.: Inference attacks on encrypted databases based on order preserving assignment problem. In: Inomata, A., Yasuda, K. (eds.) IWSEC 2018. LNCS, vol. 11049, pp. 35–47. Springer, Cham (2018). https://doi.org/10.1007/978-3-319-97916-8_3
24. Popa, R.A., Li, F.H., Zeldovich, N.: An ideal-security protocol for order-preserving encoding. In: 2013 IEEE Symposium on Security and Privacy, pp. 463–477. IEEE Computer Society, Washington (2013)
25. Song, D.X., Wagner, D.A., Perrig, A.: Practical techniques for searches on encrypted data. In: 2000 IEEE Symposium on Security and Privacy, pp. 44–55. IEEE Computer Society, Washington (2000)
26. Sun, W., Wang, B., Cao, N., et al.: Verifiable privacy-preserving multi-keyword text search in the cloud supporting similarity-based ranking. IEEE Trans. Parallel Distrib. Syst. **25**(11), 3025–3035 (2014)
27. Wang, C., Cao, N., Li, J., Ren, K., Lou, W.: Secure ranked keyword search over encrypted cloud data. In: 2010 International Conference on Distributed Computing Systems, pp. 253–262. IEEE Computer Society, Washington (2010)
28. Wang, T., Ding, B., Zhou, J., et al.: Answering multi-dimensional analytical queries under local differential privacy. In: Proceedings of the 2019 International Conference on Management of Data, pp. 159–176. ACM, New York (2019)
29. Wei, K., et al.: Federated learning with differential privacy: algorithms and performance analysis. IEEE Trans. Inf. Forensics Secur. **15**, 3454–3469 (2020)
30. Xia, Z., Zhu, Y., Sun, X., Chen, L.: Secure semantic expansion based search over encrypted cloud data supporting similarity ranking. J. Cloud Comput. **3**, 8 (2014)
31. Yang, Y., Liu, X., Deng, R.H.: Multi-user multi-keyword rank search over encrypted data in arbitrary language. IEEE Trans. Depend. Secur. Comput. **17**(2), 320–334 (2020)

Memory-Efficient Encrypted Search Using Trusted Execution Environment

Viet Vo$^{(\boxtimes)}$

Monash University, Melbourne, Australia
`Viet.Vo@monash.edu`

Abstract. Dynamic searchable encryption (DSE) is important to enable dynamic updates (addition/deletion) on an encrypted database maintained by an untrusted server hosted on the cloud. It is desired that such updates should reveal as less as possible the information revealed to the server. As a result, advanced security notions of forward and backward privacy have been proposed to categorise the leakage by via addition and historical deletion, respectively. However, recent backward-(forward)-private schemes are not efficient enough to support very large databases. In this paper, we resort to the trusted execution environment, i.e., Intel SGX, to ease the above bottleneck. In detail, we proposed Magnus that guarantees Type I$^-$ backward privacy. Our key idea is to leverage a compressed Bloom filter within the Intel SGX's enclave to verify the deletion documents with the search keyword. This optimisation minimises the communication overhead between the SGX and untrusted memory. Then, to reduce the enclave's memory, Magnus further relies on a position map-free oblivious data structure maintained by the untrusted server. This improvement is to avoid paging effect in the enclave.

1 Introduction

Dynamic searchable encryption (DSE) [11,18,22] enables users to update/query encrypted database managed by untrusted servers (i.e., cloud) securely while preserving search functionalities.

Recent attacks (e.g., file injection attacks) exploiting the leakage in dynamic operations drive the rapid development of DSE schemes revealing less information while performing updates (i.e., addition/deletion). They are formalised as backward and forward privacy notions in DSE. Newly added data is no longer linkable to queries issued before, and deleted data is no longer searchable in queries issued later. As a result, many backward and forward-private DSE schemes have been proposed [3,5,15,24]. However, we note that they often reduce the efficiency of SE, especially in the communication cost between the client and server. Therefore, recent trusted execution environment-supported schemes have been proposed to accelerate the update/search operations. For example, Amjad et al. [1] proposed Fort, the first forward and Type-I backward private SE schemes using SGX. However, the scheme is still inefficient due to the high I/O complexity between the SGX

X. Yuan et al. (Eds.): QShine 2021, LNICST 402, pp. 340–351, 2021.
https://doi.org/10.1007/978-3-030-91424-0_20

and server. Vo et al. [25] proposed Maiden, the scheme achieves better asymptotic computation. However, we find that the scheme is not memory efficiency although it can achieve Type-I backward privacy. To avoid the memory overhead, we propose Magnus, which can reduce $\mathcal{O}(N)$ memory complexity in the SGX enclave, where N is the database size.

Contributions: Our contributions can be summarised as follows:

- Motivated by the memory bottleneck during Search in Maiden, we design Magnus to achieve forward and Type-I$^-$ backward-private for supporting real document insert/addition. Magnus leverages the SGX enclave to carefully track keyword states and document deletions, in order to minimise the communication overhead between the SGX and untrusted memory. Magnus also employs a Bloom filter to compress the information of deletions, which speeds up the search operations. Magnus leverage oblivious data structures to hide access patterns on the search index and real documents.
- We formalise the security model of our schemes and perform security analysis accordingly.

2   Related Work

Dynamic Searchable Encryption: The seminal work in the field was presented by Kamara et al. [18] proposing a DSE scheme with sublinear search time. Since then, many studies have been proposed to enrich search functionality [28,31] as well as improve the security [4,24].

Forward and Backward Privacy: In dynamic SE, forward privacy blocks the old query tokens on retrieving newly inserted data. It has been used to mitigate file-injection attacks [3,23,30]. Backward privacy [5,24] prevents the adversary from knowing the historial data manipulation of the client (e.g., historical insertion time of deleted data). There are three types of backward privacy, Type-I to Type-III, in the descending order of security.

Encrypted Search with Trusted Execution: Another research direction in the field is to leverage hardware-assisted trusted execution environment (TEE) [1,8,14,19]. In general, TEE such as Intel SGX can improve the communication between the client and server by letting the SGX's enclave play the client's role in token generation (i.e., update/query). For instance, ObliDB [13] and Oblix [19] build up Path-ORAM trees to support insertion and deletion on SQL tables. HardIDX [14], POSUP [17], and BISEN [2] improve the search efficiency in supporting encrypted document search. Note that these work do not support *forward* and *backward privacy*. Hence, they are not relevant to our focus in this paper. Until recently, Amjad et al. [1] proposed three schemes supporting Type-I, II and III backward private SE to enable single-keyword query; they are, Fort, Bunker-B, and Bunker-A, respectively. Then, [26] proposed Type-II SGX-SE1 and SGX-SE2 schemes, which outperform Bunker-B in both search latency and update computation/communication. Very recently, Vo et al. [25] also proposed

Table 1. Comparison with Maiden. N denotes the total number of keyword/document pairs. a_w presents the total number of entries of addition and deletion updates performed on w. n_w is the number of (current, non-deleted) documents containing w, d_w denotes the number of deletions performed on w. D and W denote the total number of documents, and the total number of keywords, respectively.

Type-I scheme	Communication enclave-server			Enclave computation			Enclave storage
	Add	Del	Search	Add	Del	Search	
Maiden	$\mathcal{O}(1)$	$\mathcal{O}(1)$	$\mathcal{O}(n_w)$	$\mathcal{O}(1)$	$\mathcal{O}(1)$	$\mathcal{O}(n_w)$	$\mathcal{O}(W log D)$ $+\mathcal{O}(a_w W)$ $+\mathcal{O}(N)$
Magnus	$\mathcal{O}(log^2 N)$	$\mathcal{O}(log^2 N)$	$\mathcal{O}(d_w log N)$ $+\mathcal{O}(n_w log^2 N)$	$\mathcal{O}(log^2 N)$	$\mathcal{O}(log^2 N)$	$\mathcal{O}(d_w log N)$ $+\mathcal{O}(n_w log^2 N)$	$\mathcal{O}(W log D)$ $+\mathcal{O}(a_w W)$

Maiden, Type I backward privacy, that supports very large deletion and achieves better performance than Fort. However, the scheme is not memory friendly to enclave's due to paging overhead.

3   Background

3.1   Trusted Execution Environment

TEE likes Intel SGX [9] is a set of instructions forming a secure and isolated execution environment. The environment minimises the attack surface to only the CPU processor. Other components are untrusted. The trusted execution part of the application is located in a protected memory area with strong protection enforced by SGX. The untrusted part is executed as a normal process and can invoke the enclave only through a predefined communication interface of ecalls/ocalls. We refer readers to [10] for the security guarantee of Intel SGX, related side-channel attacks [21,29], and recent countermeasures [6,16,20].

3.2   Dynamic Searchable Symmetric Encryption

Here, we briefly overview dynamic SE and the notion of *forward* and *backward* *privacy* in dynamic SE. We refer readers to [3,5] for formal definition of these security notions. A dynamic SE scheme $\Sigma = (\mathsf{Setup}, \mathsf{Search}, \mathsf{Update})$ defines the client and a server via following protocols:

$\mathsf{Setup}(1^\lambda, \mathsf{DB})$: The protocol inputs a security parameter λ and outputs a secret key K, a state ST for the client, and an encrypted database EDB to the server.

$\mathsf{Search}(K, w, ST; \mathsf{EDB})$: The protocol allows to query w by using (K, ST) to generate query token q for w. Upon receiving q, the server follows the protocol to retrieve the search result (i.e., matching document) of q.

$\mathsf{Update}(K, (\mathsf{op}, \mathsf{in}), ST; \mathsf{EDB})$: The protocol takes K, ST, an input in associated with an operation op from the client, and EDB, where $\mathsf{op} \in \{add, del\}$ and in consists of a document identifier *id* and a set of keywords in that document. Then, the protocol inserts or removes in from EDB upon op.

There are two security notions based on the leakage function of dynamic SE [5]. The *forward privacy* ensures that addition update prevents using the old query token to retrieve that new added data. The *backward privacy* guarantees that when a keyword-document pair (w, id) is added and then deleted, subsequent searches on w do not reveal id. We use the notations in [3,5] to restate Type-I and Type-II *backward privacy* as follows. Let Q be the current query list, and $\mathsf{TimeDB}(w)$ be the access pattern on the non-deleted documents *currently* matching w and the timestamps of inserting them to the database. We denote by $\mathsf{Updates}(w)$ the time stamps of updates on w. Then, formally,

$$\mathsf{TimeDB}(w) = \{(u, id) | (u, add, (w, id)) \in Q \text{ and } \forall (u', del, (w, id)) \notin Q\}$$

$$\mathsf{Updates}(w) = \{(u | (u, add, (w, id)) \text{ or } (u', del, (w, id)) \in Q\}$$

Type-I *backward privacy* is the most secure [5]. It only reveals what time the current (non-deleted) documents matching to w added (i.e., $\mathsf{TimeDB(w)}$). In contrast, Type-II reveals both $\{\mathsf{DB}(w), \mathsf{Updates}(w)\}$ to the untrusted server.

4 Our Proposed Scheme

In this section, we present the system design for Magnus, our assumption, and threat model. Then, we investigate the limitation of previous TEE-supported Type-I *backward-private* scheme (i.e., Maiden), and highlight our design intuition. Afterwards, we detail the protocols of Magnus.

4.1 System Overview

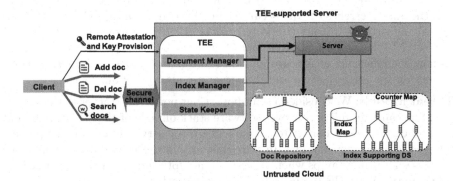

Fig. 1. System design for Type-I⁻ *backward-private* SE

In our system (see Fig. 1), the *Client* can remotely manipulate the database via Setup, Update (add/del documents), and Search operations. The *Server* manages the encrypted document repository R, and encrypted supporting data structures of index map M_I and counter map M_c. We design R and M_c using oblivious data structure maps [27] to support oblivious accesses. The *Enclave* is inside the *Server*, and it contains necessary components of *Document Manager* (resp. *Index Manager*) to perform data (resp. index) queries to the untrusted parts.

In Setup, the *Client* remotely authenticates the *Enclave* via attestation protocol [9]. Then, she establishes a secure channel with the *Enclave*.

In Update, we design the *Client* to be storage-free. Giving a document doc with an unique identifier *id*, the *Client* sends a tuple (op $= add$, in $= \{$doc, $id\}$) to the *Enclave* via the established secure channel. Then, *Document Manager* parses the doc to generate encrypted data blocks and obliviously insert them to R. During that step, *Document Manager* internally updates the local *State Keeper*. To support index search, *Index Manager* generates addition tokens for $\forall (w, id)$ in doc and obliviously insert to M_I and M_c. If Update is document deletion, the *Client* send a tuple of (op $= del$, in $=$ doc$'$, id) to the *Enclave*, where doc$'$ is a dummy document to hide the document deletion operation, and *id* is the real document identifier of the doc to be deleted. Similarly, *Document Manager* and *Index Manager* perform the same process as in document addition, except for additionally local updates within the *Enclave*.

In Search, the *Client* sends a query keyword w to the *Enclave*. Accordingly, the *Index Manager* executes the Search protocol of Magnus to only retrieve the currently matching documents of w. Then, *Document Manager* reconstructs these docs from querying encrypted data blocks from R. At the end of the Search operation, the *Client* receives the docs in a batch manner.

4.2   TEE Assumptions and Threat Model

Our Assumptions with TEE: We assume that TEE like SGX *Enclave* behaves correctly, without hardware bugs or backdoors), and the code and data inside the enclave are protected. Also, we assume the communication between the *Client* and the *Enclave* relies on the secure channel created during SGX attestation. Like many other hardware-supported works [12,19], we consider side-channel attacks [7,21,29] against SGX are out of our scope. In this paper, we only focus on how the efficiency of *forward* and *backward* privacy. Denial-of-service (DoS) attacks on the Intel *Enclave* and the server are also out of our focus.

Threat Models: We consider a semi-honest but powerful attacker at the server-side. She can gain full access over software stack outside of the enclave, OS and hypervisor, as well as hardware components in the server except for the processor package and memory bus. In particular, the attacker can observe memory addresses and timestamps when accessing (encrypted) data on the memory bus, in- memory, or in EDB to generate data access patterns.

4.3   Design Intuition

In this paper, we focus on the trade-off between the enclave's memory overhead and Type-I backward privacy. In this leakage type, we have Fort [1] and

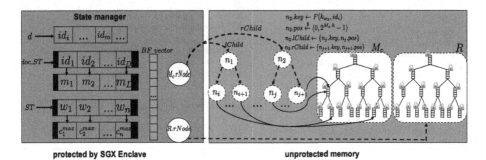

Fig. 2. AVL tree stored in Path-ORAM

Maiden [25], which are TEE-supported Type-I *backward-private* SE scheme. However, we only analyse the practical limitation of Maiden since it is more efficient than Fort. We note that Maiden requires a large enclave's storage (i.e., $\mathcal{O}W(logD) + \mathcal{O}(a_w W) + \mathcal{O}(N)$ to achieve Type-I. In details, the scheme needs $\mathcal{O}W(logD)$ to store keyword state ST, another $\mathcal{O}(a_w W)$ for Bloom filter checking, and an important $\mathcal{O}(N)$ overhead to store the states of document identifiers, i.e., $(id_i, c + i)$, mapping to w. In this way, it only needs the *Server* to store the index map M_I. However, the scheme is not memory efficient since the *Enclave*'s memory is limited at 98 MB. Exceeding usage causes paging effect in Intel SGX. Therefore, we propose Magnus, the scheme only requires $\mathcal{O}W(logD) + \mathcal{O}(a_w W)$ memory overhead in the enclave. As a trade-off, the scheme only achieves Type-I$^-$ backward privacy. The reason is that, Magnus additionally introduces a new leakage that only happens during Search operations. In particular, that is ORAM accesses to the *Server* during the operation, leaking the number of deleted documents of the query keyword w (i.e., d_w) when the *Server* records the number of visited ORAM positions.

4.4 Magnus Construction

Underlying Data Structures: Magnus utilises a key/value oblivious data structure (ODS) to build a state map, namely M_c, by using an AVL tree [27]. The AVL nodes are stored in a non-recursive Path-ORAM, where each node n_i contains the information of key/value itself and the meta data of its children nodes, i.e., $n_i = (key, value, pos, height, lChild, rChild)$, where key is an evaluation of $PRF(k_w, id)$, $value = \mathsf{Enc}(k_c, c)$ (dedicated keys k_w, k_c derived by w), pos indicates the node's leaf position in the Path-ORAM, $height$ presents the node's level, $lChild$ is a map of $(lChild.key, lChild.pos)$, and as similar with $rChild$ (see Fig. 2). With the help of this *pointer-based technique*, Magnus does not store he position map pm of $OMAP_c$ in the *Enclave*.

We note that the map lookup for an AVL node in $OMAP_c$ is reduced to $\mathcal{O}(logN)$ ORAM accesses with one for each Path-ORAM level. Hence, Magnus only spends $\mathcal{O}(d_w logN)$ round trips between the *Enclave* and the *Server* to

Setup(1^λ)	8: Initialise a keyword map ST and list del_List;
Client:	9: Initialise a document state map doc_ST;
1: Initialise $k_\Sigma, k_{BF} \xleftarrow{\$} \{0,1\}^\lambda$;	10: Init a key $M_{ck} \xleftarrow{\$} \{0,1\}^\lambda$;
2: Initialise integers l, h for BF;	11: Set tree height $M_c.h$ and a root node $M_c.rNode$;
3: Launch a remote attestation to *Enclave*;	12: Receive (k_Σ, k_{BF}, l, h);
4: Establish a secure channel to *Enclave*;	13: Initialise $BF \leftarrow 0^l$ and $\{H'_j\}_{j \in [h]}$ for BF;
5: Send (k_Σ, k_{BF}, l, h) to *Enclave*;	
	Server:
Enclave:	14: Initialise an index map M_I;
6: Initialise a key $R_k \xleftarrow{\$} \{0,1\}^\lambda$;	15: Initialise oblivious map R with $R.h$;
7: Set tree height $R.h$ and a root node $R.rNode$;	16: Initialise oblivious map M_c with $M_c.h$;
	17: Write root nodes of $R.rNode$ and $M_c.rNode$;

Fig. 3. Setup protocol in Magnus where the *Client* is *storage-free*

retrieve d_w lookup. (see Search communication in Table 1). Upon retrieving AVL nodes in buckets from the *Server*, Magnus employs a negligible *stash* to cache AVL (w, id) nodes in the *Enclave*. We note that the max *stash*'s size is about 147 blocks ($\sim$57 KB) for $Z = 4$ and the failure probability $f_p < 2^{-128}$. Then, the *Enclave* can make updates to these nodes locally (i.e., insertion and rebalancing). Before writing them back to the $OMAP_c$, fetched nodes are assigned new random *pos*, and their parents are also updated correspondingly. We also note that the $OMAP_c$ structure stored at the *Server* is bounded to $Z \cdot 2^{\Sigma(w,id)}$ blocks, to support $\Sigma(w, id)$ entries of *addition* Update. We also make use of the ODS to store the physical blocks of encrypted documents in R. We present the protocols in Magnus as follows.

In Setup (see Fig. 3), the *Client* performs an attestation protocol with the *Enclave* and provisions $K = (k_\Sigma, k_{BF})$ upon an established secure channel, where k_Σ is used to generate update/query tokens and k_{BF} is the key for computing the digest of $(w\|id)$, and l presents the vector size of the BF and h is the number of hash functions. The *Enclave* initiates R_k to later encrypt document data buckets, and set the tree height $R.h$. Note that, the document root node $R.rNode$ should always be stored and updated within the *Enclave* to allow remotely traversing the R stored in the *Server*. The *Enclave* initiates a Bloom Filter BF based on the provided (l, h). Then, it also maintains the maps ST and doc_ST, and the list del_List, where ST maintains the state of keywords, doc_ST keeps track the number of data blocks for each doc with identifier id, and del_List records the deleted ids during *deletion* Update. The *Server* holds an encrypted index M_I, the oblivious maps M_c and R.

In Update, the *Client* sends a tuple (op, in) to the *Enclave* via the secure channel, where (op = add, in = (doc, id)) or (op = del, in = (doc$'$, id))). We note that doc$'$ is a dummy document, and it enables the *Enclave* to perform insertion in R even when op = del. After that, the *Enclave* splits the doc to data chunks $B = \{b_i\}, \forall i \in \{1, m\}$, where b_i is the *value* in an AVL node n_i (see Fig. 4 lines 9–13). There is a multiple round trips $\mathcal{O}(log^2 N)$ between the *Enclave* and the *Server* to insert n_i, via R.Access(op$'$ = $update$, in$'$ = $(R.rNode, R_k, n_i)$), as presented in Fig. 2. In short, the *Enclave* obliviously traverses from the AVL root $R.rnode$ to find and insert a matching node n_i via the Path-ORAM structure

Update(op, in)		
	22:	$(u, v) \leftarrow (H_2(k_w, c), \text{Enc}(k_{id}, id))$
Client:	23:	add (u, v) to T;
1: **if** op $= add$ **then**// in=(doc,id)	24:	$pos \xleftarrow{\$} (0, 2^{M_c.h} - 1)$;
2: send (op, in) to *Enclave*;	25:	$n_c \leftarrow (key = F(k_w, id), value = \text{Enc}(k_c, c),$
3: **else** // op $= del$		$pos, height = 1, //$leaf node
4: Create dummy doc in doc';		$lChild = \varnothing, rChild = \varnothing)$;
5: send (op, in $= (doc', id)$) to *Enclave*;	26:	$M_c.\text{Access}(op' = update,$
6: **end if**		$in' = (M_c.rNode, M_{ck}, n_c))$ to *Server*;
	27:	$BF[H'_j(k_{BF}, w \parallel id)] \leftarrow 1$ for $j \in [1, h]$;
Enclave:	28:	$ST[w] \leftarrow c$;
7: **if** op $= add$ **then** //in $= (doc, id)$	29:	**end for**
8: Split doc into chunks B $= \{b_1, \ldots, b_m\}$;	30:	send T to *Server*; // in batch
//create nodes from chunks	31:	**else:** // op $= del$, in $= (doc', id)$
9: **for** $b_i \in$ B **do**	32:	$r, r' \leftarrow$ rand() from doc';
10: $pos \xleftarrow{\$} (0, 2^{R.h} - 1)$;	33:	Create dummy index node $n_i, \forall i \in [0, r]$;
11: $n_i \leftarrow (key = F(k_\Sigma, id\|i), value = b_i, pos,$	34:	$M_c.\text{Access}(op' = update,$
$height = 1, lChild = \varnothing, rChild = \varnothing)$;		$in' = (M_c.rNode, M_{ck}, n_i))$ to *Server*;
12: $R.\text{Access}(op' = update,$	35:	Create dummy data node $n'_i, \forall i \in [0, r']$;
$in' = (R.rNode, R_k, n_i))$ to *Server*;	36:	$R.\text{Access}(op' = update,$
13: **end for**		$in' = (R.rNode, R_k, n'_i))$ to *Server*;
	37:	add id to del_List;
14: doc_ST$[id] \leftarrow m$;	38:	del doc_ST$[id]$;
15: Parse doc to $\{(w, id)\}$;	39:	set dummy entries in T to *Server*;
16: $T \leftarrow \{\emptyset\}$;	40:	**end if**
17: **for** (w, id) **do**		
18: $(k_w \parallel k_c) \leftarrow F(k_\Sigma, w)$;		*Server:*
19: $c \leftarrow ST[w]$;	41:	receive T from *Enclave*;
20: $c \leftarrow c + 1$;	42:	**for** (u, v) **in** T **do**
21: $k_{id} \leftarrow H_1(k_w, c)$;	43:	$M_I[u] \leftarrow v$;

Fig. 4. Update protocol in Magnus

of R. The ORAM accesses from the *Enclave* are executed via *ocalls*, and downloaded buckets are decrypted by R_k. Visited nodes in the buckets are un-packed and cached in the *stash*. During the traverses, the *Enclave* scans the *stash* first, and perform oblivious accesses if the node is not found. To hide the data-dependent path of the ORAM currently accessing *pos*, the *Enclave* also accesses a dummy ORAM path generated from a random *pos'*. That is, the *Enclave* always retrieves buckets of two ORAM paths, one for real and another one for dummy path, from the *Server*, for every AVL node access. Magnus tries to put the node as deep as possible, i.e., *height* $= 1$, as a leaf node. Once the node is inserted, its parent node is re-balanced, recursively to the root. Finally, all accessed nodes are mapped to new ORAM positions, and ORAM buckets containing them are re-encrypted with R_k before being stored again at R. Note that Magnus only need 1 *ocall* to send all the new buckets to the *Server* in a batch. After data blocks in doc inserted, the *Enclave* will parses the doc to retrieve a list of $\{(w, id)\}$ and later update M_I and M_c (see line 14). To do so, the *Enclave* utilises the latest state $c \leftarrow ST[w]$ of w, and with $(k_w\|k_c)$ generated by $F(k_\Sigma, w)$ to generate an encrypted entry $(u, v) \leftarrow (H_2(k_w, c), \text{Enc}(k_{id}, id))$ in a temporary list T. Note that, H_1 and H_2 denote hash functions and Enc is a symmetric encryption cipher. The entry holds the mapping between c and id to allow the *Enclave* to retrieve id upon u and the known state. Then, the *Enclave* generates an AVL state node n_c of (w, id) with $n_c.key = F(k_w, id)$ and $n_c.value = (\text{Enc}(k_c, c))$

```
Search(w)                                    18: send Q to Server;

Client:                                      Server:
1: send w to Enclave;                        17: receive Q from Enclave;
                                             18: id_List ← {∅}; // currently matched ids
Enclave: //retrieve currently matched ids    19: for (u, k_id) in Q do
2: (k_w ∥ k_c) ← F(k_Σ, w);                  20:    id ← Dec(k_id, M_I[u]);
3: st_(w,c) ← {∅}, Q ← {∅};                  21:    id_List ← {id} ∪ id_List;
4: for id in del_List do                     22: send id_List to Enclave;
5:    if BF[H'_j(k_BF, w ∥ id)]_{j∈[h]} = 1 then
6:       u' ← F(k_w, id);                     Enclave://retrieve currently matched docs
7:       v' ← M_c.Access(op' = search,        23: for id in id_List do
            in' = (M_c.rNode, M_ck, u')) in Server;  24:    m ← doc_ST[id];
8:       c ← Dec(k_c, v');                     25:    for i in [0, m] do
9:       st_(w,c) ← {c} ∪ st_(w,c);            26:       key ← F(k_Σ, id∥i));
10:   end if                                   27:       n_i ← R.Access(op' = search,
11: end for                                              in' = (R.rNode, R_k, key)) in Server;
12: st_(w,c) ← {0, ..., ST[w]} \ st_(w,c)      28:       res ← value(Dec(R_k, n_i));
13: for c in st_(w,c) do                       29:   end for
14:   (u, k_id) ← (H_2(k_w, c), H_1(k_w, c));  30: Return res to Client; //in batch of docs
15:   Q ← {(u, k_id)} ∪ Q;                     31: end for
16: end for
```

Fig. 5. Search protocol in Magnus

(see line 25 in Fig. 4). In this way, the *Enclave* can retrieve the state c of w if the keyword is in the deleted doc with id in Search. Then, the state node n_c is obliviously inserted to M_c via the Access protocol, in a similar way with R. The enclave also computes a new member of $H'_j(k_{BF}, w \parallel id)$ to update BF. After all, the *Enclave* sends a batch of T to the *Server* within 1 *ocall* per a document *addition* Then, the *Server* will update M_I by using T. If Update is *deletion*, the *Enclave* generates dummy AVL nodes and inserts them to both M_c and R to hide the operation. Then, it updates *del_List* by the deleted id.

In Search for a keyword w, Magnus verifies the mapping between w and deleted id by testing the membership (w, id) with BF. If it is a case, the *Enclave* performs a look-up in the map M_c with the key (w, id) via ORAM accesses (see Fig. 5). Note that we can relax M_c to *write-only* ODS, where ORAM accesses in Search do not require writing new ORAM buckets, similar with Fort. Since the Path-ORAM of M_c is non-recursive and it has $\mathcal{O}(logN)$ levels, the communication round trips to retrieve all state nodes of deleted (w, id) pairs is $\mathcal{O}(d_w logN)$ for d_w deleted ids. The *Enclave* also performs padding with dummy accesses to ensure the *Server* sees a fixed number of ORAM buckets visited per an AVL node ($\approx 1.45 logN$). Then, Magnus retrieves the deleted state list $st_{w_c} = \{c_{id}^{del}\}$, where c_{id}^{del} is the state used for deleted ids. After that, the *Enclave* discards them from the list $\{0, ..., ST[w]\}$ to infer the states of non-deleted documents (see Fig. 5 line 12). Then, it computes query tokens in Q and send them to the *Server* in a batch. Upon receiving currently matched *id_List* from the *Server*, the *Enclave* can perform the same deterministic ORAM accesses to retrieve data blocks of **docs** in *id_List* based on doc_ST[id] (see lines 23–31).

5   Security Analysis

The security of Magnus relies on the black-box use of oblivious data structures (ODS) M_c and R, as initiated in [27]. Magnus contains the leakage of Update and Search operations. We formulate the leakage of Magnus and define $\mathbf{Real}_A(\lambda)$ and a $\mathbf{Ideal}_{A,S}(\lambda)$ game for an adaptive adversary A and a polynomial time simulator S with the security parameter λ as follows.

Let $\mathcal{L}$ be a stateful leakage function $\mathcal{L} = (\mathcal{L}^{Setup}, \mathcal{L}^{Updt}, \mathcal{L}^{Srch})$, where the first three functions define the information exposed to the *Server* in Update, and Search, respectively. In Setup, Magnus leaks the data structure of M_I (i.e., the encrypted index), M_c (i.e., the OMAP of keyword states), R (i.e., the OMAP containing encrypted document blocks). In Update(op = $\{add, del\}$, in), Magnus leaks the data access pattern T_{M_I} of encrypted entries to be inserted in M_I, ORAM positions accessed in M_c and R, denoted as T_{M_c} and T_R, respectively. Then, $\mathcal{L}^{Updt}(\text{op}, \text{in}) = \{(T_{M_I}, T_{M_c}, T_R)\}$. In Search($w$), Magnus leaks 1) the accessed ORAM positions on M_c, named $\text{ap}_{M_c}(w)$, 2) the leakage TimeDB(w) when the *Enclave* queries n_w, named $\text{ap}_{M_I}(w)$. Then, formally $\mathcal{L}^{Srch}(w) = \text{ap}_{M_c}(w) + \text{TimeDB}(w)$.

Definition 1. *Consider* Magnus *scheme that consists of three protocols* Setup, Update, *and* Search. *Consider the probabilistic experiments* $\mathbf{Real}_A(\lambda)$ *and* $\mathbf{Ideal}_{A,S}(\lambda)$, *whereas* A *is a stateful adversary, and* S *is a stateful simulator that gets the leakage function* $\mathcal{L}$.

$\mathbf{Real}_A(\lambda)$: A takes (1^λ) and returns two different computable databases DB^0 and DB^1. Then, the challenger runs the Setup(DB^b) upon a chosen bit $b \in \{0, 1\}$. Then, A makes a polynomial number of Updates (addition/deletion) with (op, in), where Z is a natural number of documents, and (op = add, in = doc_i) or (op = del, in = id_i). Accordingly, the challenger runs those updates with Update(op, in) and eventually returns the encrypted DB to A. After that, A adaptively chooses the keyword w (*resp.*, (op, in)) to search (*resp.*, update). In response, the challenger runs Search(w) (*resp.*, Update(op,in)) and returns the transcript of each operation. Upon receiving the transcript, A outputs a bit b.

$\mathbf{Ideal}_{A,S}(\lambda)$: A chooses a $DB = \{doc_i\}_{i \in Z}$. By using $\mathcal{L}^{Updt}$ and $(M_I, M_c, R)^{Updt}$, S creates a tuple of (M_I, M_c, R) and passes it to A. Then, A adaptively chooses the keyword w (*resp.*, (op, in)) to search (*resp.*, update). The challenger returns the transcript simulated by $S(\mathcal{L}^{Srch}(w))$ (*resp.*, $S(\mathcal{L}^{Updt}(\text{op}, \text{in}))$) with $(M_I, M_c, R)^{Srch}$. Finally, A returns a bit b.

Theorem 1. *Assuming OMAPs* M_c *and* R *are created with the secure oblivious map of [27], SGX Enclave are secure, and the communication between the Client and the Enclave is secure,* Magnus *is an adaptively-secure SSE scheme with* $\mathcal{L}^{Updt}(\text{op}, \text{in}) = \text{op}$ *and* $\mathcal{L}^{Srch}(w) = \{\text{TimeDB}(w), \text{ap}_{M_c}(w)\}$.

Throughout the operations, the *Server* observes a sequence of Path-ORAM positions of M_c and R, for each position is chosen uniformly at random. In addition, the map M_I always get entry inserts during the doc *addition/deletion*.

During Search, Magnus reveals n_w during the query on M_I. In addition, d_w is revealed during the communication round trips between the *Enclave* and the *Server*. This shows that Magnus has Type-I$^-$ leakage, i.e., Type-I *backward privacy*.

6   Conclusion

In this paper, we leverage the advance of Intel SGX to design a Type-I$^-$ backward private dynamic searchable encryption scheme. We carefully analyse the limitation of Maiden and propose new design to avoid memory bottleneck of the SGX enclave.

References

1. Amjad, G., Kamara, S., Moataz, T.: Forward and backward private searchable encryption with SGX. In: EuroSec 2019 (2019)
2. Borges, G., Domingos, H., Ferreira, B., Leitão, J., Oliveira, T., Portela, B.: BISEN: efficient boolean searchable symmetric encryption with verifiability and minimal leakage. In: IEEE SRDS 2019 (2019)
3. Bost, R.: $\Sigma o\varphi o\varsigma$ - forward secure searchable encryption. In: ACM CCS 2016 (2016)
4. Bost, R., Fouque, P.A.: Thwarting leakage abuse attacks against searchable encryption - a formal approach and applications to database padding. Cryptology ePrint Archive, Report 2017/1060 (2017). https://eprint.iacr.org/2017/1060
5. Bost, R., Minaud, B., Ohrimenko, O.: Forward and backward private searchable encryption from constrained cryptographic primitives. In: ACM CCS 2017 (2017)
6. Brasser, F., Capkun, S., Dmitrienko, A., Frassetto, T., Kostiainen, K., Sadeghi, A.R.: DR.SGX: automated and adjustable side-channel protection for SGX using data location randomization. In: ACSAC 2019 (2019)
7. Brasser, F., Müller, U., Dmitrienko, A., Kostiainen, K., Capkun, S., Sadeghi, A.R.: Software grand exposure: SGX cache attacks are practical. In: WOOT 2017 (2017)
8. Christian, P., Kapil, V., Manuel, C.: EnclaveDB: a secure database using SGX. In: IEEE S&P 2018 (2018)
9. Costan, V., Devadas, S.: Intel SGX explained. IACR Cryptol. ePrint Archive (2016)
10. Costan, V., Lebedev, I., Devadas, S.: Sanctum: minimal hardware extensions for strong software isolation. In: USENIX Security 2016 (2016)
11. Curtmola, R., Garay, J., Kamara, S., Ostrovsky, R.: Searchable symmetric encryption: improved definitions and efficient constructions. In: ACM CCS 2016 (2016)
12. Duan, H., Wang, C., Yuan, X., Zhou, Y., Wang, Q., Ren, K.: LightBox: full-stack protected stateful middlebox at lightning speed. In: ACM CCS 2019 (2019)
13. Eskandarian, S., Zaharia, M.: ObliDB: oblivious query processing for secure databases. In: Proceedings of the VLDB Endowment (2019)
14. Fuhry, B., Bahmani, R., Brasser, F., Hahn, F., Kerschbaum, F., Sadeghi, A.-R.: HardIDX: practical and secure index with SGX. In: Livraga, G., Zhu, S. (eds.) DBSec 2017. LNCS, vol. 10359, pp. 386–408. Springer, Cham (2017). https://doi.org/10.1007/978-3-319-61176-1_22
15. Ghareh Chamani, J., Papadopoulos, D., Papamanthou, C., Jalili, R.: New constructions for forward and backward private symmetric searchable encryption. In: ACM CCS 2018 (2018)

16. Gruss, D., Lettner, J., Schuster, F., Ohrimenko, O., Haller, I., Costa, M.: Strong and efficient cache side-channel protection using hardware transactional memory. In: USENIX Security 2017 (2017)
17. Hoang, T., Ozmen, M.O., Jang, Y., Yavuz, A.A.: Hardware-supported ORAM in effect: practical oblivious search and update on very large dataset. In: PET 2019 (2019)
18. Kamara, S., Papamanthou, C., Roeder, T.: Dynamic searchable symmetric encryption. In: ACM CCS 2012 (2012)
19. Mishra, P., Poddar, R., Chen, J., Chiesa, A., Popa, R.A.: Oblix: an efficient oblivious search index. In: IEEE S&P 2018 (2018)
20. Oleksenko, O., Trach, B., Krahn, R., Martin, A., et al.: Varys: protecting SGX enclaves from practical side-channel attacks. In: USENIX ATC 2018 (2018)
21. Shinde, S., Chua, Z.L., Narayanan, V., Saxena, P.: Preventing page faults from telling your secrets. In: ACM AsiaCCS 2016 (2016)
22. Song, D., Wagner, D., Perrig, A.: Practical techniques for searches on encrypted data. In: IEEE S&P 2000 (2000)
23. Stefanov, E., Papamanthou, C., Shi, E.: Practical dynamic searchable symmetric encryption with small leakage. In: NDSS 2014 (2014)
24. Sun, S.F., Yuan, X., Liu, J., Steinfeld, R., Sakzad, A., Vo, V., et al.: Practical backward-secure searchable encryption from symmetric puncturable encryption. In: ACM CCS 2018 (2018)
25. Vo, V., Lai, S., Yuan, X., Nepal, S., Liu, J.K.: Towards efficient and strong backward private searchable encryption with secure enclaves. In: Sako, K., Tippenhauer, N.O. (eds.) ACNS 2021. LNCS, vol. 12726, pp. 50–75. Springer, Cham (2021). https://doi.org/10.1007/978-3-030-78372-3_3
26. Vo, V., Lai, S., Yuan, X., Sun, S.-F., Nepal, S., Liu, J.K.: Accelerating forward and backward private searchable encryption using trusted execution. In: Conti, M., Zhou, J., Casalicchio, E., Spognardi, A. (eds.) ACNS 2020. LNCS, vol. 12147, pp. 83–103. Springer, Cham (2020). https://doi.org/10.1007/978-3-030-57878-7_5
27. Wang, X.S., et al.: Oblivious data structures. In: CCS 2014 (2014)
28. Wu, S., Li, Q., Li, G., Yuan, D., Yuan, X., Wang, C.: ServeDB: secure, verifiable, and efficient range queries on outsourced database. In: IEEE ICDE 2019 (2019)
29. Yarom, Y., Falkner, K.: FLUSH+RELOAD: a high resolution, low noise, L3 cache side-channel attack. In: USENIX Security 2014 (2014)
30. Zhang, Y., Katz, J., Papamanthou, C.: All your queries are belong to us: the power of file-injection attacks on searchable encryption. In: USENIX Security 2016 (2016)
31. Zuo, C., Sun, S.-F., Liu, J.K., Shao, J., Pieprzyk, J.: Dynamic searchable symmetric encryption schemes supporting range queries with forward (and backward) security. In: Lopez, J., Zhou, J., Soriano, M. (eds.) ESORICS 2018. LNCS, vol. 11099, pp. 228–246. Springer, Cham (2018). https://doi.org/10.1007/978-3-319-98989-1_12

Correction to: Topology Validator - Defense Against Topology Poisoning Attack in SDN

Abhay Kumar and Sandeep Shukla

Correction to:
Chapter "Topology Validator - Defense Against Topology Poisoning Attack in SDN" in: X. Yuan et al. (Eds.): *Quality, Reliability, Security and Robustness in Heterogeneous Systems*, **LNICST 402, https://doi.org/10.1007/978-3-030-91424-0_15**

In an older version of this paper, the "l" was missing from the last name of Sandeep Shukla. This has been corrected.

The updated version of this chapter can be found at
https://doi.org/10.1007/978-3-030-91424-0_15

© ICST Institute for Computer Sciences, Social Informatics and Telecommunications Engineering 2021
Published by Springer Nature Switzerland AG 2021. All Rights Reserved
X. Yuan et al. (Eds.): QShine 2021, LNICST 402, p. C1, 2021.
https://doi.org/10.1007/978-3-030-91424-0_21

Correction to: Topology Validator - Defense Against Topology Poisoning Attack in SDN

Abhay Kumar and Sandeep Shukla

Correction to:
Chapter "Topology Validator - Defense Against Topology Poisoning Attack in SDN" in: X. Yuan et al. (Eds.):
Quality, Reliability, Security and Robustness in Heterogeneous Systems, **LNICST 402, https://doi.org/10.1007/978-3-030-91424-0_15**

In an older version of this paper, the "l" was missing from the last name of Sandeep Shukla. This has been corrected.

The updated version of this chapter can be found at
https://doi.org/10.1007/978-3-030-91424-0_15

© ICST Institute for Computer Sciences, Social Informatics and Telecommunications Engineering 2021
Published by Springer Nature Switzerland AG 2021. All Rights Reserved
X. Yuan et al. (Eds.): QShine 2021, LNICST 402, p. C1, 2021.
https://doi.org/10.1007/978-3-030-91424-0_21

Author Index

Printed in the United States
by Baker & Taylor Publisher Services